Pierpont Morgan and Friends

PIERPONT MORGAN AND FRIENDS

THE ANATOMY OF A MYTH

BY

GEORGE WHEELER

PRENTICE-HALL, INC.
ENGLEWOOD CLIFFS, NEW JERSEY

Acknowledgment is made for permission to reprint
excerpts from the following works:

Peacocks on Parade by Albert S. Crockett, reprinted
by permission of Dodd, Mead & Company.

Reprinted with permission of The Macmillan Company
from *J. Pierpont Morgan: An Intimate Portrait* by
Herbert L. Satterlee. Copyright by Herbert L.
Satterlee, renewed 1967 by Mabel Satterlee Ingalls.

Pierpont Morgan and Friends: The Anatomy of a Myth by George Wheeler
Copyright © 1973 by George Wheeler

Printed in the United States of America

Prentice-Hall International, Inc., London
Prentice-Hall of Australia, Pty. Ltd., North Sydney
Prentice-Hall of Canada, Ltd., Toronto
Prentice-Hall of India Private Ltd., New Delhi
Prentice-Hall of Japan, Inc., Tokyo

Library of Congress Cataloging in Publication Data
Wheeler, George.
Pierpont Morgan and friends.
Bibliography: p.
1. Morgan, John Pierpont, 1837-1913. 2. Capital-
ists and financiers—United States. 3. Finance—
United States—History. I. Title.
HG2463.M62W5   332.1'092'4 [B]   73-8728
ISBN 0-13-676148-8
10 9 8 7 6 5 4 3 2 1

CONTENTS

Pierpont Morgan and Friends

THE

GOLD CRISIS

WHEN the financier Pierpont Morgan died, the event sent editors, clergymen, and men of affairs on the usual hunt through the ragbag of literature for appropriate shreds and patches in which to wind his body. The New York *World,* displaying a gaudy remnant from Shakespeare, described the financier as a man who had been able "to bestride the earth like a Colossus." Others, such as the obituary writer who mourned the passing of "the nation's bulwark against panics," were content with tattered bits from threadbare Fourth of July oratory. For the most part, the businessmen varied the theme of "patriot." Later writers, less restrained as his memory dimmed, fastened on such epithets as "the magnificent" and "the great."

Some of these mythmakers were little more than hired artisans. They would have been more appropriately employed—provided they could have absorbed the necessary stonecutting skills—in incising tombstones with no thought of what went into the inscription. Morgan's controlling links were deeply embedded in their livelihoods, as well as in the publications, the religious organizations, and the businesses of the days. The hagiolotrous sermons, obituaries, and eulogies were as uncritical as might have been expected. The later writers, swinging incense as assiduously, but with less reason, were able to reproduce the heroic image uncritically by ignoring a variety of negatives.

The chief distortion has to do with the neglect of the time factor in Morgan's career. Pierpont Morgan spent the greater part of his life in obscurity before embarking on any ventures that may be called great, yet he is presented as though he had always been at the center of large affairs. Allied with this has been the tendency to thrust into the background, or ignore altogether, powerful figures who helped or hindered him in his course. When the flow of time is restored, we see a much diminished Pierpont Morgan who was just beginning to bustle at an age when younger contemporaries, like Andrew Carnegie and John D. Rockefeller, had made their marks on the nation and already were giving thought to retirement. When this time factor as well as the numerous antagonists and protagonists who helped shape Morgan's career are considered properly and objectively, the myth that has been woven around Pierpont Morgan dissipates. In place of the strictly decorative legends emerges a truer portrait of the man, useful for showing both his constructive and disruptive contributions to the financial world he inhabited.

John Pierpont Morgan did not become a figure for the front pages of daily newspapers until 1895, when he was fifty-eight years old. Previously, his sphere had been a constricted one, his influence severely limited. His reputation was known only to those closely connected with the financial world. He had, thirty-four years earlier, flimflammed the federal government in the sale of some rifles at the opening of the Civil War, a time when such manipulations were proving too tempting to the weaker moral reeds. Later, in the infamous "Gold Room" on Wall Street, he had played a part in transactions difficult for the ordinary mortal to understand. They consisted of speculative operations that generally undermined the Union's efforts to retain its gold and they depended on an ability to follow the perverse pattern of buying when everything looks blackest and selling when everyone else was lining up for victory parades. Such reverse reflexes are not easily acquired, but Morgan developed them early. His wartime speculations were not too noticeable in a period when just about every man of substance able to avoid the draft was profiting on Lincoln's difficulties in trying to keep the Union cause on course. But they were notorious enough to lead Morgan's father to take a decisive step. Junius S. Morgan realized that his son's path was not a promising one.

The men who then were creating the postwar world of industry were a questionable lot. They ran from bad to worse; from Cornelius Vanderbilt, the old Commodore, to Daniel Drew, the old cattle drover. The Commodore subsidized sympathetic aldermen and legislators. "Uncle Dan'l" Drew pioneered a whole bag of shabby tricks by which swindlers are still taking advantage of the gullible. One of the shabbiest was his penchant for wrecking his own properties to advance his speculations. Drew, a dried-up man with the air of an unfrocked country parson, later attracted unto himself two acolytes, Jay Gould and Jim Fisk, who ultimately exceeded him in daring and deviltry. Fisk and Gould, particularly, were so exhilarated with the spirit of vice that on occasion they fleeced each other—and Uncle Dan'l—just to keep in fighting trim.

The Commodore, tall, handsome, and with a weakness even in old age for attractive female members of his large domestic retinue, had vices of his own, but there was a wide swath of villainy separating him from the likes of Drew and Gould. He played the speculative game to the full, manipulating stocks as wildly as Uncle Dan'l ever did, and he suborned lawmaking bodies on a grand scale. But unscrupulous as his methods were, their end result was to produce an efficient, working railroad—the New York Central. Drew, with Gould and Fisk, cared nothing for his chief victim, the Erie, and left it a wreck.

The Commodore and Uncle Dan'l defined the extremes of ruthlessness in the postwar period when the industrial revolution was beginning to convulse a rural America. In his office in London, Junius S. Morgan watched his son moving in the direction of these two conscienceless pirates and determined to crack the parental whip. The elder Morgan bought his son a partnership with one of his business associates, Charles Dabney, who kept close watch on the younger man. There followed three decades of less flamboyant, less questionable, and probably more profitable activity as an investment banker and agent for the older man's London house.

The profitability can be gauged from the estimate in the magazine *The Forum* in 1889 that the younger Morgan was one of the hundred wealthiest men in the United States, with a fortune of $25 million. His father was credited with a like amount; both, though, were far behind John Jacob Astor with $50 million and John D. Rockefeller, William K. Vanderbilt, and Jay Gould with $100 million each.

The event that ended Pierpont Morgan's career as an affluent but obscure man and propelled him into the headlines was the contract he signed to supply gold to the United States Treasury in February 1895. The exact nature of the role he played in that transaction, so different from the legend he helped build around it, will be examined in full, but first it is necessary to look upon the near and distant background of this incident.

In the decades since the Civil War, the country had never truly settled its monetary system. Lincoln had been forced into a token money, or fiduciary, standard to finance the war. Such a standard has great appeal for debtors, especially such a debtor as a government that must raise a nonproductive army and waste its assets on the battlefield. It is equally appealing to other debtors, especially individuals involved in large, extravagant enterprises. Creditors usually prefer a gold standard. This was particularly true during the period from the 1860s to near the close of the century, when a token money policy promised inflationary ease in paying debts whereas the gold standard, given the relatively static pool of the world's gold, implied a deflationary pledge to the creditor, a guarantee that his capital would be conserved.

The token money policy prevailed until January 1, 1879, when the country resumed the pre–Civil War practice of honoring its obligations in "specie." To be sure, the creditor class had not won a clear-cut victory over the debtors by that act, inasmuch as "specie" might mean silver as well as gold. The result was a confused standard, rather than either a fiduciary or a gold one, complicated by the instability of world silver supplies and the difficulty of maintaining a fixed interchangeability between the two metals.

Psychologically, though, the creditors had an edge. Part of it consisted of the recognition of gold as the principal standard and part of it consisted of agreement by the federal government to establish a gold reserve, a deposit of at least $100 million in coin and bullion to be held by the Treasury. For the next decade or so, the monetary fever flared up periodically, whenever weakness appeared in the economic system or whenever the gold and silver struggle swung to extremes. The gold reserve had psychological importance, especially to overseas investors in the economy, as the outward sign of the inner grace supposedly conferred by the gold standard.

The question arises whether a gold or gold plus silver standard was preferable to a fiduciary one. According to two of the ablest monetary authorities of our time, Milton Friedman and Anna Jacobson Schwartz, the answer is a qualified no. Abandonment of the gold standard "might well have been highly preferable to the generally depressed conditions of the 1890s," they contend, but they add that quitting the gold standard would have been "politically unacceptable." But this cavil takes the question outside the field of economic determinism and into the realm of politics, psychology, and the ideas that men hold to be true regardless of whether they are so or not.

This was a realm that had been constructed by men of Pierpont Morgan's class, patched together by the associates who had brought him into the 1895 gold contract and laboriously papered over and shored up by himself and later allies. It was their world. When they are accounted heroes and patriots for their acts of self-preservation, it must be remembered that they effectively drew up the specifications for their own honors lists.

As a corollary to this distinct advantage, they can be said to have had a major part in preparing the "generally depressed conditions of the 1890s," the most extreme example of which got under way early in 1893. This dislocation, the Panic of 1893, one of the worst in the history of the country, was the immediate background for the gold contract. It started on February 25, 1893, only a week before Grover Cleveland was to take office for a second time, when the always ailing Philadelphia and Reading Railroad went into bankruptcy, with debts of $25 million. The panic proper began on May 4, when the National Cordage Company announced it could not meet its obligations. The officers and directors, it should be noted, placed the blame for the bankruptcy on the contraction of credit that had been brought on by withdrawals of gold by foreign investors.

The foreigners, conditioned by the gold psychology of the time and fearful of what could be expected to follow the extraordinary expansion of the late 1880s, were trading in their American stocks and bonds for gold. It was the beginning of a vast outflow that was to lead Cleveland, the Democrat, to shake hands with the devils from Wall Street, alienate him from his party and in fact divide that party so thoroughly that it was unable to win the nation's highest office for nearly two decades—until the Republicans went through a similar division.

After National Cordage went under, business and bank failures multiplied. During July they were almost daily occurrences. By the end of that month, nineteen national banks and a large number of state banks in the southern and western parts of the country closed their doors. By October, more than eight thousand businesses had failed and 156 railroads were in receivership. The Northern Pacific had gone down in August, the Union Pacific declared itself insolvent in October, and the Atchison, Topeka, and Santa Fe, along with the New York and New England, followed in December. For the year, the score stood at 642 bank failures (about 5 per cent of the country's total) and fifteen thousand commercial bankruptcies. Of 177,823 miles of railroad in operation that year, 32,379 were in receivership.

The catalog of ruined industries and railroads is long and doleful. An additional measure of the crippling force of the panic is found in the production of a single item, pig iron, a vital ingredient for all industry in that early age of steel. "No more accurate barometer of American industry" existed, said the Boston *Herald* at the time. The newspaper went on to give these figures: in 1890, mills in the United States reached a peak of production, turning out 9,202,703 long tons, an increase of more than tenfold over the preceding three decades. Output wavered in the next two years, began to slip in 1893, and bottomed in the following year at 6,657,888, a slide of nearly 28 per cent. It was one of the worst economic dislocations to that date.

But catalogs and production statistics leave much untold. Underneath the readily perceivable corporate failures and dwindling of output spread a far more corrosive unrest among the workers, so little prepared—or rather, so little able to prepare—for such crises. In those days of inadequate, even nonexistent, relief for the victims of a depression, wage earners and heads of families were transformed into little more than beggars—and their dependents to something less. The human effect of the panic soon became apparent in a hellish outburst of working-class bitterness that threatened at times to become real revolution and was suppressed only with brutal force.

In 1890, before the slowdown had begun, there had occurred the greatest number of strikes in any one year of the century. The Homestead strike in 1892, still before the panic proper, included a pitched battle between strikers and an army of Pinkerton detectives that featured a casualty list. At the strike's height, Carnegie Steel Company head Henry Clay Frick was wounded by the anarchist Alexander Berkman.

In the panic year, 1893, violence subsided briefly, but its flames gave way to a more ominous smoldering—the gathering of large numbers of men and boys who wandered the countryside and

occasionally troubled the cities. One such embryonic revolutionary collection was the army of twenty thousand men and women
led by Jacob S. Coxey. Early in 1894, Coxey's army marched from
Ohio to Washington. The maneuver was aborted, ending in the
disbanding of the force and the arrest of Coxey for trespassing.
Despite the farcical conclusion, the event struck terror into the
country.

Far more serious unrest followed in the minefields of Pennsylvania and in the Pullman strike in Chicago in July, which
together amounted almost to a general labor insurrection. The
explosive possibilities were never realized, but in thwarting them,
and especially in his handling of the Pullman strike, Cleveland
resorted to methods that lost him the support of labor and a good
part of the general public. His Attorney General, Richard Olney,
who must bear the primary responsibility, moved federal troops
in past the peacekeeping force of state militia called out by Illinois Governor John P. Altgeld. Altgeld's troops had been doing
all that was required, maintaining order, but Olney's act crushed
the strike to the satisfaction of the railroad owners. It was a
decisive intervention that helped end Grover Cleveland's political
career. The destruction was substantially completed by the gold
contract of 1895.

The story of the contract begins with a visit to Washington by
August Belmont. He came down on the night train on Thursday,
January 24, 1895, and the next morning, as he recalled: "I went to
see Mr. [John Griffith] Carlisle [Cleveland's Secretary of the
Treasury] . . . at his own office in the Treasury building." The
Treasury was hard by the White House, but Belmont did not see
the President, although he had tried. He added: "I find that I did
call on Secretary of War [Daniel S.] Lamont on the first visit to
Washington. I called at the War Department, but my visit was
short, and was only for the purpose of having him find out if I
could see the President." Lamont sent word to Belmont at his
hotel that the President was busy, conferring with some members
of his Cabinet, and no meeting could be arranged. Belmont then
went on to the Treasury to talk matters over with Carlisle.

Belmont, who with his father had long been associated with
both Democratic politics and the great London-based merchant
banking house of Rothschild, at this time was forty-two years old.
Debonair, a man of the world, a drawing-room comedy figure,
the very model of hundreds of imitators since on stage and

screen with his thinning hair, thin-lipped sneer, hairline moustache and arched eyebrows, he would have been perfectly cast in an Oscar Wilde play. In fact, he showed himself capable of originating arrogant lines that Wilde would not have disowned.

He had the kind of bearing that made him equally capable of bantering pleasantries with a doorman, pending the lackey's good behavior, or of snarling the man into the pavement for departing too far from servility. He was later to display this capacity to good advantage with those other representatives of the lower orders, the United States senators who were impudent enough to conduct a farcical sideshow intended to be an investigation into the gold contract negotiations. But his highhandedness was reserved only for those who didn't count to his overseas principals; with the members of the Cleveland administration he maintained an easy, cordial relationship, writing letters and calling on the President and his Cabinet to offer advice that would be useful to his clients.

Among the cabinet officers with whom he was on easy terms were Lamont and Carlisle. The former was a longtime political crony of Cleveland, the friendship dating back to the President's term as governor of New York. He had been Cleveland's private secretary in the first administration, his Secretary of War in the second, and always his political chief of staff and patronage dispenser.

Carlisle, the Treasury Secretary, was a powerful Democrat. A former Speaker of the House and Kentucky senator, his fondness for his native state's bourbon kept him from the heights of even greater political office. He was once proposed as Chief Justice of the United States, but Cleveland turned on his seconder, Senator Blackburn, with: "Blackburn, you tell only part of the truth. You know why I don't appoint him. I won't appoint a man to be Chief Justice of the United States who might be picked up in the street some morning."

The suave Belmont and the rustic Carlisle went to great lengths later to conceal what they had talked about at this January 24th meeting, even to the extent of courting contempt citations at the Senate hearings eighteen months later. Of the reason for his going, Belmont then said, "My visit was brought about in a very simple way. I saw Mr. Cannon, who was a member of the Clearing House committee [in New York], and learned from him some details which I did not know respecting the condition of the reserve and the banks and the fear that was existing here. I felt it then my duty to go to Washington and do whatever I might."

Despite the reluctance of both men to detail what happened at the meeting, it is known that Carlisle learned from his party's chief link with the financial world that a sense of panic was building and that some new method to rebuild the gold reserve would have to be tried.

The $100 million fund, so important to Belmont's employers, the Rothschilds, and the wealthy clients whose money they handled, had been an irksome matter to Cleveland right from the time he took office on March 4, 1893. In fact, before his inauguration amid the first indications of the financial panic, it had been necessary for his predecessor Benjamin Harrison, to shore up the reserve with $8,250,000 in gold obtained in Wall Street by his Treasury Secretary. Otherwise the reserve would have dipped below $100 million for the first time since its creation. After Cleveland took office, the deepening crisis increased the fear of the Europeans, and Carlisle had to take hat in hand and prowl the canyons of lower Manhattan as his Republican predecessor had done.

Still the outflow continued and in February 1894 a bond issue was offered to raise nearly $10 million. But again in August, Carlisle, who in his days as Speaker of the House had flirted with the anti-Wall Street silver wing of his party, was forced to widen his acquaintance in the financial district in New York to raise another $10 million in gold in return for United States notes. Less than four months later, in November, as the depression reached its nadir, the drain had reduced the reserve by an alarming $48 million and another bond issue was resorted to.

At this point Cleveland and Carlisle realized that the "patriots" who were supplying the gold for notes and bonds were simply making gestures and that as soon as the administration's back was turned they were surrendering the paper and taking back the gold. So Carlisle threatened to publicize the names of any who resorted to that trick. One result of his pressure was that a former Secretary of the Treasury under Cleveland, Charles S. Fairchild, together with a number of other financiers, withdrew from the bidding on the government's bond issue.

This second bond issue was successful in restoring the reserve, but despite Carlisle's threat to expose the quick redeemers, the drain recommenced almost immediately. "The payments in the Treasury on account of this sale were not entirely completed until after the first day of December, 1894, and it soon became evident that the transaction had not been effectual to stop withdrawals of gold," he said at the Senate hearing later.

In other words, the buyers of these bonds—among whom, incidentally, Pierpont Morgan figured as a small part of a syndicate—were not delivering their own gold as promised. Instead, taking advantage of the grace period for the payment, they were in effect making delivery with the Treasury's own dwindling stock. Between continued withdrawals and the operations of this tricky method of bond-buying, the reserve in late January 1895 stood at about the point it had reached in November when the second bond issue was floated—about $60 million. Clearly something bolder had to be tried.

The novel and daring method was to come from neither August Belmont nor J. Pierpont Morgan; the source was Cleveland himself. He wanted the gold to come from overseas rather than from domestic supplies. His preoccupation with this system had been displayed as early as February 1893, before he took office and while he and his crony Lamont were corresponding about cabinet choices. A letter from Cleveland to Lamont recently added to the latter's papers in the Library of Congress proves Cleveland's early interest in the foreign operation and, in addition, serves to show the free-and-easy relationship of the President-elect and the Rothschild representative, young August Belmont.

Cleveland wrote to Lamont, following the discussion of cabinet possibilities:

> And this reminds me of another confidential mission I want you to undertake for me.
>
> Will you go to Belmont & Co. and see if they can arrange for the purchase *abroad* of say fifty millions of caisse bonds . . . I want in the transaction the *actual gold* brought from abroad and put in our own Treasury and I want it done promptly. . . . Of course we do not commit ourselves to the issuance of these bonds. We may be anticipated or the necessity for such action may be averted. I only want you to find out in the most confidential way possible what can be done if the contingency arrives.

The contingency, as we have seen, did not arise because Benjamin Harrison's Treasury Secretary was able to bring the reserve back up to $100 million by borrowings on Wall Street.

The principle of purchasing gold overseas was still uppermost in Cleveland's mind two years later. This is indicated in a memorandum among his own papers dated January 23, just two days before Belmont's visit to Carlisle. It emanated from the Treasury Department and was brought up to date in Carlisle's hand. To it, Cleveland added emendations in his own peculiar penmanship, consisting of a wriggly line with occasional pulses and resembling nothing so much as an anarchronistic foreshadowing of the readout of an electroencephalograph.

At one point, the report suggested bringing the reserve up to the required limit by a purchase of gold either in this country or abroad. In the latter event, some of it could be left in England, France, or Germany, the report advised. In rebuttal, Cleveland's squiggled interlineation stretches out over the sheet and angrily curls up the side of the page. "The gold ought to be in our hands and it would be very desirable to advance it from abroad," it reads.

The chances for success of this European purchase were among the major reasons for Belmont's visit on January 25, 1895. His testimony at the Senate hearings later indicated how the question came up. He told Carlisle, he said, that he wasn't hopeful of a bond sale in Europe, but he would endeavor to get a definite answer from his London headquarters. In addition he told Carlisle of the rising sense of panic in Wall Street and the feeling that any attempt to replenish the gold reserve by a sale of bonds domestically would result, as had the previous two attempts, in a meaningless shift of ownership of the bullion stored in the nation's subtreasuries, notably the one in New York.

He also tried to win from Carlisle some assurance that governmental action would be taken so that he might allay the fears of Rothschild clients in Europe. But the shrewd backwoods politician, sensing that he could soothe Belmont's constituents only by ruffling his own, told him that nothing that was being said could be construed as an offer to negotiate.

Belmont then departed, although probably not before he, as an influential Democratic moneyman, was made privy to the daily gold withdrawal reports that were being made to Secretary Carlisle. These showed that in the four days just before he had caught the late night train on Thursday, the outflow had snowballed to a total of about $7,200,000, and that on the day they had met there occurred the biggest single day's withdrawal, $7,156, 046, or nearly as much in the one day as in the preceding four. As of that Friday night, there was just $59,367,198 in the reserve.

On the Monday following Belmont's visit, Cleveland displayed his concern over the mounting crisis in a message to Congress seeking clear power for another bond sale. It was a futile but typical gesture of a President who consistently sought to thrust responsibility onto Congress by asking for renewed mandates of powers he already possessed. In the first bond issue, a year earlier, he had done the same thing and Carlisle had tried to help spur the Congress along by claiming that otherwise it would be unlawful for the administration to act.

Congress ignored the White House on that occasion, too, and when the administration was forced to rely on the powers it had under an 1878 statute, a strange spectacle followed. The lawmakers reminded Carlisle of his misgivings and called the bond issue illegal. It all made the selling of the January 1894 bond issue an exciting proposition. Congress, in effect, was loudly calling for repudiation of the bond obligation even as the administration was trying valiantly to sell as many of the bonds as possible to European investors. One commentator noted that it was as if some country noted for defaulting on its debts was coming hat in hand into the money market. The market, he observed, probably would have extended a warmer welcome to a bankrupt banana republic or a Ruritanian fiefdom held by the most extravagant of princes.

Europeans had shown their distaste for American holdings by liquidating about $100 million in American stocks and bonds during the Panic of 1893. The amount seems relatively small— about 4 percent of the total invested by Europeans—but as with so many gross economic concepts, the significance is in the change of direction. Such investments had been growing, more or less, since the early 1880s. This was the first net contraction.

Cleveland's appeal was totally lost on Congress—and on investors here and abroad. On the day he submitted his message, the gold hemorrhage had continued, with over $4 million withdrawn. In the country at large, his demand served only to intensify creditor-debtor animosities. Surveying editorial opinion throughout the nation, a powerful and liberal provincial journal, the Springfield [Massachusetts] *Republican,* noted:

The leading newspapers of the East and central West as a rule indorse the President's financial recommendations. . . . The free silver and cheap money organs in the South are rejoicing in the present situation of the national Treasury, and are lifting up their voices with one accord to protest against bond issues and the retirement of the greenbacks. The Atlanta [Georgia] *Constitution,* which is one of the worst of these shouters, and whose guiding political principle is hatred of Cleveland and opposition to everything he advocates, declares that "the people of this country, outside the hotbeds of goldbuggery and Shylockism, don't care how soon gold payments are suspended."

In the face of congressional inaction and the continued onslaught by big American and European bankers on the gold reserve, Cleveland and his Cabinet went on what amounted to a war footing. There were late night meetings of the President, Carlisle, and Attorney General Richard Olney, soon to become Secretary of State. Heightening the impression that open hostilities had begun was the presence of Secretary of War Lamont.

Also on hand, in the anteroom, was William E. Curtis, a New York Democrat whose father held a minor judgeship. Formerly a Wall Street lawyer, he had been named an assistant secretary of the Treasury at the start of Cleveland's term. During this crisis, he was drafted into service as a courier between staff headquarters in Washington and the combat zone in lower Manhattan. Charged with carrying messages of cheer to the field commander at the subtreasury on Wall Street, Conrad N. Jordan, also an assistant secretary, Curtis communicated too with the enemy's mercenaries—big bankers like James Stillman of National City, George F. Baker of First National, Belmont, and the rest.

The deterioration of the reserve, now dipping crazily toward the half-full level, brought almost daily dispatches from Jordan at his subtreasury post in New York to Curtis. On January 28, the same day that Cleveland's message reached Congress, he wrote: "Today began a run in small amounts. . . . We must have more gold from nearby points. San Francisco is too risky." He noted that the supply of coin would be exhausted "this week" and that there should be no delay between announcing a bond issue and taking bids. "If our gold is taken beforehand, & that it is certain to be—if the loan is offered for gold, we shall be bankrupt before we get any returns from the loan. . . ." Closing with the advice that "this thing may degenerate, or rise into, a panic, as you prefer," he signed himself, "Your 'Cassandra.'"

An indication of the siege conditions he was working under came in the form of a postscript to the letter that he had completed just before the closing of the subtreasury for the day: "$20,000-odd of so-called jewelers have come in at five minutes of three—after this letter had closed—how tired you must be of—" and signed off with his initials. The implication was that the panic must be getting under way when small hoarders were ready to pass themselves off as jewelers to get gold. In his next communiqué, the following day, he reported: "It begins to look as if it were a general debacle."

The deepening crisis led Carlisle the next day, Wednesday, January 30, to send his courier Curtis directly to New York to see what could be done. What happened on that occasion became predictably muddled in the Senate investigation and has since been purposely confused by partisans of Pierpont Morgan anxious to claim a preeminence for him that cannot be supported. Curtis went directly to Belmont and, fortunately, set forth the whole account of his meeting with that financier immediately after returning to the University Club, then on Madison Square, where he was staying.

The letter shows conclusively that Belmont (identified as "B") wanted complete charge of the negotiation at that point and, further, that the "other bankers" Curtis tried to see first did not include Morgan. Curtis wrote:

☞ *Please keep this. I have no copy—*

> University Club
> Madison Square
> 30 January 1895
> 10 P.M.

Dear Mr. Secretary:

I have been with B. since 7:15 & just left him. He has called to learn whether foreigners would do anything with the 5s [five percent bonds apparently discussed by Belmont and Carlisle] at all and expects an answer in the morning. He does not think it will be

favorable. He says that the selling of American securities must be stopped by inspiring foreigners with
confidence and until that is done the gold must go to
them. He says he tried to see Stillman today and
failed but saw Baker. They decided that $100,000,000
was necessary with an option for $100,000,000 more
if desired. Syndicate to be arranged to take ⅓ here
and ⅔ abroad. They think this figure only would help
situation and loan of $50,000,000 would have little
or no effect even if taken locally wholly. B. says action
must be immediate in his opinion. Jordan was here
to meet me. He lost over $3,000,000 today. Thinks he
can hold until Saturday night and tomorrow may
decide. Urges immediate action as necessary. Look at
Meline's [the government assayist] gold statement of
tomorrow morning showing transfers made and to
come. People seemed scared and panicky in the club. I
have seen no one on this business except B. and Jordan.
Reporters were on the train, at the ferry and elsewhere.
Impossible to elude them or do anything but hold
one's tongue. If you will call me up at the club here at
half past nine tomorrow from the long distance telephone in my office I would like instructions. First—to
whom shall I talk? (B. evidently would like to try to
arrange the syndicate if you decide to go ahead, but
shall we not make some advances elsewhere, through
him or personally?) Second—what representations can
I make, if any, as to the intentions of the government?
I think it should be decided at once whether a bond issue should be made, or not. If the former and to a syndicate the amount, terms, method etc. to be suggested
by B. and such others as you may name and to be approved by you. If there is to be no issue, it should be
so stated at once. B. thinks we have overstayed our
time. The question also as to the probable effect of
suspension with a bond issue pending, or advertised
for, must be well thought out. If we decide upon an
issue *by advertisement,* they should be printed tomorrow, proposals to be handed in and opened at the
Treasury next Monday. *This time* have provisions made

for allotment, if necessary, and take the highest; no "all or none." I think the country *might* respond to this. Installments after first round amount to be easy and in gold. This is a personal opinion merely. I feel the responsibility here and would like to divide it. I sent a note to F. but got no answer and think he may be away. You of course know the congressional outlook. I do not and my views are simply based on what I see here. I send this by special delivery.

Yrs. Truly
W. E. Curtis

Curtis may have held his tongue as the reporters dogged him on the train up from Washington, on the ferry across the Hudson to Manhattan, and on his journey to Belmont's home, but word of his visit, and much speculation on it, was carried in the newspapers the next day.

The accounts acted to stanch the hemorrhage. As Carlisle observed later,

> The effect of that report was that the withdrawals of gold substantially stopped for several days and some $3 million or $4 million in gold, which had been ordered, and part of which was actually taken out of the [sub]Treasury was not, in fact, shipped. Some of that which had been taken out was returned and a large part of that which had not been taken out was left there.

During these developments, Pierpont Morgan took no direct part in the salvage effort. Up to this point it looked as if the aging financier—he would be fifty-eight in two months—would be merely one among many in this and whatever subsequent bond arrangements would be necessary. It seemed as though he would move on into old age with little more to round out his obituary than his awkward attempt to profiteer on the sale of rifles at the start of the Civil War, his minor shorting of the Union in gold trading toward the close, and a bold but largely unsuccessful move in the late 1880s to impose an eastern capitalist ceasefire on the country's warring railroads.

But there were steps being taken even now to bring him out of the financial backwaters—and they were not being taken by Pierpont Morgan himself. The first suggestion of his name for a role in the recharging of the reserve originated with the London branch of the House of Rothschild, Belmont's employers, but the idea may have come to gestation among an even more powerful group, the consummate politicians of the Cleveland administration. They were certainly aware of the dangers inherent in promoting a rescue effort for the United States Treasury that would be financed by those archetypes of "international Jewish financiers," the Rothschilds.

They had only to look in the daily papers for evidences of this peril. The Atlanta *Constitution* was ranting of "Shylockism," a term more sharply anti-Semitic then than now when other ethnic groups dominate the profession of usurer. Even the powerful liberal journals operated by Joseph Pulitzer, *The World* and *The Evening World,* were not immune from references to "money-changers" who had to be driven from the Temple. And Pulitzer was Jewish.

Part of the reality of the day was an ugly resurgence of anti-Semitism. Only a year before the bond transaction, Captain Alfred Dreyfus of the French army had been arrested on trumped up charges of treason, beginning a vicious outbreak of hatred in France that took more than a dozen years to run its course. Only two months after the bond contract was signed, the French Chamber of Deputies held a remarkable debate on "the Jewish Peril." Coincidentally, two Rothschild offices in Paris were bombed. Persecution of the Jews in Russia might be termed chronic during this period.

During one of the periodic subsidences of this condition, four years before the bond contract, the Czar curiously turned to the Rothschilds for financial help. He had his finance minister enter a negotiation with the English branch for a loan.

The consecration of capital to high social purposes is rare, but the Rothschilds have occasionally taken part in that sacrament. On this occasion, no doubt encouraged by a great popular opposition in England to the Russian repressions of the Jews, the firm told M. Wyschnigradski, the finance minister, that it would withdraw from the negotiation unless pogroms were completely halted. The Czar, nettled at the arrogance of a banking house that dared act as an equal, or even victorious, state in proposing such a concession, took his business elsewhere—to a non-Jewish group in Paris.

No hint of these stirrings of ancient hatreds occurs in any of the official documentation of the gold contract, but then there is little candor in these documents about anything. It is difficult to conceive that August Belmont the Younger was unaware of the menace and almost as hard to attribute such blindness to the Cleveland associates with whom he was so familiar. But it is impossible to believe that the Rothschilds would be insensitive to the possibility that their leading role in this contract might well serve to spread the uglier forms of this poison to a new country.

Someone was needed as a cover. Who better than J. Pierpont Morgan, a solid, Protestant exemplar of capitalism able to trace his family back to pre-Revolutionary times? Besides, he was connected with a London banking house that served as an important conduit for European investment sources.

Whoever generated the idea, credit for selecting Morgan undeniably goes to the Rothschilds. The first mention of his name in connection with the reserve operation was made by their banking house, as detailed in a cable Pierpont Morgan received at his office at 23 Wall Street on Thursday morning, January 31, the day after Curtis's arrival. It came from his brother-in-law, Walter Burns, who was in charge of the London office, and read:

> N. M. Rothschild & Sons have sent for us, asked us if we would act with them Europe re U.S. Government securities. A. Belmont & Co., New York, have called them assistant secretary of Treasury coming see him today to offer 4% bond. We replied we will be most happy act in concert with them provided you A. Belmont & Co. acted together U.S.
>
> N. M. Rothschild & Sons cable A. Belmont & Co., New York, see you also that our opinion is jointly that public will not take any loan not specifically gold bonds at any price satisfactory to U.S. Government.

Belmont confirmed the fact that Morgan was ordered to the meeting from abroad, but not before trying to make the affair look like some chance encounter between two boulevardiers at the races or at their club. "I made the arrangement with Mr. Morgan . . . the next morning," he told Senate investigators later. "He [Morgan] was going over to the Treasury [actually the subtreasury, a historic building still standing across from Morgan's office at Broad and Wall Streets] and so I went over. It was rather an informal appointment."

The cable received by Morgan shows that it had all the informality of a marriage arrangement between the houses of two small and jealous Middle European principalities in the eighteenth century, a fact so patently obvious that Belmont quickly had to abandon his man-of-the-world air before the senators. He admitted that "the reason I saw Mr. Morgan was because of my dispatches from the other side. I was trying to induce them to view favorably the possibility of any purchase abroad. They wanted me to see Mr. Morgan and consult with him, which I did."

Morgan, too, played a similar shell game with the senators, first with the complete fabrication that he had received a note from Curtis. The assistant secretary, as we have seen in his confidential report to Carlisle, never even considered Morgan among the people he should try to meet. Morgan then amended that claim to say: "That morning . . . I received a cable from my firm in London, J. S. Morgan & Co. stating that the Messrs. Rothschild, of London, had called upon them and stated that Mr. Belmont had cabled them of the necessity of the United States Government in relation to gold, and that they had suggested to them that the two firms should act together in conjunction with Messrs. Belmont and my firm in New York with a view to accomplishing something, if possible, in the matter."

Through all the purposeful confusion then and since, it is abundantly clear that Cleveland and his advisers were the ones insisting on a foreign loan and that they, probably, and the Rothschilds, certainly, saw the wisdom of shifting responsibility for the transaction to someone who could not be called a Shylock or a violator of the Temple. Thus was the Morgan firm brought in.

MORGÁN IS
BROUGHT IN

ON the morning of January 31, the day after Curtis's arrival in New York and his meeting with Belmont, the latter strolled into Pierpont Morgan's office at 23 Wall Street. Both had received their cabled instructions from their respective London offices earlier. The two financiers spoke briefly, then crossed the street to the subtreasury building where they met with the two assistant secretaries, Curtis and Jordan. About an hour later, Morgan returned to his office. He then sent a cable to his brother-in-law, Walter Burns, at the London office, in response to the earlier message.

He told Burns that there were Wall Streeters with a "more sanguine" outlook than Burns had on the possibility of selling to Europeans. Adding that he "should dislike see business largely hands Speyer & Co. and similar houses," he said: "The situation . . . is critical and we are disposed to do everything our power avert calamity and assist government under the power it actually possesses."

Then he detailed for Burns the highhanded proposition he intended to lay before the government: "Would the government make a private contract with a syndicate for the sale of 50,000,-000 with option of 50,000,000 additional, such a contract to be considered a state paper and confidential and not to be divulged until syndicate issue completed?" The same inquiry, taken down in the hand of someone in the Morgan firm, was also relayed to Curtis during that day and taken by him back to Washington that evening.

The proposition indicated that when opportunity came, Morgan was ready for it. He showed himself prepared to deal with a government as an equal power, from the grand elevation that had so irked the Czar when the Rothschilds tried it. And how different were the motives. Pierpont Morgan made them explicit in the same cable. He has been quoted as observing: "A man always has two reasons for the things he does—a good one, and the real one." But that was a cynical analysis of the behavior of others. He never felt the compulsion to give "good" reasons.

In his private communication to his London headquarters he said: "We think if this negotiation can be made will be most creditable all parties and pay good profit. . . . We all have large interests dependent maintenance sound currency United States." He then spelled out another "real" reason, the profit to be exacted: "If can obtain such exclusive contract should feel inclined form syndicate on 3⅝ to 3¾ percent basis provided at least 25,000,000 could be sold or underwritten in Europe."

The proposal as outlined in the cable to Burns and in the document Curtis took back to Washington that Thursday night was a remarkable one. It showed that Pierpont Morgan was indeed ready to come out of the financial shadows and move into the dominating position that he was to maintain until the end of his life only eighteen years later. He was prepared to take his place as an agent of capital who would give no quarter, a man worthy to tread the decks of the various yachts that he successively called by the one evocative name—*Corsair.* Formerly a mere bond salesman for his father's London firm, he was ready to deal with his own government *puissance à puissance,* as the diplomats would express it. He would try to dictate terms of absolute secrecy, even from congressional prying, and he would call for a loan of $100 million when Cleveland and Carlisle wanted, and the Treasury reserve required, about half that amount.

The Rothschilds may have allowed higher considerations to bubble up occasionally, as in their dealings with the Czar in 1891, but for Pierpont Morgan there was no greater good than profits and a favorable atmosphere in which to make them for himself and his customers.

Selflessness, patriotism, even the workings of a rudimentary conscience are qualities not often sought in the operations of the agents who move capital for wealthy individuals or institutions, but they can occasionally be found. Besides the attempt to curb the Russian pogroms, the House of Rothschild indulged itself on another occasion in an elevated gesture.

That was when the London banking firm lent Queen Victoria

£4,000,000 "for a few days" to secure an interest in the Suez Canal at "the patriotic rate of three per cent," as a chronicler of the merchant bankers, Joseph Wechsberg, observes. The patriotic motive in this instance may have been slightly tarnished by the fact that the Suez venture was to mean a great deal in pounds and pence to the British Empire and, consequently, to suppliers of capital like the Rothschilds.

An earlier and purer example involved another great merchant banking house, when one of the Hambros, then living in his adopted England, declined a commission on a transaction that helped the country of his birth, Denmark. There was even a chance of loss in this loan, made for a chancy war that could have gone against Denmark. Hambro may have been ready for a loss, the Rothschilds to practice a profitable patriotism, but the ferocious-eyed Morgan, then at the height of his magnificence, a six-footer weighing a little over two hundred pounds, was to let no such weakness corrupt his grasp for gain.

The terms laid down by Pierpont Morgan, a supposed supernumerary in the reserve operation, threw Cleveland and Carlisle into confusion when Curtis returned to Washington on Friday, February 1. Curtis was sent back to New York for further discussion with Pierpont Morgan and Belmont the following day, but on Sunday the administration dispatched Curtis's private secretary to the financiers in New York with the news that the government was breaking off all negotiations.

The turndown message, which Morgan and Belmont received early Monday, was in two parts, a "communication" and a covering letter. A rough draft of the communication was preserved by Curtis and in it can be read the agitation and distress of the administration. The main part was drawn up by Carlisle. He then added and subtracted much in the typescript and Cleveland, too, made a number of changes in his odd hand. As finally corrected it read:

> Having fully considered the information communicated by you in pursuance of the suggestion of Mr. Belmont touching the negotiation of a foreign loan to replenish our gold reserve, we are satisfied that the terms upon which it could be accomplished as indicated by your advice are so different from what was hoped, and that the probable results fall so far short of

what is desired that the plan for a syndicate arrangement made in advance is inexpedient. The advantages which such a plan was supposed to offer was the hope that it might be carried out upon more favorable terms as to rates of interest, less delay in completing the transaction than would result from public subscription in the usual way, and the obtaining of the amount of gold required by the government from abroad, thus favorably and rapidly re-establishing the reserve without danger of having it immediately reduced by withdrawals. As the matter is now presented, we are not encouraged to believe that any of these purposes would be accomplished by the plan suggested and that it is therefore the duty of the government to resort to other measures for the maintenance of the public credit.

In another scrap of paper saved by Curtis, Carlisle took issue with the "secret treaty" provision, noting that the administration "can not stipulate for secrecy as to the terms of information called for by Congress." The only kind of participation possible for the United States, he added, would be to "cooperate with syndicate in effecting issue and sale to full extent authorized by law and not involving risk of loss by the Government."

The covering letter to Belmont and Morgan that accompanied the communication noted that the negotiations were being called off for the reasons enumerated in the message "and others which will occur to you." Among them would have been the syndicate's insistence on secrecy and "cooperation" by the Treasury verging on unconditional surrender mentioned by Carlisle.

But the other reason that occurred to Morgan was neither of these. It was the fact that the President and his Treasury Secretary were having their cake and eating it, too. The negotiations were having an effect without being brought to a conclusion that would be profitable to Pierpont Morgan. The run on the gold reserve had dropped sharply, beginning with the day that Curtis made his first trip to New York, Wednesday, January 30. On that day less than $2.5 million was taken out, compared with nearly double that figure on the preceding day. And the outflow had dwindled still further in the next few days.

To understand how this had come about, it is necessary to go back to the newspaper accounts following Curtis's first visit. The papers were, of necessity, printing highly speculative reports in the face of the refusal of Curtis and the others to provide any details. But even these vague recitals contained sporadic reassurances.

The arrival of the assistant secretary in New York was reported in the following morning's *World* under the headline "Bonds Must Issue—Curtis Sent to New York." At this early date there was, of course, no mention of Morgan in the front-page story. Even in Friday morning's *World*, written after the meeting of Curtis, Belmont, and Morgan at the subtreasury, he appears in only a minor role. That account was headed: "By the Rothschilds!" and included a two-column cut of August Belmont.

The account went on to say that "a very busy three hours was put in by Curtis at the subtreasury. . . . The central figure at the conference was August Belmont, the American representative of the Rothschild millions. . . . Several banks were consulted, but Belmont and Morgan were regarded as the ones whose promises were the most potent." There was a quotation from Belmont: "Nothing can be said yet; no definite conclusion has been reached." Everyone else refused any kind of comment.

These and later newspaper reports were having the effect of giving the government respite from the gold drain without the necessity of being committed to any negotiation. Morgan recalled it this way: "During Friday, it began to be whispered around that the Government were in negotiation with Messrs. Belmont and ourselves for gold, whereupon parties who had shipped gold withdrew it from the steamers and a large portion of it was sent back into the Treasury. And it is fair to say that from this time forward until our entire contract had been perfected, little, if any, gold was shipped abroad."

As a footnote to Morgan's recollection given at the Senate investigation, it must be noted that he held an exaggerated view of Belmont's and his power to stanch the outflow; there was no question of its dropping to "little, if any" proportions. According to the government assayist's reports, the withdrawals continued, although during the seesawing negotiations they moved down sharply to anywhere from a half to a tenth of the three, four, and even seven million-per-day outflow that had prevailed as the panic built up.

In any case, the Cleveland administration was reaping the

benefit of a reduction in the gold outflow, a reduction that had been brought on by rumors and vague reports of a negotiation that Washington had now aborted.

Morgan was not the type to let anyone enjoy a cake of his baking without letting him in on the feast, and Belmont was also a jealous *pâtissier*. For both, there was, of course, the consideration of "good profit." To Morgan this was to mean driving the 3¾ percent bond bargain despite the fact that he and his overseas correspondent, Walter Burns, had agreed that that figure was just a bargaining point and that their European clients would be satisfied with an eighth percent less.

Then, too, there was the more important consideration of "large interests dependent upon maintenance sound currency United States" that Morgan had mentioned in his cable. There was never any question in the minds of the two agents, Belmont and Pierpont Morgan, that theirs and their customers' were the only interests to be considered.

It also never entered the minds of the two that the message from Cleveland and Carlisle that arrived early Monday need be considered a deterrent, despite its unequivocal terms. What did the decision of the nation's Chief Executive and his cabinet officer count for when profit was to be had?

After receiving the message, Belmont conferred with Morgan and immediately called the assistant secretary, Curtis, to demonstrate how little it mattered. He said, according to Curtis, "that he would come over [to Washington] on the 10 o'clock train, and that Mr. Morgan would follow that evening with a new proposition, or words to that effect; something to give me the idea that the negotiation was not closed by the communication which had been sent over that morning."

At the Senate hearings, where this recollection was provided, Curtis was a tricky witness who tried to blur everything he said with hazy qualifications. Later, he tried to fuzz this statement over by saying the call was from "Mr. Belmont . . . or whoever telephoned me." Pietro Mascagni, whose *Cavalleria Rusticana* was then coming into popularity, could have scored this part of the proceedings. In his opera it will be recalled, the hero Turiddu is killed offstage by his rival Alfio. Both are well known to all in the little Sicilian village that provides the setting for the tragedy; the slaying is witnessed by many, and there is no mystery to anyone on stage about who has killed whom. Yet a woman witness rushes in to scream, in the tradition of the Mafian *omerta:* "Someone has killed Turiddu!" (*Hanna ammazzato compare Turiddu!*") Curtis's "someone" would have benefitted from Mascagni's tremulous strings.

Curtis was also evasive about the reason for the financiers' visit in the face of the government's flat refusal to negotiate further. However, he was at length made to admit that some new considerations had prompted the government to reopen the negotiations. Chief among them was a concession by Belmont and Morgan, who agreed to drop the highhanded demand that the syndicate be considered some sort of equal power to be dealt with by secret treaty.

Belmont's hurried trip to Washington was the beginning of what amounted to an all-out assault by the financiers, with the ultimate objective a meeting with the head of the government himself, Grover Cleveland. On arriving at the capital, he met briefly with Curtis, only for the purpose of determining Carlisle's whereabouts, and visited Lamont on the way to the home of the Secretary of the Treasury.

Belmont told the Secretary of War that Morgan would be along on the afternoon train and gave him information on "exactly how matters were getting to be in New York; that they were on the verge of a panic." He reached Carlisle's home "just before his dinner hour, about half-past six, I think. . . . I simply told him the situation in general and how serious it was . . . that a panic would ensue, that is all, and suspension of specie payments." He also began the assault on the prime target by asking Carlisle's help in securing an audience with the President. "I also told him that Mr. Morgan was coming in the afternoon," he said at the Senate investigation.

Back in New York, Pierpont Morgan, who had met with Belmont at the Morgan home at 219 Madison Avenue, went on to his office, where he telephoned Carlisle. "Upon so communicating, I learned that it was proposed to issue a public advertisement [for the planned public sale of bonds] that afternoon, and I urged the secretary in the strongest terms not to do this, and at least to delay its issue until Mr. Belmont and myself should have an interview with the President and himself, stating at the same time that in view of the negotiation which we had undertaken and in view of what we had accomplished we felt entitled at least to that consideration. The secretary, a little later, replied that the delay would be granted."

Thus Morgan, who had been urging the need for speed and knew that a delay might bring the reserve to a point at which a popular subscription could not save it, was nevertheless ready to force a postponement when it suited his purpose. The deferral would give him time to further his own plan and, as an added benefit, would help build up additional pressure on the White House that would be valuable to his design.

After winning the Secretary's assurance, Pierpont Morgan prepared to join Belmont in the assault on Washington. He took the Cortlandt Street ferry to the Pennsylvania's terminal across the river. There his private car was joined to the Congressional Limited, which left at three-twenty. On board with him were two close associates, one decorative, the other useful. They played important parts in the affairs of Morgan, so a closer look at both is called for.

The ornamental one was Robert Low Bacon, twenty-four years younger than his chief and the bearer of the kind of spectacular good looks that often prompt misgivings about the owner's ability to carry out the normal functions of life without trained assistance. But his jut-jawed handsomeness, so like the collar ad and magazine hero illustrations of the period, was the occasion of this soppy tribute from Anna Robeson Burr, the late-blooming Victorian novelist and biographer of National City's James Stillman: "When the angels of God took unto themselves wives among the daughters of men, the result was the Morgan partners," she wrote.

When he led the Harvard football team fourteen years earlier, Bacon had been described by Walter Camp, the founding father of football hoopla and publicity, as "a tall crinkly-haired blond giant, handsome as Adonis."

While at Harvard he also had rowed number seven on the university crew and had been an excellent boxer. Occasionally his sparring partner was a man his direct opposite in every way, the decidedly unprepossessing Theodore Roosevelt. To round out Bacon's athletic accomplishments, he also excelled at the hundred yard dash and the quarter-mile run. After graduation, his football prominence led to what may have been the apex of his career, when he headed a group that investigated and summarily disposed of the plebeian, non-Harvard charges that the game was physically injuring the youth of the land.

Still, despite the tortuous tribute of Mrs. Burr and the worshipful windbaggery of Camp, Bacon could use trained assistance.

Conrad Jordan, the Treasury official in charge of the New York office, was to complain of his "stupidity" in the aftermath of the gold contract negotiations, and Bacon and Pierpont Morgan were to part in another few years following an incident in which Bacon was either stupid, somnolent, or possibly venal.

The incident occurred when Morgan's arch-enemy Edward H. Harriman was buying great blocks of stock in Northern Pacific, a railroad that Morgan, then vacationing in Europe, definitely did not want in Harriman's hands. The hectic buying went unnoticed, or at least unreported by Bacon, who was supposedly watching the store. After leaving Morgan, Bacon filled out the rest of his life in a succession of diplomatic and military jobs that required the frequent wearing of colorful uniforms and state dress. He filled both ornamentally.

The other traveler was Morgan's lawyer, the very useful Francis Lynde Stetson. He recalled later that Morgan had called him as he was leaving the office for the ferry, saying, "There may be papers to be drawn and I want you." The lawyer knew little of the preliminary steps that had been taken in connection with the gold negotiation, having been out of the city for some time on other business for his client until late Sunday night. But, Stetson said, "I asked no further questions, but went. He said that it might result in a contract, and, if so, he wanted me to draw it."

Stetson, though, had a far greater value than his willingness to trot in the master's footsteps at such a command. He formed a powerful link between Morgan and the man in the White House. Cleveland had served a term as President from 1884 to 1888, the first Democrat to win that office in the years of hatred that followed the Civil War. He had lost his bid for reelection in one of the quirky contests of that era, despite the fact that he had won the popular vote, and by a greater margin than the one that had carried him into office four years earlier. The anachronism known as the electoral college had served effectively to frustrate the popular mandate.

Before winning the office back from Benjamin Harrison, thus becoming the only Chief Executive ever to serve two nonconsecutive terms, Grover Cleveland proceeded, like many others of his official family, to Wall Street. Lamont was there, along with William C. Whitney, Secretary of the Navy in the first Cleveland administration, and there were many others putting to work the knowledge and influence they had accumulated during the years of power. Lamont made money in the market with the help of Whitney, who also dabbled in municipal traction matters. Cleveland, though, turned to Francis Lynde Stetson, joining his law firm the day after leaving the White House at an office a few doors down Broad Street from Morgan's own headquarters in the Drexel, Morgan & Co. building.

Stetson was already representing Morgan, having acquired him as a client in February 1887. Nine years Morgan's junior, he was no stranger to the shadier realms of financiering. Early in his career he had had to face some severe questioning from a group of New York state senators for his part in the payment of a $500,000 bribe by his client, Jacob Sharp, an aptly named and celebrated trickster, to the city's board of aldermen for a trolley franchise.

Such were Pierpont Morgan's traveling companions on that journey of Monday, February 4. On arriving at Union Station at about seven-thirty that evening, he dispatched Stetson, often jokingly referred to as "Morgan's attorney general," directly to the White House, where he was to try to win an audience with his old associate, now the President of the United States.

Meanwhile Belmont, with the same objective in mind, was calling on Secretary Carlisle, whom he had difficulty in locating, at Carlisle's home. Neither he nor Stetson was to win an immediate appointment with the Chief Executive. Later, at the senatorial bond investigation, Stetson explained that at the White House, "I was told that the President was tired and could not see me, so that I merely stopped there to see the President on my way to the Arlington, but did not see him, and did not see him until the morning of Tuesday, February 5." If lawyer Stetson's explanation seems wordy and a bit repetitive, it had good reason to be. He was volunteering it at the bond probe in an attempt to head the senators off from the natural conclusion that he was taking advantage of his special relationship with Cleveland to drive a bargain.

While the two of them carried out their separate sapper operations, Pierpont Morgan left Union Station for a curious diversion, a solitary visit to a Mrs. J. Kearney Warren at her home on K Street. Mrs. Warren is described as an "old and dear friend of the Morgan family" by Pierpont Morgan's son-in-law and official biographer, Herbert Satterlee. In a day so devoted to punctilio, the unannounced visit should have been an uncomfortable surprise to the lady, and Satterlee assures us that it was. It lasted about an hour, after which Pierpont Morgan continued on to the great hotel to which he had earlier sent Bacon.

The hotel was the Arlington, as mentioned by Stetson. It was Pierpont Morgan's invariable command post in the nation's capital. One of the oldest, largest, and most expensive of Washington hotels, run by Theophilus Roessle and his son, innkeepers formerly of Albany and Lake George, it consisted then of a cluster of five mansions remodeled and joined together as a habitat for royalty, visiting ambassadors, and high federal officials such as Presidents-elect, vice presidents, cabinet officers, and the like. The individual homes which comprised it had once been the townhouses of similar dignitaries. But its claim to fusty glory was not its chief attraction for Pierpont Morgan. He was drawn to it for the superb strategic view it commanded of the White House. Only the sparse foliage of the park at Lafayette Square stood between it and the Chief Executive's home.

When he rejoined Bacon and, shortly after, Belmont and Stetson at the Arlington it was nearly nine o'clock on a winter night and the attacking force hadn't even the consolation of the view. But they set about changing that state of affairs. Probably at Belmont's instigation, they left the hotel for their first objective, the home of the War Secretary, patronage dispenser, and general factotum, Daniel Scott Lamont. Much later, in 1904, when the Morgan legend had reached such proportions as to blot out the importance of other mortals, and, in fact, when Lamont himself was a Morgan spearholder in the financier's Northern Pacific railroad, the Secretary of War recalled the visit in this way:

> My recollection is that Mr. Morgan came to my house late in the evening much put out because he had found himself an unwelcome visitor at Washington, and in a state of despair because he believed that the President and his cabinet were not alive to the desperate peril in which the country was and that nothing was to be accomplished by his visit.
>
> He declared that we were on the brink of the abyss of financial chaos and would be on a silver basis in forty-eight hours, and that in view of the situation he had determined to go back home and put his house in order.

Lamont, who set his recollections down in a letter to Richard Olney, Cleveland's Attorney General during the period of the Belmont-Morgan negotiations, added: "As I recall I strongly urged him to remain over and see you, and finding that you had not retired for the night, he consented and did go around to your house. . . ."

Olney then picked up the story. Not so misty-eyed about Morgan as Lamont was in 1904, he recalled that there were others in the party, including Belmont and Bacon, and even thought he remembered Lamont being part of the force that came to his home—a point that Lamont disputed. Olney wrote: ". . . Morgan stated that they despaired of accomplishing anything in Washington and were going to return to New York that night and let things take their course. . . . I think you and I persuaded them to hold on and try the result of an interview with Mr. Cleveland the next morning which we felt certain we could bring about. . . ."

It is interesting and relevant to the Pierpont Morgan myth to pause over this 1904 dialogue between Olney, the savior of the Pullman Company a decade earlier, and Lamont, who was wearing the Morgan cap at this time. It came about as an exchange of critical comments by the two on an article Grover Cleveland had just written for the *Saturday Evening Post*.

Cleveland's article was a chronicle of the events leading up to the Belmont-Morgan contract and the two former cabinet officers devoted the private exchange to straightening out some of the former President's faulty recollections. One thing that Olney, at least, seemed to find objectionable was the reverential tone used toward Morgan; the aging ex-President ascribes to him almost supernatural ubiquity, sagacity, and omnipotence. Indeed, the *Post* article is one of the founding documents of the Morgan myth, a circumstance that is not so surprising when the relationship between the two men at the time is taken into consideration.

Within a year of the *Post* article Pierpont Morgan was to select Grover Cleveland, for purely olfactory purposes, in connection with a noisome scandal that had grown up around New York's insurance industry. Cleveland had no qualifications for the figurehead post he was given other than that faint odor of sanctity that gathers around the no-longer-powerful and can be used to mask gamier emanations in the public nostril. Despite such impediments in its author, the article has since been accepted uncritically, not only by Morgan partisans, which is understandable, but by serious scholars, which is baffling. Its argument and purported facts form a subcutaneous lump, as if some deep-burrowed wood louse lay just beneath the surface, in at least three highly lauded histories of the era.

But back to our tired group of plotters. They had succeeded in their first objective. Having arranged the meeting with Cleveland for the next day through Olney, with the help of Lamont, they temporarily fell back to their Arlington headquarters. The others went to bed, but Pierpont Morgan's light burned until early the next morning. He was indulging himself in his favorite game of solitaire, called "Miss Milliken," before taking his triumphal rest.

The next day, Tuesday, February 5, dawned clear, cold, and bright. Some time around nine o'clock, Morgan, Belmont, Stetson, and Bacon came together with Cleveland, Treasury Secretary Carlisle, and Attorney General Olney in the President's office, or "outer room" at the White House. There Cleveland, despite his rejection of the offer for a private negotiation, consented to listen to whatever proposition the financiers were ready to formulate.

Both August Belmont and Pierpont Morgan began with a description of the tenuous condition of the Treasury, especially the branch on Wall Street, and of the rising sense of panic in the financial district. They were aided and abetted in their compelling presentation by the periodic appearance in the outer room of Treasury messengers with dispatches from Assistant Secretary Jordan in New York showing the up-to-the-minute withdrawals.

The previous day, as rumors continued to circulate that a solution to the gold crisis was being worked out, only $63,000 had been taken out. But as the two groups met on the fifth, some word of a breakdown must have got abroad, and withdrawals were running at six times that rate. By the end of the day a total of nearly $400,000 was to be taken out.

There was another danger. Cleveland was well aware of it, but that did not stop either Belmont or Morgan from bringing it up to add to the President's uneasiness. It was largely a matter of the psychology of investors here and abroad who set such great store by the precious metal. Although foreign investors knew generally of the country's straits in regard to the reserve, they did not know exactly how bad the situation was. Even such well informed agents of theirs as Belmont and Morgan probably were not possessed of completely accurate data on just how much remained in the Treasury. But this relatively comfortable state of generalized disquiet would last only as long as the Treasury was able to pay out gold in the form of coin rather than bullion. When it had to tap the bullion supply the panic would be on in earnest.

There were two reasons for this. First, the bullion, in the form of bulky bars and bricks, was an inconvenient and even unacceptable medium of exchange, and because there was an unavoidable loss in transforming it into coin, it was actually worth less, ounce for ounce, than coin. But far more important was the fact that it was generally known here and in Europe that the bullion portion of the reserve came to about $40 million. Once the point was reached at which the subtreasury would have to refuse to pay in coin, there would be no mystery about the condition of the reserve. To delay that moment as long as possible, shipments of all available coin were being made daily from the eight other subtreasuries and three mints scattered around the country to restock the New York subtreasury, which was at the point of maximum withdrawal pressure.

The panic point was perilously close; only about $3 million in coin remained in New York as the Wall Street forces unfolded their arguments to the President. As an instance of the mystique that surrounded the actual condition of the reserve, Pierpont Morgan was under the impression that more than twice that amount—or $7 million—was on hand, according to what he told the investigating senators later. Echoing his harangue of that morning before Cleveland, he added at the Senate hearing: "If I had gone to the Treasury Department with $10,000,000 of United States gold certificates, payable in gold, I could not have collected them in gold." He meant gold coin, of course, and he was even righter than he knew. He added: "I think the Bank of England at that time, held a great deal more gold coin than the United States Treasury."

The dramatic recital by Belmont and Morgan of conditions that Cleveland knew more about than they did not serve to sway the President. That was accomplished with a subterfuge, a suggestion that he buy the gold by contract under a disused, forgotten Civil War power granted to Lincoln. It was Section 3700 of the Revised Statutes, adopted to enable Lincoln's Treasury Secretary, Salmon P. Chase, to obtain gold under the emergency conditions of the war. It read:

> The Secretary of the Treasury may purchase coin with any of the bonds or notes of the United States authorized by law, at such rates and upon such terms as he may deem most advantageous to the public interest.

The difference between this law and the redemption statute under which he had held the previous two bond issues seems piddling, but the stolid, unimaginative lawyer in the White House was attracted by just such hair bisections. With the redemption statute Cleveland had always felt, possibly correctly, that the authority granted had been intended only to create, not replenish, the reserve. The diffidence this view had instilled in him had led him continually and typically to seek a renewed mandate from Congress—to spread the blame, cynics added. The legislators were equally constant in refusing to share the responsibility. The turndown had been especially final only a month before this meeting when he had pleaded with a Congress rendered decidedly hostile as a result of the inroads made in the 1894 election by silverites, Populists, and just plain haters of the Eastern financial establishment. Of course, the newly elected members hadn't taken office yet, but they were already making their influence felt. And the lame ducks they would displace on March 4 weren't disposed to be friendly with a President who shared the blame for some of their disabilities.

So Section 3700 was a welcome straw for Cleveland to grab at, for it satisfied his legal-fogey mind as offering clearer power than the redemption statute. His whole attitude toward the Belmont-Morgan offer changed on his hearing of it.

The laurels for suggesting Section 3700 clearly belong to Pierpont Morgan. Stetson credited him with bringing it up; so did Cleveland and so, long afterward, did Olney, not to mention Morgan's son-in-law, Herbert Satterlee. Although they all have their weaknesses as witnesses, there would be no reason to dispute them, except that this is exactly what was done by a garrulous old former editor of the New York *Post,* a writer on economic matters named Horace White.

In a letter to his old newspaper dated July 8, 1908, White, late in his own life and long after the gold contract, simply states as a fact that William E. Curtis, the assistant secretary, first discovered the existence of Section 3700 and brought it to the attention of Morgan and Carlisle. Most commentators since have accepted White's dictum and denied the claim for Morgan, a curious reversal of the usual mythmaking for the financier's benefit.

But White's letter to the *Post* has to be dismissed as incorrect. He of course was nowhere near the scene of the contract negotiations, but more important, neither was Curtis. Strangely enough in view of the important part he played and was to play, he had sent a note to Secretary Carlisle just before the meeting saying: "I will be in my office and you can send for me if wanted." He was not summoned and it would have been difficult for him to suggest anything to the White House conferees from the Treasury building in the next block.

There is further evidence for the legitimacy of Morgan's claim. At the time the statute was enacted, Curtis was about eight years old while Morgan was in his twenties and active, as a rich man's son, in the very gold market in which Chase would be putting the law into action. Later, in the seventies and eighties, Pierpont Morgan was associated with Jay Cooke and with the elder Belmont in government bond activity related to the resumption of specie payments and would have had some familiarity with the enactments then in force.

The suggestion to use Section 3700 was made early in the conference between the two sets of negotiators. From that point on Cleveland appeared to drop his resistance to the private arrangement. The only question to be determined was whether Section 3700 was still on the books. Many such emergency war powers granted before and since, even some that could be used to transform the country into a Cromwellian dictatorship, are not expunged; others are. It remained to be discovered whether Congress, in some burst of unaccustomed efficiency, had wiped the statute off the books. Attorney General Olney detached himself from the proceedings to get his staff started on this tedious task.

"The discussion on this question," Stetson recalled, "then arose and continued for four hours, the President leaving the room in the meantime for nearly an hour, going off somewhere, I do not know where, and the discussion going on with the Secretary of the Treasury in his absence."

§ 35 §

The statute was determined to be still in force before the end of the session, but in the meantime Grover Cleveland had shown that he was going to play a strong hand in the negotiation. Much as he was at a disadvantage before the potentates of Wall Street, he indicated that he was not going to surrender completely the responsibilities of his office. Seemingly a stolid, bloodless sort of fat man masking feeling and even thought in the stiff, formal speech and prose of the day, it was typical of him to rise to occasions and reveal a strong and human being buried in the flesh. In his first campaign, he had met and conquered a deadly smear, the charge of being intimate with a woman and siring her bastard child, by simply stating that he had reason to believe the child was not his. He would not stoop to the hypocrisy of denying the liaison, and the commoner (and more acceptable) Victorian practice of lying his way out of the whole thing never entered his mind.

After that display of all-too-human frailty and uncommon honesty in dealing with its consequences, he showed an uncommon bravery in dealing with a crisis that occurred only a few months after he took office for his second term. Cancer was discovered in his upper jaw. An operation removed all malignancy, but he vastly increased the discomfort and danger of the ordeal by insisting that the surgery be performed in the strictest secrecy aboard a private yacht, far from hospital facilities that might be needed in an emergency. And he imposed this trial upon himself at a time when he was troubled with the initial stages of the panic and with a tariff bill he was desperately and vainly trying to block. Finally, despite his dull, passionless look and manner, he was one of the few Presidents to bring a touch of romance into the affairs of state in his courtship and marriage to Frances Folsom while he was in the White House.

So it may not have been completely unexpected when, toward the close of the conference, he let Belmont and Pierpont Morgan know the conditions that would be exacted by the United States in return for the contract. The status of Section 3700 having been resolved, the door to the outer office continued to swing open and shut for the passage of the messengers of doom with the latest gold outflow figures from the Treasury. Amid these interruptions, Cleveland stood up to the financiers and told them there would be no question of acceding to their demand for a $100 million purchase of gold. It would be about half that, he said. He must have shaken the Wall Streeters considerably with that announcement and its implication that profits from the bond sale for the purchase would be halved. About $65 million would bring the reserve to where it was supposed to be, he continued, and that would be all he would authorize.

He then moved on to his second and most telling point. He reviewed the futility of the government's previous bond issues, the first a year earlier and the second only the preceding November. The net result had been a mere shifting of ownership tags on some of the gold that was in the Treasury, from government to bond bidder and back to government again, while the drain had continued unabated. The only way another attempt would succeed, he went on, was for the two organizers of the syndicate to pledge that at least half the gold would be physically brought to New York from overseas investors and, more important still, that every effort would be made by the syndicate participants, "so far as lies in their power," to keep the flow from reversing.

A clause embodying that promise was agreed on. Herbert Satterlee credits the financier with a bouncy reaction to the President's demand for the double-edged pledge: "Yes sir, I will guarantee it during the life of the syndicate, and that means until the contract has been concluded and the goal has been reached."

It is questionable whether he was as light-heartedly agreeable as that. That he was under considerable tension was shown in an incident that occurred at the breakup of the conference around two o'clock, when Cleveland suggested that the participants go out for something to eat. A friend of Cleveland's, John G. Milburn, recalled the story: "I remember Mr. Morgan's describing how he held a large unlighted cigar in his hand, and at the end of the conference he found it was gone, having been unconsciously ground into powder under the excitement of the occasion."

Thus the meeting ended on a light note as Pierpont Morgan brushed the dust of a shredded cigar from his knees. But the promise he had given could not, and, as we shall see, was not kept. Still, all the details needed for "final agreement," as August Belmont called it, had been worked out and a date for the drawing up and signing of the contract was set for three days hence, on Friday, February 8. The reason for the delay was Cleveland's desire to have Congress shoulder the blame for forcing him into what the newspapers were telling him would be a highly unpopular private contract with Wall Street.

He wanted to make his usual offer to share responsibility with Congress in the form of new authorization for a bond issue. He did so on Thursday, but added a curious new element that seemed designed to kill all chances for passage of the bill. He asked for a promise to repay the bondholders in gold, an obligation the United States had never before undertaken even though in practice such redemptions always had been in gold. Such an explicit declaration probably never would have gotten through any Congress, but with the group he was dealing with now, repudiated at the polls in November, it seemed calculated to produce a rebuff. Whether or not this was the case, it had that effect.

The financiers had returned to New York at the close of the Tuesday meeting. Belmont, ever mindful of the correct form, had the grace to wait until hearing that the Cleveland proposal, called the Springer Bill, had gone down to defeat about six o'clock Thursday evening. Then he caught the evening train for the capital. Not so Morgan and his party. They felt under no compulsion to keep up appearances. The trio—Bacon, Stetson, and Pierpont Morgan—had rushed back to Washington, once again in the private car behind the Congressional Limited, hours before the Springer Bill had even come up for a vote.

Their departure and the contempt for public opinion that it represented was noted by Arthur Brisbane, then in his early thirties and managing editor of Pulitzer's widely read morning paper, *The World*. His by-lined front page report, which, of course, did not appear until the following day, showed a complete grasp of what had been agreed on at the first meeting and of the charade of presenting a foredoomed bill to Congress before the final signing.

"Final action in the bond matter was delayed until the administration bill should die," Brisbane wrote, "simply because it would not have done to let the bankers, by a private arrangement, supply the money until all hope of help from Congress, in the ordinary democratic way, should be gone."

It was all play-acting in preparation for the cut-and-dried denouement on Friday, the signing of a contract that would give Wall Street—and above all, J. Pierpont Morgan—the heroic role of saving the credit of the United States. But even in the wildest contrivances of their stagecraft, the politicians and financiers never thought of introducing the hackneyed device of the pathetic fallacy—the use of natural forces to point up and mirror the drama onstage.

In what followed, the natural forces themselves took care of the oversight. Nature staged a storm that not even a fifth-rate playwright would have indulged in. Just as the economy was locked in the grip of the terrible depression that followed the Panic of 1893, so the nation became locked in a fury of wind and snow that began early on that Thursday. The elements seemed bent on emulating the icy-hearted moneymen whose "extremely harsh" bargaining "measured with little mercy the emergency of the Treasury," in the words of one observer. Men were numbed by the cold, as all of man's works, from farm to factory, were numbed by the congealing of commerce. Snow and cold froze axles, journal boxes, and bearings, blocking movement that had been rusting to a halt anyway.

The storm began in the southeast, bringing temperatures averaging about 9½ degrees along the eastern seaboard as Morgan, in his millionaire's equipage, clicked southward to Washington in advance of its approach. By that evening, in New York, cable cars were motionless on Broadway, theatergoers walked or stayed home, derelicts froze in doorways. The storm had spread over most of the country by then. "Never in the history of the weather bureau has there been such cold weather over so great an area of the United States," *The World* reported alongside Brisbane's piece.

In the Friday morning editions there was no room for gold contract news on the front page; the weather story under the two-line banner, "Ice Snow & Gales/Rule the Country," together with a spectacularly large engraving of the ice-caked harbor viewed from the Pulitzer Building, took up every column. Although only five and a half inches of snow had fallen in New York, gale-piled drifts, the biting cold, and the extent of the storm throughout the country made it "the worst blizzard" to that time, even with "The Blizzard of '88" fresh in mind.

Paradoxically, the storm, which kept Morgan off the front pages, had a hand in the creation of the Pierpont Morgan myth. It perversely delayed August Belmont's arrival until very late in the ultimate contract-signing, a condition that has enabled succeeding generations to forget that he was even there. Morgan and his party, by their arrogant early departure, were able to spend the night comfortably at the Arlington. The punctilious

Belmont, delaying his trip until after the Springer Bill had been disposed of, paid for his sense of the right form by being hung up somewhere between Philadelphia and Wilmington at the height of the storm. And on a trainful of actors, too! It was a troupe headed by Sir Herbert Beerbohm Tree, holder of the lowest form of knighthood, and they were to do scenes from *Hamlet* at the National Press Club. Delayed for more than seven hours while a force of two hundred men struggled to free the train from a drift south of Philadelphia, they didn't arrive in Washington until two in the afternoon.

Long before that the storm had ended. While Belmont fretted aboard an uncomfortable train, Pierpont Morgan and his party rose early, breakfasted, and slogged their way across the drifts around Lafayette Square.

Their route through the six-acre park planned by George Washington and laid out by Pierre Charles L'Enfant took them over much the same path that had been followed by British soldiers on their way to burn the White House eighty-three years earlier. The difference was that this time the more crucial Treasury, just to the east, was the objective. The executive mansion had been taken three days before.

As the Wall Streeters progressed purposefully through the lovely park, they had easily in view the stately procession of homes that surrounded it on the east, north, and west, homes whose dwellers had played leading, and often brutally bloody, parts in earlier dramas involving the republic that was now at their mercy. To their right, as they started, was the onetime home of Commodore Stephen Decatur, naval hero of four wars, declared and undeclared, and suppressor of the Barbary Coast pirates. He died in this house facing the northwest corner of the park on March 22, 1820, at the age of forty-one, of wounds suffered in a duel over a matter of professional honor so complexly trivial as not to be worth the recounting.

A few doors from Decatur's was the former home of one of the country's more celebrated rascal-heroes, Daniel E. Sickles, who lost a leg in a particularly foolhardy action at Gettysburg. Before the war and the loss of his limb, though, on February 27, 1859, he had pursued Philip Barton Key, son of the author of the national anthem, around this very park to shoot him down in the gutter of Madison Place, on the east side, near where the men of finance were striding. Key died shortly after in the nearby Metropolitan

Club, another of the historic Lafayette Square houses, in which he had been living. The slaying was the result of Sickles' discovery that Key and his wife had been having an affair, one that had had a gamey beginning with a quick coupling by the erring pair "in the parlor, on the sofa" of Sickles' home a year earlier.

This same Metropolitan Club passed later into the hands of William H. Seward, Lincoln's Secretary of State, and was the scene of an assassination attempt on Seward on April 14, 1865, part of the conspiracy centering on the President.

Across the park from where the New Yorkers were marching on the Treasury was another building that had housed a tragic figure. He was Major Henry R. Rathbone, an aide to Lincoln who, with his wife, was in the Presidential box at Ford's Theatre that same night of April 14. He had witnessed the killing of Lincoln and had suffered serious stab wounds in the head and neck in trying to capture the President's assassin, John Wilkes Booth. Eighteen years later, Rathbone, possibly as a result of that shattering experience, went out of his mind far from this place, in Hanover, Germany. He killed his wife, tried to kill his two children, and succeeded in wounding himself. He recovered, but spent the rest of his unfortunate life in an insane asylum.

Even a more international scale of mayhem and lawlessness was represented by the square through which Pierpont Morgan, Bacon, and Stetson were passing. Two other former occupants of neighboring houses there, Captain Charles Wilkes and Senator John Slidell, met on the high seas during the first year of the Civil War. Slidell, no longer a United States senator, and a companion, both of whom were representing the Confederacy in a secret mission to the Continent, were seized and taken from the British steamer *Trent* by Wilkes and brought back aboard the United States Navy vessel he was commanding to be imprisoned in Boston.

All in all, except for the lack of any verifiable massacres of Indians on the square, the six-acre plot symbolized in compact form the all-too-often ignored seamier and bloodier side of the history of the republic. It was unfortunate that the planners of the park had bowed to convention in placing totally unoriginal statuary in it—Lafayette in the middle, other heroes at the corners. A more creative conception could have summed up a neglected part of the nation's history in massive groups of granite, bronze, and marble representing presidential assassinations, men going mad, cuckolded husbands gunning down their tormentors, piracy, and the like.

And after this historic walk of 1895, the capital's monument planners could have added a tall business-suited bronze of J. Pierpont Morgan at the head of his entourage, striding through the snow on his mission of little mercy. It could be a hopeful symbol in contrast to the others, showing how the baser passions and vices are in a sense refined, with the shedding of money substituting for the shedding of blood in the higher reaches of plutocracy. The whole display would form an apotheosis of civilization, in which rage, wrongs, violence, and hate are transmuted, through the medium of wealth, into something not necessarily finer, but less bothersome, more socially acceptable.

The walk across this Grand-Guignol slice of American history brought the New Yorkers to the Treasury building. Here they met first with Assistant Secretary Curtis and a stenographer, in Carlisle's large office, to work out the details of the contract. It was then typed up and taken into the Treasury Secretary's private office, where Carlisle was closeted with the Attorney General. Carlisle made some additions in the four-page typescript. It was now getting on toward noon, when a message from Cleveland was to be read in Congress announcing that the private negotiation had been completed. But there was no sign of August Belmont, who was still aboard the storm-delayed train. So cable authority was obtained from London to enable Morgan to sign for Belmont and the Rothschilds. In a commanding scrawl he appended to the corrected document: "Approved J. P. Morgan & Co. for all parties of the second part, as authorized."

It happened that another two hours or so was needed for the preparation of the final form of the contract in quadruplicate. By that time Belmont had arrived and was able to sign for the Rothschilds. But the delay served to thrust the urbane Rothschild agent into the background and the first great legend of Morgan was born, the one in which he figured as the singlehanded savior of his country in its moment of sore financial extremity.

And what were the conditions for this act of salvation? The government was to get from the syndicate $65,116,244 in gold within a year. (As it happened, the delivery was completed in less than six months.) In return, the syndicate was given an issue of bonds with a total face value of $62,315,400, maturing in thirty years—that is, in 1925—and paying 4 percent interest, which comes to nearly $2½ million annually for three decades.

The government, of course, was receiving a premium, an excess of $2,800,844 in gold over the redemption value. But this was due to no sudden onslaught of generosity on the part of Morgan and Belmont. In fact, it represented just the opposite.

The premium was simply a recognition that such bonds, backed by the full faith and credit of the federal power and paying $40 annually on each $1,000, would be attractive enough to lead investors to bid more than the face value. In fact, they did, as we shall see.

To understand this, and to understand the harshness with which Morgan drove his bargain, it is necessary to go into the somewhat confusing jargon of the bond salesman. The premium on the bond itself, at the insistence of the syndicate and with Morgan taking the lead in that insistence, came to 4½ percent, or, in the more usual terminology, the bond was said to be priced effectively at 104½. This meant that the actual interest payout as promised on the face of the bond amounted to 3¾ percent. Thus it can be seen that up to the very end, to the signing of the contract on that cold February morning, Morgan was able to hold out for his figure rather than the 3⅜ percent his brother-in-law Walter Burns had said Europeans would gladly have accepted.

But this was a point of petty profiteering, compared with the full implication of his demand that the bonds be sold to the syndicate at an effective price of 104½. For at this very period, similar but much older United States 4 percent bonds were bringing 111 on the market. These issues had less than half the time of the Morgan-Belmont bonds left until they were redeemable at their face value of 100, and so would have commanded less of a premium. Thus if Pierpont Morgan possessed even the modest competence of a fledgling clerk in a bond house, he could not but have been aware that the bonds he was demanding at 104½ could be sold immediately at better than 111. And that's exactly what happened. The bonds, which were delivered to the syndicate in batches as gold was brought to the subtreasury, went initially for 112½, crept up to 119 by May, and were selling for 124 during the summer.

That increase in value was accomplished through the operation of forces Morgan could not necessarily foresee and certainly could not control. They included such factors as the discovery of additional gold reserves in South Africa, a general quickening of trade, and favorable crop prospects.

The profit that resulted has exercised many since. *The World* stormed at the time and estimated the figure at $16 million. Another source puts the amount at 7 to 12 millions. *The World's* computation is probably close to the truth if all profits to every member of the syndicate—the two London houses, their two American branches, and the principal bankers that lay in the orbits of the four—are taken into consideration. It is based on the idea that the ultimate purchaser would find a 3 percent yield attractive and thus could be charged an effective price of 133⅓. That there was such a market for United States bonds was shown by the clause that Belmont and Morgan agreed to have inserted into the contract providing for a 3 percent issue in the totally unlikely event that Congress would pass a bill specifically stating that redemption would be in gold. If 133⅓ was the price paid by the ultimate buyer, *The World's* figure was accurate.

In all events, the exact profits can never be known. At the Senate probe set up specifically for the purpose of establishing that imponderable a year and a half later, Carlisle referred all questions about profits to the syndicate, but, as will be seen later, Belmont, Morgan, and other members of that group who appeared contemptuously told the inquisitors that, in effect, it was none of their business. Records of the transaction, we are told by the successor to the House of Morgan, no longer exist.

But even the largest of the estimates—$16 million divided between the Houses of Rothschild and Morgan and further subdivided among the major banks here and abroad—dribbles into insignificance in comparison with the intangibles of power and influence the operation conferred on Pierpont Morgan. His role as "savior" of his country and as distributor of the bonds that fell to his lot propelled him to the forefront of the world stage as a premier financier. With the issue of bonds he had extracted from the government, there was put into his hands an instrument with which he built a network of financial dominance unparalleled before and since. Its dimensions would never be discovered until a rare set of circumstances produced the congressional "Money Trust" investigation in the year before his death nearly two decades later.

Even at the signing of the contract Treasury Secretary Carlisle had recognized "that the terms were hard for the Government." It was an admission he was ready to make only at the end of an exhaustive grilling by the Senate probers. A much more forcible verdict was freely given by a knowledgeable financial observer of the time, Alexander Dana Noyes, a writer for the New York *Evening Post*. His were the remarks on the harshness of the terms and the lack of mercy shown the government that already have been quoted. Of Morgan's demand for a bond priced at the equivalent of 104½ while similar government securities were selling at 111, he wrote in 1909: "This was asking a heavy concession; no such demand has been made by any Government-bond syndicate during the present generation."

Except for one important reservation, a case could be made for the financiers. It might be argued that they were entitled to their heavy tribute had they been able to accomplish the huge task they had set themselves: reversing the flow of gold from the United States Treasury.

But the reservation is all important. They could not succeed in this aim and they did not succeed. The syndicate had some success up until mid-June, then the drain began anew. The *Evening Post's* Noyes was one of the few with the grasp of events and the even more important element of courage to point up the failure. He did so on several occasions. As he was preparing his final version of the negotiation fourteen years after it had taken place, he reported that he had come under pressure from "some of the Treasury officers of the second Cleveland Administration" to change his views. He doesn't name the would-be censors, but by then, as we have seen, a considerable number of the parties to the transaction on the government's side, including Cleveland himself before his death in 1908, had moved profitably into the Pierpont Morgan orbit.

The argument put forth to Noyes by these ex-officials was that the scheme had worked for four and a half months and therefore was a success. Noyes pointed out, though, that the expectation had been that the Treasury "would be put permanently on its feet and the exhausting drain of gold ended." "In this respect," he added, "the experiment was a failure; the subsequent loss of gold was probably greater because of the artificial damming up of gold exports." He therefore refused to alter his judgment and repeated his conclusion that the "undertaking to protect the Treasury had broken down."

By the end of the year it was obvious that the effort had failed. From July to November, about $65 million—the amount that had been delivered during the first operation of the contract—had been withdrawn. During this period the syndicate, through the same kind of makeshift efforts as in previous rescue attempts on behalf of the reserve, had been able to raise an additional $20 million, but by December 31, 1895, the Treasury's supply of gold was nearly as depleted as it had been a year earlier. A new bond issue was announced by Cleveland in January 1896.

This time the effort was successful, through no fault of Morgan's. In fact, he was nearly squeezed out of any kind of participation in the wake of charges that he had attempted to impose another private contract on the government. The scandal that resulted apparently forced the President to offer the bond issue— $100 million on this occasion—to the highest bidders in a popular subscription. The response was gratifying, with the investing public oversubscribing by nearly six times the amount sought. Morgan was able to take only about a third of the issue by considerably sweetening his bid of a year earlier. Still the price he put on the bonds, 110%, made him the lowest of the successful bidders. The rest took two-thirds of the issue at prices up to 120.

3

A RESPECTFUL

INQUIRY

THERE was one final curtain to be rung down on the events of 1895–96—the senatorial investigation of the bond sales. It was to be pure comedy, both high and low, in every detail: the timing, setting, cast of characters, and dialogue. Part of this was to be expected from the composition of the inquisitorial group. These were the days when senators were chosen according to the original Constitutional prescript—supposedly by state legislatures, but actually by the greasy brood of rural or urban political bosses that ran those bodies. The United States Senate was a shame and a laughingstock until seventeen years later, when the whole farce was swept away by an amendment providing for direct election of its members.

There was another reason to expect high comedy rather than fruitful discussion. Republicans had won control of both houses in the 1894 election and had organized the subcommittee that conducted the inquiry. Ordinarily, this could have been expected to produce an investigation that would make political capital for the approaching presidential campaign; such a group would aim at embarrassing the Democratic President and his administration and at producing a record useful to the Republican candidate.

But there were complications as the subcommittee was being formed in this spring of 1896. One was the silver issue, which had laid hold of both parties. As it happened, though, it played little part in the proceedings, largely because of the ineptness of the silver partisans. A more crucial factor in defusing the probe was the importance of Wall Street and its potent financiers to the Republicans. Even then the Ohio industrialist, Marcus Alonzo Hanna, was busy among America's great corporations and banks, raising by a sort of tithing system what would be a record sum of $3½ million to elect William McKinley, a former legislator not universally acceptable in the ruling circles of the East. The Republicans in command of the subcommittee could hardly be expected to push wholeheartedly to uncover what really went on between Cleveland and the bond syndicators.

Timing provided the first element of humor in the Senate hearings. Partly through accident, partly through design, the sessions, authorized by Congress in the spring of 1896, bumbled along fitfully at first. Treasury Secretary Carlisle submitted a statement; it didn't meet with the approval of the subcommittee, so he sent in a second reply. He also passed along a Byzantine analysis, taking up over two hundred pages of the printed transcript, of all the bond issues. Then he and Assistant Secretary Curtis testified in early June. It was not until the middle of the month that the Wall Streeters, such of them as deigned to appear, were assembled. Coincidentally, the brass bands, banners, and fireworks of the Republican Convention in St. Louis began. On the day that August Belmont took the stand, June 18, the party nominated the fifty-two-year-old Ohio governor, William McKinley, on the first ballot.

In another two weeks, a much younger man, thirty-six-year-old William Jennings Bryan of Nebraska, would use a voice that was described as "golden" even by those who weren't swayed by it to declaim the "Cross of Gold" speech. That stirring and highly inflammatory address would turn the twenty thousand Democrats gathered in Chicago into a wildly shouting, hysterical mob that would acclaim him as their candidate. That was in the future, but there was even now a pervasive feeling all over the country that Armageddon was at hand.

For the country was deeply divided, as it had never been since the Civil War, and possibly more so than in that conflict. The long, depressed aftermath of the 1893 panic had split wide the patched-up fissures that separated the haves from the have nots, the capitalist from the jobless worker, the western debtor-farmer from the eastern creditor. Everyone awaited the great pitched battle looming in November and had ear only for the noisy selecting of champions in the late summer conventions. There was little interest by press or public in such a minor skirmish among advance pickets as represented by the Senate subcommittee hearings.

The delay that had resulted in this exquisite timing was partly of Pierpont Morgan's contriving. On March 25 he had begun his unvarying spring trip to London and the Continent. These voyages had started years earlier on orders of his father as annual pentitential journeys after Pierpont's Civil War escapades. But Junius S. Morgan had died in 1890 in a coaching accident near his villa in Monte Carlo. That event was to lessen greatly the terms of probation under which Pierpont Morgan had been operating during the preceding three decades, but he was not totally free until the death in 1893 of the Philadelphia financier Anthony Drexel. Drexel, one of his father's generation, was the last of a line of mentors chosen by Junius Morgan to keep a watchful eye on his son. After Drexel's death, the European visits ceased to be those of a subordinate reporting to the head of the firm or, as they had become with the passing of the senior Morgan, those of an intermediary between branch and home offices. Now more securely on his own, Pierpont Morgan had changed the name of the New York branch from Drexel, Morgan & Co. to J. P. Morgan & Co. in the very year of the bond contract. And he had taken to using the annual pilgrimage to indulge his growing pleasure in collecting great objects of art.

So in 1896, with the congressional summons imminent, he still chased after a Gutenberg Bible that had once been owned by Cardinal Mazarin, after some jewelry for his oldest daughter Louisa, customarily the only member of his family to go along with him on these trips, and after other works of art that caught his fancy. The demands of representative government counted for little in the majestic scale of values he was beginning to acquire. And he made his frame of mind clear in a lordly response to the subcommittee's summons.

"My firm cable me of your notice," he said in a wire to Senator Isham Harris of Tennessee, the subcommittee chairman, sent from London on May 26. "Regret absence from country will delay, but will sail Wednesday next week, Teutonic, and hold myself at the call of your committee. My cable address is simply Dover House, London." He signed the message simply, "Pierpont Morgan."

But at least he had cabled. There were four other financiers summoned to the hearings who never showed up. Of that number, only one—Ernest Thalmann of Ladenburg, Thalmann—bothered to excuse himself because of illness.

Even so, Pierpont Morgan was merely observing written amenities by claiming to be "at the call of" the subcommittee; he had no intention of rushing to whatever feeble judgment awaited him. He indicated his general indifference even in his choice of ship, the White Star liner, *Teutonic*. Twenty-five years earlier he had been inconvenienced by a strike of Cunard Line workers. He vented his indignation by vowing never to travel by Cunard except in an emergency—a condition he obviously did not feel existed in a semi-judicial convocation of a group of United States senators.

Leisurely arriving in New York fifteen days after sending the cable, he unhurriedly put off until the following day, a meeting with the reporters who were now following his comings and goings. At his press conference on June 11, he talked of money and politics, especially as they bore on the convention that was to begin the following week. He talked urgently of the need for a gold standard plank in the platform, an article of belief that was not then shared by the Ohioan, William McKinley.

There was still plenty of time for more important matters than the hearings. One of them was to set the Republican leaders on the path of sound money, and to that end he met with McKinley's backers, Hanna and Myron T. Herrick, aboard his yacht *Corsair*, anchored in the North River. He instructed them in the reasons for his disaffection toward their man, who had an orthodox Republican belief in high tariff but who had flirted occasionally with the silver forces. The session was most productive in getting Herrick and Hanna to steer McKinley into the more conventional and rewarding romance he was to have with sound money. And the gold standard became a feature of the Republican platform.

Thus Pierpont Morgan put to profitable use the comic element of timing. He and all the Wall Streeters were to benefit equally in the other element of comedy, the location of the hearings.

Secretary Carlisle and his assistant Curtis were questioned in Washington, but the senators moved up into Belmont-Morgan territory in New York to quiz the financiers. It was a move that brought the senators' own mandate into question. Senator George G. Vest, a sixty-six-year-old Missouri Democrat who was about the only effectual questioner on the panel, noted this curious fact in a remark to one of the witnesses: "The trouble is that the congressional statute relating to the examination of witnesses is exceedingly defective, and applies to the District of Columbia only. We can[not] enforce the attendance of witnesses here [in New York] or outside the district. They can defy us with impunity, but if we go to Washington City we can issue our subpoena. We can there enforce their attendance, and if they refuse to answer our questions, we can have them indicted. . . ."

This defect was to keep the hearings from ever being anything but a squirmingly respectful pleading for information by the senators, with the New Yorkers defying them repeatedly without any fear of consequences.

The impotent group made their headquarters at the Hoffman House, a hotel run by Edward L. Stokes, celebrated as the slayer of Jim Fiske of Erie Railroad fame a quarter century earlier. It was generally regarded as ground hallowed to the Democrats. Republicans favored the Fifth Avenue Hotel, diagonally across Broadway where that thoroughfare crosses Fifth at Twenty-third Street. It was there that the state's GOP boss, Tom Platt, maintained his "Amen Corner," so-called because there he heard the respectful so-be-it's of his retainers.

Choosing the Democratic Hoffman House may have been a concession to the minority or it may have been because the hotel featured "the longest bar in the world," a place of refreshment that faced a famed piece of voluptuary art painted by Adolphe W. Bouguereau, a Frenchman who could be described as a carnally disposed Pre-Raphaelite. It depicted in heroic and luscious detail a group of four lovely nudes apparently trying to rearouse a spent satyr. Jolly Bouguereau's bosky picturing caught a brief reposeful interlude in what must have been one of the most strenuous ravishments in all mythology and was an appropriate backdrop for what was about to happen to the senators who put themselves at the mercy of Belmont, Morgan, and the other Wall Streeters.

In addition to time and setting, farce demands a hero—preferably a slightly unprincipled one—and crackling dialogue. August Belmont played the role and, within the ad-lib limits imposed by a congressional hearing, provided the lines to go with it.

He breezed into Room 306 of the Hoffman House, the first witness of the transplanted segment of the hearings, on the morning of Thursday, June 18. He was as resplendent as could be expected of a man who would continually be chosen second-best-dressed male in the country. (The acknowledged keeper of such records, William Randolph Hearst's "Cholly Knickerbocker," habitually awarded first place to an amiable and wealthy nonentity, Evander Berry Wall, as the "Edwardian dandy and beau ideal of sartorial splendor.")

Belmont was a tamer of lions working out a holiday among house cats; a *beau sabreur* with a murderous weapon among barroom brawlers uncomfortably forced to defend themselves with fencing foils. Elegant and small-headed, trailing clouds of money and glory, his mere presence was enough to set lesser breeds like United States senators to examining their fingernails for signs of soil. Even his light tread was the product of the influence of an unmatchable set of parents combined with thousands of dollars worth of education, hundreds of thousands worth of summer and winter homes, yachts and ships and vacations such as are known only to the fabulously well-funded. His mother, born Caroline Slidell Perry, was the daughter of one of the country's ranking heroes, Commodore Matthew Calbraith Perry; his father was the chosen agent of a good part of the disposable wealth of England and the Continent.

August Belmont, Sr., had been a romantic figure of finance. He had walked with a bad limp, the result of a duel said to have grown out of his "being too gallant to another's man's wife." A leader in the society of his day—both the strictly formal world of Astors, Rhinelanders, and Goelets, and the racier café variety— he once had lost $60,000 at a baccarat game at the sumptuous gambling parlor maintained just across Broadway from the Hoffman House by the sometime congressman and all-time pluggugly, John Morrissey. As the elder Belmont, fresh from his losses, helped himself to a pair of canvasback ducks at the resplendent free buffet Morrissey set out for his patrons, he observed that at $30,000 each the ducks were undoubtedly the most expensive fowl ever served, but that the price befitted a representative of the Rothschilds.

The older man's entertainments at home were no less prodigal. He was said to have run up wine bills of $20,000 a month and he reached some sort of twin peak of arrogance and conspicuous display by employing his father-in-law, the naval hero who had opened up Japan at gunpoint, as his wine steward. It was said that he used often to send the aging commodore tottering to the wine cellar, gold key in hand, to select appropriate vintages for his guests.

The elder Belmont had died in the same year as Junius Morgan, so that August Belmont was a much younger man than

Pierpont Morgan when he succeeded to his full social, political, and, of course, fiscal, heritage. To his birthright he added some unique touches. He was a highly competitive sportsman, on the sprinter's track and on the polo field. His financial enterprises, especially later in life, were to be large—in fact, in the realm of public works.

He financed the city's first subway system, traces of whose early grandeur still shine through three quarters of a century's grime in the older stations. His name was honored in one of the city's major engineering triumphs; unfortunately, it was a tunnel fathoms down in the mud of the East River. Another of his personal ventures was the Cape Cod Ship Canal, an enterprise so magnificent that the federal government coveted it, took it over tentatively in World War I, and then permanently in 1924, the year of August Belmont's death.

The duty of supplying sprightly insolence at the hearings-farce devolved largely on Belmont and he proved equal to the task. He was cavalier with the truth in a manner that would have brought a lesser mortal to the attention of the Department of Justice in such exchanges as these:

"Did you receive any notification of Mr. Curtis's coming?" Vest asked him.

"None, whatever," was Belmont's answer. But a little later on Vest again put the same query: "You had no previous notification of his [Curtis's] coming?"

Without pause or interruption, Belmont airily responded: "Yes, I knew he was coming on. He notified me that he was coming on and wanted to see me."

When he tired of these self-contradictions, he fell back at his pleasure on the "I-do-not-recall-them-now" forgetfulness of the evasive witness. And throughout, he instructed the senators on what was "relevant" and what was "within the province of your authority."

In one brief skirmish with Vest he managed to set the investigators straight on where they stood by somehow advancing the remarkable proposition that he was not so much declining to answer a question as denying that the question even existed. Senator Vest began by asking if he had any objections to naming those associated with him in the 1894 contract, a line of inquiry specifically called for by Congress in authorizing the hearings.

Mr. Belmont: I think that is a matter of my private business.

Senator Vest: It might become a matter of some importance to us to know who your correspondents were there if we should pursue this inquiry further as to how this sale happened to be made.

Mr. Belmont: This is a mere matter of private business, as I have stated. You will have to accept that; that it is a matter of mere private business.

Senator Vest: Then you decline to answer it?

Mr. Belmont: I do not decline to answer it. I say it is not a matter coming within the scope of this inquiry.

And that was that.

The senators had been directed in the congressional resolution to investigate syndicate and individual operations in each of the bond transactions and to uncover "the profits made or to be made by such syndicate or any person or persons connected with such syndicate directly or indirectly." Belmont proceeded to stymie that high directive and to show just how powerless this scruffy band of representatives was.

He went on to defy Vest on just this question of profits, whereupon the old Missourian went through the prescribed legal form for setting up a contempt citation. Vest repeated the Senate resolution, thus getting the purpose of the inquiry into the record at that point. Then he had the stenographer read back Belmont's refusals to answer and entered them in the record together with Belmont's affirmation that he had been correctly quoted.

It all led nowhere, of course. Belmont was not even rebuked by the Congress he had defied. And in his boundless egotism, he wrote the following day to Senator Isham Harris, the chairman of the group, correcting a "really not very important" error in still another part of his testimony, in which he had denied seeing President Cleveland's familiar, War Secretary Lamont, on his first visit in 1895. He amended the record by conceding that he now remembered he had. It was all very informal and he added a postscript that for sheer arrogance goes beyond any stage farce and approaches the farcical reality of Renaissance courts.

"I see so many errors in the newspaper reports that I request a copy of the stenographer's report, to review and correct, if necessary," he wrote to Senator Harris, adding his initials, AB. The presence of bracketed matter in the final printed transcript suggests that the people's representatives hadn't the stomach to withhold this egregious privilege from the lofty AB.

Belmont was the star of the proceedings. His part was fatter than that of any of the others; he was onstage almost twice as long as Pierpont Morgan, for instance. And he was first on the witness stand, with his well-bred, often witty insolence, defining the restricted path the investigation was to take for the benefit of the financiers who were to follow.

Pierpont Morgan quickly picked up the cue when he took the stand the following day. He began with a lengthy, uninformative statement, resisted cross-examination by Vest on it, and when asked the question Congress had wanted answered on profits said bluntly:

> That I decline to answer. I wish to state that I am perfectly ready to state to the committee every detail of the negotiation up to the time that the bonds became my property and were paid for. What I did with my own property subsequent to that purchase I decline to state, except this, that no member of the Government in any Department was interested directly or indirectly in connection therewith.

Vest asked: "You decline to answer my question as to the amount of profits made by your firm?"

Morgan answered: "I do, sir."

After the previous day's experience, Vest was so browbeaten that he subsided without even reading the riot act as he had done with Belmont.

There was one more clash between the senator and the man of wealth. By any standard of judgment, even the cursory sort that a reporter might bring to the matter on his way to telephoning his account to his city desk, Morgan's responses were nonsensical, but still his burblings have surfaced often since in the Pierpont Morgan canon as proof of his financial infallibility. The exchange occurred when Vest asked why Morgan and Belmont had demanded "exclusive control" of the 1895 contract. Said Morgan: "Because it was absolutely impossible for more than one party to negotiate—to make the same negotiation for the same lot of gold. It would only have made competition."

In the latter part of his answer, Morgan showed that he felt no need even to pay lip service to the supposed keystone of the capitalistic system he was supposedly bulwarking. Vest then pressed him on the question of why the Treasury should not have had the advantage of more than one bid:

Senator Vest: If the gold was abroad, I take for granted that anybody could get hold of it who had the means to do so. If you were actuated by the desire to prevent a panic, why were you not willing that other people should do it, if they wanted to?

Mr. Morgan: They could not do it.

Senator Vest: How did you know?

Mr. Morgan: That was my opinion.

Senator Vest: And therefore you specified that nobody should have anything to do with it but you and Mr. Belmont?

Mr. Morgan: Yes.

By cutting off this exchange after the response, "They could not do it," and by ignoring the fact that Belmont and Morgan were among those who could not and proved it in the aftermath of the bond contract, biographical mythmakers have been able to present Pierpont Morgan as a sort of Old Testament figure of the new capitalism, arbitrarily but precisely giving forth the law. Some even supply italics for the last line, as though it had been thundered Jehovah-like, a reminder of eternal truth for blundering legislators. But, of course, Vest had gone on to demand how he knew, and it turned out that it was only Pierpont Morgan's opinion, not divine revelation after all. And events had proved that Morgan, even with Belmont's assistance, could not do it any more than those who had been shut out. The phrases were the first things that came to Morgan's mind and good enough for an arm of a democratic deliberative body.

There was one final frustration to be provided by the money-men as the hearings closed that afternoon. It was delivered by John A. Stewart, president of the United States Trust Company. Stewart correctly read the tenor of the hearings set by Belmont and reinforced by Morgan. He eluded the bird-dogging of Vest about the profits his group had made, referring his questioners to Morgan only an hour or so after the latter had defied the subcommittee's right to such information. He tried, too, to avoid even specifying how much in bonds his bank had received.

But this sort of arrogance from Belmont and Morgan was one thing; allowing a pipsqueak bank president to mantle himself with such a privilege was too much even for the otherwise complaisant chairman, Senator Harris. He came briefly to Vest's aid and elicited the information that the trust company got an allocation of $1,800,000 worth of bonds. But that was as far as Vest was able to go in trying to pierce the financial *omerta* of the bankers. His further attempts to question Stewart were interrupted by the chairman with: "If no other member of the committee desires to propound any other questions, I will ask Mr. Stewart whether there is any further statement which he wishes to make?"

Thus invited, the trust company president provided the final effrontery. "I think that covers all the facts of the case," he said. Vest subsided like a hound that suddenly finds itself the object of a chase by aggressive raccoons headed by its own master and the comedy was over.

YOUTH AND
EARLY MISSTEPS

THE man who was to emerge in the last twenty years of a long life as an overpowering force in world affairs in the role of a dispenser and withholder of money—other people's money—was a long time in coming to the fore. He was born April 17, 1837, the sixth generation on both sides of his family to start life in America.

The first of the Morgans to come here was Miles, who made a post-Mayflower arrival in Boston in 1636, when he was twenty. He had come from Wales.

Miles Morgan settled in Springfield, Massachusetts, and prospered as a farmer. Succeeding generations increased or preserved their patrimony in the same neighborhood. One descendant, Joseph Morgan, served as a captain in the Revolution on the side of the colonists. His son, also named Joseph, the grandfather of J. Pierpont Morgan, moved the family base from Springfield to Hartford and took the initiatives that were to propel the Morgans to prominence. He ultimately bought a total of 106¾ acres in his adopted city, operated the Exchange Coffee House and the City Hotel, both popular with the political element of the state capital and with businessmen of the briskly rising young republic and other public figures. More important, he entered into the business affairs of the day. Among his ventures was the Aetna Fire Insurance Company, which had been founded in 1819.

Joseph Morgan, the Hotelkeeper or the Innkeeper, as he was called, acquired a major interest in the firm and took a bold step in 1835 that helped solidify its position as an insurance underwriter. That is, it was a bold step in the financier's lexicon, which takes as a base such words as caution, prudence, timidity, and even cowardice.

On December 16, 1835, one of the periodic fires that ravaged New York City broke out in the heart of the commercial district, leveling most of the area bounded by Wall Street, Broad Street, Coenties Slip and Pearl Street eastward to the river. Damage to nearly six hundred establishments was estimated at $15 million.

Most of the insurance companies involved proceeded along the path of prudence, timidity, and cowardice by taking advantage of the fine-print escape clauses, but Joseph Morgan was instrumental in getting his associates at Aetna to come forward generously for its part. Mythologists of the Morgan family have attempted to equate this action with Thermopylae, Horatio at the Bridge, and the like, but contemporary evidence suggests that Joseph Morgan had taken his bold step onto ground he must have known contained a high proportion of solid granite.

Philip Hone, the diarist, headed a delegation to Albany that sought city and state relief; other prominent citizens matched the ex-mayor Hone's efforts in getting federal aid. Hone reported to his diary on January 4, 1836, in Albany that "The bills authorizing the city loan of six millions and for enabling the fire-insurance companies to settle their concerns and to resuscitate their business, have passed the Legislature with great unanimity." And Hone also noted on February 23 that twenty of the lots in the burned district "were sold . . . at most enormous prices, greater than they would have brought before the fire, when covered with valuable buildings." The increase of more than eightfold in value was brought on, he noted, by the settlement of a vexing dispute with the French and the "spirit of speculation" over the prospect of business expansion that, it turned out, was to end in a panic in another two years. In any case Morgan's gesture so impressed the merchants who were insured by Aetna that they signed for new policies at triple the old rates!

The Morgans had allied themselves by marriage with such New England names as Bliss, Bird, Stebbins, Smith, and Spencer. Joseph Morgan's son, Junius Spencer Morgan, was to tie the line into another eminent lineage that had provided the religious and intellectual life of the district with many exemplars. Its contemporary representative was the Reverend John Pierpont, whose daughter Juliet married Junius in the spring of 1836.

The alliance of the Morgans and the Pierponts provided a genetic equation that is probably insoluble, but tantalizing nevertheless. These two grandparents of John Pierpont Morgan strike strange harmonies, dissonant at times, soothing at others, that ring out through the life of a grandson both of them cherished.

Joseph Morgan was preeminently of a type that adapted himself to his world and times, improving an inheritance several-fold by looking out on that world, spotting the main chance, and taking it. Although he read his Bible incessantly and spent the entire Sabbath visiting and revisiting church, there is no evidence that he had drawn any higher view of his obligation to humanity and his God than the duty to prosper. At one point he had some of his fortune in stagecoach lines; when it became apparent that the romantic form of moving goods and people would be rudely shunted aside by the railroads then beginning to appear, he simply moved his capital from one to the other. He may even have given the order to pull out of the one and into the other between readings of the Old or New Testament.

A Congregationalist like the Morgans, the Reverend John Pierpont was made of different stuff. He had failed as an adapter to things as they were: when he had gone into business before taking orders in his twenties he had promptly gone bankrupt. Some Morgan historians have faulted him for this, as evidence that he hadn't the moral stamina to meet payrolls and hence counted for little. But there is no evidence that his grandson ever discriminated in that way. John Pierpont Morgan seemed as genuinely attached to his maternal grandparent, who survived until Pierpont's thirty-ninth year, as to his paternal one, who died when he was nine.

Grandfather Morgan was an organizer of the world as it was, an accumulator of wealth who had a clear view of the approach of the industrial revolution to America and who took advantage of it. To the ever-busy comings and goings of the man of affairs, the frequent travels to New York, to Halifax, to Chicago, to New Orleans in a day when such journeys were tedious and trouble-some, he added one unusual touch. He was an assiduous diarist, setting down primarily the number of times he read or reread his Bible, his church visitations, commercial notes and, finally, events of the day.

One entry recorded a childhood incident involving his grand-son Pierpont. On June 5, 1845, he noted that the eight-year-old "Pierpont came near drowning while fishing in Little River near Finlay's Upper Mills with George Beach's sons. He was rescued by Isaac T. Beach reaching him his fish pole."

The diary-keeping had begun when Joseph Morgan was

twelve, in 1792, and continued until a few weeks before his death on July 23, 1846. Out of this half century's chronicle only about a dozen volumes survived. This urge to record, with its implication of a sense of importance and consequence on the part of the recorder, reappeared in a slightly different form in his grandson. Pierpont acted for more than thirty years as the agent in New York for his father in London. During this period he wrote long, detailed letters twice each week to Junius, who judged them worthy of preservation in a series of letter books that survived until 1911. In that year, Pierpont Morgan tossed them into the fire in the Morgan's Dover House in Roehampton, England. "He said afterwards that he could not take the time to go all over them and cut out or delete things that he did not wish others to read, and as a great many of the people of whom he wrote were dead and gone, he thought it was better to burn them," Satterlee recorded.

Some of the letters escaped the 74-year-old Morgan's conflagration. From them and others he wrote it can be inferred that an irreplaceable record of the beginnings of industrial America was burned. The reports ran to several pages apiece and were full of candid commentary on men and events. They may have been superficial, especially during the early years when Pierpont Morgan would have been an agent's agent and not given to thorough analysis, but as the decades wore on they would have provided an unexampled view from one who was present at the takeover of finance capitalism from the undisciplined promoters and entrepreneurs who built the railroads, the steel mills, the oil facilities, and the other engines of wealth.

Pierpont's heritage from his maternal grandfather for the most part appeared only sporadically. From the Reverend John Pierpont and his daughter Juliet Pierpont Morgan, his clearest inheritance was an unfortunate one, a disposition toward facial skin eruptions, especially on the nose. Grandfather, mother, and son suffered from the tendency; in Pierpont Morgan's case it was to give rise to a disfigurement that late in life became awful to bear, puffing his nose to a great size and, at times, covering it with a warty growth. James Henry Duveen, whose art-dealing family owed much of its success to Morgan's collecting mania, was one of the many to comment on the feature:

> . . . I was unprepared for the meeting with him [at Morgan's London home at Prince's Gate when the

financier was in his seventies]. I had heard of a disfigurement, but what I saw upset me so thoroughly
that for a moment I could not utter a word. If I did not
gasp I must have changed colour. Mr. Morgan noticed
this, and his small, piercing eyes transfixed me with a
malicious stare. I sensed that he noticed my feelings of
pity, and for some time that seemed centuries we stood
opposite each other without saying a word. I could not
utter a sound, and when at last I managed to open my
mouth I could produce only a raucous cough. He
grunted.

The other characteristics of the Reverend John Pierpont were
not so clearly transmitted. After his failure in business and his
becoming a minister at the age of thirty-four in 1819, he was less
inclined to temporize with the world around him. He looked
about him and decided that the evils he saw—slavery and in-
temperance and debtors' prisons—were not to his liking. He
stormed at them from the pulpit of the Old Hollis Street Church
in Boston in a brave and highly unpopular cause for the New
England of his time. The Abolitionist movement was gaining
adherents, but the more widely held attitude was that such
matters were outside the sphere of ministerial commentary and,
anyway, running slaves and rum was an acceptable kind of trade
for a region whose prosperity was so closely linked to shipping.
Pierpont had no patience with such views and his continued
anathemas against both evils brought him into conflict with his
parish around the time of Morgan's birth.

In 1838, a group constituting a bare majority of the parish
asked him to avoid "exciting" subjects in his homilies. His answer
was that the only kind of subject he would avoid would be one
that was not "exciting."

The group then brought up written charges, including one of
"moral impurity" for Pierpont's use of the word "whore" in one of
his discourses. His response was to insist on a trial where the
charges and the defense could be weighed. In the context of the
time, when the comfortable assumptions held by the majority
were increasingly being brought out of their hypocritical hiding
places and displayed for what they were by the Abolitionists and
others, the majority wanted no airing of the matter in a trial. The
congregation reacted typically by simply and quietly cutting off

the pastor's salary. But he refused to oblige them with a quiet withdrawal and ultimately succeeded in getting his trial before an ecclesiastical council.

It took place in 1841, lasting for six months and arousing a great deal of public interest in a country that was becoming polarized around the great issue that would lead to civil war two decades later. The outspoken minister was largely upheld, with the congregation being given a few crumbs of criticism of some of his actions in the verdict. There was no cause for his removal, it was decided. The verdict was appealed to a Supreme Judicial Court of the church, but here, too, Pierpont was sustained. After winning official vindication, he resigned his pastorate.

He went on to immerse himself in politics, first with the Abolitionists and then with more pragmatic groups such as the Liberty Party and its successor, the Free Soil Party, which led to the organization of that Republican Party later so dear to the interests of his grandson, but an organ of revolution at this point. He later served as a chaplain in the Civil War and his eightieth birthday, a year after the end of the conflict, became a sort of victory celebration for the antislavery forces. Tributes came from William Lloyd Garrison and other leaders of the cause who attended the function in Washington.

Throughout, Pierpont supplemented his public stands and actions with his writings, issuing his sermons as pamphlets and collections and contributing to *The Liberator* and other journals. He also turned out a variety of occasional or ceremonial verse, one example of which, Warren's Address to his Soldiers at Bunker Hill, became a favored schoolboy recitation of his grandson's day.

On the Morgan side of the family was practicality. Grandfather Morgan took account of the prevailing beliefs of his time, of the structure of society, and of the ordering of business. Joseph Morgan would as soon think of grappling with them as would a sea captain try to subdue wind, wave, current, or undersea obstacle. These were the things that one sailed by, taking advantage of the one to cancel out the other, avoiding this one or waiting for a better disposition of that. Thus his journey was smooth and prosperous.

Not so for the Reverend John Pierpont, it seems he never learned to bow to the things of man's own making as though they were natural forces. To him, what man saw fit to join together or keep asunder was to be examined for its contribution to God's scheme of things, not man's. Whatever fell short was to be changed. His winds, tides, and bearing points were more elemental than Grandfather Morgan's.

For that, most would regard him as superior to Morgan the Hotelkeeper. There is one cloud, though, on this easy hierarchical distinction. Slavery, the only one of the Reverend John Pierpont's beastlinesses to end in his lifetime, withered more because of activities of people like the Morgans than because of the scoldings of New England divines. It already had atrophied in other countries where the industrial revolution began earlier. It is hard to see how even the most intense humanitarian factors, whether expressed reasonably or with Biblical thunder, would compare with the elementary fact that this ultimate form of paternalism could not meet the demands for profitability made by capitalistic industrialism. Capitalism needed, and got, a proletariat—a work force that could be cut loose to fend for itself at the close of a twelve-, fourteen-, or sixteen-hour day, or during slack, unprofitable periods, or at the introduction of the labor saving machinery which was even beginning to change the character of the agricultural world during the 1830s and 1840s in America. It needed, and got, a work force that above all could be discarded at the end of its useful life.

Slaveholding could never meet those tests. Even poorly treated slaves required some kind of twenty-four-hour-a-day year-long and life-long care. As Gustavus Myers noted, "so-called free white men, women and children of the North, . . . toiled even harder than the chattel black slave of the South, and . . . did not receive a fraction of the care and thought bestowed, as a corollary of property, upon the black slave." There may be sentimentalism in this view, to judge by experiments in slave labor conducted in some of our leading civilized states subsequent to Myers' writing, but by and large even the expense of maintaining security puts slavery beyond the reach of the most openhanded of capitalists.

Whether a cynical view of this sort had anything to do with it, Grandfather Morgan's traits were the more important influence in the life of Pierpont Morgan, especially later when, with the death of his father in 1890, he began to make those bold strokes late in his own life that would carry him to the pinnacle of world finance. But, occasionally, the romantic, rebellious, larger view of

Grandfather Pierpont surfaced, as inevitably as the occasional bouts of ill health that came down to him through his mother and her father.

This direct physical trouble manifested itself almost at birth and remained acute until he was in his twenties. From old family records, his son-in-law reports that when he was ten months old and was cutting his teeth "he was very ill and almost died." A month later, in March 1838, he suffered a series of convulsions and was not expected to live. "Toward the end of the month his mother was taken down with scarlet fever. They both survived, but he was desperately ill again in April."

He contracted scarlet fever himself in 1841. As a little boy, friends recalled his "having indefinite, unnamed illnesses which kept him from going to school at an age when he should have been there and which prevented him from taking part in a good many of their activities." The ailments took various forms, sometimes earaches, and continued to interfere with school and play until he entered English High School in Boston, an institution that the old rebel, the Reverend John Pierpont, had helped found. He was able to complete the course, though with interruptions.

The ailments to this point were vaguely described for the most part. In the summer of 1852, when Pierpont was fifteen, he suffered his most serious illness, specifically diagnosed as inflammatory rheumatism. On July 29, the boy had sat on the ground to watch the Trinity College commencement. "Soon afterwards he was taken very ill and had a high fever and much suffering. When he recovered he was very weak. One of his legs was shorter than the other and it was feared that he would be lame all his life." He was out of school for nearly a year, but the fears proved to be ill-founded because of another set of contradictions layered onto the pragmatic-romantic nature of his personality. Although sickly, he was robust in constitution. This had not come about through any sort of triumph of mind over body, as was to be the case with the weakling who made himself strong, Theodore Roosevelt. Morgan never particularly liked exercise and his competitive spirit never took the form of wanting to excel in sports. He walked and rode, but only as recreation and his participation in games was minimal. Still, he was developing into the powerful six-foot, 210-pounder that he would become in his maturity.

Two playmates of this period, his cousin James Goodwin and another boy, James Burbank, recalled later for the family biographer that in appearance

> he had plenty of straight, dark brown (almost black) hair, a well-shaped head and a strongly built body, although he had not the appearance of good health. His eyes were dark hazel and looked straight at you. His nose and chin were well-molded, complexion ruddy, with a good rather full-lipped mouth and medium-sized, closely set ears. His hands, in boyhood as in manhood, were strong and notably well formed.

The response of his family to the rheumatic attack was an unusually Spartan one. After three months of rest, during which he made little progress toward recovery, his parents sent him abroad, alone, for a stay at Horta on the island of Fayal in the Azores. He was accompanied on the journey aboard the bark *Io* by Charles W. Dabney, a friend of his father's and American consul in the Portuguese possession, who was returning with his daughter and a friend of hers after a visit to Boston. Morgan, still so lame he could not walk, had to be taken to the gangplank in a carriage and carried aboard the *Io* on November 8. His quarters aboard ship were separate from those of the Dabney party, and when he arrived in Horta he stayed by himself in a hotel while the Dabneys went on to their home.

The thirteen-day voyage improved his health to the point where he was able to leave his cabin and join the Dabneys at times. But it was a strange convalescence for a boy whose father had gone from wealth as a storekeeper in Hartford to greater wealth and importance as a Boston merchant. A few letters from the period survived and in one long one to his parents, begun on November 23, a few days after his arrival in Horta, and completed on December 11, he wrote: "My health has been pretty good since I have been here, but not so good as it was on the voyage, during which I did not feel neuralgia at all. But I am well satisfied that I am much better and am getting better than I was. You will see by my journal of Dec. 10 that I am getting able to walk again as well as ever." The young Pierpont was as avid a diary keeper as his grandfather, Joseph Morgan, and he included the current volume in the packet with the letter.

Good health did not continue for him, despite the fact that he was able to record in the reports on his health he sent his parents that he weighed 126 pounds, a twelve-pound gain during his first month in Horta. Later, toward the end of his stay, he reported an increase to 150. But there were interruptions of illness. He was in bed for several days in late January 1853 with an attack of influenza. Again the following month he was "wretchedly ill" with a return of the same malady, Satterlee says. "He had to stay in bed and could not read, but Mr. C. W. Dabney called on him every day and looked after his comfort and by the end of the week he was sitting up and was soon out and about again."

The misery of a boy nearing his sixteenth birthday confined to a room of a colonial hotel thousands of miles from anyone close to him, visited only by an acquaintance of his father's generation, and unable even to read, was, fortunately for Pierpont, not a chronic condition. He was able to get about much of the time, to enjoy the picturesque, red-tiled hillside town of Horta, to savor, if not enjoy, the lives of the islanders, and on occasion to take more extended walks to indulge a fondness for romantic, craggy mountain views. He dreamed often of climbing Mount Pico, one of the peaks he could see in the distance.

A passage from his diary of this period is a compound of the normal homesickness expected from a boy his age with the more precocious urge to be informed of the larger events taking place on the national stage, an urge that developed in him early in life. He wrote on March 4, "Franklin Pierce, I suppose, was this day inaugurated President of the United States of America. Should like to know very much who composes his Cabinet." He had no way to get closer to these events, but at least he could remedy the need to rely on conjecture as a substitute for fact. He was able to get copies of the London *Times* and London *News* at the Dabneys, but he wrote to his parents around this time, asking them to send American periodicals. "I shall expect on the return of the *Io* a large bundle of letters and papers. I should like you to save me the Traveller, Transcript, Witness and Courant . . . and Harpers Magazine."

But probably the most enjoyable, and surely the most therapeutic of his experiences was the opportunity he had to gorge himself with fresh oranges. Early in his stay, in the November 23 letter, he wrote that Dabney "has a most delightful garden back of his house, and I often go there and eat as many oranges as I choose." Once, when he went there and found the young people away, together with their parents, he chose to eat twenty of them "fresh-picked."

It was not all delightful gardens and fresh-picked oranges, though. In addition to his periods of invalidism, there was a melancholy, even morbid, event that stayed with him. Shortly after his arrival he had made friends with another of his father's generation, a Dr. Cole, a friend of the Dabneys who also was in the Azores for his health. Together they played chess and whist, the only kind of competitive play Morgan ever bothered with, and read or took long walks during breaks in the rainy season. It must have been a welcome change from the sieges of sickness for the young boy. "We can amuse ourselves together very well," he wrote back home, and added, that Dr. Cole "intends if nothing happens to go to America in the spring."

Something did happen though. In early April young Pierpont wrote of the death of the doctor, "who had been gradually sinking after a hemorrhage of the lungs." The recollection of the tubercular's death was buried deep in Morgan. Fifty years later he made a sentimental detour on one of his European visits in order to stop at the island of Fayal. He made his way to the English cemetery at Horta to visit the grave of Dr. Cole, which, along with "the graves of many others [in the Azores] he had known and loved as a boy . . . made his visit very sad."

The young convalescent made many plaintive appeals to be allowed to end his Azores stay. Shortly after his sixteenth birthday he was permitted to leave Horta. He sailed on the *Great Western*, bound for England, where his parents were traveling.

It was on this trip that his father took a step that was to have profound importance in his own and his son's life. The older man made the acquaintance of an emigré American financier who had risen in the ranks of great investment bankers of London. He was George Peabody, who for nearly two decades had been building up an agency for the development of American resources with European capital. He had been successful despite the American panic and depression of 1837 and in the face of highhanded financial skullduggery that characterized the early days of railroad and canal construction and the occasional predilection of several of the states to repudiate their debts. Peabody had helped preserve the credit of his native country and also had lent a hand to the repudiators by buying their depressed bonds and holding them until financial prospects improved.

Junius S. Morgan's Boston firm, J. M. Beebe, Morgan & Co., was the agent for Peabody's banking house. The elder Morgan impressed the London banker and the visit led Peabody, the following spring, to invite Morgan to join him as a partner. Pierpont's father had no hesitation in uprooting his family for an opportunity of this magnitude, nor in leaving his own aging mother in Hartford. An estrangement had developed between his family and that of his wife, so there was apparently no regret at abandoning the rebellious old minister John Pierpont. At least no consideration was given in the family's record. Junius was ready to make the move by October 1, 1854. In the meantime, Pierpont had completed the course at English High School and, after a quick tour with cousin Jim Goodwin of the northeast as far west as Buffalo and north as Maine, he was enrolled at a boy's school, Bellerive, at Vevey, Switzerland.

The school was an educational refuge for boys from the economic strata occupied by Pierpont Morgan, or "Pip," as he was nicknamed. During the three years he spent there, his vague ailments continued. He also began to suffer more severe attacks of the all-too-well defined skin eruptions of his nose and face.

Pierpont had had the normal youth's eye for girls ever since his Hartford days, when he and his cousin Jim Goodwin used to tease "The Drapers"—the girls from the Draper School. He had his picture taken during a visit to Geneva and wrote to Goodwin: "Grandmother will be rather surprised I know to hear that anyone with such an eruption on my face should have had their portrait taken; but M. [Edouard] Sillig [the headmaster at Bellerive] insisted that I should try it, and as I found that photography showed no defects of the kind I consented and was very much pleased with the result." The disfigurement wasn't causing the nineteen-year-old Pip to isolate himself from girls either. He reported in the same letter that he and some friends had organized a series of balls at Vevey. Expenses were split among the fifteen organizers.

After the first three of the entertainments had been held, Pierpont exulted:

> How I have enjoyed myself! They are not those stiff, formal reunions which I so much detest, especially here on the Continent where the gentleman stands on one side of the room and the lady is seated solitary and alone upon the other, but everything was perfectly

free and easy. You could dance and talk with whom, as often, where and as much as you liked. The company is very choice and select and everything goes off in capital style. It costs me about $5.75 a night, but that is dog cheap when you can laugh, talk and dance with such a beautiful girl as Miss H. as much as you choose.

"Miss H" was further identified only as a Miss Hoffman.

Still, such facial outbreaks were troubling, as they would be to any one of Pierpont Morgan's age, and he expressed a plaintive hope to Jim Goodwin in the same letter that his mother might visit him in Vevey and bring him to Paris "to see if anything can be done for my face." The skin trouble continued through his stay at Bellerive and plagued him during his one-year term at the University of Gottingen. A schoolmate there, W. Parker Prentice, later recalled that Pierpont had failed to appear at an important function at the university, the President's ball, held during the Christmas season in 1856, because "he had some sort of eruption or inflammation on the upper part of his face, around his temples and brow."

Although he had periods of invalidism, he was flourishing physically. A Bellerive classmate who became a lifelong friend, William Riggs, remembered being "much impressed with my friend's energy and strength. I recall that on one of our excursions (our tutors would take us about Switzerland, mainly mountain climbing) he picked up and carried to a distant inn an American fellow student, who had sprained an ankle, stumbling over a boulder when his alpenstock slipped." A diminutive man, Riggs remembered too that even in his sixties, Morgan would pick him up and hug him in midair. "His strength was so great that one could not realize that he was no longer young," he said.

Pierpont Morgan's academic career did not glow with scholarship. There are a couple of legends extant about his mathematical ability, one from a teacher at Bellerive who recorded that Morgan could do cube root and lengthy decimal problems in his head, and another from Professor Ulrich at Gottingen, who was said to have urged the young man to remain at the university instead of going into business and to have added that he would do what he could to make the American boy his successor as professor of mathematics. Both Morgan and Ulrich are said to have recalled the incident much later and it found its way into some of the fulsome obituary material for the financier in 1913, but the event seems to have mellowed and ripened with age and the increasing stature of its hero.

In any case, there is no other evidence to point to Pierpont Morgan as a master of theoretical mathematics. And in early life he had several outbreaks of the romantic rebelliousness bequeathed him by the Pierponts, during which he sickened of business as a lifework, yet he never evinced any inclination to take up mathematics or any other academic pursuit. As early as the visit to Horta he was showing aptitude for the simple fingers-and-thumbs juggling of rates of exchange, conversion of money, and the like, the kind of elementary toting up and discounting that would be all that would be required for a buyer and seller of stocks and bonds. He was no doubt sent to the two foreign schools for that final polish his father Junius thought he would need and for further development of that interest in the affairs of his own country and the world that he was evincing even in his fifteenth year, rather than for any spirited intellectual awakening. The youth sent such evidences as he had of progress to his father, who kept his copybooks and compositions proudly and carefully at his London home.

To gain more of the polish that was the object of his education Morgan was sent to Gottingen. He plunged merrily into the beery, oom-pah-pah of a German university town's social life. He became a member of one of the student corps, although, like the other Americans, he refused to take part in the duels that provided the facial nicks and scars so highly prized by the German students. He drank beer and wine with them, attended fêtes featuring German bands at the hotel, the Krone, visited picturesque country inns, and attended concerts. "These concerts are great places for sociability," he wrote to his cousin Jim Goodwin in Hartford, "the fair sex abound in the greatest quantities, and while the maternals or the old-maidish aunts are sewing or knitting, the younger portion are engaged in a very agreeable (to all appearances) conversation with the beaux. Plenty of German beer is to be had, and I may as well add that plenty of it is drunk."

Gottingen, the university of such Americans as Benjamin Franklin, Edward Everett, George Bancroft, John Lothrop Motley, and Henry Wadsworth Longfellow, saw Pierpont no more after the early summer of 1857. Even before he left, his father had arranged to place the twenty-year-old youth with the firm of Duncan, Sherman & Co., the agents for George Peabody and Junius Morgan in New York. The young Morgan's status amounted to that of a commercial spy at the 11 Pine Street office, for he received no pay from Duncan, Sherman. His living expenses were borne by his parent, to whom he sent full reports by every outbound ship for the British Isles, a twice-a-week routine that he continued until his father's death thirty-three years later.

His apprenticeship with Duncan, Sherman coincided with a time of trouble and panic for the financial world and near disaster for the Peabody, Morgan partnership. Pierpont Morgan's early reports must have been of great help to the London firm, inasmuch as they contained records of conversation within the Duncan, Sherman office, including shrewd and accurate records of gossip and surmise there, together with a broader view of the talk and mood outside the office, along Wall Street. Pierpont Morgan plunged immediately into what amounted to the career of a journeyman reporter, displaying the notable dash of a gossip columnist and political analyst almost from his first day on the job. He even injected a touch of the sob-sister in consoling his father in a time when the London firm came near foundering.

Although Pierpont was developing as a trusted agent for his father, he was progressing slowly in the world of finance. He took part in two transactions during this period, one of which was daring and succeeded, but apparently it was too breathtaking for his employer, and cost him his job. The other was shot through with tawdriness, if not downright criminality, and cost him the trust of his father. The first occurred in 1859, when Pierpont Morgan traveled to New Orleans on Duncan, Sherman business. While there, he spent some of his free time prowling the wharves along the Mississippi, gossiping with officers of the commercial vessels and with dockside agents. On one of his rounds he came across the captain of a vessel that had brought a cargo of coffee from Brazil.

The captain had a typical waterfront tale of misfortune. The company to whom the cargo was consigned had gone out of business. The ship's owners at the time had ordered the captain to pick up another cargo and he was faced with the dilemma of trying to make a quick sale of his coffee without loss in order to be able to carry out the order without delay. Over the next few days, at dinners with J. Lawrence McKeever, an acquaintance who also happened to be in New Orleans, Pierpont told of the incident, describing how he had taken a chance on a profitable resolution of the captain's dilemma. He picked some samples of the cargo, then shopped around among the city's coffee merchants and got quotations from them.

He then stepped out boldly by taking the whole cargo, paying with sight drafts for which he had had no authorization. McKeever was horrified about the foreseeable reaction from Morgan's superiors. "Oh, I telegraphed them and, of course, they won't like it; but by the time I get their answer I will have the coffee all sold and I think they won't object to the results," said Morgan.

He got the indignant telegram he had expected from the New York house, of which he was not even a paid employe. But by that time he had broken the cargo down into small shipments and disposed of it to a number of the coffee merchants, at a profit of "several thousand dollars." He mailed the checks back to New York and received part of the profit, he told McKeever.

The experience was a profitable one all around, according to the family chronicle, but it must have thrown a fright into the staid old firm of Duncan, Sherman & Co. about what he might do next. Such impromptu rescues of wharfside castaway captains are not in the ordinary way of business for the representative of one of the biggest merchandisers of American securities in Europe. Junius Morgan had been trying for some time to get his son a partnership in Duncan, Sherman but the firm had resisted. Shortly after the New Orleans coffee episode, Pierpont Morgan left the 11 Pine Street firm and late in 1859 went into business for himself at 54 Exchange Place.

There, with no restraint acting on him other than what his father could bring to bear from three thousand miles away, Pierpont Morgan became embroiled in a slick bit of profiteering at the opening of the Civil War that his heirs and their employees are still, at great expense and toil, trying to explain away. The facts are complicated, in no small part because almost everyone involved was acting on the most sordid and devious of motives. It was part of a story that filled court, congressional, and executive department records. It figures in the works of polemecists, both those concerned solely with robber barons and those whose interests were the prevention of fraud in wartime procurement. As late as the 1940s, a Morgan partner, R. Gordon Wasson, was dispatched to clear the boss's name in a heavily documented book. The part of the recital that is not in dispute is relatively simple and goes like this:

In the confusion of the start of the war in 1861, Lincoln, a president who had won a mere 39.91 percent of the vote against three opponents, had the greatest of difficulty in organizing his own constituency, not to speak of the job of unifying an army that had and has always included a generous representation of southerners. Four months after the declaration of war he had just begun to make headway. Whether because of the divided loyalty up and down the rank and file, plain human cussedness and corruption, or the eternal verity that armies not actually at war are always just a little out of step, the supply sections of the federal force were engaged in the peculiar business of both buying and selling munitions of war.

Among those being offered for sale were five thousand ten- to thirteen-year-old rifles, known as Hall's carbines, stored in a government armory in New York. The rifles were obsolete, having the old-fashioned, inaccurate smooth bore; to bring them up to date by rifling the bore to increase range and accuracy was an inexpensive machine shop operation, which probably was performed eventually right in the armory where they were stored.

A couple of slick operatives, one of whom, Simon Stevens, knew Morgan, were aware of what the left hand of the government was doing, while the right was buying. The other, Arthur M. Eastman, who hadn't the price of even one of the weapons, bid for the lot at $3.50 each and sold them, unrifled—at a quick profit on nothing invested—to Stevens at $11.50. Stevens had no money either, but through his sister, a former teacher of Morgan's at Hartford public school, and his brother Henry, a federal officer in London with contacts at Peabody & Co., he had prospects. He also knew General John C. Frémont, then trying to raise and equip a force for the western department at St. Louis. He got Frémont to agree to get the government to buy the weapons at $22 each.

The cheap, sleazy shell game was financed by Morgan, who on August 7 lent Stevens $20,000, taking title to the rifles as collateral. As part of the agreement, Morgan had the rifling of the barrels carried out, after which Stevens completed delivery to Frémont. In September Morgan received $55,000, the first half of the $110,000 payment that the government was making for rifles it had sold for a total of $17,500 three months earlier. Out of that Morgan took $26,345.54 "to repay himself with interest and commissions, expenses of packing cases, insurance, etc.," and presumably the cost of the rifling. That was the end of the matter for him.

Stevens was to pay Eastman out of this first installment, leaving about $11,000 for himself, plus all of the second $55,000. But about this time, the tremendous job of organizing for war was beginning to bring to light this and other mean and shabby acts of profiteering. The government simply refused to make further payments on this and many other similar deals.

Meanwhile, just as Eastman and Morgan had done, Stevens unloaded his responsibility by selling his rights to the transfer of the weapons. They were bought, probably at deep discount because of the government's show of stubbornness, by "Pierpont's old friends," Messrs. (Morris) Ketchum, Son & Co. Over the next few years, which included the darkest days for the North, the Ketchums pressed for payment in the Court of Claims, and despite the heaviest censure by Congress and a special commission of the War Department set up to investigate matters like this just short of treason, it was paid in full. The congressional report said to those who took part in such actions: "He cannot be looked upon as a good citizen, entitled to favorable consideration of his claim, who seeks to augment the vast burdens, daily increasing, that are to weigh on the future industry of the country, by demands on the Treasury for which nothing entitled to the name of an equivalent has been rendered."

Morgan's participation in this deal escaped any important censure until after his late emergence as a financial power. He was in his seventies when Gustavus Myers published his *History of the Great American Fortunes,* in which that crusading devourer of government printing office publications devoted a section to pillorying the great man.

Morgan's official biographer, Satterlee, says, "If Morgan ever heard of this book he treated it with entire indifference." Not so Satterlee, who devotes considerable space to giving the family's version, and not so R. Gordon Wasson, whose energy expenditure in trying to exculpate the deceased founder of his firm has increased over the years. A new edition of Wasson's *The Hall Carbine Affair* is imminent.

It's true that Myers does exaggerate Morgan's part in the

transaction in order to attach to him the final evil—the fact that
the claim made in the name of Stevens and eventually won by
the Ketchums opened the floodgates of what were termed "dead-
horse claims" against the government, but in the final analysis,
the attempts to find Morgan blameless just won't wash. So that
the Morgan heirs will not further detach partners better suited
for other work than the dusty task of research and dispute in old
records, the account here has been taken entirely from Satterlee
as far as fact and incident is concerned. The only defense available to the Morgan apologists is the plea that he had no knowledge of the nature of the transactions nor of the perpetrators. To
make this argument believable, however, Pierpont Morgan has to
be portrayed as a person who passed on $20,000 to a pair he did
not know for purposes that he was ignorant of. The absurdity
becomes patent with another look at the first transaction, the
New Orleans coffee purchase of two years earlier, and the proof
comes right from Satterlee.

When Pierpont Morgan's friend McKeever congratulated him
on his "luck" in having the coffee transfer come out profitably,
Morgan took exception to the term:

> He said that it was not luck at all, since he had
> found out that he could sell the coffee at a profit before
> he bought it: the only risk he ran was that the coffee
> would not come up to sample and might be rejected.
> But he had made his own estimate of the captain's
> honesty and believed him when he said that the coffee
> was bagged and shipped by perfectly reputable people
> in Brazil; and so he laughed at Larry's fears, which
> had proved to be unfounded and treated him to a very
> good dinner.

It thus comes down to whether one can believe that a twenty-
two-year-old Morgan could show that kind of resourcefulness in
getting needed information about character and merchandise
along the docks and in the coffee warehouses of a strange city
and yet, two years later, display culpable innocence in a far more
serious matter in his own backyard. Little was recorded of Arthur
M. Eastman, who had come from Manchester, New Hampshire,
but Stevens was a well-known Tammany politician who, it developed, had been involved in custom house frauds about the time

Morgan carried out his coffee coup. The Ketchums were respectable enough at the time by the rubbery standards that prevailed in the world of successful business ethics, where the success counted for a great deal more than the ethics. But any defense of Morgan has also to rest on the legal fiction that he had no part in the transaction subsequent to repayment of his loan nor in the introduction of Stevens to the Ketchums. Morgan partisans say he had nothing to do with introducing Stevens to his friends, but it is impossible to absolve him completely because Pierpont Morgan went on to embark on another questionable transaction with young Edward Ketchum, whose father was relieving Stevens of his obligations in the rifle deal.

This second prank proved a little more costly to the North, for Morgan and Ketchum divided up about $160,000 as a result of it. The shady transaction, occurring in 1863, consisted of driving up the price of gold by quietly accumulating a great deal of it. For this Pierpont Morgan and young Ketchum used several million dollars' worth of the credit of their parents' firms. The government, to maintain its at times shaky credit abroad and to pay interest on its bonds both here and in Europe, was the largest customer for the commodity, and would have contributed a good part of that profit.

It was done apparently with the knowledge of Morris Ketchum, but whether Junius Morgan knew of it is problematical. The accumulation took place during an uneasy equilibrium between the Union and the South. In the fall of 1863, when gold reacted by dropping in price and buyers were lulled into the eternal sense of security of those who believe that things will go on getting cheaper, Morgan and Ketchum struck by announcing the shipment of their hoard to Europe. Immediately there was a scramble for gold. The price shot up from 143 on October 5, some time after the Morgan-Ketchum group began their buying, to 149 on October 10, when *The New York Times* observed that $1,150,000 of a very large shipment of gold for England had been traced to "a young House in Exchange Place respectably connected on the other side, but whose regular business in exchange would be called large at 10 percent of the sum." The price went on up to 156 on October 16, when the two speculators reaped their profit.

All this unprincipled activity, by Morgan and others, took place in a hideout, a sort of financial speakeasy at the corner of

William Street and Exchange Place called the "Gold Room," operated by a resourceful curb broker named R. H. Gallagher (or Gallaher). The official name was the New York Gold Exchange and associated in it were members of the New York Stock Exchange, including J. P. Morgan & Co. The reason for its hole-in-corner location was the perennial desire of the stock exchange to maintain its reputation for patriotism by keeping its unpatriotic operations as far out of public view as possible. Congress and state lawmakers had become exercised over the gold trading activity and in Washington ineffectual laws were passed to prohibit it. They were quickly repealed when Morgan and others complained, but in deference to the popular tumult the gold dealings were kept separate from the august exchange.

The Gold Room, around the corner from the exchange, was a colorful place. The exchange's official attitude of censuring gold speculation, of course, had nothing to do with the private activities of its members, and they crowded the room for "trading sessions [that] were the wildest Wall Street would ever know" as bidding followed news and rumor of the fortunes of the North and South during the fateful year of the war. An added, tawdry touch, was the singing of "Dixie" over the noise of the bidders when the price of gold rose in response to news favorable to the South, and of "The body of old John Brown" on southern reverses. It had all moved Lincoln to a fury in mid-year: "What do you think of those fellows in Wall Street who are gambling in gold at such a time as this? For my part I wish every one of them had his devilish head shot off."

There was little chance of that for Pierpont Morgan—and the rest of the bidders, too, for that matter. Pierpont had begun to develop a new ailment—fainting spells—around the time the North was beginning to stake out recruiting stations. The medical history was piously recorded by his son-in-law long after, like some posthumous affidavit for a draft board. Following the practice of the time, Pierpont Morgan had also hired a substitute, paying over his volunteer bonus, possibly from part of the profits of the rifle sale. "He kept in touch with this man (whom he called 'the other Pierpont Morgan') and helped him for years after the War," says Satterlee, who never gives his real name, nor why he needed help.

All the insulated business-as-usual trading among the speculators of the Gold Room took place in 1863, the year that "saw the greatest successes and the heaviest reverses of the Union army, Gettysburg and Vicksburg and Chattanooga against Chancellorsville and Chickamauga." The North had been routed at Chancellorsville in May. Then followed the two great Union victories of Gettysburg and Vicksburg, climaxing on the same day, July 4. Union forces invested Chattanooga in September, but choruses of "Dixie" predominated in the Gold Room as southern forces conquered at Chickamauga and menaced the Northern Army of the Cumberland in the nearby city. But a month after Morgan and Ketchum had pocketed their profits, the southerners were decisively smashed at Lookout Mountain and Missionary Ridge in a three-day battle ending on November 25.

Pierpont Morgan's part in all this is hardly defensible, and his devoted son-in-law ignores the incident totally in his detailed record of the year. But Pierpont Morgan may have expiated some part of his sin in what followed, however. From this point on it was obvious that the South could not win, and the game of gold speculating became very chancy. Still, young Ketchum continued to play his hand, backing his bluff with the credit of his father's firm. When the bluff was called at the end of the war, the firm went into bankruptcy and young Ketchum to prison on the discovery of the forgery of $1,500,000 in gold drafts. For those who hanker after the old Greek retributive god Nemesis, there is balm in the fact that some of Morgan's money went with the debacle.

At Ketchum's trial, a Morgan employee pegged the loss in checks forged by Ketchum at $85,000, or just about what he had made in the earlier attempt at a corner. Parenthetically, it might be added that old Morris Ketchum, the friend and former partner in Hartford of Junius Morgan, also ended equivocally. In a California gold operation of 1863, he handled the sale of three quarters of a float of 100,000 shares of stock at $100 a share. Two years later at the time of the downfall of the firm, the shares were worth eight cents each.

Whether or not Nemesis hovered over the Gold Room scene, there was one interested human watcher. Junius Morgan, from London, observed his son going from mild profiteering to the cynical choruses of Dixie in the Gold Room to the final ignominy of his association (and a losing one, at that) with Edward Ketchum. The elder Morgan decided that his son was incapable of handling his own affairs and needed strict supervision. Such a move had been doubly desirable ever since October 1, 1864, when George Peabody retired from the firm to return to America and the London house was newly styled J. S. Morgan & Co. It wouldn't do for the head of that prestigious house to have it known his son was getting involved in such scrapes.

There may also have been some need to take a little tarnish off his own reputation. The standing of old Peabody, an enlightened philanthropist during his active business career and later after his retirement, was generally high, as was that of the firm, which had been hired by the North as agent for the vast bond placements needed to support the war. But there was gossip, possibly baseless, that the firm during the war had contributed to the English favoritism for the South, a bias based on the simple economics of England's need for the South's principal product, cotton.

The gossip surfaced in the Springfield *Republican* eighteen months after the close of the war in an article that was reprinted in *The New York Times* on October 31, 1866. The motives of newspapers at any particular time in carrying such attacks are difficult to fathom, especially in that era of highly personal journalism. But the *Republican* was a paper of good repute and undoubtedly the most powerful newspaper in the country outside New York City. It was controlled and edited from 1844 to 1915 by three generations of Samuel Bowleses. The second, "and probably the ablest," was in charge at this time, and his decision to carry the article lends it some weight. Even if untrue, though, the report probably rankled with the new head of the Peabody firm and strengthened his resolve to put his firstborn under some kind of restraint.

Accordingly, just a month after he assumed leadership of the London firm, Junius Morgan arranged a change in the firm's agency in the United States. This shift of highly profitable business from Duncan, Sherman, the firm that had refused his son a partnership, was accompanied by a shift of one of its chief employees, Charles H. Dabney, a cousin of the man Morgan had accompanied to the Azores and well known to Junius. In December 1864, as the supremacy of the North was daily becoming more clear, the following notice appeared in the Bankers Magazine: "Messrs. J. Pierpont Morgan & Co. and Mr. C. H. Dabney (for several years of the firm of Duncan, Sherman & Co.), have associated together as bankers, under the firm of Dabney, Morgan & Co., 50 Exchange Place."

The issue carried a further artful item noting that "Messrs. Duncan, Sherman & Co. have transferred their London account, late with Messrs. George Peabody & Co. to the banking firm of Messrs. Finlay, Hodgson & Co., a concern of very old and wealthy standing. The withdrawal of Mr. Peabody and his large capital and experience will doubtless induce a number of other changes in American accounts in London."

The young Morgan also had been giving his father cause for worry for several years with outbreaks of "Pierpontism" in his personal life. There survives from the 1911 holocaust of old letters and reports one that gives evidence of scolding and expressions of abandoned hope on the part of the concerned parent. It is a seven-page letter that apparently had been misfiled with George Peabody's papers and turned up at the Essex Institute in Salem, to which Peabody had bequeathed those papers. Dated September 19, 1862, it is one of the young Pierpont's full reports to his father. The detailed summary out of the way, he gives petulant voice to a complaint: "I must say that I don't see that I have done anything to warrant your saying that the advice that you give me on my point has not the slightest weight. If there is anything I aim to follow it is that but it is very disheartening to be told the contrary." The older man's letter has not survived, so we have no way of knowing what it was that brought out the timeworn parental refrain, "You never listen to anything I say."

Sometime toward the end of 1859, after the great coffee transaction, Morgan definitely had broken with Duncan, Sherman & Co. It is impossible to say whether the break grew out of the firm's refusal to offer him a partnership, its continued refusal to grant him a salary so that his father's subsidy could end, or the assumption of responsibility in the New Orleans visit that was more than the firm liked to see taken on by a decidedly junior agent of twenty-two years. But the step coincided with the start of the wildest, most uncharacteristic, most romantic action Pierpont Morgan was ever to undertake. For a brief period the spirit of old John Pierpont—the spirit of one man against the world in a hopeless cause—totally occupied him. Having spent its force, it left him forever. From that point on through the rest of his life, he displayed what passed for daring or boldness only in situations in which all the cards were carefully stacked so that there was almost no chance of his failing. But in this case, his courtship and marriage to Amelia Sturges, there wasn't a chance of success.

As a rising young Wall Streeter, Pierpont Morgan had been sharing bachelor quarters with friends like Joseph Peabody, son of the head of the London firm, or his cousin James Goodwin in what was then the fashionable part of town, first on West Seventeenth Street and later in the East Twenties. After working hours, there were sociable rounds of clubs and restaurants and, above all, the congenial homes of attractive women, then, as always of the greatest importance to the handsome man about town. To one of these, the home of Jonathan Sturges and his family, Pierpont Morgan was particularly drawn. The Sturges household provided a faintly Bohemian relief from the moneyed class in which Morgan moved. Mrs. Sturges was an accomplished pianist and was said to have owned the first grand piano ever seen in the city. And the house was the gathering place for the artistic, literary, and musical lights of the day. Among them were the pianist and composer Louis Moreau Gottschalk, the pioneer compiler of slave tunes and cakewalks from his native New Orleans, and J. F. Kensett, a "Hudson River School" painter somewhat outshone since by the better-known Thomas Cole and Asher B. Durand.

It must have been a heady atmosphere for the embryo financier, and even though it seemed to have no influence later in his life, during his almost maniacal collecting days, he was not alone in this fault for the vagaries of academic and professional opinion buried both Gottschalk and the Hudson River School in undeserved obscurity a decade or so later.

The glow of the Sturges circle was greatly enhanced for young Pierpont Morgan by the presence of their daughter, who was nicknamed Mimi. He fell helplessly in love with "this high-minded young girl of good New England ancestry . . . refined and well educated, very sweet-looking, with beautiful teeth and a delightful smile." The words are those of Morgan's son-in-law, who may just possibly be echoing those of an old man discussing his bittersweet memories of a doomed love many decades later.

For Mimi, like her namesake, the heroine of Henri Murger's *Scènes de la vie de Bohème,* was a consumptive. Giacomo Puccini, who has immortalized the stage Mimi, didn't present *La Bohème* until 1896, but Murger's stories had been published in the 1840s and a theatrical version, by Murger and Théodore Barrière, which is essentially the same as the opera's libretto, had a "triumphant success" in 1849. Pierpont Morgan, always susceptible to music, could not have known the cascades of Puccini

melody that have made tuberculosis very nearly the most romantic and seductive of maladies, but he may have seen a later
production of the sentimental play during one of his teenage
grand tours that included Paris.

Amelia Sturges' illness was not apparent during the early
period of Morgan's courtship and both families seem to have
approved of the match. He was welcomed at the gatherings of
his beloved's family at their townhouse at 5 East Fourteenth
Street and in their summer quarters. His own family showed
their approval with an invitation to Mimi to visit them in
London.

But in the spring of 1861 she came down with a severe cold
that soon manifested all the symptoms of the disease, which was
then nearly always fatal. He responded in a manner worthy of
Murger's hero Rodolphe, telling friends that they were engaged.
During this same period he also took another decisive spiritual
step by leaving the Congregational church of both his grandparents. On March 29, 1861, with the Reverend Stephen H. Tyng
officiating, he was confirmed in the Episcopal Church. The scene
was St. George's, then on Beekman Street, and it was to be his
church for the rest of his life.

Within a few days came the declaration of the war in which
Morgan, was to play anything but a romantic part. Some months
later, while he was deeply embroiled in the Hall's carbines affair,
Mimi's illness increased alarmingly. He determined to marry her
and seems to have had some idea of saving her life through a trip
abroad like the one that brought him back to health nine years
earlier.

The Sturgeses were horrified at the thought of his marrying a
girl who, given the state of the art of healing at that time, had
only a few months to live. His family seems to have opposed the
match equally. The headstrong and willful Pierpont overcame
the Sturges' objection, but none of his own family appeared at
the strange wedding that took place at the Sturges' townhouse on
October 7. The disease had progressed so far that Mimi had to be
carried downstairs by the bridegroom to the back parlor where
Dr. Tyng performed the ceremony. Her condition was also such
that she could not join the guests for the wedding breakfast in an
adjoining parlor. Dividing doors between the two rooms were
parted just long enough for the group to observe the brief ceremony; then the doors were closed and the glum feast went on

without her. The bride and groom left immediately for England, where Pierpont Morgan's family continued to show their opposition to the morbid match by not greeting them. They continued on to Algiers and to Nice, where Mimi died a little over four months after the wedding. Mrs. Sturges joined her bereaved son-in-law in Nice. She spent more than two months abroad consoling him, before they brought the body home for burial.

The sad marriage may have played a part in initiating Morgan's interest in collecting paintings, the hobby which was to consume so much of his later years. About the time of his return, he attended a fair held by the city's Sanitary Commission on Fourteenth Street and "bought his first oil painting." it was a portrait by George F. Baker of a "young and delicate looking woman." The price was $1,500. This reminiscence of Mimi hung for many years over the mantel in the library of Morgan's home at 42 West Twenty-first Street.

The marital episode was to be the last outbreak of romance and rebellion on the part of Pierpont Morgan. Henceforth, he buried himself in the affairs of the financial district, devoting himself to his gold speculating until his father brought him into harness three years later with the stick and carrot—the formation of Dabney, Morgan and the transferral of the lucrative J. S. Morgan & Co. agency.

The new restraints showed themselves in his second marriage, to Frances, or Fannie, Tracy. The Tracys were anything but Bohemian, and in marrying into their family Pierpont moved out of the orbit of the intellectual Sturges circle. His new father-in-law, Charles S. Tracy, was a lawyer who was to be associated until his retirement with Pierpont Morgan in that capacity.

In marrying Fannie Tracy on May 31, 1865, Pierpont seemed to be filling a precocious marriage prescription he had penned to his cousin Jim Goodwin when he was nineteen. Goodwin and he, mutual confidants in matters of the heart, had been discussing the former's attraction to a girl who seems to have somewhat resembled Mimi Sturges. She was studying to be an opera singer and Pierpont dashed Cousin Jim's aspirations with: "Your career in life like mine depends on our own individual exertions, our courses though widely apart will both be in the mercantile sphere and from this cause it becomes our duty to select for our wives those who, when we go home from our occupations, will ever be ready to make us happy and contented with our homes."

That pompous idea of mating was forgotten a few years later when he married Mimi, but apparently it surfaced again when his father reined him in toward the close of 1864. Out of the union with the stately and decorous Fannie Tracy were born four children: Louisa Pierpont in 1866, John Pierpont in the following year, Juliet Pierpont in 1870, and Annie Tracy, known as Anne, three years later. The last traces of the old rebel, the Reverend John Pierpont, who lived on until the year the first child was born, are evident in the names of the first three. The last was named for a sister of Fannie's.

THE
GREAT BARBECUE

THE disciplinary steps taken by Junius S. Morgan to curb his impetuous son are obscure, except for the creation of the partnership that put Charles Dabney in charge of the young man. But their effects were obvious and dramatic. For the quarter century that the older man was to live, after the Civil War, Pierpont Morgan's activities were greatly circumscribed. He arrived at the point of notoriety early in the period on one occasion, in connection with a minor engagement of a minor battle in the long campaign for control of the Erie Railroad, a campaign that was itself only a part of the greater upheavals that characterized the building and operation of railroads throughout the country.

Of course, he was growing in wealth and power, even as the agent of the overseas banking house operated by his father, and, toward the end of this period, in the late 1880s, he made moves, some successful, others not, to wield influence in the anarchic world of railroading. His success was largely local, in New York State; failure came when he tried to move beyond those boundaries.

Meanwhile he was prospering, quietly, and was becoming better known in the financial and social worlds of his day. He and Fannie moved to a more fashionable part of town on upper Madison Avenue and the year after his marriage Morgan joined a club that was to be his favorite throughout the rest of his life, the Union Club, then at 42 West Twenty-first Street.

It was at the time "the citadel of the 'jeunesse doree' and, open all night, it afforded a refuge for the gilt-edged, who did not dare to go home," says one chronicler, who also reported that two years later James Gordon Bennett, the younger son of a newspaper publisher generally hated by those of Morgan's class for his irreverent notions of news, was able to buy his way into a lifetime membership. From that point on, members of the club "were sacrosanct in the Herald office." "How in hell can I be expected to carry the names of all the members of the Union Club in my mind," one editor complained in connection with the list of "sacred cows."

Morgan was displaying his increasing affluence, too, in selecting the right bank of the Hudson, opposite Garrison, New York, as the location for his family's summer home. It was called Cragston, a sprawling place among similar holdings of railroad presidents, bank officers, wealthy lawyers like his father-in-law, and other men of wealth. However, despite many later attempts to postdate a blank check of power to him at this period, he figured not at all among the financial potentates whose moves were chronicled in the generally awestruck financial press and in the records of Wall Street observers.

One of the ablest of them was the Reverend Mathew Hale Smith, a minister from Portland, Maine, who was captivated by the rival religion of money and its high priests and temples in Wall Street. A generation older than Morgan, he had also practiced law in New York since about 1850 and had contributed articles, later collected into several books, to the Boston *Journal* under the name of "Burleigh Letters."

In one of the collections, there is a sort of *Who's Who* of Wall Street in 1870, listing all the important and many of the unimportant denizens of the financial capital. Morgan's name hardly appears. In a catalog of the twenty "leading banking houses" beginning with "one of the largest on the street, J. & W. Seligman & Co.," and going on to "one of the oldest," Clark Dodge & Co., Dabney Morgan & Co. appears in sixteenth place. Dabney is mentioned in the entry, as is Senator Milton Latham of California, "one of the ablest bankers in the States," who is credited with Dabney Morgan's success in San Francisco. No other member of the firm is singled out.

This was in a period when New York financial circles included the land-holding Astors; the railroad manipulators Daniel Drew, James Fisk Jr., and Jay Gould. It was the day of merchants like Alexander Turney Stewart, Leonard W. Jerome, and Thurlow Weed, of the Tammany bully John Morrissey, of the Bennetts and of stock-plunger Jacob Little. It included the notorious and beautiful Tennessee Claflin and her equally dangerous and attractive sister, Victoria Woodhull, both of whom gave spiritualistic stock tips to their first impresario, Commodore Cornelius Vanderbilt, from an office he was said to have financed on Broad Street.

Pierpont Morgan, although obscure, moved among them, still retaining the gregarious, man-about-town habits that had carried over from his bachelor days. His "town," the financial district, was then as now a small one, compact in size and in population, restricted to the people who would count to the agent of one of London's major banking houses. It included among lunchtime haunts, as it still does in an enlarged building, the celebrated Delmonico's at Beaver and South William streets. Up at the edge of the financial community, in Fulton Market on the East River, stood the unlikeliest of popular eating places—Dorlon's.

The "very elite" of the city, merchants, governors, ex-governors, ex-presidents, congressmen, union officers, rebel soldiers, writers, clergymen (including the Reverend Mr. Smith), noted vagabonds, and notorious men of all grades—both Wall Streeters and aristocrats—pinched by one another down the long narrow alley that barely permitted two abreast to approach Sidney Dorlon's Seafood House. It had been operated since the 1840s by Dorlon, a Long Islander who took over his father's oyster business and became something of a mogul in the mollusk trade. "A room cramped, cribbed and confined," it was "a little den of a place, fitted up in the plainest style—mere stools without cushions, tables without cloths, and stoneware instead of porcelain. Amidst hucksters, venders of peanuts, oranges and vegetables, Dorlon's establishment stands. . . . Here can be found, daily, from 11 o'clock til 4, the richest and the most gorgeously dressed people of New York."

One of Morgan's favorite haunts was the Fifth Avenue Hotel, where he maintained a room for nights when he had to remain in town finishing up the twice weekly letters to London. At Fifth Avenue and Twenty-third Street, on the northwest corner, the hotel was beyond the outer boundaries of Wall Street by day, but at night it was in the heart of the financial district during these feverishly speculative years right after the war. In the booming reconstruction of the North as well as the South, activity in stocks and bonds of mushrooming railroads and industries burst the time restrictions of the exchange and curb markets.

The exchange closed at four, when the big operators would move uptown, for a spell of decorous carriage riding in the new Central Park if so inclined, or on up to Harlem Lane, now St. Nicholas Avenue, to indulge themselves in the more spirited craze of the moment, trotting. The fad drew the aging sport, Commodore Vanderbilt, the elder August Belmont, and others, young and old, prominent and obscure, of the financial, newspaper, and theatrical worlds.

But around six, the Wall Street contingent repaired downtown to Twenty-third Street and Broadway where, just after the close of the war, R. H. Gallagher, late of the Gold Room, had opened his evening exchange in Republican headquarters. The politicians used it during the day, the brokers at night. That lasted only a brief while, until the New York Stock Exchange, reacting to the scandal of the Ketchum forgeries, forbade its members from trading there and it closed down. "For a while, however, New York had 'round the clock trading, the only place in the world with this innovation."

There remained, though, an evening exchange of sorts at the Fifth Avenue Hotel that lasted into the 1870s. First it occupied the lobby, until the management objected. Then the action was restricted to "a little bit of paper, three inches by ten, pasted up in the vestibule," which provided quotations on the curb's late action. It was the center of great interest.

"Brokers come in from a ride, to take their dinner, and then drift down to the hotel; when they left the street they left millions at stake. The last quotations may benefit or damage them to the amount of hundreds of thousands of dollars." The Reverend Smith, beguiled equally by trade in oysters—$15 million a year in New York alone—and by the doings of thugs and prostitutes in such stews as the Five Points, and, above all, by the diversions of the financial potentates, continues with a vivid description of the procession of the mighty at the hotel:

> You can touch and handle the famous Bulls and Bears:—that is Vanderbilt, a tall lithe, clerical looking gentleman, with nearly eighty winters upon him, yet erect as a Mohawk warrior, and as lithe and subtle as when he was thirty years old. All give place to the great millionaire and he walks through the open pathway, to the little room where his friends are gathered.

August Belmont walks in. A short, thick-set dark looking man, dressed in English style. He would give fifty thousand dollars if he did not limp. The center of that group is Richard Schell, familiarly known on the street as Dick Schell. He is a short, thick-set man, stoutly built, with heavy, stolid features, indicative of dogged resolution. He throws his head back as he walks, and has a quick, energetic pace, as if he had to make his account good at the bank, and was a little late. Fisk drops in, a large specimen of the Fat Boy of Dickens—short and chunky, with a face easily caricatured—with sandy hair, parted in the middle and curled. He flashes all over with jewelry and walks with the air of a man who controls Erie.

James Fisk, Jr., certainly had every right to the air of a man who controls Erie; with two other men not part of Smith's tableau, Jay Gould and Daniel Drew, he actually was in control of the great railroad. Drew, a pinch-faced pretender to great piety, was probably in his hotel room giving it out that he was busy saying his prayers; Gould, unlike his flamboyant crony Fisk, thought little of appearing in such glittering assemblages, especially when doing so would put him in the company of his occasional opponent, the rangy Commodore.

The three partners, Drew, Fisk, and Gould, with whom Morgan was to have a minor brush, were the arch-villains of this period of America's growth, a trio whose evildoing formed a spreading stain that "led into the parlor of the President." The president was Ulysses S. Grant, who was linked in some way that is still unexplained to Gould's attempt to corner gold in 1869, and the comment was made confidentially by James A. Garfield, then a congressman conducting the investigation of the manipulation, who saw to it that no public shame should come to his fellow Republican in the White House. This was, clearly, not an era for casting stones. Garfield himself was caught up in the Credit Mobilier scandal.

These were the actors in the most shameful period ever seen in American life, a period not even matched by the skullduggery of the Harding administration at the opening of the 1920s. It was a period of dishonor afflicting every aspect of the nation's being, from the lofty ideals of black and white equality that had heartened a people at war and that were being traduced in the aftermath, right down to the government of cities.

"The period was congenial to . . . juggling with public credit and legislative pledges," says one observer, Noyes, who felt called on by the spectacle to interrupt his singleminded concentration on financial and business affairs to make a moral judgment.

> Socially, financially, and politically, it stands out quite apart from any other decade of the century. It comprised, in the United States, such a succession of episodes as the plundering reign of the Tweed cabal in New York City; the impeachment of President Johnson for purposes of political revenge; the infamous gold-market conspiracy of 1869, into which the ringleaders very nearly dragged the Federal Administration; the rise of vulgar and dishonest railway speculators to public eminency; the notorious corruption of the courts by such adventurers; scandal fixed upon Congress by the Credit Mobilier disclosures and on the Administration by the Belknap impeachment trial. Moral sense seemed for a time to have deteriorated in the whole community; it was a sorry audience, at Washington or elsewhere, to which to address appeals for economy, retrenchment, and rigid preservation of the public faith. The government's financial recklessness was readily imitated by the community at large; debt was the order of the day in the affairs of both.

The Civil War itself, and, even more, the industrial revolution that it had caused to explode in a predominantly agricultural world, was largely responsible for this moral swampland of the postwar years. The war cost an estimated $20 billion, in balance sheet terms, or 620,000 lives in terms that transcend the casting of accounts. Yet both charges were met, through the astounding recuperative powers of a country rich in resources and tides of immigration.

The war had been a "modern" one—cruel, destructive, vicious —in ways that the prancing cavalry-charge contests conducted elsewhere in the world were not, in ways, in fact, that only began to be matched eighty years later in World War II. The First

World War was bloody, but it lacked the wholesale destruction of the total war between the states. While Lee and his generals were executing textbook field exercises that gallantly won, and lost, battles, Grant and Sherman were less spectacularly destroying his confederacy—civilian, soldier, factory, railroad, and plantation—down the Mississippi and across Tennessee and Georgia. Only then did they engage in the war of attrition, the classic bloody clash of armies that ended in the destruction of the Confederate forces. It was the way to win a war, but it provided a terrible object lesson to the survivors on both sides: to the ruthless goes the victory.

It was a lesson not lost on the burgeoning industrial establishment that was supplying the victorious army with uniforms made of "shoddy" boots of paper, meat from diseased cattle and hogs, and exorbitantly priced guns of dubious value, such as those Morgan had had a hand in selling. Among the costs of the war have to be accounted the decade and more that followed in which men, especially those in positions of power, acknowledged no check of conscience or sense of justice or fair play. It was a period in which Morgan could have been thankful that he was subjected to the firm hand of his father.

The postwar period was one that can be told in terms of a railroad—the Erie. Most of the principal actors played parts in the farce—the Commodore, Richard Schell, his broker and link with Tammany Hall; Daniel Drew, the miserly, Bible-reading wrecker; James Fisk, Jr., the loudmouthed blusterer with a fatal weakness for women; and Jay Gould, the consummate evil genius whose ambitions made the other three look like petty thieves dipping into church poorboxes.

It is a story that, though often told, still strains the art of narration, for each of the principals operated on more than one set of motives continuously and simultaneously. In the case of Gould, there were several main directions to his plotting, plus the subordinate ones of trying to outwit each of the other three. A proper account of him probably requires the use of multicolumned pages, as in a polyglot Bible. And because part of the action took place in Fisk's Grand Opera house on Twenty-third Street and Eighth Avenue, a genuine enough showcase for good music, the full scenario would need a synchronized vocal and orchestral score along with the general narration. The early part of the story concerned Morgan not at all; later he appeared in a minor, spear-carrying role. But he learned much during the battle for Erie, in the course of which appeared many of those techniques that would be further refined by Pierpont Morgan and his partners—"blackmail" transportation lines, watered stock, convertible bonds, and similar mechanisms of usurpation.

The Erie can be likened only to an unfortunate class of human being, the types that may have helped shape the Marquis de Sade's lopsided thinking. They are the unfortunates whose characters twist a cringing helplessness around an excess of servility to a point where they invite persecution, exploitation, and ultimate, utter degradation. Such humans could provoke brutality from a St. Francis of Assisi; it is to be supposed that the good man spent most of his life among birds, beasts and serpents and so met few such; the Marquis must have been surrounded by them. And Erie encountered no saints during its life, anyway. Conceived in corruption in 1831, its early history was full of accusations, investigations and receiverships.

The Erie had been planned on a more grandiose scale than any of the other pre-Civil War roads. Most of them began small, usually as connections between nearby cities, and later were amalgamated. The New York Central, for example, was a combination of eleven lines that were little more than interurban trolley tracks joining communities between Albany and Buffalo. But the Erie was envisioned by its early promoters as a connection from New York to Chicago and ultimately as part of a vast transcontinental link with the West. Even the more modest aim wouldn't be reached for decades.

Leaving these ultimate ambitions aside, it grew to adolescence in a queer, lumpy misshapen form: from its birth in 1831 until 1878, a period during which it had to endure the vicious rate wars of up to four competitors, it consisted of a single set of tracks. The others each had two and were able to easily add a third and fourth for fast, efficient service and peace of mind for the riders. To make matters worse, the Erie's lone track was freakish. It had a wide, six-foot gauge between wheels that made the line's equipment uninterchangeable and forced agonizing and expensive transshipments or alterations any time it made a connection. The standard gauge adopted by nearly all other roads was four feet, eight-and-a-half inches.

The choice of wide gauge was only one of the Erie's many peculiarities. The roadbed had been laid out without much regard for grades—at one time it was planned to elevate a good part of the line on pilings in its passage through rugged terrain. That plan was wisely abandoned, but it left the railroad running up and down hills and mountains in what must have formed a spectacular forerunner of the Austro-Hungarian empire's transportation system through Montenegro, Serbia, and its other Balkan possessions later in the century. To negotiate the different levels heavy and powerful locomotives were needed. It was thought that such motive power would require the wider gauge.

That at least was a defensible line of reasoning. A more important consideration to the state legislators who approved participation in the venture, however, was the "childish theory" that the mismatching of guages would prevent the railroad from connecting with lines that would lead traffic out of the state away from New York City to Boston, Philadelphia, or Baltimore. The result was that the Erie had to be saddled with an expenditure of $25 million for extra maintenance and for the changeover to the common gauge in the closing years of the 1870s.

The hill-and-dale careening of the Erie was another impediment that put it at a disadvantage in competition. The New York Central system, which was merely an afterthought linking up several small separately conceived short lines, turned out to be one that opened the Great Lakes and the West to the region East of the Hudson and New York through the Mohawk Valley, the natural east-west passageway through the great Alleghany range. If it had been planned, it could not have taken an easier route. For the Erie there was no search for the easy way. Its promoters had no thought of compromising with nature. They were out to conquer and subdue all obstacles—and to take the bows for success. But the Erie was never a clear-cut success, so there were no bows. The railroad throughout its life paid the price for scaling lofty mountain ranges, flinging itself across gorges, and plunging into fertile valleys.

This maladjusted mass of iron and wood came to the attention of Daniel Drew around 1864. It had an immediate appeal to the sixty-seven-year-old "Uncle Dan'l," promising him a few good rounds in the perverse sort of capitalistic game he had come to love. Born in Carmel, New York, he began his career as a drover of cattle herds from Eastern pasturages to New York City. He had amassed a small fortune and gone on to the more lucrative field of finance as a banker to other drovers. The financial vocabulary was enriched by Drew, who had his drovers feed the cattle plenty of salt as they approached the city. Just before being weighed the beasts were permitted to slake their salted thirst with all they wanted to drink. The process added tons to herds of six hundred to a thousand head and "watered stock" was a term that followed Drew into Wall Street. He went there with a stake he had raised in a "blackmail" transportation operation at the expense of Cornelius Vanderbilt. It was a trick that the Commodore had often played earlier. In Drew's case, it consisted of painting up an old tub and merely threatening to cut prices in the Hudson River steamer traffic dominated by Vanderbilt. The Commodore paid well to abort the Drew threat, and Uncle Dan'l was ready to go to work on Erie.

Tall and lanky, eyes constantly on the lookout for the jugular, and with the heavily tanned and lined face of one who had spent many years among the lowing kine, Drew assiduously cultivated the appearance of a country bumpkin, possibly a rural deacon so unworldly as to have been done out of his parish. His walk was catlike and among his affectations was a carefully nurtured, rustic manner of speaking. He called the railroad "Ary" and spoke of buying "sheers" in it. The Commodore was "C'Neel" to him, when they were on speaking terms.

Whenever he met with frustration, he had a habit of repairing to his room in the sleazy hotels he frequented. There, no matter what the weather, he would seal the windows, lie down under four comforters, and, hotel Bible in one hand and water glass full of whiskey in the other, drink and read himself into a stupor. When sober, he liked to quote a few lines of holy writ that had penetrated through the alcohol.

He had the distinction of being the only major American financier of the nineteenth century to have taken up arms on behalf of the country they were all supposed to be devoted to. In fact, it was with the bounty he collected as a volunteer in the War of 1812 that he began his cattle operations.

As a financier, his way was labyrinthine, tortuous; he was the principal bear of Wall Street. He loved the game of "shorting," a complicated method of playing the stock market in which all rules of making money are reversed. Stocks are borrowed, not bought. The "short-seller" makes a profit only if the price of the stock goes down. It is a complicated process, like trying to tie a bow tie in front of a mirror. Most men who try either go down to defeat, like uncoordinated babies.

With all its danger, shorting frightens most speculators, but this was particularly its appeal for men like Drew. Losses for the long-buyer are limited; even if he has bought on margin, or credit, he can be ruined only within the limits of his credit and can start over. But there is no limit to losses for borrowers of stock. In a sharp rise, especially the kind of explosive movement possible with a "corner" in those ungoverned days, the cost of replacing the borrowed stock could rise to two, five, ten, or a hundred times the original commitment.

In 1864 Drew had taken a short position in Harlem railroad stock at 30 at a time when his rival, the Commodore, was preparing to corner the stock and take possession of the company. Vanderbilt succeeded in buying up just about all the available stock, running the price up to 285. Uncle Dan'l had to scrape up more than nine times the price at which he had borrowed the stock to pay for the borrowed shares and he lost millions in the deal.

The narrow escape supposedly led Uncle Dan'l to creative endeavor, and he composed a couplet that is still current in the financial district:

> He who sells what isn't his'n
> Must buy it back or go to prison.

Drew probably crept under the covers with a bottle and Bible in a sealed hotel room on that occasion, but otherwise the loss didn't slow him down appreciably. He had begun playing a highly profitable game at the expense of the Erie Railroad a decade earlier, and it continued to be a multiplier of his fortunes.

Erie, as has been said, was conceived on more expansive lines than any of its contemporaries in the first flush of railroad building in the country. And that expansiveness in everything from ultimate goals right down to financing was to be typical of the postwar continent-spanning engineering feats that were to follow in the routes to the Pacific.

Like the transcontinental routes, Erie was nominally a private enterprise. Actually, the "capitalists" who built it provided no money of their own. A wide swath of land was supplied by the state and paid for by the taxpayers' money either directly or after condemnation proceedings under the right of eminent domain. The immense construction costs were advanced directly by the state, or indirectly through state guarantees on bonds and mortgages.

A railroad operated the way the Erie was would fit into Drew's scheme of things the way the cattle he drove fitted into a slaughterhouse, and as inevitably. He came early to Erie, around 1854, when the road was forced to borrow nearly a million dollars from him. The loan was secured with a mortgage on nearly all the 445 miles of main line of trackage, land and improvements. Drew also became a director and, for a time, treasurer of the Erie, positions that he complemented by having his brokerage firm take up bearish positions in Erie stock at a time it was falling from 80 to 43. For such activity, he became known as "the speculative director."

Another bearish blessing for Drew was his ownership of two other transportation projects. One was a railroad, the Buffalo and State line; the other an Albany to New York steamship company, the People's Line. He used both to benefit Erie's rival, the New York Central, through preferential rates for connections, whenever he wanted to see Erie's stock go down. Presumably he could reverse the procedure, too, whenever he wanted. Although he preferred making money perversely by gambling for disaster, he probably thrust his thumb onto one or the other pan of the scale frequently.

He was associated throughout this early period with Vanderbilt. He and the Commodore looked vaguely alike, both being lean and hungry and with that soft feral tread that put the Reverend Mr. Smith in mind of a Mohawk warrior. But their personalities were poles apart. The Commodore was loud and blustery, ungrammatical, favoring oaths when he wanted to emphasize a point. He chewed plug tobacco and had an eye for the girls. Generally he acted like what he was, a former ferryboat operator in New York Harbor and later a ship operator who had defied the power and prestige of Fultons and Livingstons by running nuisance blackmail lines in the Hudson and on Long Island Sound. The Commodore could never fathom the switchback bearishness of Drew. Like most plungers before and since, he was usually straightforward, a bull, speculating for the rise. Even his nuisance lines were intended to dominate, not wreck.

By the end of the Civil War, when he was approaching his seventies, he was a millionaire many times over. At an age at which most men would have rested on earlier accomplishment, he was keen enough to see the importance the railroad would play in the country's development and wanted to be in on it. He set to work to control the route from New York to Chicago. He never quite reached that total goal, but he brought his lines far enough to meet the Lake Shore and Michigan Southern—a railroad that was brought, two decades later, under the control of the Vanderbilt system by his son.

The Commodore began with the Harlem Railroad, at the time little more than a trolley line reaching just beyond New York City. Taking it over was comparatively easy, for the road had never paid a dividend in its history and the shareholders were ready to take 30 cents on the dollar to give up their investment. He began buying in 1863, drove the price to 92, and then, by a corner, elevated it in August of that year to 179. But even though he had raised the value of his earlier purchases to the level of a modest addition to his fortune, the prize of control eluded him. The following year he manipulated another corner, the one in which Drew was caught at 285.

With his profits from the Harlem operation, he moved on to the Hudson River Railroad, another essential link in his plan, buying nearly all of its stock. The Hudson River line, together with the Harlem, linked New York with the east bank of the Hudson, just opposite Albany. In buying the Hudson River stock he nearly doubled its value and then proceeded, in a fashion quite unlike Drew's modus operandi, to bring efficiencies to the management of the two lines. He soon was able to begin paying dividends to the few Harlem stockholders outside his family, and he doubled the earnings of the Hudson River line during the 1865–69 period.

It was an easy matter for him then to move in on the New York Central, formed in 1865 of an amalgamation of small roads reaching from Albany to Buffalo. He incorporated his second and third possessions in 1869 as the New York Central and Hudson River Railroad, but he appeared to have some sentimental and highly profitable weakness for his first acquisition. The Harlem was retained in the family and was leased at a high valuation to the Central. The Vanderbilts also saw to it that the Central guaranteed a large dividend on the Harlem's stock.

As he completed the consolidation of his system, the wily old Commodore realized that the Erie represented a threat that it would be better to have under his jurisdiction. He accordingly set about buying its stock.

As Vanderbilt moved in on the Erie, two younger men were enlisted as allies by the crafty Drew. It was a fateful recruitment for Drew, for his new cohorts would carry out his defense against Vanderbilt triumphantly, but in the process they would sell him out, leaving him to die a bankrupt in 1879. The new mercenaries were James Fisk, Jr., and Jay Gould. Fisk, whose early life is obscure, was a few years younger than Morgan. In 1863, when Pierpont Morgan's wildness was beginning to worry his father, Fisk's similar contempt for convention was a source of pride to his mentor, Drew. He first came to the attention of the sixty-six-year-old bear in that year by getting a good price for an unprofitable steamboat line, the Stonington, belonging to the older man. As a reward Uncle Dan'l put him on the board of directors of Erie.

A native of a small town near Brattleboro, Vermont, Fisk had worked at one time with a rural circus troupe. Then he had taken over his father's small village-to-village peddling business, expanding it with a few circus touches. His caravan consisted of brightly painted wagons and his own vehicle included a sprinkling of frequently changed village belles to keep him company in his rounds. "It was his fashion to astound the unsophisticated folk of New England by the splendor of his four-in-hand, the lustre of his bright red van, and the beauty of the lady who accompanied him, seated high in air, upon the box of his magnificent vehicle." He moved on from that colorful mode of life, in which his father had become a paid helper, to the more prosaic dry goods business of Jordan, Marsh & Co. of Boston during the Civil War. Here his ambition and initiative manifested itself.

He expanded into the business of supplying the fighting army with clothing. A characteristic vagueness cloaks this enterprise, too, although there are indications that he may have been among the purveyors of shoddy blankets and uniforms and paper shoes. Just before the close of the war and his opportune meeting with Drew, he is said to have lost a fortune of fifty or sixty thousand dollars, his profits from the Jordan, Marsh connection, in Wall Street speculation. A fat fop with a taste for uniforms and titles, Fisk was the least of Erie warriors, but he was among the most articulate, despite the strong suspicion that he could neither read nor write. Always portly and good-looking in the "fat boy" style noted by Mathew Hale Smith, he affected a mustache whose waxed ends protruded several inches beyond his chubby cheeks. He regularly wore the full regalia of an admiral of the United States Navy in a day when dress uniforms lived up to that title, all on the strength of his operation of the Narragansett Steamboat Line.

He also took on the title of "Prince of Erie" during the period when he was engaged in trying to wreck his principality. His palace was the great marble Pike's Opera House at Twenty-third Street and Eighth Avenue, torn down in 1960. It cost about $1,500,000 for land and building: Pike sold it for $1,200,000 after a brief, unprofitable season. The Erie predators refurbished it with $300,000 worth of carved woodwork and doors, stained and cut glass partitions, gilded balustrades, splendid gas fixtures, artistic frescoes, grand staircases, telegraphic communication systems, "desks such as a coquette might desire for her boudoir, so ornamented and tastefully arranged are they," furniture, mirrors, and statuary by noted artisans of the time, all installed under the personal direction of the Prince from Vermont.

But it was in his role of mouthpiece for the thieves of Erie that the Admiral-Prince outdid himself, bringing a deep furrow of worry across the thoughts of such contemporary moralists as Charles Francis Adams, Jr., and his brother Henry. He was widely quoted across the country in an age when newspapers gave the kind of space to railroad promoters and stock jobbers that later they would provide for flagpole-sitters and marathon dancers, and, later still, for movie stars and directors. One of the early and often cited Fisk legends, dating back to the peddling days, had it that a customer complained that he had lied and gypped her out of a shilling (about sixteen cents). "What!" said Fisk. "Do you think I would tell a lie for a shilling? Pooh! That would be petty larceny."

During the Erie war, when the Drew forces fled the splendor of the Grand Opera House for the rundown Taylor Hotel in Jersey City, he tickled newspaper readers with his response to the questions about where it would all end. "Can't tell just yet," he replied, "but it'll either be inside of marble halls in New York or stone walls in Sing Sing."

The Adams brothers saw in these eagerly retailed witticisms a foreboding change. Henry conceded that "Mr. Fisk's redeeming point was his humor, which had a strong flavor of American nationality. His mind was extraordinarily fertile in ideas and expedients, while his conversation was filled with unusual images and strange forms of speech, which were caught up and made popular by the New York press."

Henry Adams' stuffy New England attic of a personality was ready to offer a sneaking admiration for Fisk, and he even allowed that the Grand Opera House was vulgar in style but "certainly not more vulgar than that of the President's official residence (the White House), and which would be magnificent in almost any palace in Europe." In that one comment Henry Adams evened aesthetic scores with those who had succeeded to his grandfather's and great-grandfather's power and with the equally contemptible parvenus of European society.

His brother, Charles Francis Adams, Jr., went beyond petty sneers. He noted that anecdotes glorifying the Erie wreckers pushed out of currency those earlier myths of folk heroes like Franklin, Washington, and the revolutionary founders of the country, leading him to comment that

> The present evil has its root deep down in the social organization, and springs from a diseased public opinion. Failure seems to be regarded as the one unpardonable crime, success as the all-redeeming virtue, the acquisition of wealth as the single worthy aim of life. Ten years ago such revelations as these of the Erie railway would have sent a shudder through the community, and would have placed a stigma on every man who had had to do with them. Now they merely incite others to surpass them by yet bolder outrages and more corrupt combinations.

The towering figure in the Erie manipulations was Drew's other choice for the board in 1863, Jay Gould. Like Drew and Fisk, he was another country bumpkin out to meet and best the slickers of the financial world. Gould was just eleven months older than Morgan, having been born May 27, 1836, in Roxbury, a Delaware County community about 140 miles upstate from the metropolis.

Later in life, he was to tell a senate committee a tearful tale of having been taken advantage of by his first employer when he was about fifteen. Gould had wangled a good education, considering his background and the times, from his father, a farmer, and was working as a surveyor. His employer told him he'd get no pay until the job was completed, but that in the meantime his bills for meals and board at neighborhood farmhouses would be taken care of. At his first stop, however, the owner of the house flew into a rage and threw him out.

"I came to a piece of woods where nobody could see me and I had a good cry," he told the senators. "Finally I thought I would try my sister's remedy—a prayer." Then everything turned out all right, he said.

The memory of his teenage piety and sorrow nearly overcame Gould as he addressed the senators in 1883 and he had to be reminded to keep his voice up. "It is a lot of silly stuff, but you have got me into it," he said. He was reassured by the chairman who said: "No, it is not so; and I wish you would give it to us as minutely as you can."

There probably wasn't a dry eye in the house at the hearings, which were a strange set of perambulations across the country by the senate in which voluntary witnesses were encouraged to give what they could of a picture of the relations between capital and labor in the 1880s. Gould had appeared in many municipal, state and federal court processes, and under subpoena had bedazzled many a legislative group probing into his doings. No wonder he waxed sentimental at one of the few hearings at which he volunteered his presence and the only one in which he wasn't threatened with the possibility of a jail term.

Gould was the antithesis of the other three Erie wreckers. He was small and slight in contrast to the six-foot septuagenarians, Drew and Vanderbilt; he was even smaller than Fisk, who was of average height. His silence and stealth also contrasted with the "large, florid, gross, talkative, and obstreperous" Prince of Erie, but he had a habit of talking to the point and was as much the master of publicity as his fellow director. During the later stages of the Erie war, he was able to score tellingly at times when Vanderbilt had the upper hand by testifying at hearings, giving interviews and inspiring hacks in his hire to write on the dangers of "monopoly," specifically the kind of monopoly that the Commodore represented in attempts to control Erie.

He also transcended his allies and opponents in ways that were beyond their powers of comprehension. Gould not only fought the Erie war to a personal financial victory, but at the same time, like some master check kiter, he got more than face value out of each of his wins, thus widening his power in Tweed ring politics, and consequently his influence in city and state government. He was the interlocking director among most of the major corruptions of the post-Civil War period, a fact he often concealed from even a close associate like Fisk. He aided and was aided by the Tweed group; he suborned courts at the municipal, state, and federal levels; he mastered state legislatures and the United States Congress. At one point, his soaring ambition brought him just short of controlling the country's money supply and interfering with its banking system. In furtherance of that scheme, which culminated in the ruinous "Black Friday" panic of 1869, he rang in President Grant's own family and at least one of his appointees. As master of ceremonies at this outrageous saturnalia, he even caused Grant to play a questionable role. And all this was mere prelude. He went on from that to greater railroad wrecking on a continental scale, ending with his bringing the Union Pacific into bankruptcy in the 1880s.

The Erie war, including both Vanderbilt's long struggle to win it from the other three freebooters and the further agony of Gould's control, went on for a dozen years, from 1863 to 1874. But it was no ordinary war, an outbreak from peace to a war footing and then a return to peace, as might be the case among belligerent nations. For the first seventy years of its history the Erie, both before and after the so-called war, was continually being robbed, looted, abused, violated, and subjected to other indecencies. Vanderbilt, Drew, Gould, and Fisk simply multiplied the abnormalities and, instead of confining the debauchery to the line's stockholders and creditors, extended their field to include the people of the state and of the nation.

During the struggle, in addition to using every form of political corruption developed since the days of Rome, the four principals used every weapon of financial skullduggery, illegal and barely legal, that existed. Where the old weapons were unserviceable, they forged new ones.

One of the first was hammered out by the inventive genius of Drew, who was not loathe to violate laws that others hesitated about transgressing. Vanderbilt was trying to gain control of Erie by buying a majority of the 250,000 shares of common stock outstanding. He bought and bought and still there were plenty of Erie shares. In what amounted to an obscene travesty on the miracle of the loaves and the fishes, the more he bought, the more the stock multiplied. "If he wants 'Ary' let him have it," cackled Uncle Dan'l. The market became so flooded that a legend grew up that Drew, Fisk, and Gould were turning the certificates out on a printing press. That wasn't so. Actually Drew used three methods of twisted finance.

The first consisted of a violation of the state railway act of 1850. That law permitted the roads to issue bonds to raise money "to complete, equip, and operate" the line. To help sustain the value of the bonds, a "sweetener" was allowed in which the buyer could convert the bond into a share of common stock. The theory was that the buyer would pay a better price for the bond and thus maintain its value if he knew that later, when the stock rose above par, he would have an additional profit through the conversion feature. But Drew had his own theories. He had the company issue the bonds in violation of the legislative provision that they were only to be brought out for the specific purposes cited, and he immediately used the convertible feature despite the fact that the stock was far below par.

A second method was to vote himself stock in return for his loans to the company, which now aggregated about $1,500,000.

The third procedure, one used also by Vanderbilt for railroad wrecking and stock watering, was to raise money on the stock of worthless railroad and other properties which were sold to the Erie for substantial amounts of cash, bonds, or stock, and sometimes all three. Vanderbilt had been robbing Erie in this fashion in collusion with a group that had formed the useless Boston, Hartford and Erie Railroad Co., but Drew outshone him with his Buffalo, Bradford and Pittsburgh Railroad.

This twenty-four-mile phantom cost Drew and his associates about $250,000. It consisted of little more than a franchise and some land. On this they issued $2 million worth of bonds—eight dollars' worth for each dollar they had put up. Uncle Dan'l and Company then put on their Erie hats and agreed to lease the railroad for $140,000 a year, representing seven percent interest on the bonds, plus the right to pay themselves Erie stock at par for Buffalo, Bradford and Pittsburgh stock at par. The agreement had the further unfortunate consequence of obligating Erie eventually to build and equip the branch from a treasury that was sadly depleted by just such tricks as these.

Faced with rivers of Erie stock manufactured by these and cruder manipulations, Vanderbilt turned to the courts, thereby letting the judicial branch of the state government in on the venality. He was helped in this by his close ties to the Tammany Hall ring headed by William Marcy Tweed, a group whose contempt for public opinion and private conceptions of morality was unbounded. They also combined brutality with corruption. For crimes ranging from petty thefts on up to murder and incitements to riot, the omnipotent villains of the Italian Rennaissance, who so fascinated Marlowe, Webster, Jonson and other great Elizabethan dramatists, were as holy innocents in comparison with Tweed and his forty—or more—thieves.

The Commodore had easy access to the ring. A power in his New York Central, and in fact, the chairman on his death, was Augustus Schell. Schell was chosen to succeed Tweed as grand sachem of Tammany when the boss was dethroned in 1871. Said a Tammany historian: "This appointment was a wise one, for the public knew that Mr. Schell was too old to be very actively dishonest whatever his worst inclinations might be." Another Schell, Edward, was among the committee of six leading citizens headed by John Jacob Astor and handpicked by Tweed, that closed their eyes to fraudulent claims of more than $15 million and other peculations during an early attack on the Boss. The committee came up on election eve of 1870 with "the most perfect piece of whitewash conceivable" for the benefit of the Ring. It was said the six prominent committeemen received especially tender and thoughtful care from the city's assessors and tax gatherers for the next three years in return for their philosophical handling of the charges. They were supposed to have paid no taxes on their considerable properties during the period. In extenuation, though, it has often been noted that a more forthright judgment of Tweed might have taxed them right out of the city.

Another of the Schell family was Richard, who figured in the Reverend Mr. Smith's tableau at the Fifth Avenue Hotel. He was Vanderbilt's broker. Tweed himself, early in the Erie fight, was said to be "one of Vanderbilt's agents on the floor of the senate."

Evidence that the corruption in corporate affairs could be matched or bettered in the political arena began with a singular judge of the state Supreme Court, George G. Barnard. He had been personally railroaded into office by Tweed early in the Boss's career and had a number of idiosyncrasies. His career on the bench gave birth to a pearl of judicial wisdom: "It is better to know the judge than to know the law."

Charles Francis Adams noted that he issued injunctions like hailstorms and at one juncture developed a new legal process that Adams called an "electro-writ." This was a writ of assistance, an archaic legal form more appropriate to France before the Revolution than to a New World democracy. But Barnard modernized it by having it transmitted by telegraph. He wired one from New York to the Albany sheriff and claimed for it the full power of a legally served paper. In this he may have been following the lead of Boss Tweed, who was devoted to ageless corruption but was ever ready to press into service the latest technology to further machine politics. In the same 1868 election, Tweed, knowing that upstate Republicans had the votes to beat his candidate for governor, John T. Hoffman, had his democratic cohorts in strategic upstate locales use the telegraph to estimate pluralities. Thus he had instantaneous electrified intelligence on which to base his ballot-box stuffing in New York. He wanted no nasty surprises developing days later when votes from the backwoods precincts would be tallied. Tweed wrought victory with Samuel F. B. Morse's invention. Hoffman won handily.

The Erie war dragged through 1868, counterpointed early in that year by one of the worst railroad wrecks in the early history of the iron horse. An Erie train was derailed on April 15 in Pike County, Pennsylvania, killing and injuring seventy-five. The cause was faulty maintenance, a branch of railroading that the Erie management always had slighted for the more challenging realms of fixing courts and legislatures. A month earlier, the general superintendent, Hugh Riddle, had reported to the president, John S. Eldridge, a Vanderbilt man, about the condition of the road after "three months of unusually severe winter weather":

> . . . there is scarce a mile of your road, except that laid with steel rails [a total of about ten miles] between Jersey City and Salamanca or Buffalo, where it is safe to run a train at the ordinary passenger train speed, and many portions of the road can only be traversed safely by reducing the speed of all trains to twelve or fifteen miles per hour, solely on account of the worn out and rotten condition of the rails.

This report, unfortunately, coincided with a climax in the affairs of Erie. Vanderbilt, who claimed to have lost $7 to $10 million by the Drew-Gould-Fisk stockjobbery, had momentarily obtained the upper hand in the Tweed courts. The response of the Erie managers was to flee the jurisdiction of Barnard and the other Tweed judges and set up headquarters in the Taylor Hotel in Jersey City, close to the "Long Dock" terminal of Erie. The flight occurred on March 11, when all the books, papers, and records of Erie, together with "bales containing six millions of dollars in greenbacks," were packed up at the railroad's executive offices, then on West Street, between Duane and Reade, and ferried with most of the officers across the river.

There sapper operations were conducted in the New York and New Jersey statehouses over the next half year, with Gould's satchel of $500,000 making up the entrenching tools and explosives. Major and minor engagements were fought in the courts and the local journals were subsidized in a propaganda war, largely paid for by Gould, to enlighten the public on the evils of monopoly as represented by Commodore Vanderbilt.

During this period, reports persisted that Barnard was masterminding a plot to kidnap the fugitives to bring them back to New York where they would be under his jurisdiction. Nothing was ever proved of this but Barnard did admit during one of his sessions that he was spying on the litigants through private detectives. "I am now doing as other people have been doing: I have been followed by detectives for four or five weeks all over the city and now I am following others. . . ."

This part of the Erie agony climaxed in the movement of the field of action to the Albany area, where the representatives of the people positively slavered over the possibilities for enrichment that had been eluding them of late.

Before long it began to appear that Vanderbilt had come to some agreement with his opponents and was withdrawing.

Charles Francis Adams wrote:

> Then the wrath of the disappointed members turned on Vanderbilt. Decency was forgotten in a frenzied sense of disappointed avarice. That same night the pro rata freight bill, and a bill compelling the sale of through tickets by competing lines were hurriedly passed, simply because they were thought hurtful to Vanderbilt; and the docket was ransacked in search of other measures calculated to injure or annoy him.

The frustrated solons adjourned, though, and forgot the matter as other opportunities presented themselves in subsequent sessions. There is no record that the gnat-stings that resulted ever seriously inconvenienced the Commodore in his search for the greatest good for himself. A few months later, the settlement he had made came to light: The Erie treasury was robbed to mollify him for his $7 to $10 million in losses. Gould and Fisk went on to ruin their former partner, Drew, in a pitiless manner. The railroad was further mismanaged by the pair until Fisk was murdered in 1871 by Edward L. Stokes, a frustrated would-be blackmailer.

Gould carried on alone until the following year when he was deposed in a final flareup of the Erie war. This segment was brought about by one of the greatest rascals of American history, General Daniel Sickles. A one-legged veteran of a foolhardy act on the battlefield of Gettysburg, and the slayer of Philip Barton Key in an affair of "honor," Sickles had bragged that he could wrest the Erie from Gould and the other directors and make it a first-class railroad through the agency of legal proceedings. Fond of discoursing on the efficacy and purity of the courts of New York State, he backstopped this lofty faith by spreading $300,000 worth of bribery among the Erie's directors to induce them to step down voluntarily. Gould was won over by an irresistible market tip: "If you resign," said the General, "Erie will go up fifteen points. You can make a million dollars."

The General was a lot less daring in the financial field than he had been at Gettysburg. The rise was twenty points, which meant that Gould pocketed a profit about a third higher than Sickles had foreseen. And there were other emoluments to allay the sorrow of parting; another $1.5 or $2 million was thrown Gould's way, a totally unnecessary bonus. He was ready to move on to bigger and better wrecking operations anyway in the Chicago and Northwestern and Union Pacific railroads. The violation of Erie went on without him. His successors, installed by Sickles for the English interests, went on to such typical Erie behavior as selling bonds in order to pay an unwarranted dividend and the like.

The operations of the Erie wreckers have intrigued legions of commentators since, none of whom have outshone the Adamses, whose hot-off-the-press accounts required courage not demanded of later chroniclers. Charles Francis Adams, Jr., fired off his first blast, "The Erie Railroad Row Considered as an Episode in Court," at the height of the first fierce battle. It appeared in the

American Law Review in October 1868, a time when assault and battery, kidnapping, and even death were overtaking many who got in the way of the titanic Drew-Vanderbilt struggle.

Again, in July 1869, when critics were still being featured in police blotter homicide entries, he published "A Chapter of Erie" in the *North American Review,* a magazine edited by his brother Henry. A book-length account, with chapters by one or the other brother, followed in 1871, when it still could be registered as an act of bravery.

Charles, the older of the two brothers and thirty-three at the time of his first salvo, exemplified in his life a lofty concept of the responsibilities to be borne by people whose wealth put them beyond the nagging care of earning a living and whose forebears and associates were intimately bound up with the birth and maturing of the republic. Only two years older than Pierpont Morgan, his life and work was a constant contrast to the narrower, self-centered, and often selfish career of the financier. Adams used his position as an American aristocrat to expose and flay the Goulds and the Fisks and to recruit from the ranks of decent citizens what little opposition there was to the public immorality of the time.

He did even more. He combined the usually incompatible trade of the intellectual with that of the businessman and public servant. His state, Massachusetts, pointed the way for the rest of the country in recognizing the need for railway regulation. In 1869 it established a railway commission, a forerunner of similar bodies in other states and of the federal Interstate Commerce Commission, which did not come into being until 1887. For many years Adams served as chairman of the Massachusetts commission. Later, he got right into the business itself, serving as chairman of the Union Pacific after one of the many reorganizations undergone by the line formerly run by Jay Gould.

Like Morgan, Adams too came to an important landmark in his career in the 1890s, when both were entering on old age. Morgan, released by his father's death, plunged into the business world; Adams turned from it in disgust. "Indeed, as I approach the end," he wrote,

> I am more than a little puzzled to account for the instances I have seen of business success—money-getting. It comes from a rather low instinct. Certainly,

as far as my observation goes, it is rarely met with in combination with the finer or more interesting traits of character. I have known, and known tolerably well, a good many successful men—big financially—men famous during the last half-century; and a less interesting crowd I do not care to encounter. Not one that I have ever known would I care to meet again, either in this world or the next; nor is one of them associated in my mind with the idea of humor, thought, or refinement. A set of mere money-getters and traders, they were essentially unattractive and uninteresting.

For all this excessive protest, though, Adams, like most who have come into contact with Erie crew, couldn't resist the temptation to pick a favorite villain. For Adams, the Lucifer among lesser devils was Cornelius Vanderbilt. Far from seeing the Commodore as "essentially unattractive and uninteresting," Adams was fascinated by his "steady nerve and sturdy gambler's pride."

The selection of one evildoer over another in the rampant vice of the Erie struggle is a difficult choice, and in making it many commentators have passed over Adams' nominee and settled instead on Jay Gould. For sheer vaulting ambition, the quality that recommended Lucifer to Milton, he well may deserve the palm. But the best corrective for any tendency to admire his role in connection with that much put-upon railroad is the facts. In the nine years from 1864 to 1872, the bonded indebtedness of the company increased 48 percent, from $17,822,900 to $26,395,000, and the common stock, issued by the Drew-Gould-Fisk "printing press," rose from 242,280 to 780,000 shares, or over 221 percent. This against an increase in mileage of 53 percent and a rise in net earnings of only 22 percent. "No more disgraceful record exists for any American railroad," said an authority more than thirty years later. "The stock was not issued for the sake of improving the road, and it was subsequently shown that the road was not improved; but it was thrown upon the market at critical times in support of bear operations by the Erie managers, while portions of it, on at least one occasion, were bought back wih the funds of the company to aid speculation for a rise."

The occasion mentioned was in late 1868, when Gould, under the tutelage of crafty old Uncle Dan'l, learned how a wider objective than Erie could be gained. In the learning process, Gould pitilessly stripped his mentor of wealth and power. For Gould, it was a rehearsal for the maneuvers that were to culminate the following year in the Panic of 1869, bringing the economy to a near standstill.

In the 1868 prelude, Gould and Fisk, occasionally abetted by Drew, developed a new adjunct to the printing press. With their combined resources, they discovered they were able to "lock up" the unprecedented sum of $12 million in cash. In other words, what amounted to a considerable portion of Wall Street's ready funds would follow their lead. Their purpose was to depress the value of Erie by taking up the "short" position, but they found that the follow-the-leader effect extended to the entire list of stocks and beyond. The monetary stringency they brought on continued to spread until the normal financing of the nation's October crop and even government revenues were threatened. The Erie gang observed the whole operation with great interest.

And they learned from the next step, which was taken by the government. President Johnson's Secretary of the Treasury, Hugh McCulloch, had been committed to a tight money policy in trying to dry up the supply of liquidity let loose by Civil War financing. But the consequences of the 1868 squeeze nearly forced him to change his strategy and he let it be known that he was ready to reverse himself with a distribution of $50 million into the economy. The threat was sufficient. Gould marked the lesson well and realized that before his next coup he would have to get control of the U.S. Treasury.

Gould and Fisk had been ready to change tactics anyway, and McCulloch's response merely hastened their shift. During the rise that followed that they tapped the Erie treasury and at the same time managed to squeeze the old bear Daniel Drew right out of the financial world.

The experience was an exhilirating one for Gould and in the following year, shortly after Grant took office for his first term, he must have seen possibilities for a monetary operation beyond anything he had ever dreamed of before. He took Fisk fitfully into his plans, letting him know just enough to enable him to carry out his part of the plan. The scheme rested on another "lock-up" similar to the one of 1868 but on a much grander scale— specifically, $50 million compared to the $12 million of the earlier operation. Ultimately, the aim would be to corner all the gold outside the Treasury.

The purpose was much more ambitious than the mere beating

down of Erie stock. Having seen the effect of the previous tightening of the money supply on western farmers, eastern industrialists, and the government itself, Gould this time set out with high hopes of paralyzing the entire economy. There was only one imponderable. He had to have the cooperation of the United States Treasury—or at least he had to *appear* to have its cooperation. Gould realized that it didn't matter whether the assistance was actual or mere seeming, and it has never been clear which method was used. The amount of gold in circulation at the time was about $20 million compared with $75 million to $100 million held by the federal government. Any attempt at a corner of the circulating supply could easily be foiled by the release of some of the government supply. In fact, the government used precisely this method to stabilize the price of gold at 135. Gould had to deploy his whole collection of tricks to keep the government flow to a minimum.

A key figure in his plot was an elderly adventurer named Abel Rathbone Corbin, a speculator, lobbyist, and follower of other such "hazardous pursuits," as Henry Adams termed them. A few years earlier, as he was about to turn seventy, he had married Grant's sister and the newlyweds went to live in New York. Through Corbin, Gould had access to the President. Throughout the summer of 1869 he cultivated the Chief Executive through Corbin. He won an invitation to meet Grant at Corbin's house in June. Gould improved on that occasion by getting Grant to attend a performance at the Grand Opera House in Fisk's private box. The following day the President was ferried to Boston aboard one of Fisk's ornate steamers. Both events were extensively trumpeted by the press to the public, which was left to ruminate as it would on the spectacle of a Chief Executive among such riffraff.

The voyage up Long Island Sound included a dinner that offered further opportunity for Gould and Fisk to impress themselves on the President. During the meal and after, Gould, as adept as ever at developing plausible reasons for his machinations, laid down a smokescreen that would make a plan for his personal enrichment seem like a public benefaction.

The proposal, as he outlined it to Grant and the other guests, went like this: a rise in the price of gold from 135 to 145 or so, if it came in the fall around harvest time, would have the effect of raising the value of exported grain by roughly 8 percent. This was surely a worthwhile result for merely letting the price of gold fluctuate a little more than usual, Gould told the assemblage as the smoke of rich Havanas floated upward in the grand dining salon. His dark eyes flashed, his bulging forehead glistened as he hinted that a tighter hand on the government's gold would bring rich blessings to the farmer and possibly earn his gratitude at the polling place. The lollers in the salon of course were aware that a higher-priced crop would bring added revenues to Gould's railway, the Erie, on its way to eastern ports, but this slight element of self-interest seemed merely to lend more force to Gould's plan. His listeners had no suspicion of his actual goal, the effective takeover of the United States Treasury for whatever period of time pleased him. Larceny on such a scale did not occur to the happy excursionists during the pleasant trip up the Sound.

It all seemed so right to Corbin, whose ethical sense, vestigial at best, was further atrophied by what Gould promised he would get out of the scheme. Grant, too, seemed to have been beguiled by the idea. Apparently only the harmless diversion of extra profit to the farmers was all that met Grant's eye. At least it is unlikely that he would have entered into a conspiracy with the little Mephistopheles of Wall Street. On the other hand, his venal associates deserve no such assumption of innocence. In any case, from this point on coincidences and happenstances occurred to further the Gould scheme.

One of them was the appointment of a military man, General Daniel Butterfield, as assistant treasurer, with the job of watching over the principal supply of governmental gold at the New York subtreasury. Whatever the General's prowess on the battlefield may have been, his chief claim to a secure place in history must rest on a relatively homely accomplishment: he is credited with creating the end-of-day bugle call, Taps. Butterfield had been a general with the unscrupulous Sickles at Gettysburg. Both were under the overall command of General Joseph Hooker. Charles Francis Adams, Jr., was a cavalry captain there and recalled the three with distaste. "All three were men of blemished character," said Adams. Butterfield got his job of seeing that none of the gold got out to upset the plans of Gould through the agency of Corbin. Like Corbin, he was put in the way of some profit, it was said.

Around August 20, 1869, Gould began to bait his bear trap. Forming a pool with two other speculators, he bought gold surreptitiously so that there was little change in price. On September 3, Grant exceeded Gould's fondest expectations in furthering the scheme. While on a visit with Corbin in New York, the President, pressed by his brother-in-law to do something about Gould's scheme for benefitting the farmers, agreed to write to Secretary of the Treasury George S. Boutwell about the matter. The letter was not made public, but Boutwell, at a congressional investigation of the gold panic, recalled enough of its substance to indicate that it could have been written by the chief conspirator himself. It bid him instruct his department to "send no order to Butterfield as to sales of gold until you hear from me."

The whole substance of Grant's response, and possibly even the letter to Boutwell itself, was communicated to Gould by Corbin immediately. Thus assured, the financier moved to further prepare the trap. He gave orders to buy. His agents in the Grant retinue continued the pressure as gold made its way up. Then, late in September, Gould began to perceive that his efforts to neutralize the government supply of gold were beginning to break up. Grant was starting to listen to some of his more high-minded advisers, who were pointing out that siding with an unscrupulous and notorious stockjobber was an untenable position.

Realizing that Grant soon would countermand his orders to Boutwell, Gould gave orders to sell heavily. Ordinarily such sales would have depressed the quotations and caused him terrible losses, but Gould had a plan to take care of this; he simply transferred the risk to his partner, Fisk. Fisk, who had no knowledge of the shift in strategy, continued to bull the price of gold until it reached 162 in the disorderly panic of Black Friday, September 24. Henry Adams reported:

> The bubble suddenly burst, and within fifteen minutes, amid an excitement without parallel even in the wildest excitements of the war, the clique brokers were literally swept away, and left struggling by themselves, bidding still 160 for gold in millions which no one would any longer take their word for; while the premium sank rapidly to 135. A moment later the telegraph brought from Washington the order to sell, and the result was no longer possible to dispute. Mr. Fisk

had gone too far, while Mr. Gould had secretly weakened the ground under his feet.

Gould had betrayed his jovial partner, but between two such consummate crooks that mattered little. A small stab in the back from a friend made little difference to Fisk, who was able to say as the value of his holdings evaporated that day, "Nothing is lost save honor."

Anyway, Gould only appeared to be betraying Fisk, for Fisk immediately repudiated his debts—with the full assistance of Gould—thus unloading the losses on the men who had been foolish enough to act as his brokers. When the congressional committee investigating the gold corner asked him where the money had gone, he insolently answered with a nonsense phrase that became a catchword of the day: "It has gone," he said, "where the woodbine twineth."

Fisk was chipper enough to turn the inquisitors' attention to pastoral byways only because he and Gould had escaped a probable beating on Black Friday. The Prince of Erie had had the foresight to direct a couple of his lovelier retainers, girls from the chorus line of the Offenbach and Strauss light operas that he featured at his opera house, to reconnoitre the financial district. When these scouts brought back reports about the size and ugliness of the crowd gathered at his broker's door, he and Gould decided it would be expedient to remove themselves from the commercial center for some time.

The angry mood didn't last. As after any financial catastrophe, the ruined melt away, to throw themselves in one or the other of the convenient pair of nearby rivers or to take up residence in the derelict areas around the Five Points at Chatham Square or the Bowery. In no time the financial world returned to normal—or at least that giddy, chancy state that it likes to think of as normal. Little more than a month later there occurred a pair of spectacles—high and low comedy—that demonstrated how completely Wall Street had forgotten the September gloom.

Both events came about because of the ego of one man, Commodore Vanderbilt.

The Commodore planned and commissioned a colossal monument to himself, to be unveiled on November 9. It was carried out by one of his employes, Albert de Groot, a onetime riverboat captain, with the help of a sculptor, Ernest Plassman, of no great

renown but of sufficient technical competence to translate the old
riverdog's ideas into fifty tons of bronze, bluestone, granite, and
marble. The overawing cyclorama was put up on the Hudson
Street terminal of Vanderbilt's New York Central and Hudson
River Railroad, between Laight and Vestry Streets.

The unveiling was attended by Gould and Fisk, which shows
the extent to which the lynching spirit had subsided since Black
Friday. Also on hand were Tammany Mayor A. Oakey Hall,
August Belmont, and Vanderbilt's recently hired junior counsel,
Chauncey M. Depew, together with the rest of the people who
counted.

What the crowd saw as the cloth barrier across the block-long
terminal parted was an awesome memorial to bad taste. The
monument stretched over half the building. The centerpiece of
the 150-foot long, thirty-one-foot high opus was a twelve-foot
statue of the Commodore, just about double life size. The representation was arrayed in fur-lined, fur-collared cloak, just as was
the original in the crowd below. The bronze Commodore, surrounded by intricately detailed castings of his possessions,
seemed to be scanning the horizon for new victims.

There were effigies of ships, smaller craft, railroad trains and
track, switchmen and their shanties, and, among the smaller
refuse of the jumbled composition, detailed relief of nuts, bolts,
gears, chains, hawsers, bananas, pineapples, and other carefully
wrought objects—even a raccoon, presumably memorializing the
source of the Commodore's collar and coat-lining. It was a
veritable nightmare of all he had seen, touched, and twisted to
his use.

Liberty, the emblem of the Republic, and Neptune were there,
at the furthest remove from the central statue and placed at a
properly subordinate level. There was even a jumble of railroad
gear piled up to the Commodore's right, giving the impression of
a wreck—a detail that may have reminded onlookers of Vanderbilt's connection with the Erie.

Over on Broad Street, an irreverent group of brokers, clerks,
and runners chose this day to give their own tribute to Vanderbilt. A statue was unveiled. Lacking the means to pay a foundry
for the casting of twelve-foot bronzes, the group enlisted one of
its members—"a tall figure draped in white, with a face expres-
sive of little but idiocy"—to play the role. He bore in one hand a
watering can labeled "207," the price the Commodore had run

Central stock to during a phase of the consolidation. The burlesque symbolism was considerably more deft, and of course more to the point, than that of Vanderbilt's scrambled concoction, but to make sure it passed over no one's head, the chairman delivered a mock-eulogy:

> It is the use of water, not as a beverage but as an element of public wealth, which has been the distinguishing characteristic of the achievements of Commodore Vanderbilt's later years. . . . We may say of him not only that he commenced life as a waterman, but that water has been the Central idea of his life.

At one point the burlesque was interrupted; a messenger appeared with an injunction to halt the proceedings issued by "G. Bennerdo"—reference to Vanderbilt's former handmaiden, Supreme Court Justice George G. Barnard.

An interesting sidelight to the event was the fact that most of the city's papers ignored the burlesque, as though fearful of dignifying the proceeding by taking notice. Only Horace Greeley's *Tribune* reported the shenanigans in full the next day. Then the *World* took notice and on November 11 put the whole event in what it considered the proper context. The *World* said: "The Commodore is the realized ideal of every one of them [at the mock unveiling]. . . . He has done what they all admire and envy him for doing, and what they would all do if they could."

The editorial apparently mirrored the feeling of those who were burlesqued. This was a time when all the newspapers in the city, except for the *Times* and to some extent the *Tribune,* were courtesans for the Tweed ring, highly paid in one way or another. The extent of the ring's grip was yet to be shown. As the *Times* and *Harper's Weekly* mounted the attack that was to end the ring's rule, one of the best newspapermen in the city, Charles Nordhoff, tried to enlist the New York *Evening Post*, of which he was managing editor, in support of the battle. He was fired as a result by William Cullen Bryant, good green poet and owner and publisher of the paper.

In one way or another, criticism of the movers and shakers was suppressed. Mark Twain and Charles Dudley Warner managed to ridicule the popular delusions of the day and gave a deeply ironic name to the eight-year period of the Grant administration.

They called it "The Gilded Age." Washed by time of its critical implication, the phrase has been taken up by succeeding generations to describe the period as seen through a golden haze of nostalgia. A less ironic name for the era has been put forward by Vernon Louis Parrington, an incisive observer of the literary past and its underpinnings in the world of the Vanderbilts, Astors, Adamses, Morgans, and Rockefellers.

His phrase for the time was "The Great Barbecue," but it hasn't been taken up. No generation likes to think of its fathers, grandfathers, or great-grandparents as participants in a disorderly and unbuttoned excursion into gluttony, so the apt title has never supplanted the term Gilded Age. Parrington develops his barbecue theme in this passage:

> To a frontier people what was more democratic than a barbeque, and to a paternalistic age what was more fitting than that the state should provide the beeves for roasting. . . . As a result the feast was Gargantuan in its rough plenty. . . . More food, to be sure, was spoiled than eaten, and the revelry was a bit unseemly; but it was a fine spree in the name of the people. . . . Unfortunately what was intended to be jovially democratic was marred by displays of plebeian temper. Suspicious commoners with better eyes than manners discovered the favoritism of the waiters and drew attention to the difference between their own meager helpings and the heaped-up plates of more favored guests. It appeared indeed that there was gross discrimination in the service; that the farmers' pickings from the Homestead Act were scanty in comparison with the speculators' pickings from the railway land-grants. The Credit Mobilier scandal and the Whisky Ring scandal and the divers other scandals came near to breaking up the feast, and the genial host—who was no other than the hero of Appomattox—came in for some sharp criticism. But after the more careless ones who were caught with their fingers where they didn't belong had been thrust from the table, the eating and drinking went on again till only the great carcasses were left. Then at last came the reckoning. When the bill was sent in to

the American people the farmers discovered that they
had been put off with the giblets while the capitalists
were consuming the turkey. They learned that they
were no match at a barbecue for more voracious
guests, and as they went home unsatisfied, a sullen
anger burned in their hearts that was to express itself
later in fierce agrarian revolts.

The barbecue was not confined to New York, with its Tweed
ring, and Washington, the center of the pilfering of the Credit
Mobilier, the construction company that stole from the govern-
ment-backed Union Pacific with the connivance of even a future
president, James Garfield, and the current Vice President,
Schuyler Colfax. The groaning board was set from border to
border—and beyond. There was corruption in the Navy Department, among ministers to England and Brazil, among customs
collectors in New York and New Orleans. The thieving Whisky
Ring, headquartered in St. Louis, the mismanagement of Indian
affairs, graft in local and state governments in Pennsylvania,
Illinois, Iowa, Minnesota, and California testified to the breadth
of the criminality.

The Great Barbecue did not include Morgan; he was under
virtual house arrest by order of his father for excesses committed
before the grand, brawling feast began.

He did, it was true, play a small part in the backwoods
skirmish related to the Erie war in 1869, right about the time Jay
Gould was readying his panic. Pierpont Morgan seems to have
acted as a well-dressed bully-boy for the management of the
Albany & Susquehanna, a gentlemanly but formidable counter-
balance to the goon squads of Tweed ring hangers-on who had
been imported when the Erie gang tried to take over the line.
The 140-mile Albany & Susquehanna linked the New York Central terminal at Albany with the Erie's terminal at Binghamton in
a northeast-southwest direction roughly paralleling the Susquehanna River. It would be a valuable prize for either of the great
trunk routes, but Gould and Fisk seem to have been first in
attempting to capture it. Defending it was rough work that
included a great pitched battle between the Tweed recruits and
the Albany & Susquehanna's own workers. At one point two rival
boards of directors were installed. Among the highlights of the
struggle, when operations moved into the judicial atmosphere of

Tweed judges *versus* their rural counterparts beholden to the railroad, was the finding of the dead body of the son of the president of the Albany & Susquehanna floating in the Hudson River. The last he was seen alive was when his father, finding it impossible to serve Fisk and Gould with ordinary process servers, sent him to New York as a substitute officer of the court.

AFTER
THE FEAST

THE Great Barbecue lurched on, from the relatively minor panic of 1869 to the much more serious one of 1873. The earlier one had, after all, inflicted some partial paralysis on the economy, but its major effect was in vaporizing the water pumped into securities values by such experts in high-pressure hydraulics as Commodore Vanderbilt. Jim Fisk had been caught, but he was able to laugh off, with Jay Gould's help, the cries of outrage from the brokers he had bilked. But the panic of 1873, the crowning achievement of Grant's second term, was a far more serious matter. It tumbled from the heights a financier who had been looked on as almost as much of a Civil War hero as Grant had been. He was Jay Cooke. "The war," Parrington observed, "was as great a godsend to Jay Cooke as it was to Grant, for alone amongst our moneylenders he realized the problems and foresaw the profits in a popular system of war financing."

Along with the diligent halo-burnishing and retroactive distribution of credit for great financial feats that emerged in Pierpont Morgan's last two decades on earth, there have been attempts to hail him as the man who knocked Cooke out of the counting house. Unfortunately for Morgan's hagiographers, there doesn't seem to be much evidence for this claim. The myth relies largely on what happened in connection with the sharing between Cooke and J. S. Morgan of a governmental bond issue during the panic year. Each took up a half, or $150 million worth of the issue. According to the myth, this division was due to the energy, initiative, and general genius of the thirty-six-year-old Morgan and was done over objections by Cooke. But there is no evidence that Cooke had objections. He had suggested as far back as 1861 sharing government business with Drexel & Co. Since that time some bitterness had grown up over Drexel-inspired attacks on Cooke and his Northern Pacific railroad financing. But other than the fact that Morgan had become a Drexel partner in 1867, there is nothing to show that he led the Philadelphia firm in an effort to take business from Cooke.

All the evidence points to a continuance during the postwar period and the Gilded Age that succeeded it of virtual confinement to quarters for Morgan. His physical disabilities seemed to trouble him more, particularly the reddening of his nose and forehead, and he even contemplated retirement.

This desire to withdraw, which ultimately he was able to conquer, only because of constant prodding from his father was manifested in an almost insatiable impulse to travel. Some of his extensive trips combined business with sightseeing, as when he went out, as an early pioneer, to the West Coast only months after the completion of the Central Pacific–Union Pacific transcontinental link. Some were aimless wanderings, the padding through European splendor that was being indulged in by other empty wealthy men, in their thirties, like Morgan, or a little older. Travel seemed to relieve some of the disfigurement, the aches and pains that visited him more often. "He seemed to feel better when he was actually traveling than when they settled down anywhere," says Satterlee.

One of the journeys, though, was not aimless and brought more to him than simple physical relief. He may have been simply following the fashionable world in going to Egypt, but the place soon had him in its spell. There was something that appealed to a part of Morgan that hadn't even awakened yet in a land where a chosen handful had reached the apex of human magnificence, flourished briefly, and had left monuments of such colossal magnitude that they have never been duplicated. Egypt became one of his favorite spots on earth; and he returned again and again to Memphis, Luxor, the Valley of the Kings, Khargeh —six visits in all. Three of them came in each of the last three years of his life, almost as though he were fending off approaching death, bargaining for one last look at the crumbling memorials to pomp before joining the Pharaohs himself. The last visits coincided, too, with extensive diggings and restorations undertaken there at his instance—to be sure, he grumbled at the expense—by the Metropolitan Museum of Art.

Of course, Morgan's travels were often far more prosaic. His lengthy trip by rail to the West Coast in 1869 was undertaken partly to report on the condition of the transcontinental railroad to Dabney, Morgan, and his father, and partly to confer with his father's representative in San Francisco, Milton I. Latham. There was also a good deal of visiting and sightseeing. Morgan, his wife, her sister Mary K. Tracy, and his cousin Mary Goodwin, Jim's sister, started out July 5, less than two months after the last spike joining the Central Pacific and Union Pacific was driven at Promontory Point, Utah, opening the first rail route through to the Pacific. The party visited in Chicago, and then went on to St. Louis where the journey west was made in high style in one of the early Pullmans. Sightseeing in Salt Lake City, a visit with Brigham Young, more visiting and gaping, plus business with Latham in San Francisco and a tour of the Yosemite occupied them until August 21, when they began the return journey. They were back in New York by September 1, just in time for the sortie in upper New York involving the Albany and Susquehanna railroad.

For the next two years little was recorded of Pierpont Morgan's doings. It was a time when the firm of J. S. Morgan & Co. took part, on behalf of its English stockholders, in promoting the efforts of the unspeakable General Sickles to unseat Jay Gould, the insufferable.

Pierpont Morgan may have had some part in these dealings, although the principal backer of Sickles was Pierpont's old firm of Duncan, Sherman & Co. and most of the decisions and actions emanated from that group. One of the few facts that is clear from this period is that in September 1870 he represented his church, St. George's, for the first time at the triennial Episcopal diocesan conference, a practice that he was to continue throughout most of his life.

The following year there occurred some sort of crisis in his affairs about which we have only occasional bits of information. Sometime in the early part of 1871, he appears to have suffered an even more virulent return of the skin eruption, headaches, and possibly the fainting spells that had first appeared around draft time in 1861. This flareup coincided with the ending of the Dabney, Morgan & Co. partnership, after less than ten years.

The Dabney, Morgan breakup was said by the family biographer to have resulted from a set of remarkably fortuitous mutual desires, but if this is so, they were synchronized in a way that strains belief. First Dabney was supposed to be ready to retire, which he may have been. But Jim Goodwin, after nearly as long a period as Pierpont Morgan in the heart of New York's financial district, was said to have wanted to return to Hartford to help with his father's affairs. Goodwin was the boon companion and cousin who, together with Pierpont, had teased girls at the Draper Academy, had compared notes throughout youth and early adulthood on that same all-consuming subject, and had toured the Northeast and Europe together with Pierpont.

We don't know if they parted under estranged circumstances, but from that point on Goodwin and his cousin never had any business connections and very little social contact. The inseparable companion of Pierpont Morgan's youth showed up occasionally three decades later at yacht races and other ceremonial occasions, and Morgan appeared to be friendly to Jim and his wife around the turn of the century, visiting them for a few family dinners. But certainly their close friendship, reinforced as it was by blood ties, virtually ended with the breakup of the partnership in 1871.

The other contributing factor to the dissolution of Dabney, Morgan was Morgan's illness. To some extent this flareup of his physical ailments may have been precipitated by a growing restiveness under the yoke that his father had imposed. The record, of course, was carefully destroyed by Pierpont Morgan himself. We do know, though, that at this point Morgan seriously considered retiring. Word that his son would take his place among the jaded has-beens of America's idle rich at the age of thirty-four appeared to have ignited Junius Morgan, who immediately came up with a substitute probation officer to replace Charles Dabney. He was Anthony J. Drexel of Philadelphia.

Drexel was the son of Francis Martin Drexel, a Swiss painter who had emigrated to America a half-century earlier to win success both as a portrait painter and as a banker and founder of Drexel & Co. In 1847 Anthony, with his brothers Francis and Joseph, became a partner in the business, which already had a Paris outlet, Drexel, Harjes & Co., but wanted a New York office. At the modest price of taking over Charles Dabney's surveillance duties, the Drexels got just such an office, Drexel, Morgan & Co., complete with a connection with the major American house in London, J. S. Morgan & Co.

The London branch, important in the promotion of American securities since the days of Peabody, was just adding to its stature in a wider, more international way during the Franco-Prussian War. After the defeat of the emperor at Sedan and while Paris was still under siege, Junius Morgan went to Tours, where he agreed to lend the exile French government there 250 million francs—or $50 million—on 6 percent bonds which he was getting at 80. Morgan was exacting a stiff price from the French, but then many investment bankers weren't lending to the defeated country at any price. At one point he was forced to buy in the bonds to support the price, but ultimately the move was crowned with success as the energetic republic that succeeded Louis Napoleon's empire went on to create wealth sufficient even to repay the $1 billion indemnity set by the Prussians.

Pierpont Morgan agreed to ally himself with Drexel in return for a concession from his father and his new partners that he be allowed to take a protracted vacation during this supposedly crucial first year of the combination. The extended leave was based on advice from the Morgan family physician, Dr. George T. Elliot, who wanted him to give up business entirely and take his family abroad for a long vacation. Otherwise, the doctor said, a breakdown would be inevitable.

This lengthy trip took him out of the country with his family less than two weeks from the starting date of the Drexel, Morgan & Co. partnership on July 1, 1871. The new firm took over the old Dabney, Morgan office at 53 Exchange Place. Pierpont Morgan was not to return to the business for nearly two years, by which time the Drexel Building, a six-story white marble structure costing $945,000, had been erected at the corner of Wall and Broad streets, a corner still dominated by Morgan interests. Anthony Drexel's brother Joseph acted as partner in charge while Morgan sought health and relaxation in London, Paris, Karlsbad, the Austrian Tyrol, Salzburg, Vienna, Munich, Rome, and in his first trip to Egypt in December of 1871. The family continued traveling during most of the following year.

It was while he was on this tour that Morgan bought Cragston, a great rambling country place at Highland Falls on the west bank of the Hudson, near where he had often vacationed. The place was to serve him as more than a summer retreat; for it was here that he was to begin his herds of prize cattle and his kennels of champion collies. A sprawling old house unlike the splendid country homes the rich were beginning to affect, it was a comfortable retreat for him and the family. They would move up each year in the spring and stay until late summer while Morgan commuted to Manhattan, sometimes by train; later more often by boat.

While such domestic considerations and the state of his health were monopolizing Pierpont Morgan's attention, the truly dominating financier of the Gilded Age or the Great Barbecue, Jay Cooke, was embroiling himself ever deeper in deals that would help bring on the panic of 1873 and that would effectively bring an end to his power over the affairs of the country.

Jay Cooke, the Philadelphia banker, can be called the first modern American businessman. When he undertook to finance the Civil War, he realized the need to construct an almost overpowering piece of machinery, not one of iron and steel, puffing pipes and whirring gears, but of something less substantial and therefore far more refractory, of people and influence welded together into a machine of salesmanship and promotion. Cooke was the financial counterpart of those visionaries of the time who were flinging bridges across rivers and rails across the wilderness, who were harnessing natural power in great engines to bring abundance into being. He sold the government's bonds with floods of advertising that swept every city, town, and hamlet. The message was that the civilian must back the fighting man with his dollars. Cooke subsidized agents everywhere to supplement the direct advertising appeal. They were in newspaper offices, both metropolitan dailies and rural weeklies, in banks, in pulpits. Hack writers churned out copy that was scattered broadcast.

Because the aim of these efforts—to support and win the war—was generally felt to be praiseworthy, his success in creating the whole institutional apparatus for selling securities met with general approbation. And he didn't stop with the United States. He had a superbly efficient extension of his machine in Germany, where thirty newspapers were under subsidy and his paid agents lived in ducal palaces.

In addition, innovator though he was, Cooke never hesitated to adopt the ideas of others. He succeeded in handling the original war financing alone, but as refinancing began in the decade of the 1870s, he introduced the "underwriting syndicate" in which the risk is "laid off" on a group. The system had been developed by French financiers. In 1871, the year that Drexel, Morgan & Co.

was formed, Cooke launched the first such syndicate in this country in order to sell part of an issue of $500 million worth of government bonds.

Cooke was of an autocratic and overbearing turn of mind from his earliest days. In the first year of the war, when he was nothing more than a fledgling banker, he boldly suggested that Secretary of the Treasury Salmon P. Chase divert all Treasury operations to his firm. The forty-year-old Drexel & Co. in Philadelphia reminded Chase that "We could not be expected to leave our comfortable homes and positions here without some great inducement and we state frankly that we would, if we succeeded, expect a fair commission from the Treasury in some shape for our labor and talent."

This proposal didn't win acceptance, but humility never infected Jay Cooke. More than a decade later, during the Credit Mobilier scandal, he wrote to his brother Henry, horrified over the government's proposal to halt payment on interest-bearing coupons of the Union Pacific: "Now I want you to go to the Attorney General at once and tell him how wrong this whole procedure is. This whole persecution of the Union Pacific is nonsense, and is damaging our credit abroad." The letter is a highhanded anticipation of a more celebrated proposal to be made three decades later by Cooke's successor in arrogance and finance, J. Pierpont Morgan, who would suggest to a President of the United states: ". . . send your man [the Attorney General] to my man and they can fix it up."

But in 1873 it was too late for Cooke to be dispatching underlings to the President's menials to patch things up. He had transferred his methods, sufferable when they involved government funding, to the railroad sphere. Now his offhand ways with government officers, his gifts of cigars to a President and fishing equipment to his son, could be misunderstood.

Cooke was deeply involved in the disastrous attempt to build the Northern Pacific. His high-pressure promoters, so readily accepted when they were working for the federal cause, were now the cause of public anger and, what was worse, ridicule. He put forward exaggerated claims aimed at bringing Americans and foreigners to the Northern Pacific's territory, and after some of his unprincipled and ignorant copywriters had described imaginary groves of fruit along the Nebraska-Montana right of way, the area was satirically nicknamed "Jay Cooke's Banana

Belt." Cooke was laughed at; congressmen even dared to mock him.

At the same time, Cooke was being menaced by other financiers greedy for participation in the federal financings. Among them were the firms of Morton, Bliss & Co., and Drexel, Morgan & Co. The grumblings of the uninvited ultimately reached Congress, where the House Ways & Means Committee heard testimony in January 1873.

As one of his first duties for his new firm, Morgan went to Washington, where he began his long association with the Arlington Hotel. "Pierpont was always given the same rooms in the old red brick dwelling house that was part of the hotel. There was an old-fashioned parlor with an open fire, and his meals were served there when he had guests. When he was alone, however, he always liked a particular table in the hotel dining room, and all the waiters knew just what he wanted to eat and drink. He always felt very much at home there," Satterlee recalled.

Morgan may have been at home in Washington, but he played only a minor role in the congressional area. The spokesman for the group was Levi P. Morton, but before the committee listened to him it heard from Pierpont's old boss, William Butler Duncan of Duncan, Sherman & Co., who urged the government to dispense with all banking intermediaries and sell directly to the citizens. Bankers like Cooke and the others who arranged syndicates, he said, took "United States bonds out of the hands of small investors and put them in the hands of bankers, brokers and large investors, where they were liable to be affected by the frequent fluctuations in the money market." If this were not done, Duncan said, the refunding, in which it was proposed to substitute 5 percent bonds for the 6 percent bonds that had been necessary during the war, would be "a very doubtful operation." An attempt in 1871 had nearly failed and "I doubt very much whether in the present condition of the markets of the world another effort in the same direction would be nearly as successful as that one has been."

When he got his turn to speak, Morton ridiculed Duncan's contention that the government should deal directly with the holders of the earlier bonds: "Some gentlemen have argued that the Government should wait for buyers to come to the Treasury Department for the conversion of their bonds; in my opinion the Government would have to wait for a long time before it would make any conversion of 6 percent bonds into 5 percent bonds."

Of course, this was all talk—financial talk of the kind reserved by businessmen for governmental agents. The purpose was not to guard against fluctuations or to benefit the small investor. The small buyer might have come in handy in the 1860s, when the bonds were more in the nature of IOU's issued by a threatened federal power that might not even exist long enough to redeem them.

But now, with the industrial machinery of the nation humming, the Treasury was honoring these obligations as though they were promissory notes payable in gold. This was the time for taking the bonds away from the "small buyers" who had so gullibly swallowed Jay Cooke's patriotic pitches and to distribute them among the wealthy realists who wanted no part of them while shots were being fired at their issuers. So the only result of the hearings was to widen the circle of financiers who were now ready to exhibit faith in the government.

After the hearings, Treasury Secretary Boutwell determined to divide the refunding issue, with $150 million going to the syndicate comprising Cooke and the Rothschilds in England and a like amount spread among Morton, Bliss, Drexel, Morgan, and their European counterparts, J. S. Morgan, Morton Rose, and the Barings. The consideration for selling the bonds was the extremely modest sum of $150,000 to be cut among all the participants. However, the members of the syndicate were to be allowed to sell the bonds and retain the payments without interest charge until December 31, when a delayed accounting would be made to the Treasury.

That consideration was worth thousands of dollars for Jay Cooke, who was then juggling the fragile structure of Northern Pacific. It also brought with it the possibility of remaining solvent. He needed just that kind of gift from the government. But it wasn't enough to help Cooke, and on September 17 his house failed, bringing on the terrible Panic of 1873. On September 20, while the precipitous drop in securities continued, the New York Stock Exchange had to take the unprecedented step of closing its doors. The interruption helped stem the slide in securities prices but had no effect on the depression that then set in and continued for another six years.

The finagling of Cooke and of the businessmen and politicians in both his Northern Pacific venture and the even more scandalous Credit Mobilier, together with all the other speculations, high and low, contributed to the economic paralysis, but the domestic panic was part of a larger experience. Germany, France, and England felt the slowdown. The net inflow of foreign capital that had helped over the past eight years to double railway mileage to 70,268 miles and to push total investment to $3.78 billion in the year of the panic was halted as European investors called in their American loans. Overexpansion of agriculture, so much more important in that era, produced surplus crops that could not be marketed abroad at satisfactory prices after the Franco-Prussian War.

The latter half of the Gilded Age, Grant's second term, ended in depression, an elaborate national centennial celebration of independence at Philadelphia, and a corrupt election. All the while, Pierpont Morgan was drawing closer to the sources of power, but he hadn't arrived yet. He would accompany Morton to congressional hearings and do his part in trying to take business from Jay Cooke, but his role was still that of an apprentice financier. Some later observers of the period profess to see him setting up traps and imposing proposals "in the shadows," but the evidence is lacking. One such commentator notes that "contemporary opinion" observed the power of "the great house of the Drexels," but failed to discern Morgan as "the active moving force, although still comparatively unknown beyond the inner circles." The contemporary opinion referred to was that of Henry Clews, a Vanderbilt associate and chatty chronicler of Wall Street doings for more than forty years. He was a prominent member of the financial community and when he singled out a name like Drexel and ignored a Morgan, it would be on the basis of accurate information. If Clews failed to discern Morgan's power at this period, it would have been because that power did not exist.

Andrew Carnegie also testifies to the errand-boy character of Morgan at this period. He had met Junius S. Morgan in London and suggested a sale of railroad bonds, demanding that the elder Morgan give him 25 percent of the profits if there were any in the Carnegie idea. But during the panic of 1873, "Mr. Pierpont Morgan . . . said to me one day: 'My father has called to ask whether you wish to sell out your interest in that idea you gave him,'" Carnegie recalled.

"I said: 'Yes, I do. In these days I will sell anything for money.'"

Carnegie sold his interest ultimately for $70,000, but throughout the transaction the principals were himself and the elder Morgan. Pierpont Morgan simply relayed messages and checks.

In fact, more typical of Morgan's conduct during this panic year was his joining with Morris K. Jesup, William E. Dodge, Sr. and Jr., and others active in the Young Men's Christian Association to form that ultimate in moral vigilanteism, the New York Society for the Suppression of Vice. Members of the group, as always in such extralegal associations, were safe from its nosiness; the purpose was to impose its narrowminded ideas of decency on the defenseless majority.

To that end the society catapulted into prominence one of the all-time American pests, Anthony Comstock. For more than four decades he harassed the unfortunate middle and lower classes of the country by outlawing the cheaper forms of gambling, snooping into widespread vulgarity, and drawing fig leaves over any display of nature that he considered offensive by his dim lights. Although he destroyed the New Orleans lottery, there is no record of his ever having taken exception to any of the opportunities for gaming likely to be patronized by his superiors—like Saratoga or the gambling houses run by Morrissey or Canfield. His fig leaf obsession was ridiculed in a drawing by Charles Dana Gibson in *Life* for January 13, 1888, showing "A scene in the moral future." The drawing shows a stagecoach full of people horrified at two naked children skipping along at the side of the road, while every horse, a dog, and bird at rest or flying—even an elephant occupying a zoo cage in the background—is swathed in voluminous drapery.

This was a day of corruption on a grand and national scale. It was a time when the Drews, Vanderbilts, and Goulds could use a railroad as a toy and rob it of money needed to prevent forty-fatality accidents; when members of Congress and the Grant administration could be drawn into a Credit Mobilier and into doing the bidding of a profiteer like Jay Cooke; when legislators could be bought, not once but again and again, as Horace Greeley pointed out, and the judiciary was as easily taken by the highest bidder. It was an age when the boss of Pennsylvania, Senator Simon Cameron, could define an honest politician as "one who, when he is bought, will stay bought."

By a quirk of the mind not difficult to fathom, people like the YMCA group to which Morgan gave his support managed, in the face of all this corruption, to convince themselves that the burning civic question of the day was the need of the masses for moral laundering. Their utopian view envisioned a world filled with the stuffiest, most emasculated, and most uplifting of reading matter, the elimination of all forms of wagering small enough to tempt the poor, and statuary in which primary and secondary sexual characteristics were replaced by drapery and foliage.

It might be noted that few of the principals was unacquainted with the kind of corruption that really needed expunging. Morgan's intimacy with it already has been detailed, and the Dodges, too, were in a position to suggest some more fruitful fields of reform. Just a few months earlier, their importing firm, Phelps, Dodge & Co., compromised a tax fraud charge brought by the government on complaint of one of the few zealously honest men ever to enter the Custom House in New York, B. G. Jayne. The settlement came to about twenty-five cents on each dollar of discovered fraud.

Among the accusations against the Dodges was the charge of using a sly method of getting around the heavy duty on imported lead and zinc. The metal ingots were brought in under the much lighter customs duty applicable to "works of art" by being reworked overseas into crude and lumpy Dianas, Venuses, and Mercurys. The people of the ruling class who unleashed Comstockery, as George Bernard Shaw called it, had to have a sense of humor. The Dodges' mirthful pedigree is clear on the evidence. Anyone in the messy metal importing trade, a business of tramp steamers, of untidy foundries and crude machinery, who can put on a straight face at the customs inspector's table and set up as an art dealer is clearly a comic spirit. But what of Morgan? While he was using Comstock as a sort of surrogate nose to be poked into the business of his inferiors, we know he was noted as a great gallant who enjoyed the company of beautiful women and generally behaved himself in a way that would have drawn writs, warrants and summonses from the vice-baiting Anthony.

The year of the panic and the year that saw Morgan enrolled as a public crusader against impurity also witnessed the completion of his family with the birth of Annie Tracy on July 25. She was named for a maternal aunt, but called herself simply Anne as soon as she got around to expressing an opinion. There were now Louisa Pierpont, seven; John Pierpont, the younger, or Jack, six; Juliet Pierpont, three; and Anne.

Little Anne continually showed a streak of unexpected independence. Elizabeth Drexel, whose father was Joseph Drexel of Drexel, Morgan & Co., and who grew up not far from the Morgan home at 219 Madison Avenue, recalled that Anne, "a thin lanky child with an elfin face and penetrating eyes . . . had a personality and a will as strong as . . . [Morgan's] own and a disconcerting habit of putting her elders in the wrong." Once Anne was trotted out to amuse the guests at a dinner party and her father asked her what she intended to be when she grew up. " 'Something better than a rich fool, anyway,' she replied with infinite contempt, and the scornful child's voice rang through the room, making more than one millionaire look uncomfortable," Elizabeth Drexel recalled.

Domestic life still loomed as the most important aspect of his life for Pierpont Morgan during the decade of the 1870s; there was little exploration of the business world. One year, 1874, was so uneventful that the family biographer was forced to write: "There are few records of what the Morgans did during that year. We only know that they spent the summer at 'Cragston' and the cold months at 6 East Fortieth Street." But there was a return of Pierpont's illness and more traveling, including a trip to Bar Harbor on a commercial steamer in 1875.

The following year, there was the voyage across the Atlantic that included another journey up the Nile. With Fannie, the four children, and two nurses, Morgan left New York on June 14 to spend a little more than a month at Dover Court, his father's country house outside London. In August and September there was a trip to the Lake Country, then Scotland, with Pierpont breaking off his journey for occasional stints at his father's office in London.

There were periods of ill health, too, including a serious spell of headaches. As the year waned, they went on to Paris and made arrangements for the trip to Egypt. His visit to that country in 1871 had brought him face to face with an experience that he would continue to pursue throughout his life. He was only thirty-four when he first beheld the ruins of antiquity in the Valley of the Kings. He wasn't yet one of the mighty whom Shelley's Ozymandias commanded to look and despair, and even if he had been he would not have obeyed. Even less would he have appreciated the poem's ironic comment on human vanity. The works he looked upon may have filled him with the desire to emulate the kings and pharaohs of old, for he certainly left the obvious kinds of imitation behind in the form of buildings and collections. He also left imitations of ancient glory of a not-so-obvious kind—the organization of monumental works of human energy in the manner of the men who harvested the desert in the Nile Valley and in the manner of his other favorites, the Romans.

Pierpont Morgan recognized his affinities. A year before his death, when he was making his sixth visit to Egypt, someone asked him which places on earth he favored. He ticked them off on his fingers. "New York, because it is my home; London, because it is my second home; Rome and Khargeh." When the questioner laughed, Morgan became annoyed. "No, *I mean it,*" he said, and he pointed out that the Nile steam yacht built for him by Thomas Cook & Sons was named *The Khargeh,* for the great oasis four hundred miles southwest of Cairo, where there were remnants of both his favorite civilizations—the Egyptian and the Roman. And Morgan did not name yachts frivolously, at least not when he became mighty. Early in his career there had been a small boat, the *Louisa,* named the way other rich, yacht-owning mortals name their craft, for a favorite female member of the family. But when Morgan became a serious yacht collector, his personal vessels were designated with only one carefully chosen name: *Corsair.* He may have been related to the pirate, Sir Henry Morgan, who harmonized the dual career of freebooter and Elizabethan colonial officer and who distinguished himself not only by his cruelty in sacking Caribbean cities but also by cheating his own lawless associates in the division of the spoils afterward. Pierpont Morgan stopped short of taking his nomenclature from the annals of Elizabethan piracy, but he got across the idea by using the term that identifies the equally bloodthirsty Barbary buccaneers.

Morgan's leisurely peregrinations through the British Isles, Europe, and North Africa in 1876–77 coincided with the end of Grant's second term, when the Great Barbecue entered its last grimy phase, the election fraud of 1876. The sweaty, greasy guests at the head tables had eaten and drunk too much and their conduct was becoming outrageous. They may even have started to dine on one another, for cannibalism would not have been greatly out of character for James Garfield and the other Republican leaders who perverted the electoral machinery to put Rutherford B. Hayes into office.

The corruption and filth were extensive enough already, but

with the election of 1876 they took on monumental proportions. The use of repeater votes by Tammany Hall, the hasty certification of immigrants, the theft of elections, and the buying of legislators, judges, and executives in cities and rural areas had proliferated until the stain spread "into the parlor of the President." But now the occupant of the parlor spread his own stains as "the most daring conspiracy in American history" got under way.

It began on election night, 1876, when crowds all across the country went to bed after celebrating the victory of Samuel J. Tilden, the Democratic canadidate and governor of New York by virtue of his triumph over Tweed. He had a popular plurality of about 250,000 votes. But an inquiry that night was made by a high Democratic official to *The New York Times* about the figures for South Carolina, Florida, and Louisiana. It was a tipoff that the Democrats were uncertain about those three states, all of them in the grip of Republican carpetbag overseers, and the news of their uncertainty was hastily conveyed to the opposition. The Republicans lost no time in arranging that the uncertainty for the Democrats would be turned into assurance for both. The carpetbaggers saw to it that the balloting would give the presidency to their candidate, Rutherford B. Hayes, governor of Ohio, by one electoral vote. Grant was equal to the task of backing them with the Army and naming the proper sort of Republican politicians for the commission that would certify the vote. Among them was John J. Sherman, a hack ward heeler who, as a reward for his services to Hayes, was to be made the Secretary of the Treasury. It so happened that he filled that job creditably, but that could not have been foreseen from the history of his undistinguished legislative career.

Garfield was another member of this certification commission. A startling judgment of him was made after his assassination in 1881 by Andrew D. White, first president of Cornell University and one of those charged with the hazardous commando work of keeping open the lines of communication between the academic world and the Republican party. "Looking back over his life, I have a strong feeling that his assassination was a service rendered to his reputation," White concluded.

And it was. Had he not been murdered, Garfield would be remembered only for his lying and stupidity in connection with the Credit Mobilier, for his deft work with red herrings in the Gould gold corner business, and for his part in confounding the will of the electorate in 1876. As it happened, he died a martyr and gained honor.

It must be noted, though, that the Republican shenanigans were ably forwarded in many ways by the Democrats, who were still badly divided eleven years after the close of the war, in large part because of the character of their candidate, Samuel Jones Tilden. "A great lawyer, he was seldom seen in court; a brilliant political leader, he rarely appeared upon the platform," it was said, and, as the 1876 contest grew ever more ugly, the sixty-two-year-old bachelor retreated into his study.

He failed to act on a suggestion made the day after the election by Henry Watterson that he take the initiative as Governor of New York to invite Hayes, as Governor of Ohio, to join with him to form a committee to proceed to Louisiana to survey the count. It's true the telegram with Watterson's suggestion was delivered by Western Union Telegraph Co., a tool of the dominant party, to Republican headquarters before it arrived at Tilden's door in Gramercy Park, thus enabling Grant to get the jump on Tilden in any action he took. But the point is he took none.

He could possibly be excused for the lack of fire and ambition on his own account, but his timidity was a betrayal of more than the fortunes of one man. In permitting the minority of 4,033,950 to elect the President, Tilden sold out the 4,284,885 people who had voted for him. He chose to sit in his library at Gramercy Park preparing worthless statistics on previous elections and dreaming of a law suit while Hayes and his advisers, having created a contest where there was none, further consolidated their position by undermining Tilden among his none-too-ardent Southern constituents. With that the die was cast and Tilden had to content himself with reading, on the day of Hayes's inauguration, a consolatory letter from Charles Francis Adams, father of the two gadflies of Erie and a near candidate of the Liberal Republicans in the preceding presidential contest.

"It has been many years since I ceased to be a party man," wrote Adams. ". . . It is a source of gratification to me to think that I made the right choice in the late election. I could never have been reconciled to the elevation by the smallest aid of mine of a person, however respectable in private life, who must forever carry upon his brow the stamp of fraud, first triumphant in American history."

7

ENTER
COSTER

THE hundredth anniversary of the country's founding marked a nadir in its fortunes, with even the national electoral process perverted. But for Pierpont Morgan, 1876 was an auspicious year. On January 1, Joseph Drexel retired, to be replaced by Egisto P. Fabbri of the firm of Fabbri and Chauncey. In dissolving his old firm, Fabbri brought with him an associate "who showed unusual ability," in the words of the family biographer. The associate was Charles Henry Coster. Twenty-four years old and fifteen years Morgan's junior, Coster drew sharply limited praise from the Morgans. Pierpont Morgan's son said much later that "his mastery of detail was complete, his grasp of a problem immediate and comprehensive, and his power of work astonishing." Others, though, were less reserved. Coster rapidly wore himself out in the service of Morgan and died on March 13, 1900. Describing him as "a genius at working out plans of reorganization," John Moody said: "It is asserted that all the successful Morgan reorganization plans up to the time of Coster's death were his work."

It took Coster time to work his way up in the Morgan hierarchy. He was not made a partner until 1884, a significant date. This was about the time when Morgan was just beginning to assert himself. Whether he had proved to his father by then that some relaxation of the house arrest was in order or whether he made the move on his own account is difficult to say. He may have been given fuller trust because of his capable junior partner.

In his own house Morgan was the master of all public relations, so that in relation to Coster nothing but the formal applause of Morgan's son and son-in-law survives. But it can be

§ 137 §

noted that the most enduring of the House of Morgan's accomplishments came during Coster's time with the firm. They were the railroad reorganizations that survived into the 1920s. Coster was a realist who was able to assay accurately the worth of abused property like the Erie and to get operations started again. His was not the genius of fantasy, of the wild overcapitalization of later Morgan ventures—United States Steel, the fiasco of International Mercantile Marine, the sheer lunacy of the New York, New Haven & Hartford operation. These latter were "imaginative" conceptions that required plenty of pelf to keep afloat; Coster's reorganizations had their own buoyancy.

After Coster's death, Morgan began flinging money about without restraint. His acquisition of art objects matched his profligacy in business. He began emptying Egypt of treasure at such a rate that on one of his visits he was scolded by Lord Kitchener. Then a representative of the British Raj at Cairo, Kitchener read the great financier out the way he would a Sherper ammunition carrier suspected of filching from Her Majesty's small stores.

The extravagant splurging reached the point where Andrew Carnegie was unsettled by it. When Morgan purchased the Carnegie Steel Corporation, the nucleus of United States Steel, Carnegie realized a prize of nearly half a billion dollars, at least double his most exuberant earlier valuation. But he was nagged by the feeling that Morgan had paid too readily and might have given more. Meeting Morgan some time later, Carnegie had his misgivings confirmed when the financier admitted he had been ready to pay almost any price to get control of Carnegie Steel.

These were not Coster's methods. He was recalled by Moody as "a familiar figure in Wall Street—a white-faced, nervous man, hurrying from meeting to meeting and at evening carrying home his portfolios." He rode the railroads he was studying, watching roadbeds from the back platforms of trains, never getting a chance to relax until he took off six days in the spring of 1900 for a bout of pneumonia. At the end of the sixth day he was dead.

Coster came from a family that arrived in New York from Haarlem around the time of the Revolution and quickly gained prominence in the shipping field, bringing in textiles and Holland gin from the homeland and shipping rum, sugar, and coffee from the West Indies. First to arrive, just before the outbreak of the War for Independence, was Henry A. Coster. A few years later,

John G., the Morgan partner's grandfather, who had been trained as a doctor, joined his brother in the shipping firm. Both had large families. Marital and mercantile ties brought their sons and daughters into contact with some of the most prominent families of the city. They mated with Depews, Delanceys, Primes.

Henry had a son named Washington Coster, and John had one named George Washington Coster. Family tradition has it that the first President stood godfather to one or perhaps both children.

John's fifth son, George Washington Coster, married Elizabeth Oakie, or Oakey, daughter of another of the city's merchants. On July 24, 1852, while the family was vacationing at Newport, then a fashionable resort but not yet the symbol of sumptuary spending that it was to become later in the century, Charles Henry Coster was born. Apparently he got his early education privately and there is no record that he went on to college. His father died on April 17, 1869, and his mother a few weeks later, on May 20. According to Charles Henry Coster's son, when George Washington Coster died, "the family found itself much less well off than had been expected, so that he did not go to college."

He joined Chauncey & Fabbri around this time and appears to have kept up his education himself. He read both Italian and French, which may have been a routine accomplishment for a young man brought up in the mercantile tradition. In the year he entered Drexel, Morgan he published a book that indicated his purposeful, scholarly way. It was a 250-page history of "local" stamps, the kind issued by private postal companies for deliveries within cities, with an illustration of each stamp and information about the issuer. Coster, who enjoyed a reputation as a knowledgeable philatelist from his sixteenth year, prepared the work for J. W. Scott in both English and French.

Realizing that he wasn't going to have time for quaint researches in obscure byways of history at Drexel, Morgan, Coster disposed of his stamp collection at a sale in Paris in 1878, but Coster's own copy of his book indicates that he intended to continue with the work at some time. This copy contains, bound into the book, correspondence about the work, including a letter from a deputy postmaster in 1891 suggesting an error in one of the entries. Bound with the letter is a refutation of the criticism by Coster and other extensive notes.

During his twenty-four years in Pierpont Morgan's office,

Coster took part in all the major railroad reorganizations that made Morgan's early reputation. The railroad operations began with a major transaction on Commodore Vanderbilt's New York Central three years after Coster was hired.

While President Grant, the Republican Party, and the United States Army, among other amateurs of corruption, were fastening on the country the victory of Rutherford B. Hayes, Commodore Vanderbilt, a professional in jobbery, was drawing out his last illness. He died on January 5, 1877, too soon to see the final triumph of the forces he had helped unleash on the country. But by this time he may have changed his attitude toward stock watering, manipulating prices, buying judges, governors, and legislators. He had always appeared, even to those who hated him for other things, as a man who, unlike the Bible-quoting Drew, was no hypocrite. The Commodore, in contrast, was loud and profane. He had a reputation for chasing his prettier female domestics, and he gambled on his own breakneck trotting abilities on Harlem Lane. His sins had been plentiful, but hypocrisy had not been among them. So the signs of deathbed repentance evinced by the Commodore have to be given some credit.

He took an unconscionable length of time expiring, beginning in April 1876. He lived to express his condolences to the family of one doctor who began treating him when he fell ill and was getting ready to offer them to another when his own death supervened.

Only eight years earlier, when he was seventy-three and in the midst of fighting for his life against Gould, Fisk, and Drew, he had taken his second wife, a beautiful southern widow with the odd name of Frank A. Crawford. Their married life was full: it encompassed Vanderbilt's desperate struggle against the threat of ruin in the Panic of 1873 and his expensive efforts to shore up the market; it included his rate wars. Then there were his amusements, his breakneck drives, often with Frankie sharing his daredeviltry on Harlem Lane, and more reposeful long winter evenings with her singing southern ballads in the parlor.

For the Commodore, there was spiritualism, and possibly earthier hanky-panky with the two Victorian beauties, Tennessee Claflin and her sister, Victoria C. Woodhull. The former practiced "magnetic healing" and the latter claimed direct communication with the Greek orator Demosthenes. Finding himself in a tight squeeze in 1873, the Commodore tried to have Victoria exorcise the ghost of Jim Fisk for some spectral tips on the future of the market.

But there was neither spiritualism nor southern ballads as the end drew near. The profane old Commodore had become used to the ministrations of a spiritual adviser, the Reverend Dr. Deems, for whom he had built a church called the Church of the Strangers. His well-prepared-for passing saw the full assembly of his relatives in the death chamber. There were scriptural readings. Toward the end, Vanderbilt said, "I shall never cease to trust Jesus," and Frankie launched into one of his favorite hymns,

> "Come ye sinners, poor and needy,
> Weak and wounded, sick and sore."

He had often before chimed in with the responses: "I am poor, and I am needy," but now his voice faltered. Possibly he contemplated the approach of a stern and final judgment that would not wink at the spectacle of a man with $104 million rattling on wistfully about his poverty and need. He was able to form a brief prayer, which he followed with the evaluation: "That was a good prayer," before he died at 10:52 in the morning.

In life, the old man had antagonized every one of his children. He had exiled his son, William H. Vanderbilt, to Staten Island because he didn't think too highly of the younger man's abilities. But William was able to return to favor through overreaching his father in some sly way in a deal involving shipments of horse dung that restored the old man's pride in his offspring. Like Morgan, William, or Billy, as he was called, was a late starter. Born May 8, 1821, his exile in Staten Island almost exactly corresponded to the period of life in which Morgan was under banishment. Billy was just short of his fifty-sixth birthday when his father died and he was able to get his hands on one of the greatest fortunes in the country. But with Billy the late start was going to be more detrimental than it was to be with Morgan. Pierpont Morgan lived on to his seventy-sixth year, but Billy Vanderbilt had only eight years of stewardship, during which he would double the patrimony but do little else to stamp his personality on his time.

In fact, his active period of management of the great fund was marked by a determination to erase his own personality. He was the Vanderbilt who coined the phrase that seemed so appropriate

to the robber barons: "The public be damned." But the problem
was that Billy didn't really mean it whereas his father, who lived
by and acted on this sentiment, knew better than to articulate it.
The public was to be flattered; not even representatives and their
laws were to be damned.

Made fun of, ridiculed, perhaps. When a friend told the
Commodore that "each and every one" of a series of moves in
connection with one of his transportation lines was "absolutely
forbidden by the statutes of the State of New York," Vanderbilt
wryly replied: "My God, John! You don't suppose you can run a
railroad in accordance with the statutes of the State of New York,
do you?" On another occasion he had roared: "Law! What do I
care about law? Hain't I got the power?"

Billy may have pronounced damnation on the public, but he
was frightened out of his wits by it. He proceeded to take steps
to mollify the great beast. The state legislators had always had a
handful of bills in the hopper ready to go when the old Commodore acted in a manner fiscally disappointing to them. State
lawmakers can always draw up laws that seem to affect a broad
class of industry but in actuality apply only to the specific company that needs to be taught a lesson. Such legislation need not
be particularly constitutional; it has nuisance value only, and as
soon as that nuisance value pays off, the law will be withdrawn.
Of course if by chance it goes into effect, the injured company
can always have it voided as unconstitutional, through a series of
suits and appeals in the shooting gallery atmosphere of the costly
court system.

A number of such bills were ready to go into effect, both in
Albany and in New York after the Commodore's death. Billy
Vanderbilt melted before the threat. As the oleaginous Chauncey
Depew, who had been hired by the father and trickled down to
the son, put it:

> Mr. Vanderbilt, because of assaults made upon him
> in the Legislature and in the newspapers, came to the
> conclusion that it was a mistake for one individual to
> own a controlling interest in a great corporation like
> the New York Central, and also a mistake to have so
> many eggs in one basket, and he thought it would be
> better for himself and for the company if the owner-
> ship were distributed as widely as possible.

Depew also cited another possible reason for Vanderbilt's desire to efface himself from the Central. Just before the Commodore's death, Depew had been visiting England, where Prime Minister William Gladstone commented about the social dangers inherent in a large fortune, such as Vanderbilt's, that carried none of the social landlord-tenant obligations of the great English landholdings. Gladstone said to Depew:

> I understand you have a man in your country who is worth $100,000,000, and it is all in property which he can convert at will into cash. The government ought to take it away from him, as it is too dangerous a power for any one man to have. Suppose he should convert his property into money and lock it up, it would make a panic in America which would extend to this country and every other part of the world, and be a great injury to a large number of innocent people.

This wasn't the damned public talking, nor Karl Marx. It was the head of a government that was highly permissive toward great industrial fortunes and did not lightly talk of confiscating them. This may not have been the kind of argument that would have swayed the proud Commodore, but Billy was something else. Homely and stout, William H. Vanderbilt never would have been taken for a Mohawk warrior, in appearance or spirit, even in his youth.

Of course, Billy was under more important pressures than those brought to bear by childishly vindictive legislators and the philosophical bellyaching of England's prime minister. Chief among them was the last and most efficient of the state's railroad probes, the Hepburn committee hearings. Even the inspiration for the probe was unusual. It originated with as unlikely a body as the New York Chamber of Commerce, which on February 6, 1879, memorialized the Assembly with a charge that the railroads of the state—particularly the Erie of course, but including the Central—were abusing their powers by unjust discrimination in rates, by subordinating the rights of stockholders to those of privileged management, and similar abuses.

The city chamber was not alone in expressing indignation. Although the final scope of the inquiry was defined by the city's chamber, together with the Board of Trade and Transportation, it received the support of commercial groups throughout the state.

All of this frightened the railroaders. The chambers and boards were acting uncomfortably like the revolutionary Granger movements in the West, which had taken steps—widely regarded as confiscatory in the boardrooms of the New York Central and the Erie—to limit the owners' control of the lines. And some of these Granger acts were even then being upheld in the courts. It was enough to make the Goulds, the Vanderbilts, and the Morgans lose faith in the country's judicial system.

Besides originating with commercial social groups that were ordinarily expected to play the part of mutual admiration societies, the investigation committee headed by Assemblyman A. Barton Hepburn also failed to come up with the usual legislative buffooneries that had characterized early investigations.

The Hepburn committee fired its major rounds against the always vulnerable Erie, but Vanderbilt also was called to testify and did not escape lightly. The Hepburn group made known secret agreements between him and the oil refiners. Complaints were aired of his "tyranny" over the cost of milk in New York, as a result of which a good part of the state allegedly paid tribute to Billy. It also exposed such Vanderbilt methods of serving the community as the extra-fare "Merchants' Express," an operation in which regular freight service was held to a crawl or sidetracked to let the fast express by. This forced shippers to choose between paying for the premium service or accepting something less than normal scheduling.

Vanderbilt also rigged rates to help such a customer as A. T. Stewart, the richest department store owner in the city, an importer of near-indentured labor, and a builder of cathedrals, cities, and other monuments who hardly qualified for preferential treatment on grounds of need. The practice showed that Vanderbilt was "deliberately making the rich richer and the poor poorer . . . through the instrumentality of the freight charge," the committee's counsel said sarcastically.

Altogether, the public Billy Vanderbilt was ready to damn was getting to know too much about his operations. Then, too, his connections with the oil refiners, the group that would later form the Standard Oil complex, were beginning to open his eyes. "I was surprised at the amount of ready cash they were able to provide," Vanderbilt said, referring to their ability to raise $3 million almost instantly to buy out a pipe line company that would have threatened his rail carrier service. To the Hepburn group he said: "There is no question about it but these men are smarter than I am a great deal. . . . I never came in contact with any class of men as smart and alert as they are in their business. They could never have got into the position they now are. And one man could hardly have been able to do it; it is a combination of men."

Vanderbilt was shrewd enough to see that the day of the lone tycoon such as his father had been was drawing to a close. The individual provided too much of a target for the wrath of the public and its representatives. In the big operations of the future it would be combinations of men that would count. He determined to sell out enough of the 87 percent of New York Central's $100 million in capital stock that he held to make him no longer a majority holder.

Vanderbilt did business through a number of brokerage houses in the financial community. Henry Clewes among others, but a transaction of this magnitude, he knew, would have to be spread as widely as possible, either partly or wholly overseas. Any attempt to sell locally would have greatly depressed the stock. For such a venture, the well-established Peabody firm in London now operated by Junius S. Morgan was one of the few with the required capabilities. Vanderbilt's decision to use the Morgan firm, rather than Belmont-Rothschild or any of the smaller houses, was a momentous one. It brought the forty-two-year-old Pierpont Morgan into contact with one of the country's biggest railroad operators and provided the budding financier with the opportunity to work out methods that he would use again and again on an ever-widening stage. It also provided him with a sizeable profit.

That was always an important matter for Morgan, as was illustrated in a spectacular maneuver his firm had recently concluded. Following the Army-backed victory of Grant and the Republicans over the Democrats and the South in the execrable election of 1876, the Democratic majority in Congress, elected despite Grant's power, retaliated by refusing to appropriate money to pay for federal mercenaries in the fiscal year beginning just three months after Hayes's inauguration.

Morgan, in a forerunner of some of his later splendiferous gestures, offered to stand treat for the army that had helped resolve the election so much to his satisfaction until Congress got ready to act intelligently and appropriate the money. It was the firm's "obvious and sacred duty," Morgan wrote to the Secretary of War, to supply $2.2 million to the men who had barred unworthy Democrats from the ballot boxes and were then off disposing of the Indian problem. (The Indian was a problem too. Only a year earlier, in June 1876 Custer and a force of 265 were slaughtered at Little Big Horn. Despite the fact that his Indian and white scouts evaporated into the brush at the sight of so many hoof-prints in the area, Custer pressed for the unfortunate showdown with Sitting Bull, in hopes, many said, of winning a battle that would give him the Republican nomination that Hayes won later that summer.)

Morgan's duty was obvious, sacred, and above all profitable.

Many years later Major General Hugh L. Scott paid an equivocal tribute to this Morgan generosity. Scott's tribute referred to an occasion when he had just pulled in "ragged, dirty and hungry" to the mining hamlet of Helena, Montana, after more than six months of Nez Perce pacification duties. He had with him a pay voucher of $125 and was directed to take it to a local bank, where $120 was returned to him after a 4 percent discount was exacted. The soldier, who thus surrendered about a week's pay for the greater glory of Drexel, Morgan & Co., recalled later, in more affluent circumstances, that "all the people of my day have always been very grateful to Mr. Morgan for his action at that time. When we needed a friend—he was that friend." Congress came to its senses in November 1877, appropriating the funds to make good the vouchers within about six months. Thus Pierpont Morgan's generosity cost its recipient about 8 percent per annum.

For Vanderbilt, the cost of the friendship was even higher. Morgan placed about 215,000 shares of Billy's stock with English investors at the going rate of $130 per share. For that, Vanderbilt received about $25 million in cash, which he put into United States government bonds, safe from the predations of New York legislators. Morgan's New York and London syndicate pocketed just under $3 million, or nearly 11 percent.

Morgan executed the 1879 transaction without any fanfare—in fact, in great secrecy, a necessary condition to prevent the price of the New York Central stock from dropping as the great block went on the market. In exchange for this secrecy he got Vanderbilt to agree to two conditions. One was that a place on the

Central's board of directors be provided to Morgan or one of his associates so that the buyers of the stock would have representation. The other was a guarantee by Vanderbilt that the 8 percent dividend be continued for at least five years. The guarantee lasted only for that period, but then it was never secured by any ironclad arrangement, such as the one that was to assure the Vanderbilts the return on the Harlem River railroad throughout all eternity.

In the entire transaction, Morgan kept his part of the bargain, though. It was five months before newspapers in New York and London stumbled over the details.

During this period, as Morgan was trying out his ability to shift millions and tens of millions in capital for the powerful, the world of industrial America was struggling to be born. It hardly deserved to be called chaos yet. Only with the imposition of some order would it deserve that term. Elements of it—the first struggles of labor, for instance—Pierpont Morgan would be almost unaware of. Possibly he'd harrumph and turn the pages of the *Evening Sun* with an extra snap and a snort in his chair in the Union Club on reading of some outrageous demand for rights on the part of a group of working men. But that would be all.

With the growth of industry came the somewhat belated realization on the part of the workers that at the Great Barbecue the few were being stuffed while the many were starving. Unionization was slow in coming, but sporadic protests that ended in bloody strikes began in the wake of the Panic of 1873. In the same year, the coal miners of Pennsylvania, objecting to working conditions and the housing forced on them by mine owners, walked out by the tens of thousands. In Illinois, Indiana, Missouri, Maryland, Ohio, and New York, strikes broke out in a number of industries. Then in July 1877 workers on the four eastern trunk lines struck rather than submit to a fourth reduction in wages in seven years. The most recent wage cut had been airily announced simultaneously by all four managements.

During one week in July traffic was totally suspended on the Baltimore & Ohio, the Erie, the Central, and the Pennsylvania. The rebelliousness of the railroad workers spread in Pennsylvania, culminating in riots in Pittsburgh. All of the anthracite coal miners walked out, followed by most of the soft coal miners of Ohio, Indiana, and Illinois. The unrest in this year proved beyond the capacities of the states to control; President Hayes had to send federal troops into many of the states and he had to issue a proclamation commanding all citizens to keep the peace. Clashes between militia and workers were frequent.

Fatalities were high during the year of the "Great Strike" of the railroad workers. To Morgan, this inchoate striving and reaching out for power by the laboring man was something from another world, fit only for an occasional rattling of a paper in a clubroom or an outraged compression of the eyebrows over a drink with a fellow buccaneer. He was only vaguely aware of its connection with his own activities, that it was a natural concomitant of the similarly anarchic growth of corporate power.

The disorderly growth of corporations, particularly railroads, was closer to Morgan's ken. The proliferation of railroads was of vital interest to his principals, the wealthy Englishmen who were customers of Junius S. Morgan & Co. Charles Francis Adams, Jr., who found British capitalists "singularly fallible" in their judgment of American securities, professed to be unable to understand "this curious infatuation" for railroad stocks, particularly when they were fully priced or, more likely, considerably watered beyond that point. The infatuation, though, is easily explained. The United States ended the Civil War with little more than the eastern trunk lines completed; in other words, 35,000 miles of rails had been laid in a system that would reach the incredible high water mark of 400,000 miles at the close of World War I, fifty-five years in the future.

These statistics may be dull, but the story they tell is in the highest degree exciting. After hunger and sex, the most powerful human drive is avarice, but the components that satisfy this third great longing are almost universally despicable, gritty, and boring to the mass of mankind. People can be gratified by almost any aspect of food-preparation, even to enjoying the reading of a recipe for broiled clams, and the attractions of anything tinged with sex hardly needs elaborating on. But economic statistics are a bore to be avoided. From such trivialities, however, the great trends of avarice can be detected; everyone wants to hear about the trends, but few want to busy themselves with the trivialities.

The trivialities for the railroads during the period of Morgan's adult life spelled out a formula for fantastic profits the like of which probably never will be seen again for such a protracted period. Eight years after the end of the Civil War, mileage of the roads doubled to over 70,000. In another thirteen years it had nearly doubled again, to more than 136,000 miles. Again, sixteen years later, in 1902, came the third doubling, to 274,000. In the year of Pierpont Morgan's death, 1913, total mileage operated stood at 379,508. This amounted to a compound rate of increase, through some of the darkest panics of the industrial age, of from 4½ to 9 percent in what might be termed plant expansion alone. Profits were not recorded with such care as track mileage, but their increase was probably more phenomenal.

In view of this extraordinary record it is little wonder that the men of Morgan's class who had any connection at all with such wonderful wealth-producing machinery were able to collect expensive wives, mistresses, homes, art treasures, and, more important, the judges, mayors, aldermen, assemblymen, state and national senators and congressmen, and even Presidents that would adorn, amplify, and legitimize their positions.

This growth was naturally harder to see while it was occurring, but the profitable possibilities would have been apparent to the representative of any English investors well-heeled enough to stand the inevitable short-term fluctuations. And if the future was obscure, there was no blinking the past. The railroads of the United States had not been much of a drain on the men who controlled the issuance of their securities, for up to 1880 they were built largely with public money. At that point, according to one estimate, federal, state, and local governments had contributed $700 million in cash for railroad construction. To further sweeten the pot the three levels of government had donated 155 million acres of public lands, an empire of 242,000 square miles, or more than the total area of France and four times the size of New England. "About 40 percent of the legitimate construction costs were paid by public money," says one transportation expert. A biographer of Morgan, Lewis Corey, extrapolates this figure on up to 100 percent by adding in the probable profits the railroaders made from the sales of parts of the great swatches of territory that were donated to them. The 100 percent figure does not seem exaggerated. For example, the reported cost of building the Northern Pacific was $70 million, but in 1917 the railroad reported gross receipts from land sales of nearly twice that amount. And it reported that it still retained possession of a large part of its most valuable lands!

At the close of the 1870s, these great corporations, although they were to more than double in the decades ahead, were substantially completed as far as their general functions and terminals were concerned. What remained to be added were spurs to new centers of population or of industry, doubling or quadrupling of trackage for greater efficiency and safety in handling bigger freight or passenger loads, as well as multiplication of trackage as the pressure of speculative investment forced competitive duplication, a factor that was to occupy Morgan and his firm in the following decade.

At this point, there were the four great eastern trunk lines, the New York Central, the Pennsylvania, the Erie, and the Baltimore & Ohio, joining the East Coast cities of Boston, New York, Philadelphia, and Baltimore with midwestern terminals at Chicago and St. Louis. The railroad system of the South was still in the formation stage, but short lines linked some of the principal cities. The great transcontinental systems were in place—the Northern Pacific and Great Northern providing separate routes between Duluth, Minneapolis and St. Paul, and the cities of the northwest coast; the Union Pacific and Southern Pacific joining Chicago and Kansas City with just about every city of consequence on the West Coast; and the Atchison, Topeka & Santa Fe linking Chicago with San Francisco and Los Angeles via a wide southerly sweep that brought rail transportation within easy reach of much of Texas, New Mexico, and Arizona.

There are seeming non sequiturs in the overall picture—the Pennsylvania deadheading at St. Louis, and the two northernmost lines ending nowhere in Minnesota. Actually, two smaller roads, the Chicago, Burlington & Quincy and the Illinois Central, provided the junctions that brought the whole structure together in midcontinent. Both were to be very important to Morgan in the years ahead, for they were to involve the only setbacks that he would have to own up to in his career. Both defeats were major and, moreover, both were inflicted by the same man, Edward H. Harriman.

If this was a time for the forging of the great railroad machine that was to carry Morgan to limitless power, it was equally a time for bringing forward a new set of manipulators who would people Morgan's world in the decades ahead and would work with or against him. The panic of 1873 was the watershed for the men of power. It smashed Jay Cooke, the man who had helped the government out of its extremities on two occasions during the Civil War. His postwar extension into Northern Pacific development threw him into bankruptcy; he even lost "Ogontz," his estate in Pennsylvania staffed with a full retinue of clerics. It happened that the reverse was not of long duration, however, for Cooke made a lucky gamble in a silver mine and it paid off handsomely around 1880. He recaptured the vast estate and lived on until 1905, but no longer was he a power to reckon with.

The panic undid Cooke while it made men like James J. Hill, Harriman, and, outside the railroad world, John D. Rockefeller. The myths of capitalism are studded with accounts of how thrift, resoluteness, honesty, and dependability—the innumerable cardinal virtues that are supposed to be responsible for the winning to success of young men—paid off handsomely during these heroic years. Seldom is it even implied that some young men win success by virtue of being the offspring of wealthy parents, as Morgan was. And never is the chief selective process for manufacturing the new rich and disposing of the old featured in the myths. Cooke was destroyed by the same process that created Hill, Harriman, and Rockefeller. He was the possessor of immense amounts of old values, which were being shaken out by the panic, while they had modest amounts of money ready to go into the squeezed-out values and, even more important, ready to be multiplied in the upswing to follow. While the publicists and editorialists, the fashioners of tiny epic, sing of pluck and luck, strive and thrive, fair and square, and catch and scratch, the real success story is simply to have the means, a little money, plus the inclination to invest it at the right time, a time of depressed values.

The panic that wrecked Cooke to all intents and purposes simply wiped out his values and placed them in the hands of James J. Hill, who had the good fortune to be in the right position at the right time to buy the St. Paul & Pacific, a little railroad running a couple of hundred miles west from St. Paul, with a branch joining the Northern Pacific at Brainerd, Minnesota. It had been a part of Cooke's Northern Pacific.

Hill, a little younger than Morgan, was a slow starter too. He was born in Guelph, Ontario, on September 16, 1838, was educated there, and came to St. Paul with his family at about the time he was eighteen. He had been intended for the medical profession, but there was no money for schooling when his father died. A number of great opportunities had passed him by when the panic of 1873 threw the whole countryside around him into turmoil because of the convulsions besetting the Northern Pacific.

By then, Hill was something of a character in town, where he kept a coal and wood store. Short, stocky, long-haired, with only one eye, he would sit in front of the store talking of the events of the day and of his favorite ambition—to make the St. Paul & Pacific a real railroad. He was more than just a village character though. He had organized steamboat lines on the Mississippi and used a section of the railway to transship freight across the state to Breckenridge on the Red River, where another shipper, Norman W. Kittson, hauled it in two little stern wheelers to Winnipeg.

The bankruptcy that struck Jay Cooke's Northern Pacific and its tiny subsidiary, the St. Paul & Pacific, was quickly recognized by Hill as just the kind of opportunity he had been missing in the past and would probably not see too often again. Of course, he didn't have the money, but he had the gift of gab, whetted assiduously in front of his fuel store. He proceeded to let it loose on a couple of Canadians, Donald Alexander Smith, then commissioner for the Hudson's Bay Company and greatly dependent on Hill's transportation efforts for shipments up and down the Mississippi, and Smith's cousin George Stephen, then head of the Bank of Montreal. Smith later became Lord Strathcona and High Commissioner for Canada and Stephen became Lord Mount Stephen.

To the latter fell the job of "Costerizing" or "Morganizing" the Dutch who had bought Jay Cooke's bonds and stocks. We are told by one source that the task was to make the Dutchmen take thirty cents for each of the dollars they had laid out a few years earlier, but there is other evidence that ten cents on the dollar was about what they were getting for the $27 million that had gone into the construction of the 380-mile road. In fact, the two Canadians put up $280,000 in cash for the road, renamed the St. Paul, Minneapolis & Manitoba, and then voted themselves $15 million worth of stock, to be divided among Hill, Stephen, Smith, Kittson, and two others who had taken part in the operation.

At that, they were only divvying up part of what they had in effect stolen from the Dutch; a few years earlier, a Gould, a Fisk, or a Drew would have seen to it that the full amount or even a multiple of it was taken. To Gould a road once worth $28 million would again be worth that or, preferably, would be made to seem worth double or triple that amount.

Edward Henry Harriman, a decade younger than Morgan, was also profiting to a degree from the panic and depression that stretched on for six years in the decade of the 1870s. He was born February 25, 1848, in Hempstead, Long Island, the son of the Reverend Orlando Harriman, the hard-pressed rector of St. George's Episcopal Church. At the age of twenty-two he raised the price of a seat on the New York Stock Exchange and during this period bought a Hudson River boat. He married Mary Williamson Averell of Ogdensburg, New York, and through his father-in-law he bought the rundown Sodus Bay & Southern Railroad that served that vicinity. Later he sold it to the Pennsylvania Railroad.

His father-in-law, William Averell, was president of the Ogdensburg & Lake Champlain Railroad and Harriman became a director of that line in 1880. A few years later, having improved an acquaintance with Stuyvesant Fish, a vice president of the Illinois Central, he became a director of that company. Less than two decades later, in 1897, Harriman would further improve the acquaintance to the point where he would repay his benefactor by eliminating him from the management of that important North-South link.

For Andrew Carnegie, seven months younger than Morgan, as for John Davison Rockefeller, a little more than two years younger, the depression period provided an opportunity to consolidate an already tight grip on industry. Both were industrial prodigies. They were at that time not only wealthy men, but on the threshold of the greatest steps of their respective careers.

Carnegie's early acquisition period had not been modeled on the buy-at-the-bottom principle, nor on the eugenic one of Morgan in choosing the right set of parents, nor had he taken the nuptial route to wealth that Harriman had. Most of his biographers borrow a piece of legend and attribute success to a couple of "daring" moves as an apprentice railroad telegrapher. Such daring would, and probably did, get hundreds of youths before and since fired, but supposedly it just happened to tickle Colonel Thomas A. Scott, general superintendent of the Pennsylvania Railroad at the time. As a result, the Colonel gave him tips, inside information, and the like.

But Carnegie's later career suggests a more understandable reason for his becoming Scott's protégé: Carnegie was a born courtier, adept at outrageous but irresistible flattery. By the mid-seventies he already had extensive interests in bridge building, telegraphy, and sleeping cars, and during this depressed period he was to make the move into the steel industry which was to dominate the rest of his business career.

At the start, in 1872, he displayed that sycophantic skill that became his hallmark: his first extensive steel plant was not named for himself or any of the associates that contributed to making the place a reality. It was called the Edgar Thomson Works, for the president of the Pennsylvania Railroad. Carnegie suppressed whatever urgings a thirty-five-year-old captain of industry might have to indulge in self-glorification as he embarked on the biggest project of his career. Thomson's name was chosen to help patch up an estrangement that had come about between them. The name was intended to indicate to friend and competitor alike that there was no bad blood between the two. The selection was also intended to cement future relations between Carnegie and the railroad, a line that would become of great value to him both as a customer and as the provider of transportation for his enterprises. And that was only one of his fawnings. The list, as usual with any practiced flatterer, could easily be extended to thirty or forty other excellent examples.

Rockefeller's career was somewhat different. He had early determined that he would control every process connected with sucking the oil out of Pennsylvania and Ohio and refining it in the northeast. He was a wealthy and successful businessman at the age of twenty-three, and by the time of the great panic of 1873 he was well on his way to perfecting his particular contribution to financial skulduggery, the trust. It was a device, probably the only one short of Aladdin's lamp, by which monopoly power, once the perquisite of kings, and great ones at that, could be wielded by an ordinary citizen.

It was one of the greatest financial ideas since the invention of the kited check, and contained some of the elements of that often helpful stratagem. In essence, both were ways of using the financial powers of others—banks in the case of check-kiting, wealthy stockholders in the case of the trust—for the benefit of an individual or group possessing few resources.

In kiting checks, the promoter opens an account in one bank with a small deposit, then writes out large checks on it that he deposits at a second bank. For a brief period, until he is caught, he has sizable financial resources. But this is penny-ante stuff and retribution is swift, inasmuch as the victims haven't surrendered any of their powers. The trust requires larger resources. Rocke-feller and his associates, for instance, pooled $1 million to begin the Standard Oil of Ohio trust in 1882. Then they substituted trust certificates for the unwieldy double checking account sys-tem of the check-kiter. The certificates were passed out among the holders of at least $70 million worth of securities in the companies making up the trust.

The certificates promised nothing and, in fact, transferred all powers of the stockholders to the Rockefeller group. Why would presumably rational stockholders make such a capitulation?

The answer ranges from pure speculative greed, roused by the known moneymaking ability of the associates, down to pure fear, roused by equally known cases of arson and violence that had overtaken those who tried to withhold something the Standard Oil gang wanted. And John D. Rockefeller, an otherwise pious Baptist, had perfected many coercive devices, including the rebate, the preferential rate system, and espionage, in addition to the judicious application of conventional violence. All of them formed a pistol held at the head of the holder of a desirable property.

This coercive element of trust formation attracted little atten-tion from lawmakers. The other aspect—acts in restraint of trade such as setting prices or territories—were illegal under laws then in force and were further outlawed by such special statutes as the Sherman Antitrust Act of 1890. But trusts were a natural devel-opment of capitalism in areas where monopolies were possible or likely, so that laws prohibiting them had about as much effect as decreeing a change in the tides would have had. The coercive aspect, the amassing of necessary large pools of capital by the usurpation of the stockholders' rights, was left untouched. It comes as no surprise, then, that dealing with Standard Oil put fear into the heart of even Billy Vanderbilt, although his power was considerably greater than that of most of Rockefeller's vic-tims. Billy told the Hepburn inquisitors: "They are mighty smart men. I guess if you ever had to deal with them you would find that out."

As time went on, of course, refinements in the conventional morality governing such matters dictated that the pistol should he loaded with blanks, and when he came of financial age Pier-pont Morgan favored that style of gunslinging. Even Rockefeller eased off. After the 1870s it was no longer necessary to demonstrate how a rebate could rip the competition. It was a fact well known. Only a fool would require a demonstration. The all-important coercive element in trust-forming softened as blackmail replaced gun-toting.

Blackmail entered into Morgan's next move into the industrial jungle, but that came some years later, in the middle of the 1880s. Meanwhile, as his rivals continued to consolidate and increase their power, Pierpont Morgan remained essentially a private citizen. Toward the end of 1877, Pierpont's father made one of his rare excursions out of London, to come to America, where an elaborately planned dinner was tendered him by the leading citizens of the financial community. It was a function at which all the myths of wealth were trotted out. One of them represented what must have been an advanced stage of sophistication and casuistry even for the initiates in the mysteries of pelf who made up the guest list. It was given by Samuel J. Tilden, the reluctant reformer, the eradicator of Tweed, and the defaulter to Hayes. In what must have put the audience, which included John Jacob Astor and the elder Theodore Roosevelt, together with others whose aggregate capital totaled about $1 billion, into a near swoon of delight, he said:

> The men I see before me are owners and managers of colossal capitals. You are, doubtless in some degree, clinging to the illusion that you are working for yourselves, but it is my pleasure to claim that you are working for the public. [Applause, says the newspaper account.] While you are scheming for your own selfish ends, there is an over-ruling and wise Providence directing that the most of all you do should inure to the benefit of the people. Men of colossal fortunes are in effect, if not in fact, trustees for the public.

The mighty Tilden proferred this fawning bit of flattery—which would seem to justify any crime or betrayal as long as the perpetrator had money—before a group that less than a year earlier had helped steal from him the most valued prize in American public life! Here was a courtier richly deserved by Junius Morgan and his well-wishers.

This ceremony marked a change in Pierpont Morgan's life. It was as though his confinement to quarters was being relaxed and he was being encouraged to free himself from the family ties that had bound him for so long. Shortly after the elder Morgan's return to London, Pierpont followed him, remaining on "important business" with his parents at their home at Prince's Gate until early in the New Year. This was his first absence from his children during the Christmas season and must have been a painful experience to the older children especially. Louisa at the time was eleven, Jack, ten. It was the beginning, however, of a new pattern of longer and more frequent absences.

These began in the spring of 1878 with a brief railroad inspection tour to Harrisburg, Louisville, Nashville, and New Orleans, followed by his annual spring visit, alone, to his parents. He left on April 6 and returned on May 8. The following year the parental visit was made in the company of his daughter Louisa and a playmate of hers. They crossed just before Pierpont's forty-second birthday, which was celebrated at sea. Included in the six-week trip was a stopover in Paris.

This year also saw Junius repeat his visit of two years earlier, this time to direct the Vanderbilt rescue operations, another underscoring of Pierpont's decidedly junior position when it came to major operations such as relieving Vanderbilt of part of the ownership of the New York Central. The transaction was concluded November 26 and the elder Morgan celebrated a particularly appropriate Thanksgiving at the home of Pierpont's father-in-law, Charles Tracy. There was the usual spring visit to Junius and Juliet in 1880, with Morgan this time bringing daughter Julie, nearly ten at the time. This was another six-week outing for Morgan that included a stopover in Paris, with the gallivanting husband just making it back on May 30 in time to celebrate his fifteenth wedding anniversary the following day.

At about this time Pierpont took another important step, buying a solid twenty-five-year-old brownstone at 219 Madison Avenue and having it remodeled by one of the more stodgy of fashionable architects, Christian Herter. It was to be home for him and his family for the rest of his life; the place to which he always returned with his collections, where he would hold the vestry meetings as he became more deeply involved in St. George's affairs, and where even great financial moves would be worked out, as in the Panic of 1907. Behind it, on thirty-seventh Street, he would have Charles McKim erect the lovely white marble library that would be such an appropriate monument to him.

The purchase of a home notwithstanding. Pierpont's annual trips abroad continued. The earlier excursions away from wife and hearth proved to be a mere prelude to the extraordinary absences that began late in 1881. There was the usual brief six-week spring report to Junius and the usual Paris side trip, this time with his older daughter Louisa, that year. They returned May 28, in time for the sixteenth wedding observance.

The great trip started in December 1881, just before Christmas. None of Pierpont's direct family accompanied him to his parents' home in London, but he was joined by a couple of his wife's cousins. There was a Christmas celebration at Junius Morgan's, but the main purpose of this trip was to tour the Mediterranean aboard a yacht that the older man had arranged for. First there was the inevitable Paris stopover at the Hotel Bristol, with a variation this year in the form of a trip to Nice, where the party boarded the steam yacht *Pandora* of the Royal Yacht Squadron on January 12, 1882. The yacht trip took the party east as far as Jaffa, with a jaunt to Jerusalem and a tour of Christian holy places that affected Pierpont Morgan deeply, according to letters he wrote back to Fannie. Describing to her the visit through the four-foot-high doorway into Christ's sepulchre, he says: "There is the slab on which He was laid. Impelled by an impulse impossible to resist you fall on your knees before that shrine."

Reflections of piety, however, were not sufficient to squeeze out the Pierpont Morgan stirrings toward opulence. Before the trip started, he had taken an option on a yacht of his own, a 165-foot craft commissioned by a New York Stock Exchange broker at Cramp's shipyard in Philadelphia. Thoroughly enjoying the trip aboard the *Pandora,* Pierpont's mind was made up. He cabled back to a friend, George Bowdoin in New York, to buy the yacht, which was to be the first of a line of four *Corsairs.*

Morgan's yacht trip with his father was completed in April and it was planned to have Fannie join him at Prince's Gate. But she was delayed until May 2. Three weeks after she joined her husband, he steamed back to America aboard the *Britannic* to take over his new toy, the steam yacht. Fannie remained abroad until August 12.

In other words, during a period of about eight months Pierpont Morgan and his wife were together for no more than about three weeks, a remarkable record of Christian connubiality, especially for a man who spent a good part of that time mooning around among the sentimental dustheaps of the faith. This, together with the shorter absences of the ordinary annual visits to his father, possibly may have been the key to his successful marriage. Married couples ranking lower on the economic scale are forced to spend their lives together, particularly the expensive vacation periods, and thus they are less resistant to the temptations of legal separations and divorces.

References to these aspects of Morgan's career, together with allusions to his well-known but supremely well-hidden predilection for the society of beautiful women, might properly be overlooked except for one set of circumstances. These include the evident delight Pierpont Morgan took in the trappings of Christianity, leading the hymn sings on Sundays in a very public manner, attending annual diocesan conventions, and entering wholeheartedly into discussions of faith and morals in the Episcopal church. On at least one occasion he combined his love of religion with his love of earthly beauty by taking along a reigning glamor girl to one of the triennial conventions of the church.

In addition, we must recall, Morgan was active in imposing and fostering his views on others. He helped fasten on the backside of society the vice-lover Anthony Comstock, a man who could see depravity in unclothed birds. Comstock even saw evil in the plays of George Bernard Shaw, who made Anthony and all his countrymen pay for that stupidity by coining the word "Comstockery" to describe the prevailing canons of artistic criticism in the former colonies. Comstockery, ardently supported both financially and spiritually by Morgan, was a festering evil that outlived its namesake, continuing on in the person of one John Sumner. Its effect has been to make some thoughtful natives of other lands wonder how seriously to take any expression of the American spirit.

In the period from 1879, when Billy Vanderbilt with the help of the Morgans cut down his visibility as head of the New York Central, to the mid-eighties, Pierpont Morgan seemed to lose touch with the world of railroading and financiering. He gave more attention to his new home at 219 Madison, to his yacht and his extensive trips than he did to the activities of Jay Gould, who was applying his wrecking principles on a broader transcontinental railroad stage.

Nor was he attentive to another new face in the transportation world, Henry Villard. Born in 1835 as Ferdinand Heinrich Gustav Hilgard, the son of a Bavarian Supreme Court judge, he changed both his name and his homeland after a quarrel with his father in 1853. After holding a number of odd jobs in Ohio and Illinois and trying vainly to set up a "free soil" German colony in Kansas, Villard drifted into newspaper work about the time he was twenty-one. Married to the daughter of the abolitionist William Lloyd Garrison, he worked as editor and correspondent for a number of papers and periodicals, including the New York *Staats Zeitung*, Frank Leslie's, and the New York *Tribune;* he served as war correspondent for the *Tribune* and then the *Herald,* for his own news agency, and then for the Chicago *Tribune.*

After a tour of war corresponding abroad in 1866, he returned to play a major part in the great post-Civil War railroad boom. He had had some success with the Kansas & Pacific Railway and in 1882 his Oregon & Transcontinental Company acquired the road that had ruined Jay Cooke, the Northern Pacific. Villard's sources of capital included the Deutsche Bank of Berlin and Dutch and German investors, partly through his own connections and partly as a heritage from the Jay Cooke primacy.

Morgan had some connection with the line, selling its bonds to his English customers, but when he at last began to give his close attention to the railroads, he moved on a more confined scale with the New York Central, the eastern trunk line founded by Commodore Vanderbilt. Cornelius's son Billy had gone his advisors one better in divesting himself of a controlling interest in the Central. Billy, who spoke so enviously to the Hepburn committee about the way the Rockefeller group could raise millions, liked the idea of raising cash by selling stock to such an extent that he left himself with very little of the Central's securities a few years after Morgan got him started.

It was almost too late by the time Morgan and Chauncey Depew, who had become president of the railroad, interested themselves in his holdings. Morgan's attention had been drawn to the sorry state of Central affairs during his annual hegira to London in 1885. English investors pointed out that five years earlier they had relieved Vanderbilt of $25 million worth of New York Central stock on Morgan's assurance that the 8 percent dividend would be maintained for a minimum of five years. The clock had barely finished tolling the minimum when, in early 1885, the rate was halved.

The trouble with railroads went back to the beginning of the decade. In 1880 and 1881, whatever balance wheel worked to keep railroad expansion in some kind of synchronization with demand broke down completely. In those two years, 29,000 miles of new railroad lines were created as the result of an outbreak of speculative fever. This amounted to an addition of 34 percent to the existing mileage. As one contemporary said, "Of these new railroads, about one third were justified by the existing demand, one third more would become useful at some time in the future, and the others would never be of any value to anyone, except, perhaps, to the promoters, if they succeeded in selling out."

It was the latter class, aptly named "blackmail railroads" by a victim and occasional practitioner, George B. Roberts, president of the Pennsylvania Railroad, that was causing the trouble. All that was needed to set up a railroad was a state charter granting the promoter the right to pass among the rubes and slickers and sell bonds. One of the earliest of the blackmail roads was the New York, Chicago & St. Louis, more familiarly known as the Nickel Plate. The syndicate that built it, said Vanderbilt's broker, Henry Clews, "had solely for their object to land it upon either Gould or Vanderbilt."

Running between Buffalo and Chicago, it would complement either Gould's Erie or Vanderbilt's Central. But Gould was out of the picture by the time the line was finished, so the disposition of the Nickel Plate fell to Vanderbilt. He bought it finally, but only after throwing some temper tantrums before meetings of the "pool commission," the assemblages of trunk line officers at which rates and routes were set. At one point he demonstrated his antagonism by boycotting meetings at the commission's office, sending only an underling from the Michigan Central. When he did buy the line he paid much more than the overcapitalized railroad was worth and much more than he could have gotten it for a few months later, so he became shy about making ready advances for blackmail after that.

A new threat came when Gould assembled a group consisting of General Horace Porter, George M. Pullman, and General Edward F. Winslow to build the New York, West Shore & Buffalo Railroad, which ran from Weehawken to Buffalo on a course largely parallel to and sometimes in sight of the Central's tracks on the other side of the Hudson River. Porter, a West Pointer and son of a governor of Pennsylvania, had been an aide to Grant both during the war and during the presidential years.

A holder of the country's highest decoration, the Congressional Medal of Honor, he was with his chief during Gould's 1869 attempt at a gold corner and at one point Gould tried with a half million dollars to bribe him and some other associates of the President.

Porter declined the offer, but he seems not to have passed that information and other facts he had concerning the gold conspiracy on to his chief. It was surprising, though, to find him turning up in Gould's retinue during the railroad blackmailing days. Pullman's presence was easily explained. His Pullman Palace Car had been ignored by Vanderbilt, who had adopted the Wagner Parlor Car for the Central Lines. Any opportunity to repay that oversight would be welcome to the Illinois car manufacturer. Winslow was in the scheme as a friend of Porter's, but even more important, as the president of a 270-mile railway running from Oswego to Middletown, New York, that was to be an important adjunct to the proposed West Shore. Its treasury of $10 million was also to be important. In addition to these three, a broker named Charles T. Woerishoffer was involved in the speculative enterprise. He had at times been aligned with Morgan in opposing Henry Villard in the Northern Pacific.

Another complication was provided by the presence of two other Morgan men in the West Shore hierarchy. One was Charles Lanier, a close associate and, in fact, a member of the exclusive Corsair Club, which at this time consisted of only five men hand-picked by Pierpont Morgan. They met regularly aboard the yacht in season and at each other's homes during the winter. Lanier's partner, Edward D. Adams, and an adherent of Morgan's by virtue of that connection, was also active, holding a directorship in the company that was to build the line, the North River Construction Company. Adding to the conspiratorial fog surrounding the project was the rumor, later to be confirmed, that Pennsylvania's President Roberts and some of his allies were also financially involved.

Besides the menace the West Shore represented to Morgan's interest in the Vanderbilt lines, the new railroad also caused him personal discomfort when the noise of construction between the river and his summer place at Cragston disturbed his vacations. And of course it caused him even more discomfort when he had to listen to the complaints of those who had bought Central shares on his representations back in 1879.

The West Shore got under way with its Weehawken to Buffalo

run in January 1884, to the applause of stock and bond holders who were told that it was bound to make more profits than the superlatively watered Central and the much abused Erie.

They weren't long in finding out that was not to be the case. At the end of the first year, the managers reported a loss of $840,000. The line went into the hands of receivers in the spring of 1885. Then it came out that the road, capitalized at $70 million, owed that, plus $6 million to the construction company, which consisted of the same managers with different hats.

The failure of the line could be attributed, in part, to the panic of that year, but the principal cause of the West Shore's bankruptcy was Billy Vanderbilt's determination not to be taken again by a blackmail railroad as he had been in the Nickel Plate transaction. He again mounted a murderous rate war, as he had done in the Nickel Plate prelude, but this time he kept it up until it meant "not merely bankruptcy, but utter annihilation" for the West Shore.

Vanderbilt continued the pressure into the time of the West Shore's receivership, showing that he was intent on annihilation, or at least on being able to buy the property at annihilation prices. His course was almost as deadly to his own line. The rate cutting had reduced profits, it was estimated, to 1 percent of revenues, an amount insufficient even for paying the half rate dividends that were agitating Morgan's European clients. On top of this, Vanderbilt was spending money on some blackmail railroading of his own.

This involved a phantom line, the South Pennsylvania Railroad. Chartered by the commonwealth in 1854 as a road paralleling the Pennsylvania, right through the established line's Clearfield bituminous region, it was seized on by Vanderbilt in vengeance. He was certain that a good part of the West Shore's unwillingness to die resulted from encouragement, financial and otherwise, from the Pennsy.

Probably because of its value as a source of embarrassment to the Pennsylvania, the South Pennsylvania won support from other rivals of the Pennsylvania, the Philadelphia & Reading and the Baltimore & Ohio. Both invested in the South Pennsylvania, along with numerous widows and orphans who were relying on the word of their investment counselors. The Reading even undertook a heavy capital construction program to prepare for a junction with the new line.

Another investor was the sly old Scotsman, Andrew Carnegie,

whose motives were as Byzantine as ever. Carnegie, the Pennsylvania's assiduous courtier, had been treated by his patron to a stiff rise in freight rates. He entertained briefly the idea of inspiring a torchlight protest, like the Chartist demonstrations of his Caledonian forebears, in the streets of Pittsburgh. Cooler counsel, though, pointed out that such organized spontaneities occasionally grow genuinely spontaneous. With his steel mills having recently cut wages by more than the freight rise, troublemakers among the protesters might easily swing the crowd's attention to Carnegie. Altogether, investment in a line that could provide competition for the offending Pennsylvania seemed a better mode of attack.

The South Pennsylvania was not a complete phantom, although it would have served its purpose just as well if it had been. Many mere proposals to parallel existing lines were worth hard cash to their promoters in the shaky condition of railroading at the time. But during the summer of 1884, some money was spent on showing the sincere purpose of the South Pennsylvania entrepreneurs. Forests were leveled for roadbed, tunnels were bored, piers for bridges to nowhere were built. Lives were lost, some said as many as two thousand. This substantial portion of the phantom was to serve, more than half a century later, as part of the country's first autobahn, the Pennsylvania Turnpike.

But all work on the blackmail railroad had ceased by July 1885. A violent clamor arose from all the investors in the $15 million operation, ranging from the widows and orphans right up to the master steelmaker, Carnegie, who went on railing against the fate of the South Pennsylvania for another four years. His complaints reached a climax in an address to the state legislature at Harrisburg in 1889 in which he taunted the lawmakers for permitting the killing of the railroad, "your courts and your constitution to the contrary notwithstanding."

What had happened was a long time in coming out, precisely because of the irregularity noted by Carnegie. When such of it as was ever going to be revealed was laid before the public, Morgan was to enjoy one of those fitful spells of notoriety that marked his early career. It would be another ten years before he would again emerge from the errand boy status decreed by his father, but when he emerged, he emerged clearly and unequivocally, in the gold contract arrangement of the closing years of the second Cleveland administration.

Pierpont Morgan, it developed, had returned from Europe in

June 1885, whether by design or by accident, on the same ship as William H. Vanderbilt. After having heard the critical comments of the English investors about the New York Central stock, he no doubt had much to talk of with Billy concerning Vanderbilt's handling of the West Shore threat in a rate war as suicidal to the Central as it was murderous to the opposition line. They must also have discussed Vanderbilt's adventure in Pennsylvania.

When such law and order as existed for the terribly rich finally caught up with him, Pierpont Morgan deigned to give a grudging account of what had happened:

> When I came from Europe in June of this year, I became satisfied that it was necessary that something should be done with a view to securing harmony among the trunk lines, and after conversations with various parties here, and also with friends in London, I made up my mind that the principal thing was to secure a harmony between the Pennsylvania and the New York Central.

Toward this end Morgan called on Frank Thomson, the vice president of the Pennsylvania, and noted "that there were two sores that had to be healed" before there could be a settlement. "One was the West Shore and other was the South Pennsylvania," Morgan said, adding, "I told him I thought from my conferences with the New York Central people that they would be willing to take the West Shore if the Pennsylvania was ready to take the South Pennsylvania."

Thomson wasn't ready. Or more properly, his boss, George B. Roberts, president of the Pennsylvania, was not. As Morgan recollected it, Thomson told him that, "Mr. Vanderbilt having seen fit to go into Pennsylvania, he did not see why the Pennsylvania people should give him back his money expended in the South Pennsylvania." Rebuffed on this first attempt, Morgan returned to report to Chauncey Depew and others at the Central office and to find what progress was being made in getting Vanderbilt to buy the West Shore at the knockdown price it had reached. Probably in a mood of levity, he told the Pennsylvanians who were probing into the matter, "Of course, the New York Central folks repudiated any idea of responsibility for what Mr. Vanderbilt might do with his own money."

In early July, Morgan said, he returned to Philadelphia for

another talk with Thomson, together with Roberts this time, about the proposition. The specifics dealt with what Vanderbilt and his associates were to get for the $6.5 million or so that they had sunk into the $15 million phantom. What the widows, orphans, Carnegie, and the Reading and B&O officers were to get for posting the remainder was not a question they bothered to go into. Court records indicate that their claims were extinguished at about seven and a half cents on the dollar; Morgan's clients in contrast, were to be compensated at a rate far closer to what they had put up.

"I suggested to Mr. Roberts and Mr. Thomson that if the Pennsylvania Railroad Company was prepared to take the South Pennsylvania for bonds or any other security that bore 3 percent, assuming that the sum would amount to $5,600,000 or over, I thought the thing could be carried through," Morgan recalled. But the Pennsylvania officials still had their doubts. These doubts rested on the supposedly solid bedrock of the commonwealth's constitution, adopted in 1874, particularly Section Four, Article 17, which "specifically prohibits the consolidation or merging of competing railroads or other carrying corporations."

State constitutions carried little weight with Pierpont Morgan. He decided to make a third attempt, this time amid the luxuriously appointed surroundings of the black-hulled *Corsair*. Stretched at ease under the awninged stern of the great yacht, his alien guests would surely see that the best resolution of the matter would be for Vanderbilt to take the West Shore and for the Pennsylvania interests, through some subterfuge that would leave the letter of the constitution intact, to take the South Pennsylvania off the New Yorker's hands. Only through such an agreement could the discord and confusion of unrestrained competition be prevented. Surely Roberts could be made to see that.

Accordingly, the president of the Pennsylvania and his first vice president, Thomson, were invited one hot morning late in July to partake of the kind of regal hospitality Pierpont Morgan could provide aboard the *Corsair*. Bringing the two out-of-state railroad potentates around promised to be a difficult task. Both Roberts and his railroad were unlike anything Morgan had had to deal with up to this point.

In the first place, the railroad was conceived, brought into being, and staffed by professionals whose chief interest was pro-

Morgan at the Pinnacle. A photographic portrait made in 1908, when he was seventy-one. He had reached a period of consolidation; behind him were his great successes and failures: U.S. Steel, International Mercantile Marine, the Panic of 1907. Ahead was the Pujo investigation.

August Belmont, the elder. Active in finance, Democratic party politics, and the social whirl of post-Civil War times, Belmont, he of the
"pronounced limp," played a major role in shaping the country during
the period of Pierpont Morgan's apprenticeship.

PHOTOGRAPH BY BYRON , THE BYRON COLLECTION
MUSEUM OF THE CITY OF NEW YORK

Edward H. Harriman in the unlikely getup of a French courtier, beribboned pumps, hose, silk kneebreeches, and all. The man who worsted Morgan on two occasions is shown with his daughters at the James Hazen Hyde ball in 1905. The occasion was significant. Public indignation at the extravagances manifested brought on a major investigation in New York of the insurance industry of which Hyde was a part.

Panic of 1907. Frightened investors—and gawking spectators—fill Wall Street from building line to building line, with the focus of the scene the knot of anxious depositors seemingly storming the entrance to the Trust Company of America (white facaded building in center). Since it was the repository of Tennessee Coal & Iron stock deeply desired by Pierpont Morgan, there was really no cause for panic at its gates.

Confused depositors mill around the front door of the Lincoln Trust Company shortly after closing time at the height of the Panic of 1907. The trust, at Twenty-sixth Street and Fifth Avenue, together with the Knickerbocker Trust, further uptown, did a big part of its business with individual depositors from the fashionable residential world of mid-Manhattan. According to one contemporary observer, the Lincoln and the Trust Company of America (see previous photo) were subjected to "such a run as was probably never witnessed in the history of banking."

COPYRIGHT 19
BY PACH BROS.

James J. Hill, the "empire-builder" of the Great Northern transportation complex. The photo was made in 1904 when Hill, a year Morgan's junior, was sixty-six. This is a few years after he had helped rescue Pierpont Morgan from the intrigues of E. H. Harriman in the Northern Pacific corner.

A penciled note on the back of this old print reads: "the only photo he liked." Morgan is stepping off the pier to greet a General Fred D. Grant at a garden party at Governor's Island in the summer of 1904. He might well have liked it. He was unaware of the camera and so did not lock himself into his usual "ferocious financier" pose. What results, despite heavy retouching, is a true portrait of him, a big man of big stride and large gesture, with a streak of radiant affability he generally kept hidden.

John W. "Bet-a-Million" Gates (right foreground) at a steamship pier in 1908. This was during one of his many voyagings financed in large part by funds derived from Pierpont Morgan when Morgan bought him out in the creation of United States Steel several years earlier. Boy at right seems to have just been told by his father: "Look! There's Bet-a-Million Gates."

James R. Keene, master stock manipulator who was in charge of the guy wires and ropes holding aloft United States Steel stock at its creation. This undated photograph of a painting softens but does not obliterate the ferrety quality of countenance of this "celebrated manipulator of speculative values."

Henry Clay Frick, who formulated a sort of aesthetics of finance with his: "Railroads are the Rembrandts of Investment." Morgan made him rich with U.S. Steel stock; he made himself richer by selling it when it was high.

John D. Rockefeller, center, comes out of retirement for a trip to court in 1910, during the lengthy legal proceeding that broke up the Standard Oil trust in that year.

James Stillman, "an elegant little man" who headed the "Rockefeller bank," the National City, and who served as a link between that powerful set of forces and those of Pierpont Morgan because of Morgan's admiration for him. He was also "the little man who wasn't there" when state or federal investigations loomed, notably during the Pujo hearings of 1912.

Robert L. Bacon in a photo probably taken around the mid-1890s, when he enjoyed Pierpont Morgan's favor and played a big part in such activities as the gold contract of 1895. Later, he was to prove inadequate, to say the least, in the Northern Pacific corner. In this photo, he is apparently attempting some sort of semi-beard, just under the lower lip.

The bar at the Hoffman House as it looked about the time the gold contract hearings of 1896 were going on upstairs. Bouguereau's callipygian nymph has the top-hatted patron enthralled.

August Belmont, the younger, at left, in costume for the James Hazen Hyde ball, January 31, 1905. Belmont the elegant, Belmont the debonair, strikes a pose that he must often have assumed in the presence of inferiors such as doormen, photographers, and the United States senators who questioned him during the bond hearings of a decade earlier.

Andrew Carnegie, the "little fellow" whose methods were so galling to Pierpont Morgan that he was ready to pay any price to remove this Scottish nettle. Carnegie was equally willing to move into higher spheres. He wanted to go on to advise kings, emperors, presidents, and popes on how to run their respective hegemonies. The photo was taken at his desk in his Fifth Avenue home in the early 1900s.

"The Corner" at 23 Wall Street, which Pierpont Morgan took over after the death of Anthony J. Drexel in 1893. Just before his own death, Pierpont Morgan ordered the building torn down and replaced with the lower structure that now stands at that corner of Broad and Wall.

An old photo of Pierpont Morgan, probably taken when he was in his fifties, before he had joined the movers and shakers of the financial world.

Dedication of Commodore Vanderbilt's 150-foot long monument on November 10, 1869, at the Hudson River Railroad Terminal on Hudson Street, New York. The central, fur-coated statue of the Commodore now stands overlooking Park Avenue from Grand Central Terminal.

"Commodore Cornelius Vanderbilt at Home" reads the caption for this old magazine illustration made from a photograph. It is a rare scene of domestic felicity for the high-living Commodore. The child is probably his son and successor, William H. Vanderbilt.

An early Morgan splendor, Cragston, the family's summer retreat at
Highland Falls, New York, on the Hudson. It was bought in 1872.

219 Madison Avenue, at the northeast corner of Thirty-sixth Street,
Morgan's home from 1880 on to the end of his life. Solid and obviously the home of a powerful man, it still lacks the pretension of the
palaces and chateaux erected in other parts of the city by his contemporaries, even some of those he had helped to fortune such as
Henry Clay Frick.

Samuel Untermyer, at right, with some of the members of the Pujo committee. The organizer of the "Money Trust Investigation" sports his usual home-grown orchid boutonniere.

Pierpont Morgan heads for judgment at the Pujo committee hearings in Washington in December 1912. He is accompanied by his daughter, Mrs. Louisa Satterlee, and his son, J. P. Morgan.

A somewhat wilted and crumpled Pierpont Morgan appears to be sitting in the pitiless glare of the final, apocalyptic roll-call. The effect was largely the result of the unfortunate lighting conditions in the Pujo hearing room and, of course, Morgan's advanced age.

viding transportation. It wasn't a poor abused Erie, seemingly conceived to provide remote and splendid sites for railroad wrecks, nor even a New York Central, assembled out of tiny bits by a man whose chief interest had been augmenting his fortune and only incidentally providing a public service. This is not to say that the Pennsylvania was an impossibly idealistic enterprise that had succeeded to its current dominance without stain. It of course maintained the kind of relations with the state government that any railroad had to establish in the days of the Great Barbecue. In fact, at one point the current president, Roberts, had served as the liaison man "in charge of" the lawmakers, much as Jay Gould had served in that capacity in New York. And in rate setting, granting of favorable rebates, and the like it was not surpassed by any of the other carriers of the country. Still, it had been remarkably free of the kind of excesses of capitalization that had brought trouble to other lines.

In the second place, its president, George Brooke Roberts, was a new experience for Morgan. He was just a few years older than the New Yorker and had been named president of the great transportation complex only five years earlier, at the age of forty-seven, on the death of Thomas A. Scott. Like Morgan, he was of Welsh descent, although only of the fifth generation to Morgan's six. His family was of some consequence, owning a farm in Montgomery County, Pennsylvania, but Roberts apparently owed more to his own ability in his chosen field of engineering than to any advantage his parents were able to provide.

He completed his secondary education very early, at the age of fifteen, and then went on to Rensselaer Polytechnic Institute at Troy where, in contrast to Morgan's rather haphazard schooling, he completed the three-year engineering course in two. He then worked his way up in the construction gangs that were throwing the Pennyslvania's right of way through wood and mountain in the rugged Appalachians.

At the age of twenty-nine, he was selected for a signal honor. J. Edgar Thomson, the Pennsy's first president, hired him away from the construction company he was then working for to be his assistant. Such recruiting was rare then and subsequently with the railroad, which preferred the policy of raising up its executives from its own ranks. Thomson, though, had had the brilliant young construction engineer under close observation for some time. A Quaker, he was capable of being aggressive when that

course was called for. He was slight—"delicately constructed"—
but with strong features. His jaw was powerful, he wore a walrus
mustache, and his eyes were hooded in that cobra fashion that
makes a man a formidable poker antagonist regardless of how he
handles his cards. Morgan would have his work cut out for him if
he was going to try to break through this man's antipathy for
accommodating William H. Vanderbilt or the New York Central.
In fact, it took an entire day's cruise.

Pierpont Morgan, together with the Central's president,
Chauncey M. Depew, steamed over to the Pennsylvania's pier in
Jersey City about ten in the morning to pick up Roberts and
Thomson. The slow moving *Corsair,* whose top speed was about
fourteen knots, took more than four hours to steam up to about
West Point on the Hudson. The trip back included a turn around
Sandy Hook and then back to the Jersey City pier. Carl Hovey,
the earliest Morgan biographer, who is generally credited with
doing his homework, gives this account of the *Corsair's* maiden
trip through railroad financiering.

> Mr. Morgan said very little; he smoked black cigars.
> Mr. Depew related the experience that the Central had
> had with the West Shore. He showed how it was pos-
> sible for a great railroad, no matter how prosperous,
> to be cut into and weakened in all its resources by a
> rival line of no standing whatever. He suggested that
> in the end the Pennsylvania would find it much more
> costly to stand out than to accept Mr. Morgan's pro-
> posal.
>
> "That's right! That's right!" exclaimed Mr. Morgan.
> "Can't you see it? In the end you would have to come
> to it. In the end you would have to buy or control this
> other road only to make your connections. You must
> come to this thing now."
>
> Hours slipped away; luncheon had been served; the
> sun no longer rode high; everybody, except Mr. Mor-
> gan, had smoked more of the black cigars than were
> good for them. Still the Corsair churned along.
>
> "But why," objected Mr. Roberts, "should we make
> ourselves responsible for others' mistakes—why pull
> them out of the hole they have got themselves into?"
>
> Mr. Depew drew him aside. It was clear that this

man was standing out, because he thought someone should be punished for getting the railroads into all this mess. He thought the big backers should be taught a lesson. Depew put it to him that these men, those big, rich individuals with their lack of sound railroad knowledge and their willingness to throw their cash into the wrong places, had already received severe punishment. It was true, in the scaling down of debts, in the sacrifice of interests, the backers were bound to suffer. "Oh, no," said Mr. Morgan, striding over, "they'll not get out whole."

At seven o'clock in the evening, President Roberts interrupted the silence that had fallen upon all. "Well," he said, "I agree. All right, I agree."

"At that meeting," Morgan testified later,

> there was practically an agreement reached on the plan as ultimately carried out. The amount was to be ascertained, the accounts were to be examined with a view to arriving at the cost of construction of the South Pennsylvania Company or something which should pass through that channel. The one thing stipulated was that the security to be given to the subscribers should bear the absolute guarantee of the Pennsylvania Railroad Company. Having obtained that from Mr. Roberts we went to work again with Mr. Vanderbilt and his associates, and early in August the details of what was required to be done was sent to me by Mr. Roberts. I think the letter was dated August 5.

The hitch was the state constitutional provision forbidding any buying by one railroad of a rival road, but that had been worked out with what Pierpont Morgan thought was a pretty slick maneuver. At the *Corsair* meeting, according to Morgan's testimony, Roberts was apparently the originator of it.

> Mr. Roberts said it would be necessary that some one should become purchaser and not have the purchase made directly by the Pennsylvania Company. As a firm, we [Drexel, Morgan] could not do this, but as an

individual, feeling the importance of what was at stake, I was prepared to do what I could to give the use of my name and signature to act as purchaser of one for the other, and the papers bear that out. On the 20th of August the papers were practically settled, consisting of a form of contract for the subscribers to sign, the guarantee that the subscribers required from me to protect them from any further calls from the purchasers or from any parties to whom I might transfer the property and an agreement to deliver all the property, and after having been through several hands in New York, Mr. [Francis Lynde] Stetson took them to Saratoga, where they were ratified by Mr. Roberts on August 23.

With that display of boldness and insolence, in which Pierpont Morgan not only aided and abetted a scheme to flout the laws of Pennsylvania, but had the arrogance to detail it only two months later in answers to questions from the state's attorney general, the incident closes, in most accounts.

The *Corsair* conference and its consequences usually are regarded as early proof of the grand manner that became typical of Pierpont Morgan in later major transactions. As usual, though, considerable liberty has to be taken with the truth to turn the 1885 railroad operation into a transcending triumph. Actually, the transaction was never completed according to Morgan's plan. True, he was able to prevent the construction of a railroad that probably would have visited ruinous competition on the Pennsylvania, but that seems to have happened through forces beyond his control. After a lengthy litigation of several court cases, the Pennsy had to take back its bonds and the Vanderbilts their abortive railroad, but by that time Billy Vanderbilt was dead and his heirs were having enough trouble living in grand style off the Central without thinking of completing the South Pennsylvania.

The West Shore absorption went off with only a minor hitch. Billy Vanderbilt was able to complete that part of the bargain, which was what he had been aiming at anyway, a short time before his death on December 8, four months after the *Corsair* conference. The unfortunate William H. Vanderbilt, whose development was stunted far more than Pierpont Morgan's by a parent who was overbearing rather than strict, died on that early December afternoon at the age of sixty-four, while "chatting pleasantly" with Robert Garett, president of the Baltimore & Ohio and a fellow blackmailer in the South Pennsylvania scheme. He never knew that the plot worked up by his banker, Pierpont Morgan, would be undone.

It had to be. Even during the most repulsive courses of the Great Barbecue a sovereign state could not permit the kind of transparent hokum whereby Morgan, acting on behalf of the Pennsylvania Railroad, bought up the rival line for the purpose of later turning it over to the Pennsy. The hue and cry grew to tremendous proportions as work ground to a halt on the South Pennsylvania following the *Corsair* conference. And there were important voices heard—Andrew Carnegie for one, and his friend, Henry Oliver of the Oliver Iron Works. The two of them, together with a few Pittsburgh associates, had raised about $5 million of the needed capitalization.

Another complainant was the Reading line's Franklin B. Gowen, who had succeeded in riding the presidency of that line up to the bankruptcy point of the railroad and then reappearing on the other side as receiver. He had put up $100,000 and one of his subordinate executives on the Reading had posted a like amount. Another, E. C. Knight, put up $200,000.

Then, of course, there was the Reading itself, with a capital spending program already under way to accommodate the now abandoned railroad. These were not the mute and powerless widows and orphans, the western farmers and rural bank officers that railroad financiers could ignore. They raised a fearful howl, captured newspaper columns, began court actions, and hounded the commonwealth into taking action. Just about the time the last sound of hammering and sawing was dying away along the route of the South Pennsylvania, the commonwealth's attorney general, Lewis C. Cassidy, swung out with one of the roadshows that passed for official investigations at the close of the last century.

It was a true roadshow, for apparently no one would come to Cassidy in Harrisburg. He had to open in Philadelphia, with Examiner John H. Weiss presiding at the hearing in the Continental Hotel. That was on September 30. There were more one-day stands there and in other parts of Pennsylvania, and on October 13 the whole court apparatus took the ferry over to Manhattan "to accommodate J. Pierpont Morgan, whose evidence was desired in the case," the *Tribune* said.

The judicial arm of the nearby state was prepared to go to

almost any lengths for such accommodation, even to the point of permitting Morgan to testify right from his desk at the Drexel building, but "the lack of proper facilities" interfered with that. So the visiting luminaries, who included Pennsylvania Railroad's president, George Roberts, and Wayne McVeagh, the lawyer for the carrier, together with the local stars, Morgan and his firm's lawyer, John C. Bullitt, among others, repaired around the corner to the office of Bangs and Stetson at 45 William Street.

Stetson's office, of course, was as much partisan territory as was the Drexel building. Even though he wasn't to become Pierpont Morgan's lawyer for another two years, when the latter's brother-in-law, Charles Tracy, joined the firm, he had acted as messenger for Morgan in carrying the South Pennsylvania papers to Roberts in Saratoga.

He had other claims to prominence, too. In the previous year he had helped in the nomination and election to the presidency of Democrat Grover Cleveland, the first member of his party to hold that office since the Civil War. Also aiding in that campaign was William C. Whitney, who had served as chairman of the board of the ghostly South Pennsylvania until he was rewarded for his efforts on behalf of Cleveland with a cabinet post, Secretary of the Navy. An added bit of incidental, confusing intelligence in connection with this 1884 presidential election was the fact that Morgan, for the first time in his life, refused to vote for a Republican and cast his ballot for Cleveland. It was said he didn't care for the GOP standard-bearer, James G. Blaine.

The questioning by Cassidy set no forensic records. The legal system being primarily concerned with the shoring up of things as they are, cross-examination tends to be at its most brilliant in the browbeating of those who have suffered a loss of popular esteem, such as people under criminal indictment and those of their supporters who are willing to act as witnesses. There are very few examples of courtroom fireworks directed against the rich. And so it was in this not very serious attempt by Cassidy to find out why the constitution of the commonwealth of Pennsylvania was being treated so uncivilly by Morgan and company.

At one point Morgan made the mealy-mouthed response: "Mr. Roberts doubted the policy or the ability of the Pennsylvania Railroad Company, as such, to buy off, or in any way interfere with, what might be rival roads." What he meant, of course, was that Roberts had pointed out that it would be against the law to do such a thing, but he was allowed to leave this mushy statement unchallenged on the record.

At the hearing he spoke proudly of another evasion, an elaborate fiction that he naïvely thought the court would accept. Inasmuch as the law forbade the Pennsylvania Railroad from buying a rival road directly, Morgan figured there surely could be no objection to his buying it and selling to the Pennsy. His windy wording of his sly subterfuge went like this: ". . . as an individual, feeling the importance of what was at stake, I was prepared to do what I could to give the use of my name and signature to act as purchaser of the one for the other, and the papers bear that out."

The court was not impressed. In fact, the lawyers who were arguing the Morgan side in the subsequent appeal ignored the deceit totally, knowing that it might be disastrous if the case came, accidentally and against the odds, before some high-minded jurist. But the bit of pettifoggery has impressed most of Morgan's biographers. To them, it makes Pierpont Morgan out as a man of cunning, a confounder of mere judges and lawyers.

The transplanted attorney general, Cassidy, was understandably fearful of pressing anything too far. After all, Stetson might have asked him to leave if he grew too obstreperous. He settled the fact that the papers that were readied for Roberts' signature on August 23 and rushed to him in the racy vacationland of Saratoga on that Sunday had passed through the hands of an army of lawyers with great speed. Obviously, this high legal velocity was needed to wreck the South Pennsylvania before the ponderous machinery of enforcing the state's law could be brought into action. He got Morgan to admit that Stetson (then representing Harris McK. Twombly), Charles Tracy, Bullitt (representing himself) the ever-present Chauncey Depew (representing the Central), and two other lawyers exercised their combined legal talents in reviewing the papers. After all that, Cassidy asked: "Was there anything said about getting the business through speedily?"

Morgan was well qualified even at this point in the art of blunting official inquiry when it threatened his interests. "I do not remember anything in particular, nor in general. When I have business on hand I think it is better to have it done quickly. That is my experience." This pompous evasion also went unquestioned by the state attorney general. However, he did show some spirit in the exchange that followed his asking Morgan why the group went on the yacht.

"Because it was a convenient place," Morgan said.

Cassidy's frame of mind can be well imagined in his next question amid the hostile office force of Bangs and Stetson, associates and supporters of the man in the White House. Cassidy was an attorney general, a holder of an office of high public trust, but that was only in Pennsylvania. What did he amount to here in this foreign state, to which he had come to "accommodate" the man who was sitting in the chair facing him? Still, he pressed ahead: "Then it was not for the purpose of having nobody know what business you were engaged in?"

Morgan angrily dispensed with platitudes this time. "I do not know that that was a part of the consideration. It might have been," he conceded. "I fixed upon that place, but I do not know of any special purpose or view in that connection."

Despite Cassidy's willingness to subordinate the purposes of the commonwealth to the convenience of witnesses like Morgan, he did manage to get on the record a hazy indication that there had been unseemly haste and purposeful concealment in mind in the *Corsair* conference. Above all, he established that the conference was held to give Roberts and the Pennsylvania Railroad a 60 percent ownership of the South Pennsylvania.

In view of the uproar caused by the railroad wrecking, there could be but one outcome, but the opportunity for judicial delay being what it is, the process took about seven years. In 1892 the Pennsylvania Supreme Court ruled that the Pennsylvania Railroad could not carry out a commitment to violate the state constitution. The Pennsy "settled its moral obligation [to the Vanderbilt syndicate's South Pennsylvania] by the payment of $1,500,000 with interest at 6 percent . . . plus compensation for certain counsel fees, the total running to something over $1,800,000."

Thus the sale was blocked. Once the plot was uncovered, it was foiled. It is true that Pierpont Morgan prevailed partially. By the time the legal case was completed, in the early nineties, Billy Vanderbilt was dead, the Panic of 1893 was in preparation, and the Vanderbilt interests, more diffused now, were preoccupied with holding what they had rather than pursuing competitive fantasies in Pennsylvania.

But the clear winner was George Roberts and his railroad. He snuffed out a threat at a bargain price. Even up to a few decades ago, the Pennsylvania Railroad was profiting from the fiasco. In the 1930s, during the construction of the Pennsylvania Turnpike over much of the South Pennsylvania's route, it was found that some of the railroad's rights had survived the dusty old court order of "permanent" injunction and the carrier received about a million dollars to extinguish any claims.

FRIGHTENED CAPITALISM

BEFORE the death of his father in 1890 closed off the important preparatory or apprentice period of Pierpont Morgan's life, he made an attempt to assert himself as a bringer of order to the anarchic world of railroading. He would endeavor to get railroad men from all across the country together as he had done on a more limited stage in the *Corsair* conference. The purpose would be the same, except on a continental scale. All the railroads in the country, the great transcontinental routes as well as the Eastern trunks, would be brought together in harmony and cooperation.

Morgan's meeting was set for December 1888. It made no difference to him that a year earlier Congress had specifically prohibited such harmony and cooperation in the Interstate Commerce Act. His attitude toward such laws had been expressed a few years earlier at the time of the completion of the West Shore absorption by the New York Central. Former Judge Ashbel Green, who had been a receiver in part of the West Shore bankruptcy, was selected by William H. Vanderbilt when Pierpont Morgan asked him for someone trustworthy to help with the legal work. The financier had drawn up a set of procedures indicating the sequence that was to be followed in the elimination of the West Shore as a New York Central competitor and handed it to Green. The former jurist took the program, which was apparently largely the work of Coster, to his office, pondered it for two days, and then came back with the pronouncement that it couldn't be done legally.

Green's opinion triggered a typical reaction from a man who was growing into the habit of directing that things be done, rather than seeking counsel on how to accomplish them. Later his reaction would often be unreasonable; but on this occasion he replied: "That is not what I asked you. I asked you to tell me how it *could* be done legally. Come back tomorrow or the next day and tell me how it can be done."

Of course, Morgan never allowed himself to echo Commodore Vanderbilt's opinion that a railroad could never be run within the statute books, but he held to the view throughout his life that lawyers were flunkies, like electricians, plumbers, mechanics, and other specialists, who would be well advised to steer clear of troublesome matters of ethics and morals and keep in mind the task at hand, the most efficient solution of the problem whether it be installing electrical outlets, providing a new watercloset, or combining two major corporations.

Much later, he told Elbert H. Gary almost the same thing. Gary, another former judge who became associated with Morgan in the great U.S. Steel formation in 1901, also retained much of the dust of pettifoggery even when he began bulling his way upward in the ranks of commerce. "I don't think you can legally do that," he told Morgan in reference to some railroad problem. Morgan reacted "stormily" according to Gary's admiring biographer, Ida Tarbell, saying, "Well, I don't know as I want a lawyer to tell me what I cannot do. I hire him to tell me how to do what I want to do. . . ."

Pierpont Morgan's attitude toward the law itself was well illustrated by the name he chose for his new organization. It was to be called the "Interstate Commerce Railroad Association" and no doubt its founder intended it to be a much more potent body than the puny Interstate Commerce Commission set up by Congress in the 1887 Act. It could hardly be otherwise, for the commission, intentionally weakened at birth by Congress when it was given no power to fix rates, was further emasculated by the highly reactionary Supreme Court of the time until one of the members of the Court, Justice John M. Harlan, was moved to remark that the commission was "a useless body for all practical purposes." The commission itself, in its 1898 report, concurred in this walrus-and-carpenter verdict. Another decade was to pass before it was strengthened.

Pierpont Morgan called the railroad men to a meeting in the drawing room of his home at 219 Madison Avenue on December 21, 1888. The meeting continued for several days, until shortly before Christmas, when it was adjourned to January 8. Included were the "Western presidents," Charles Francis Adams, Jr., now running the Union Pacific, Marvin Hughitt of the Chicago & Northwestern, R. R., Cable of the Rock Island, Frank S. Bond of the Chicago, Milwaukee & St. Paul; Jay Gould and his son George, of the Missouri Pacific; and A. B. Stickney of the Chicago, St. Paul & Kansas City.

A stenographic report of the meeting has survived, parts of which have reached print. There was no one present, though, who could give the kind of description called for by the presence of Adams, the moral auditor for Gould, and his subject, in the same room together. Gould was probably well able to maintain his equanimity, and within a few years Adams would be ousted from his post, largely because of conditions created by Gould's mismanagement.

Morgan opened the gathering with:

> The purpose of this meeting is to cause the members of this association to no longer take the law into their own hands when they suspect they have been wronged, as has been too much the practice heretofore. . . . This is not elsewhere customary in civilized communities, and no good reason exists why such a practice should continue among railroads.

One of the easterners, the professional railroad man, George B. Roberts, objected to that kind of talk from a banker. "Speaking in behalf of the railroad people of this country," he said, "I object to this very strong language, which indicates that we, the railroad people, are a set of anarchists, and this is an attempt to substitute law and arbitration for anarchy and might."

Stickney, of the Chicago, St. Paul & Kansas City, objected to the secrecy, which was even then being breached with mysterious leaks to the newspapers. "The public are sure to think we are conspiring to do something that we ought not to do," he said, but he won no followers in trying to open the meeting.

Roberts, displaying continued sensitivity to the problem of "blackmail railroads" that had first brought him into collision with Morgan four years earlier, said that such a paralleling of lines was at the bottom of all railroad problems and he blamed it on Morgan's fellow bankers, who could stop it easily by refusing to furnish the speculative funds. He again complained about Morgan's blunt talk, saying, "I cannot help but feel that it is a little harsh language for us to hold here, but I can stand it, I suppose, if the others can."

Morgan went right to Roberts' major objection:

> In regard to the remarks made by Mr. Roberts in re-gard to the bankers and the construction of parallel lines, I am authorized to say, I think, in behalf of the houses represented here, that if an organization can be formed which shall accomplish the purposes of this meeting, and with an executive committee able to en-force its provision, upon which the bankers shall be represented, they are prepared to say that they will not negotiate and will do everything in their power to pre-vent the negotiation of any securities for the construc-tion of parallel lines, or the extension of lines not unanimously approved by the executive committee. I wish that distinctly understood.

Adams, probably fixing Gould and his scion with a frosty New England look, laid transportation problems to the caliber of person the industry attracted to its management. He did not except anyone in the Morgan drawing room.

> . . . The difficulty in railway management does not lie in an act of legislature, state or nation, but does lie in the covetousness, want of good faith and low moral tone of railway managers, in the complete ab-sence of any high standard of commercial honor. Now the question we are to decide here today is whether any gentleman representing a railroad company is prepared to stand up and say before the public and before us that he is opposed to obeying the law, and, further, that in matters of controversy he prefers to take the law into his own hands rather than submit to arbitration. That is the whole thing in a nutshell.

Despite these arguments, the western railroad presidents, such as Hughitt, were not prepared to subordinate the interests of their shareholders to a board of arbitration and they remained outside the organization. Without them, the conference had little pretension to a national scope. Pierpont Morgan made another attempt, at a follow-up conference two years later, on December 15, 1890, to get the western lines to reconsider, but the heads of the roads still resisted. Even the agreement that was subscribed to by the eastern railroads indicated the "fundamental futility" of the ambitious proposal. The only significant outcomes were that the easterners agreed to make no private concessions to shippers in the way of rate cutting and that a board to hear complaints of undercutting was appointed, with the power to levy fines.

Despite the discouraging outcome, Pierpont Morgan met the press at the conclusion of the 1890 meeting and said: "I am thoroughly satisfied with the results accomplished. The public has not yet appreciated the magnitude of the work. Think of it—all the competitive traffic of the roads west of Chicago and St. Louis placed in the control of about thirty men! It is the most important agreement made by the railroads in a long time, and it is as strong as could be desired."

Bold words; not necessarily true words. Morgan at this point at the opening of the 1890s was talking for his British principals, who, on the eve of the 1893 crash, were growing leery of American investments. Among the causes were the new outbreaks of rate cutting, rebating, and threats of "blackmail" competition, all of which Morgan's "Interstate Commerce Railroad Association" was powerless to prevent because of the pressures of overspeculation and the equal counterpressures when the speculation reversed itself. He failed, and it goes almost without saying that the purposely impotent Interstate Commerce Commission did no better.

But in the course of the decade Morgan succeeded in another and more permanent manner. He was able to substitute the control of a wholly different class of person for the rough-and-ready adventurer who up to that point had held sway in railroading. The new dictator, with a completely new set of values and principles, was the bond salesman—himself. The railroader who had grown up since the Civil War was able, through many special circumstances, to heap up profits regardless of whether he built a fairly reliable and efficient transportation route, as Commodore Vanderbilt in his later outbreaks of public decency did.

These "special circumstances" included a willingness by the people of the United States—just about everyone down to the lowliest of farmhands—to pay premiums blindly to make sure that no railroad passed them by. Under these circumstances, the Daniel Drews, the Jay Goulds, and the Jim Fisks could gather money as well by wrecking railroads as by building them. The experience of a railroad like the Erie suggested that Gould and those like him were able to profit out of setting up systems of mass public execution as they squeezed and robbed and adopted, as a matter of policy, methods that ensured the maximum of real railroad wrecks on their lines.

Morgan, through his long period of probation brought on by his Civil War adventuring, had sloughed off this tendency toward raw profiteering. He was now a peddler of bonds. The transition, incidentally, brought no word of praise from his London-based jailer. "Pierpont's father had never complimented him on anything that he had done," says Satterlee, but he unbent at the time of the *Corsair* conference to tell his son's wife: "Pierpont handled that West Shore affair better than I could have done it myself."

Of course, the withholding of praise could be expected of an old autocrat like Junius S. Morgan. The old man, "physically large and massive" like his son, "and presenting the ponderous figure of an East India merchant prince in an old English play," displayed his real feelings about his sole surviving son only in those shelves of bound letters received twice a week from his trusted agent and, going even further back, the copybooks containing schoolboy compositions from the days in Switzerland and Germany. It may be wondered whether the lack of expressed appreciation together with the admiration confessed by that collection contributed to the regrettable act at Dover House in 1911, when Pierpont Morgan fed the volumes one by one into the fireplace.

Morgan's railroad operations have qualified him in the eyes of many as a sort of natural force in the development of capitalism. He squeezed out the adventurers, snuffed out the competitive anarchy, amalgamated and combined and introduced order and harmony into the carriers that moved men and goods. To many, especially those with a nodding acquaintance with Darwin, this seemed to mark the course of a natural evolution shaping industries as well as fishes and birds, from the simple, anarchic, and destructive to the complex, harmonious, and constructive.

Although Darwin resisted the temptation, his popularizers

were not so successful in avoiding a seductive corollary to the theories of natural selection, the idea that any newer form is inherently superior to older forms in every way, simply by virtue of its newness. All Darwin said was that the later form is better able to survive, not that it better deserves to survive. It is an idle mental exercise, of course, at this late date to express a nostalgia for dinosaurs; however, we need not hold that every species that has supplanted the dinosaur represents an unalloyed improvement. To do so is simply a violation of the truth.

Morgan, as the embodiment of natural forces, brought out a more highly developed form of capitalism, but it was not necessarily an improvement. He simply substituted the values and principles of a more cautious group of moneyholders for those of the adventurers who had preceded him. He was the bond salesman, acting for wealthy people and institutions in England who wanted their capital lent out at a profit, but with little risk.

This made the management of enterprises of some importance to Morgan, whereas to Gould and his friends nothing could be less important than management. They did it themselves as part-time amateurs. They were out to create wealth and risk was an important element of that creation. Morgan's clients were out to augment already existing wealth and risk was antagonistic to that concept.

Morgan's role as agent of foreign capital brought with it a sense of responsibility. He was a merchant who had to keep the interests of his clientele in mind because he would have to return to them again and again to succeed in his own business. The Goulds and the like were gamblers, ready to loot a given set of people on one turn of a marked card; then they would move off to where a new set of victims could be found. They had no responsibilities.

Morgan thus made capitalism safe for people with capital, where it had not been a few decades earlier. But he was to become reckless later and capitalism once more would present dangers to its beneficiaries. Of greater importance, though, would be its growing weakness and timorousness in Morgan's hands. One of its most important functions, to encourage risk-taking and new ventures, would to a great extent atrophy. Where choices were possible, the new fearfulness dictated the selection of the lesser risks. Thus Morgan's associates backed the form of electricity favored by Thomas Edison. The untutored genius of

Edison had adopted direct current almost as an article of faith, whereas the trained mathematical genius working for General Electric, Charles Steinmetz, grasped the truth that direct current was useful for children's toys and flashlights, but that the full development of electrical power depended on the maximum use of alternating current.

Because the Edison company was well established while General Electric was an audacious newcomer, the Morgan group funneled capital to the better known institution. The verdict has since come in: direct current is for toys and flashlights, while alternating current is infinite in its variety and portability. But its supremacy was established at great cost, great waste and inefficiency, for which the frightened capitalism of a Morgan is partly responsible.

The railroad organizations of this period were patterned on the procedure followed in 1885 in which the New York Central extinguished the West Shore. The process has been called "Morganization," although it seems more proper to refer to it as "Costerization," after Charles Henry Coster, who had been made a partner in the firm as of January 1, 1884. Satterlee says that Coster "had been of great help in carrying out details of the West Shore reorganization," but the official biographer breaks out of the family habit of patting Coster on the head for his "details" in a later comment, when he notes that Coster "was ably assisting Pierpont in his railroad operations and was of the greatest help . . . in the fight for the control of the Richmond Terminal and in the reorganization of the Richmond & Allegheny Railroad." The busy partner

> was now a past master in railroad organization and had an extraordinary power of recognizing the essentials in a piece of business without neglecting the minor details. In drafting documents he had great clarity of expression and fertility of invention. He continually had to invent forms and devise methods to meet the problems on which Pierpont was working. For the next few years, until Francis L. Stetson became counsel for Pierpont's firm, he did what was really legal work. He was in charge of the details of all the great reorganizations carried out by Drexel, Morgan & Co. after the West Shore.

§ 183 §

Coster's "details" had harsh consequences for the unfortunate stock and bondholders of the West Shore, but of course the blame really lies with Gould, Pullman, and the military men, Generals Porter and Winslow. Gould was said to have been able to slip out, leaving the others holding the bagful of bad paper. The railroad, 426 miles from Weehawken to Buffalo, had cost $58 million to build. That was much less than it had cost to build the Central and the Erie between the same two points, during the early days of railroading, but it was a considerable increase over the price per mile that had prevailed a decade earlier at the height of the transcontinental building boom.

The West Shore cost $136,000 a mile, more than two and a half times the $50,000-a-mile cost of the earlier period. During its first year of operation it promptly went into the red with a loss of $840,000 and receivers were appointed. Those who held the $50 million in "first mortgage" bonds (that is, bonds supposedly secured with a mortgage against the property), which paid 5 percent, were invited to turn them in at fifty cents on the dollar and at a reduction of 1 percent on the interest rate.

An added debasement was the turning over to the Vanderbilt interests of $25 million worth of the new bonds, the identical amount that the old bondholders were getting. Two of the old bonds, in other words, would be turned in for one of the new ones, and for every new bond that was being issued to the hapless holders, Chauncey Depew, the Vanderbilts, and the Morgan faction were laying up one of the new ones in the care of the Central's management. The latter were to be used for the development of the blackmail line. The bondholders screamed mightily at these terms, which recall the old "stand and deliver" of the armed highwayman. But to no avail.

At that, the bondholders fared better than the buyers of West Shore stock, which was simply recalled with no compensation. In return, the Central interests promised a long lease and a guarantee of the principal and interest of the new bonds, which were secured by a mortgage, just as the old ones were. But, of course, in the process of manipulating the shells across the board, the hand that was quicker than the eye was backing $25 million worth of bonds with a railroad that had cost $58 million. None of Pierpont Morgan's English customers could have taken exception to this. It was a dehydrating process; water was being sluiced off, squeezed out, and the last traces evaporated in these Costerizing moves.

The initial impact on small bondholders could easily have been fatal, but the process almost guaranteed a working railroad. With all the hokum that goes into security values, that fact meant that in the long run the holdings would creep back to something approaching true valuation. Coster operated with all the seeming heartlessness of a skilled surgeon, tearing away cancerous tissue and occasionally damaging some healthy parts.

Coster began his waterletting at at time when there was plenty of opportunity for it. The decade had begun with 93,262 miles of rail in place in the United States. The 1880s would see the all-time peak of new construction, with an average of seven thousand miles laid annually. But at the same time as actual steel and timber were going into place and equipment was being added, the adventurers were losing no opportunity to man the pumps. For every mile of track, oceans of water were forced into the capitalization.

This was not just the opinion of academicians or wild-eyed reformers and malcontents. *Poor's Manual,* the authority for investors, stated in 1884 that in the previous year almost $4 billion—just about all the capital stock for the railroads of the country—represented nothing but water. In the three years ending December 31, 1883, $2 billion of capital and debt had been created and "the whole increase of share capital, $999,387,208, and a portion of the bonded debt was in excess of construction."

Following the West Shore reorganization, Morgan and his able lieutenant carried out a similar squeezing and recapitalizing of the Southern Railway system, a network of roads that had been mismanaged to the point of chaos by a group of New Yorkers and Virginians who had control through the Richmond and West Point Terminal. The drastic Costerization was completed in time to help the Southern weather the storm of the 1893 panic. Before completing that operation, Pierpont Morgan and his firm had let the property slip in and out of their hands on a number of occasions as the dissident stockholders lost and regained control.

Morgan then found a way of barbing the hook so it would not slip out. To do it, he brought to perfection a device called the voting trust, which had been pioneered by John D. Rockefeller a couple of decades earlier. The simple, textbook definition of the trust goes about like this:

> Under this form of combination, the stockholders of the various constituent companies of the trust place

their stock in the hands of a small board of trustees,
giving to these trustees an irrevocable power of attorney to vote the stock as they see fit, or in accordance
with specific instructions given at the beginning.

This definition had been formulated by Jeremiah Whipple
Jenks, who was by no means so innocent as to think it made the
slightest difference what the stockholders did or didn't do. The
vantage point of the stockholder was not the place to start the
definition of a trust, which, as Jenks well knew, was an obscenity
being imposed on the stockholder. Being a man with American
and European degrees, a teacher at Cornell, and the United
States Industrial Commission's chief investigator of trusts in the
monumental report that group made on corporations in 1902,
Jenks could not but have realized that the place to start was with
those who conceived and imposed the device on the stockholders—the trust officers. This point did not escape a far more
realistic student of trusts, Samuel Untermyer, who will enter this
narrative more fully later in the great gladiatorial contest provided by Congress's Money Trust investigation.

From that more logical focus, it can be seen that the trustees
were carrying on a process, begun with the corporate form itself,
of diffusing responsibility to lessen risks and appropriating control from those who had possessed it by virtue of their possession
of capital. What was left to the shareholder was a vague understanding that some form of profit would come back to him. The
sop that induced him to permit the emasculation of his capital
contribution in every other way was the elimination of all or most
responsibility for acts that would be performed by his investment. The trust was a further extension of each of these characteristics.

In the case of Rockefeller's Standard Oil combination, the
purpose had been to provide capital without the incumbrance of
the capitalist who was supplying it. As John D. Rockefeller wrote
in 1885: "I think a concern so large as we are should have its own
money and be independent of the 'Street.'" Indeed, lack of capital was at the heart of all the troubles of industry and the
railroads. "It is astonishing the amount of working capital you
must have in a great concern," Andrew Carnegie recalled. "It is
far more than the cost of the works." But the method of seques-
tering the capital from its owners emerges only in the masterful

analysis of post-Civil War capitalism prepared much later, in 1913, by Samuel Untermyer and the staff of the Money Trust investigation:

> Thus, on the reorganization of the Southern Railway Co. by J. P. Morgan & Co., in 1894, a majority of its stock was placed in a voting trust, which deprived the stockholders of all representation and voting powers and vested the absolute control of the company in the trustees, J. P. Morgan, George F. Baker, and Charles Lanier, who, upon the transfer of the stock into their names, issued the usual trust certificates, which were listed and traded on the exchange instead of the stock certificates.

These new certificates were neither bonds, backed by any collateral, nor equities representing any form of distant control. They simply represented a vote of confidence by the holder that the Morgan trusteeship would do the right thing by him eventually. A further shaking out of the holders was provided by setting a limit to the life of the old certificate, thus forcing the holder to turn in old certificates for new versions of the engraved bits of parchment. Untermyer noted that holders of 183,938 shares of the original Southern certificates held out against the Morgan demand for a new vote of confidence.

"The result was that those not assenting to the extension of the trust and hence not taking new trust certificates found themselves with a security not listed on the exchange and therefore without a ready market and not available as collateral," he reported. In other words, the old certificates were without value.

This trust concept, in many cases, went through a number of mutations as various forms of it were outlawed in one jurisdiction or another. Some, though, were a long time in mutating. Rockefeller's Standard Oil was outlawed by an Ohio court in 1892. The trust simply ignored the decision, brightening its reputation among the army of admirers of lawlessness.

Among the new forms that ingenuity would create was the holding company, a corporate form of trust that took advantage of further division of ownership and control and the evaporation of responsibility provided by incorporation. It was said to have been first conceived by Pierpont Morgan's lawyer, Francis Lynde

Stetson, in 1893 for the creation of the Metropolitan Traction Company in New York. After its peculiarities were explained, one of the officers, Thomas Fortune Ryan, was said to have breathed reverently: "Mr. Stetson, do you know what you did when you drew up the papers of the Metropolitan Traction Company? You made us a great big tin box."

By such processes of dehydration and appropriation did the Morgan group reorganize the Erie, the Hocking Valley (a system of roads in the Middle West), and the Northern Pacific after Henry Villard completely lost control of it. Other roads in which the firm played a part, although not an exclusive one, were the Baltimore & Ohio and the Atchison, Topeka & Santa Fe. The Lehigh Valley and the Central of Georgia were also given new life.

Another Costerized line was the Philadelphia & Reading. Many officers of the Reading had little use for Pierpont Morgan because of his part in crushing the South Pennsylvania, in which they had heavy investments. But in the fall of 1887 he was able to put through a reorganization which included a cash levy on the securities holders as well as a devaluation of their holdings. However, no trust device was used to keep control in the hands of the Morgan firm, and as a result it came under the power of the man known as the Napoleon of the railroad world, Archibald A. McLeod.

The Reading consisted of 1,586 miles of railroad, of which the majority, 1,152 miles, was only leased. But its value lay mostly in its ownership of anthracite coal. At least half of the hard coal supply in Pennsylvania was owned or controlled by the railroad.

McLeod began to work out an ambitious plan as soon as he took office as the head of Reading. His idea was nothing less than the monopoly of coal production and distribution in the northeast. He came so close to achieving his goal that he was able to dictate coal prices and bring the wrath of Congress on his head.

An investigation followed, but that wasn't the cause of McLeod's downfall. That occurred when his overextended borrowing and speculation in other railways came apart in the 1893 panic. Pierpont Morgan stepped in again, upon which McLeod resigned, saying, "I would rather run a peanut-stand than be dictated to by J. P. Morgan." This time Pierpont Morgan saw to it that the recapitalization would endure by installing a trusteeship.

The inner working of Coster's system were explained nearly

forty years later by Thomas W. Lamont. First there was a careful analysis of the railroad's earnings, interest charges, dividends, operating and maintenance costs, equipment and management, said Lamont. Then came an analysis of "the extent and nature of the fixed charges that . . . [the railroad] might be able safely to undertake." Then Coster would work out a plan to bring the fixed debt obligations down to within this minimum earning capacity. This was the part that brought forth screams of outrage from stockholders, for the reorganization might involve inducing the bondholder to exchange one bond for another paying a lower rate, or for preferred or common stock, or a combination of all three. It also could mean, as in the West Shore case, asking the bondholder to be happy at receiving a new $1,000 bond for two old $1,000 certificates. The holders of stocks were frequently assessed to provide working capital, a sort of reverse dividend, and on occasion, as in the West Shore case, their holdings were simply and highhandedly declared to be worthless.

The results, from Coster's point of view were excellent; his employer received a notable bargain. Even for the investors— certainly those who lived long enough to see the long run—the wringing out process was eventually profitable.

But the larger viewpoint—that of the people, the industries, the regions that were supposed to be served by the carriers—was totally ignored. Reorganizations usually ended with harmony and higher rates. "Five years ago," an Interstate Commerce commissioner reported in 1903, "the crying evil in railway operations was discrimination, mainly discrimination between individual shippers. . . . Not so today. . . . The discrimination is disappearing, but in its place comes that other danger which always attends monopoly, the exaction of an unreasonable charge."

These reorganizations, largely ascribable to Coster, took place before, during, and after Pierpont Morgan took part in the effort to supply gold to the government. This period represents the apex of his career. He had begun in the closing years of the 1880s with tentative attempts to impose order on the country's transportation system. His scope widened in the wake of the panic of 1893, which provided him with the opportunity to attain his goal by the indirect means of salvaging wrecked railroads. He began also to grow in magnificence in other ways, too, but the 1890s were for Pierpont Morgan years of solid growth on lines largely laid down by Coster.

With Coster's death in March 1900, the rationality he had contributed to the organization melted away. From that point on, Pierpont Morgan adopted the spending habits of a sailor on shore leave. Where Coster's railroads, once wound up, could run through depression and panic, the post-Coster magnificences that Morgan indulged in coughed and sputtered. The great United States Steel combination, a waterlogged venture almost the direct opposite of anything Coster was connected with, was a hydrocephalic freak that had to be nursed through birth pangs and subsequent bad times by the great stock manipulator, James Keene.

This wild spending also marked Morgan's private ventures, especially in the art world. During the outburst of eulogies that followed his death, a London source struck a discordant note by pointing out that his departure "caused something akin to consternation in art dealing circles in London"—not because of his knowledgeable collecting but because of the inflated prices he paid. "His example stirred the ambition of others and the threat of his competition stimulated other wealthy collectors," it was said, and "American art collectors for some time to come will be less ready to pay from £5,000 to £100,000 for a picture or a piece of tapestry." *The Economist* of London concluded, "As a collector, it is said he was too hasty and uncritical, and too dependent upon art dealers. The great prices which he willingly paid did much to produce the present demoralization in the art market."

Some of this, of course, may be attributed to the always discernible tendency of the English to sneer at lesser breeds without the law that presume to ape the homegrown variety of art dilettante. The gibes grow excessively rancorous toward the former colony and its denizens, especially when they have been guilty of scooping up works of art from financially pinched earls and dukes as Morgan had. For a nation that had been filching antiquities before and since the days of Lord Elgin and that regarded Egypt as something less than a colony, Morgan's usurpations in that cradle of civilization must have been especially galling.

Morgan had grown to be the kind of collector who deserved this sort of criticism, but that was not the way he had started. He seems to have possessed a genuine appreciation for good music and the fine arts; and his interest in literature did not confine itself to the acknowledged masterpieces of safely dead authors, the conventional sort of interest with which the cultured wealthy often convince themselves of the impeccability of their taste.

In music, it was a family joke that he had a faulty sense of tune, yet Satterlee, who still seemed convinced that the joke was well-founded, recounts an episode that gives the whole legend the lie. The joke was especially pressed by his wife's relatives, who used to say that "Pierpont could not turn a tune," and teased him about not being able to differentiate "Home, Sweet Home" from "Yankee Doodle."

Satterlee records that he once called the bluff of Fannie's sisters and bet them that he could sing twenty-five hymn tunes so that they would be recognizable. The girls accepted the bet and he proceeded to hum the first of his old favorites in his "deep, resonant voice." "He proved his musical memory and tested their knowledge of the hymnal by humming twenty-four others in succession, and winning his bet."

Again, the family biographer recalls that he had a deep affection for opera that weakened, as it often will, later in his life. But "his special favorite," which he never missed, was Giuseppe Verdi's *Il Trovatore,* certainly not the kind of musical drama that appeals to the casual opera-goer. Musicianly commentators, like Ernest Newman and Francis Thompson, point out that in its fourth act it contains one of the greatest scenes in Italian opera. Morgan "was very discriminating as to how the different numbers were sung. It [*Il Trovatore*] was his standard of comparison for all operas, and there were very few that in his estimation came within measurable distance of it." His musical taste no doubt contained a great element of sentimentality, as in his early fondness for the beery oomp-pah-pah of his Gottingen days, but he developed considerable discrimination later in life.

His accretions in the fields of painting, sculpture, ceramics, and the like quickly acquired a pecuniary tinge and no doubt owe much to his growing conception of himself as a Medici prince or even a pharaoh. In his later collecting days, when he was exploited by dealers like the Duveens, who had even less genuine interest in the works than he had himself, he found a way of giving expression to his role as a magnifico.

Satterlee recalls that he began exploiting the exploiters by taking whole collections on approval. "None of the dealers liked this method, but none of them dared object to it." In this way

Morgan was able to keep the material on view and get a considerable amount of valuable critical opinion about it from other dealers and experts who were invited to look at it. Then when he finally consented to buy, he very frequently would pass the stuff on for loan to museums or galleries and "almost always, the payment was deferred for three, six, or nine months, and sometimes, in the case of a collection, for a year." This was the kind of arrogance he was developing in his business affairs, but few except London editorial writers could grow critical at his displays of haughtiness at the expense of such a breed as art dealers.

His adventures among the masterpieces also called forth the puckish kind of humor he seemed to favor. On one occasion he came back from a collecting spree and Satterlee asked him what he had been doing all day. "He said with a smile, 'Making trouble for my executors.'"

Again, James Stillman, the cryptic genius of finance who headed the National City Bank and who found it expedient to bob up in Europe any time troublesome congressional investigations threatened at home, passed on the story of a time when he pointed out to Morgan a gorgeous tapestry that he might buy.

"I suppose I oughtn't to, but it's a great temptation," Stillman said. Morgan, unconsciously paraphrasing one of Oscar Wilde's favorite and most often used epigrams, answered, "Always resist everything, Stillman, except temptation."

The art collections were quickly loaded with Romneys, Reynoldses, Watteaus, Fragonards—works that had attained a cachet before Morgan ever thought of acquiring them. There was more evidence of independence in his literary collecting, which began in 1888 with the purchase of a Thackeray manuscript from a friend of his nephew, Junius S. Morgan. Thackeray was hardly controversial, but the literary reputation of an author who had died only twenty-five years earlier was not in the same safe realm of antiquity as the painters Morgan favored.

This was to a certain extent true, too, of John Keats, whose *Endymion* manuscript was an early purchase of Morgan's, and it was even more true of Charles Dickens, who had died in 1870. Dickens's enormous popularity tended to overshadow the fact that he was a vigorous social rebel who put the ruling class to considerable trouble not only with his sharply satirical pen but also with his great popular appeal. Not the least of his targets were industrialists and stock manipulators, yet he became an early favorite of Morgan's, who collected first editions of the great Victorian novelist and other memorabilia, including the equally satirical original drawings by Phiz (Hablot K. Browne).

Voltaire and Molière, whose works he also collected, may have been defused by the passage of time, but another Frenchman, Emile Zola, was not. Among the Zola items acquired by Morgan was the manuscript of *Nana,* which Mme. Zola later tried to repurchase. Morgan had bought it at a time when the great French writer was in the midst of his indictment of industrial society, the *Rougon-Macquart* series of which *Nana* was a some-what lighthearted part, and it immediately preceded the period when Zola would do his utmost as a troubler of things as they are in his partisanship for Captain Alfred Dreyfus.

The growth of the collections was only part of the emergence of Pierpont Morgan during this period. The 1890s began with the most significant act of emancipation possible to him. More than fifty years of preparation and apprenticeship imposed upon him by his father, Junius S. Morgan, abruptly ended in April 1890.

The older man, taking the sun on the Riviera in advance of his son's annual visit, had gone out for a drive in an open carriage drawn by a spirited pair of horses. The coachman had taken the road from Beaulieu to Ezen where it ran near the railroad. A passing train startled the horses and they bolted out of control. Junius Spencer Morgan was thrown from the carriage and onto a pile of stones by the roadside. He lingered in a coma for four days until April 8, when he died.

This violent end was communicated to Pierpont Morgan in a brutal manner such as only the well-intentioned can contrive. He was at sea when his father died, and on docking at Queenstown he was handed a series of telegrams from some family source. The brainless intention had been to hand them to him in some sort of progressively worsening sequence, on the supposition that that would soften the blow.

Instead, he was handed the whole packet and, of course, tore open the last first. Following that distressing incident he pro-ceeded to France to make arrangements for sending the body home in the season when he ordinarily would be celebrating his birthday on April 17.

At the age of fifty-three Morgan for the first time in his life was on his own. His mother had died six years earlier. Yet the actual completion of his years of preparation would not occur until June

30, 1893, when Anthony J. Drexel would die and the Drexel name would be dropped from the firm.

But the passing of his father was crucial. From the financial structure built by his father on the Peabody beginnings in London depended all that Drexel, Morgan meant—certainly in New York, and to a great extent in Philadelphia. Morgan was now to take the commanding position in that structure. He marked the occasion only two months after Junius S. Morgan's death by ordering a new yacht.

Among the clubmen he knew at that citadel of respectable opulence, the Union Club, was J. Frederic Tams, a yachtsman to whom he awarded the contract. He made only three conditions for this new bit of splendor. It was to be completed within a year. It was to be larger than the current 165-foot *Corsair* but "not too large to turn around in the Hudson River opposite Cragston." And there was to be no fanfare. Tams was to keep the whole thing quiet until the yacht was ready. Even Morgan himself was not to be told about progress on the project. To that end, he handed Tams a book of blank checks at a dinner at the club at which the few details were worked out. "When the builders need money, you draw the checks until you are stopped," he said.

It was the beginning of a new blank-check style for Morgan. Tams never was stopped and he handed the commission to naval architect J. Beavor Webb. The result, ready in the autumn of 1890, was a bolder and bigger successor to the first *Corsair* and would still bear that piratical title. She was 204 feet long at the water line, a third again as long as *Corsair I*, had three engines, and was black like her predecessor. The second *Corsair*, too, would pass, to be succeeded by two more, each bigger and more magnificent. But this second holder of the title was to end up with considerable distinction. It helped augment the United States Navy, no less, as a gunboat in the first line of the battle of Santiago eight years later. For the patriotic gesture of disposing of his eight-year-old yacht, Morgan collected a quarter of a million dollars from the Navy. Even at that, he was reluctantly patriotic and "tried to put them [the Navy's purchasing agents] off in every way," even offering to build and equip a similar vessel to the government's specifications if only he could keep the *Corsair*.

But he had to give in, so he solaced himself, first by renting a big steamer, then by ordering another *Corsair,* bigger and better than the second one in some ways, but a costly duplication of it in others.

For example, he demanded that the carpeting on the second yacht be reproduced for the new one. The stuff was no longer in stock, so patterns had to be arranged on looms to turn out the new material. He gave J. Beavor Webb, again the designer, complete latitude in the design of the hull and power plant, but resisted adding any of the new sundecks and topside dining rooms and lounges that were coming into fashion in the world of millionaire's yachts. Morgan could afford to indulge his old-shoe fondness and so the main deck of the new *Corsair* was almost a reproduction, writ slightly larger, of the old. The latest *Corsair* was nearly half again as big as its predecessor, 302 feet at the water line, and, of course, glossy black. He got his first look at the magnificent new craft on his return from his annual spring trip to Europe on June 16, 1899.

The Morgan splendor was growing on land as well as at sea. This expansion, too, was stamped with his own mark. He was not tempted at all by the mansion-building impulse that was gripping nearly every other titan of finance and industry, especially during these closing years of the century and during the first decade or so into the new one.

All of them seemed to want to outdo each other in translating their power and glory into solid masonry, marble, and bronze fortresses that would spell out their power and grandeur on Madison Square and along Fifth Avenue.

Since their power and glory pretty well boiled down to sheer acquisitiveness, there wasn't much to express, and the fashionable architects who catered to the successful moneylenders, iron fabricators, stock manipulators, streetcar operators, and insurance agents had to fall back on borrowings. These included Norman castles, Greek temples, Venetian and Florentine palazzos, Spanish monasteries, and especially the exquisite hideaways that had been thrown up by French kings for their concubines. Most were simply calipered and tape-ruled, then reproduced on this side of the Atlantic. One traction magnate, though, had parts of several monasteries disassembled, crated, and shipped over to be reerected for the greater glory of himself.

This was not Morgan's manner. The brownstone at 219 Madison Avenue served as a spacious, but certainly not ostentatious, home to the end of his life. The Highland Falls summer retreat, Cragston, was obviously the home of a man of wealth, but it, too, had the faintly seedy look of his city place. Both expressed Morgan's contempt for fad and fashion. The Hudson River Valley had long since been supplanted as a warm-weather resort by Newport, Southampton, and other playgrounds, but Morgan showed his disdain for the mindless movement of his class by staying put. There appeared also to be something of that spirit in his insistence on keeping to the backwater of Madison Avenue when Fifth would so obviously have been the appropriate habitat of a dominant capitalist.

Satterlee quotes him as declaring his lack of interest in real estate, both from a business point of view on the model of his grandfather, Joseph Morgan, or from a desire for a personal memorial. He needed only "a place to live in and a lot in the cemetery," he often said.

Still, at this period he naturally came into possession of property inherited from his father, notably Prince's Gate in London, and there were other accretions. He hadn't a simple cemetery plot in mind when he bought about a thousand acres, including a sizeable body of water, Lake Mohican, in Hamilton County in northern New York.

He had visited the place, called Camp Uncas, in 1894 on a trip to the Collis P. Huntington property on nearby Racquette Lake. Huntington, active in the Union Pacific, had bought his "camp" from W. West Durant, whose father owned a couple of hundred spreads of the size that Morgan was to buy. Durant was preparing Camp Uncas for himself, with a main house fronted by lake and backed by towering pines and spruces, and he took Huntington's house guest over to see it.

Durant invited Pierpont Morgan back for a winter visit three years later and apparently took the occasion to let Morgan know he was short of ready cash. The financier agreed to lend Durant "a very substantial amount" and took a mortgage to cover the advance. A year later, the unfortunate Durant was in deeper trouble and had to sell all his holdings. Morgan became the owner of Camp Uncas in satisfaction of the mortgage. Later he added another twelve hundred acres.

Thus the owner of Cragston and 219 Madison began in 1898 to take on an imperial dimension. In fact, like Bad Ischl, for forty years the unpretentious summer home of one of the few remaining actual emperors, Franz Joseph of Austro-Hungary, Morgan's new domain, Camp Uncas, lay among two-thousand-foot peaks, at a point where the Alps are fairly well matched by the Laurentian chain known as the Adirondacks.

Actually, of course, Morgan, a potentate in a vigorous, growing empire, gave no thought at all to emulating a ruler whose outmoded empire was even then in the early stages of dissolution. Franz Joseph, seven years his senior, was not the kind of royalty to draw Morgan's interest. The Holy Roman Emperor had a private existence almost as melancholy as his public one, presiding over a disheveled dual monarchy that matched his disheveled domestic domain. His son and intended successor had committed suicide under noisy, scandalous circumstances at Mayerling in 1889 and this year, 1898, his empress Elizabeth was assassinated. First though, she had thoughtfully, but with a characteristic sloppiness, provided him with a mistress to allay his sorrow over Rudolph's death and her own indifference to him.

The loose, unbuttoned decadence of Vienna was not for a rising majesty like Morgan; he was drawn more to the young King of Prussia and emperor of Germany, William II, so controlled, so muscular, and so dynamic that he nearly blew the world apart in 1914. And he favored Edward VII, King "by the grace of God, of the United Kingdom of Great Britain and Ireland, and of all other British Dominions beyond the Seas, King, Defender of the Faith, Emperor of India."

Kept like Morgan from the center of power by a domineering parent until late in life, Edward mercifully died after a rule that was too short for him to exercise all of his peculiar talents. Of the Kaiser, because of the lack of candor among his lackeys, little is known except that he probably should have been institutionalized early in life; of Edward, from the evidence that has emerged despite British libel statutes designed to repress such revelations, it is certain that he should have been similarly treated. Both were more circumspect than old Franz Joseph; but despite the fact that the old gentleman accepted a mistress at the hand of his queen, he probably never even in fantasy could bring himself to think along the lines that were habitual with the former Prince of Wales.

Even by the unspeakable standards of the European aristocracy of the time, Albert Edward, the Prince of Wales who was later to rule as Edward VII, apparently managed to squeeze his considerable bulk through and beyond the pale. Even Kipling, who found empire and its trappings so remunerative to a modern minnesinger transplanted to the United States, could not bring himself to include the Prince in his odes of Enfield rifle chivalry. "Corpulent voluptuary," Kipling called him, which was simply a high-toned translation of the common man's term: "fat slob."

His qualifications as a slob are legion and sickening. One of the most recent is in the account Christopher Sykes gave about a wealthy uncle of his, one among many whom Albert Edward had suffered to ruin himself financially in supplying entertainment of all sorts to the heir apparent.

Some of the Prince's playful sports were no financial strain, however. He delighted in pouring brandy over Sykes's head, provided there was sufficient audience to appreciate such pleasantry, at Sykes's home, Brantingham Thorpe. Or the future monarch "by the grace of God, etc. etc." might vary that jape with another consisting of snuffing out his cigar on the back of his host's hand.

The crowning whimsey, though, was when Sykes would dive playfully, hooting and giggling, under the billiard table, whereupon His Royal Highness would take his stout billiard cue and rattle it around under the table with the object of bruising, possibly even maiming, his loyal subject. Sometimes H.R.H. would hand the cue on to another of the belted and gartered guests for a go.

The idea was surely to engage an eye, a nostril, an eardrum, a kidney, or some of the more yielding and more private parts of the prey. There is no record of his success or failure; in fact, British libel law being what it is, there's no record at all except the recollection set down by Sykes' nephew more than fifty years after the event.

It must be remembered that these three examples were not private vices, but were witnessed by many. The brandy-pouring might not cause a parliamentary crisis but the other two acts would come under the definition of criminal violations in any part of the civilized world and in many less advanced areas. We tend to think that the full meaning of such conduct was not recognized until the popularization of Freud early in this century, but even at the time the darker pathology behind such acts would have been understandable to qualified practitioners who had read Kraft-Ebbing and other pioneers in abnormal psychology.

On a more sunlit level of his life, Albert Edward specialized in sheer vulgarity, reaching the ultimate when he permitted Lily Langtry to have her bedspread at Regal Lodge, Newmarket, emblazoned with his personal standard and colors. "Whatever qualities he may later have developed as King there is little that can be said . . . at any other time in favor of the Prince of Wales as a man," says a recent English commentator.

With such a man Pierpont Morgan may have shared a mistress. The facts are obscure and, as they must be in such intensely private matters, inconclusive. Once again, it might be said that they could remain private were it not for the fact that Pierpont Morgan dabbled and busybodied himself sufficiently in the morals of others, especially those defenseless contemporaries who had to put up with Anthony Comstock.

"Roundsman of the Lord" was the title that Heywood Broun and Margaret Leech hung on Comstock at a safe distance after his death, when it was possible to be amused by his antics. Comstock may be characterized as pounding a beat for the Almighty, but he drew his pay from Pierpont Morgan and the other well-heeled founders of the Society for the Suppression of Vice. Their roles as paymaster for this passel of snoops in this instance prevent them from asserting the privacy that might ordinarily be claimed.

The woman was Maxine Elliott. Morgan had been linked often with glamorous beauties in his long voyages, yacht trips, spectacular entertainments, and even on his private car trips, surrounded by bishops, deacons, and other acolytes, to the triennial conventions of the Episcopal church that he attended religiously. But hers was the only name that ever got past the solid barrier of respectability that he always maintained.

Gossip had it that Morgan had financed the building of Maxine Elliott's Theater, as she named it, on Thirty-ninth Street and Sixth Avenue in Manhattan in 1907, the year of a panic that kept him very busy trying to maintain the banking system as it then existed. Satterlee and others deny the story.

Morgan himself denied it. The pair were aboard the same boat returning from Europe in September 1908, when reporters asked her if the rumors of Morgan's interest in her theater were true.

"Let's ask him about it, shall we?" was her response, and she produced the usually elusive financier for an impromptu press conference. "The only interest I have in Maxine Elliott's Theater is that I'd like to get a free ticket on opening night," he said.

The imputation that she needed Morgan's help is unfair to her, Morgan's son-in-law says, which seems true in the light of what was known about her financial abilities. The daughter of a Maine sea captain, Maxine Elliott was one of the ranking beauties of the time. A star of the London and New York stages, she was a statuesque brunette with violet eyes and ivory skin whose interest in money and its creation caused one contemporary to remark: "If Maxine had been a man, Schiff would have been her secretary and Carnegie her office boy." A fellow actress has recalled the fascinated attention with which Miss Elliott followed a long dinner table talk on the formation of United States Steel by its first president, Charles M. Schwab.

Beauty of the spectacular sort that Maxine Elliott had was always an attraction to Morgan. When to it was added intelligence and a genuine fondness for the acquisitive spirit, the combination must have been irresistible. She was thirty-nine years old the year she built her theater and at the peak of a career that was to last for thirteen more years. It could have continued beyond that, but by then she had amassed enough to afford a splendid villa in the south of France and a life of leisure. That was enough for her.

Whether or not Morgan had any connection with her theater, he and Miss Elliott were on terms of great intimacy during this period. Morgan, of course, never discussed such relationships, but Maxine, who was alternately discreet and swaggering, told a friend once as they drove near the Brandenborg Tor that she had once driven under it in company with the Kaiser. This had occurred in 1911, while she was a guest of Morgan aboard the *Corsair* at Kiel, she said.

The friend noted that Miss Elliott added a characteristic touch, a feminine complaint about the *Corsair:* "The arrangements on board Mr. Morgan's yacht were ridiculous. He had the cabins on a lower deck where there was no light, and the dining saloon on the upper deck. I had him change the whole thing so we could dine below, where we needed no outside light, and all the sleeping cabins could have proper portholes." Another actress reports having come upon the two of them "several times" dining privately in a hotel in Boston, where the star was opening in a new play.

Maxine Elliott was more open about her relations with King Edward VII, which probably indicates her opinion of the relative importance of the two. The powerful financier had a reputation; the impotent king had none. She apparently made up her mind early to seduce the king, if such a term is appropriate to so pliant a monarch. She met him once through one of his mistresses, or, more accurately, through the mistress's husband, who, it was said, allowed his better half "to be a favorite of the King, knowing that her manners were impeccable." Manners would seem hardly relevant in such a situation; in the case of the cigar-smoking ruler, possession of readily graftible skin would seem more to the point.

In any case, this meeting was inconclusive, so, Maxine Elliott set about laying a trap of her own devising. It was typically Victorian, typically repulsive, and almost unhealthy, as the elaborately Byzantine seductions of that period tended to be. It happened in the busy summer of 1908, just before she returned aboard the *Adriatic* with Morgan.

She intercepted the King at Marienbad, where he was taking the cure for the numerous unspecified ailments that beset him. Marienbad was a resort of the highest type, where everyone pretended that Edward was somebody other than the King of England and left him to his own devisings. Maxine, with another woman, took quarters in a hotel near his and carefully posed herself like some Burne-Jones figure in his path one day. She pretended to be reading a book.

The King, accompanied by his retinue, passed, paused, and passed on while one of the retainers, detailed procurer for the day, detached himself from the group and invited the actress to attend a dinner that Edward was to grace with his presence that night. It's a story worthy of *My Secret Life* or other dreary volumes of Victorian sex life, and Maxine had no hesitation in telling it.

Over the next two seasons at Marienbad, England's Queen Alexandra had to put up with another claimant to her husband. Then Miss Elliott bought an English country home, Hartsbourne Manor, in Hertfordshire, probably at the ruler's suggestion, so that the idyll could continue while he was engaged in running the empire, or whatever occupied him during the remainder of the year. The house was rebuilt to include a discreet private staircase connecting to a second-floor suite referred to as "the King's." Unfortunately, the sybaritic monarch was said never to have had the opportunity to twang the bedsprings. His fun-filled life ended May 6, 1910, when he went wherever it is that a welcome is out for those who like to stub out lighted cigars on the hands of those they have wrecked—possibly a place where such pyrotechnical displays attract little notice.

If Maxine Elliott's reticence about Morgan is a tribute to his magnificence at this period, it may be noted that he supplied tributes of his own of a similar nature. He had always a touch of arrogance, excused by his family on grounds of his shyness about his appearance. The trouble with his nose had settled into *acne rosacea.* The infected organ matched his growing splendor in its own way, becoming bulbous and almost continuously red from the 1890s on.

This considerable embarrassment may explain Morgan's overbearing arrogance with people he looked down on—inferiors at work, newspaper reporters, and the like—but it is insufficient to explain his highhanded ways with powers and potentates. Here he gives evidence of a growing conviction of his own magnificence.

For instance, during an earlier social call on the German emperor, in July 1902, he received the Kaiser aboard the *Corsair* at Kiel. The score of other guests on board, together with the Kaiser's functionaries, withdrew in accordance with protocol, to leave Morgan and the ruler alone. "The Kaiser, according to his habit, began walking up and down. After about two turns of the deck, Mr. Morgan evidently felt that he had about as much exercise as he wanted, and when they approached the chairs on the quarter-deck, he suggested that they should sit down."

For a commoner to make such a suggestion was definitely not in the rules recognized by the *Almanach de Gotha,* but the emperor did sit "and threw his staff into consternation."

The Kaiser, a man accustomed to thinking of himself as the spokesman for God and also accustomed to mentioning the fact frequently, was not behindhand in arrogance, but perhaps he may have had some glimmer of which of them was the real potentate. In any event, he sat and talked with Morgan for a long time.

The man who could put the Kaiser in his place had no difficulty with the German's kinsman, whose position in the British empire was much less autocratic. King Edward came to Prince's Gate to take tea a few years later and to see some of the paintings and other works of art that his country was being despoiled of. He looked, then sat with Morgan and Satterlee in the library, where his eye fell on the Lawrence portrait of the Countess of Derby.

"The ceiling is too low in this room for that picture. Why do you hang it there?" asked the King.

Morgan studied the portrait then turned to his royal questioner. "Because I like it there, sir," he said. The answer was not quite as abrupt as it might have been if the question had come from some lesser busybody, but Morgan by his response showed that the British empire and its august ruler were severely restricted under his roof.

It was hardly an exaggeration of the great dialect humorist Peter Finley Dunne, creator of "Mr. Dooley," to present Morgan in this fashion:

> Pierpont Morgan calls in wan iv his office boys, the prisidint iv a naytional bank, an' says he, "James," he says, "take some change out iv th' damper an' r-run out an buy Europe f'r me," he says. "I intind to reorganize it an' put it on a paying basis," he says. "Call up the Czar an' th' Pope an' th' Sultan an' th' Impror Willum, an' tell thim we won't need their sarvices afther nex' week," he says. "Give thim a year's salary in advance. An', James," he says, "Ye betther put that r-red headed book-keeper near th' dure in charge iv th' continent. He doesn't seem to be doin' much," he says.

The death of his father and Drexel's passing freed Morgan for the climb to this magnificence, but the real turning point seems to date to a period some time after that, following the great gold contract negotiation of 1895.

We have seen that Morgan's role was distinctly secondary to that of August Belmont and that all initiatives, including the invitation to Morgan, originated with the Rothschilds' representative. But on November 10 of that year—after the difficult and unsuccessful operations of the summer and, even more important, at a time when the Cleveland administration was preparing further maneuvers to replenish the gold reserve—a dinner was held at the Chamber of Commerce in New York that truly started Morgan on the path to national and international fame.

The principal speaker was John G. Carlisle, the Secretary of the Treasury, who, knowing that Morgan had been promised a leading part in any new borrowing, "gave him full measure of praise."

The president of the chamber, Alexander E. Orr, also saw to it that any tendency to overlook Morgan as the singlehanded savior of the United States was corrected. He had, said Orr, saved the Treasury from bankruptcy. From that point on Morgan was the oustanding figure of the operation. Even Cleveland was blinded by the propaganda, and when he came to set down his recollections of the event nine years later, Morgan was the hero. The ex-President's version has been accepted uncritically ever since.

With such advance agents preparing the way, Morgan's grandeur was multiplied. A year later his sway was extended into the political sphere, when his blessing was actively sought by Republicans who were promoting the candidacy of William McKinley. He gave it grudgingly, because McKinley as a congressman had favored silver, the soft, inflatable currency that was anathema to bond distributors on Wall Street.

Morgan returned from Europe aboard the *Teutonic* on June 10, 1896, and testified before the Senate committee investigating the Cleveland gold reserve transactions nine days later, the day after McKinley was nominated in St. Louis. Sometime between the tenth and the eighteenth, Morgan had a visit from the Cleveland banker, Myron T. Herrick, who was seeking financial support for McKinley. Herrick got Morgan and Marcus Alonzo Hanna together aboard the *Corsair*.

Only a month earlier, Hanna had been urged to have McKinley mollify eastern financiers by speaking out in favor of a gold standard and had responded, "I don't give a damn what Wall Street thinks of McKinley's silence; they can go to hell down there. We are not going to nominate McKinley on a Wall Street platform."

Hanna, a wealthy Cleveland businessman who, with Herrick, had rescued McKinley from bankruptcy in 1890 and had been trying to secure the presidential nomination for him since, saw the error of his words. Following the *Corsair* conference, a statement by McKinley pledging support of "our present standard," that is, gold or silver, was artfully changed by Hanna to read "the existing gold standard."

Later in the campaign, as money began to roll in from Pierpont Morgan's part of the country, McKinley would abandon even that equivocation and come out directly for the gold standard. Hanna raised a campaign fund of more than $3.5 million, an unheard of sum up to that time. He put double entry bookkeeping and modern business methods into politics. More than half his funds came from New York, where he had spent a pleasant hour or two with J. P. Morgan aboard the *Corsair*.

But it was not the levies he imposed, on a strictly proportional basis, on banks and businesses that elected McKinley, the "advance agent of prosperity," as Hanna billed him. That came about largely because an act of nature gave the lie to the economic arguments of the Democratic candidate, William Jennings Bryan.

America was still an agricultural power, a situation that was to prevail for another decade or more. Throughout most of 1896, the effects of the panic three years earlier and of the borrowings of gold were being felt throughout the economy, but most of all by the farmer. In August, wheat touched the extraordinarily low price of 53 cents a bushel, a profitless figure for just about every grower. But then came a failure of the crop in India; a scramble for the American output was on and the price rose rapidly. In election week, it had nearly doubled to 94 ⅝.

Bryan's managers yelped, accusing the "money power" of artificially propping the price to beat their man. Their reasoning was faulty, but they read the signs correctly. McKinley was swept into office with heavy majorities in Populist-Democratic farm states such as Ohio, Michigan, and Minnesota and a plurality of 602,555 in the popular vote, nearly double the "landslide" margin of Cleveland in the previous national election.

Morgan's multiple grappling for power on the grander levels of politics and business were matched by his increasing collection of personal property that had once been the exclusive possessions of kings, popes, emperors, princes, and dukes, grand and petty. The little room in the basement of his home at 219 Madison was crammed to bursting. Some of the booty lay still wrapped in the packaging that had been used to transport it, having been opened only for quick and unsatisfying examination and then giving place to later acquisitions.

The collecting mania was filling a storage room at "the Corner" at Broad and Wall, so extra space was reserved at a warehouse on East Forty-second Street. Morgan lent out many of the books and other material to libraries and museums that could be trusted. Still, something more had to be done. Storage space where the trophies of his increasing hunts through Europe and North Africa could be properly displayed was needed.

In filling this need, Pierpont Morgan displayed some of the characteristic flamboyance he was developing.

He commissioned one of the country's foremost architects, Charles W. McKim of McKim, Mead & White, to draw up plans for a Greek temple of simple classical line to house his art works and collections. McKim was equal to the task of dealing with men of grandeur. He usually thought in terms of Pennsylvania Stations and similar monumentalities, but he reminded Morgan that the Acropolis and other Grecian buildings had a simple and hardly observable peculiarity, compared with those of Rome and the later Gothic and Renaissance triumphs: the Greeks had wrought their miracles of line and form without cement. There was nothing superior about the method; it just happened that they knew nothing of mortar. So each block of marble or granite had to be laboriously chipped and honed to a smooth fit with its neighbor to provide long-lasting joints.

McKim confessed it had long been his dream to construct a building according to this outmoded foolishness, but, of course, he told Morgan, no one had been able to afford to indulge him, since it would add as much as $100,000 to the cost of the library, for instance.

That was just the touch needed to inveigle Morgan into approving. It would put him one up on the Medicis, the Sforzas, the builders of Mont St. Michel and Chartres, and far beyond the local grandees with their Fifth Avenue palaces all bonded with concrete.

Go right ahead, he told McKim. Confide your dreams to this Croesus and they shall come true.

Morgan bought every piece of property on the Thirty-sixth Street block between his home at the Madison Avenue corner and the home of another famous architect, Cass Canfield, at the Park Avenue corner. Then he swept them clean of buildings and told McKim to put the library on the vacant lot that resulted.

The construction began about 1900. It had to include refresher courses in the 2,500-year-old construction methods, for modern-day stoneworkers would have to be taught to leave their trowels and concrete floats at home. But Morgan was unhurried. The building was completed, a jewel in white marble and archaic construction, and hung with Ghirlandaios, della Robbias, and other treasures, by the end of 1906. It was finished just in time to provide Pierpont Morgan with a setting of truly anachronistic magnificence during the Panic of 1907, when he set to work to patch up another outworn remnant that was exhibiting alarming symptoms of decay—the country's banking system.

Morgan's climb to magnificence erupted in another direction, very much more trivial and unimportant than the building of monuments, the acquisition of property, and the collections of the prize works of all civilizations. He had throughout his life displayed a playfulness that is at odds with the ferocity that stares out of his portraits.

Once, back in his early twenties, he had exhibited this impulsiveness in an incident witnessed by a young female friend of the family who later described it to Satterlee. Pierpont Morgan had caught the train at Garrison, the Hudson Valley town where he had been vacationing. He joined the girl, Cordelia Babcock, and her mother, but then excused himself to step down to the station platform to talk to some acquaintance he saw there. The train began to move and Mrs. Babcock called out, "Pierpont, aren't you going to New York?"

"Yes, indeed," he responded, but instead of running for the steps at either end of the car, he grabbed the sill and hauled himself head first through the window at the side of the alarmed Babcock family.

"Pierpont, why did you do that," asked Cordelia's mother.

"Oh, by the time the car steps would have got to where I was standing, the train would have been going too fast for me to get on," he explained matter-of-factly.

Again, much later, he displayed this same fondness for the reckless, the foolhardy grand gesture. But this time he was sixty-two years old. He had steamed out in the *Corsair* for its customary meeting with the liner bringing members of the Morgan family home from Europe in September. The liner was the *Oceanic* and aboard were Mrs. Morgan, her daughters, and Satterlee, who observed the drama that was to be enacted.

The quarantine officer had just left the *Oceanic* via a ladder hanging down the ship's side when the *Corsair* launch, carrying Morgan, drew up. He impulsively reached for the ladder just as the launch dropped down into the trough of a wave, leaving him dangling above the boat. In the swell, it would take many minutes of delicate maneuvering to bring the launch back into position to pick him off the ladder and it would also take time for the *Oceanic* crew to rig up some kind of rescue apparatus.

Ahead was the equivalent of a climb to the top of a six-story building; moreover a climb up a ship's ladder is a good deal more strenuous than any staircase ascent. Satterlee, who was looking over the rail, later reported:

> In Mr. Morgan's mouth was a cigar. He looked up once, then fixed his straw hat more firmly on his head, and with his teeth clenched on the cigar, he started up. . . . I knew that he was sixty-two years old, weighed about 210 pounds, and never took any exercise, and it seemed to me that his progress was very slow, although he never stopped and came steadily upward. Some of those on the yacht turned away, too frightened to watch him. The time was long enough for the sporting element on the decks of *Oceanic* to make bets as to whether he would ever reach the rail. If he should fail, there was very little chance of doing anything for him in that tideway. When his face, dripping with perspiration, appeared over the rail, and he got where he could throw his leg over it, he waved aside all the outstretched hands and asked, "Where is Mrs. Morgan?" and without pausing followed the steward down to her cabin. It really was a very dangerous exploit for a man of his age who had not climbed in years.

Morgan agreed with the family judgment about the rashness of the act and promised never to do it again.

9

THE PARADE STARTS:
U.S. STEEL

IERPONT Morgan's pomp, glitter, and ostentation flowered with the closing of the nineties, but all in the more frivolous activities of his life. He attended Episcopal conventions, making the occasions of the great triennial gatherings of that church stages to swagger on, excuses for rolling out sumptuous private railroad accommodations (owned, not by him, but by his railroads) and occasions for ostentatious gifts of expensively bound catechisms and scriptures. An irreverent group of Episcopal clergymen, probably made up of those not invited to share the railroad palaces or the gifts, dubbed him Pierpontifex Maximus.

He lived up to the antique title. Among his splendors was the staging, practically singlehandedly, of the America's Cup races, taking on the lion's portion of the syndicate shares to build the expensive yachts that won. All the while his collections of lordly bric-a-brac grew apace.

But such monarchical extravagance and openhandedness had had no place in business. During these years, Charles Henry Coster prevailed, with his wringer tactics of paying fifty cents, twenty-five cents, sometimes even nothing, for a dollar's worth of securities in a troubled railroad. But Coster died on the threshold of the new century. He developed a cough on Wednesday, March 7, 1900, packed up his ever-present homework, and headed for his home at 37 East Thirty-seventh Street. Pneumonia developed and the following Tuesday he died.

Morgan hurried home from Palm Beach to act as pallbearer, along with Stetson, Bacon, and other partners or associates, for the burial at Greenwood Cemetery. It was almost as though they also were burying the tight-fisted methods that Coster had developed, because from that point on splendor and magnificence were to mark Morgan as a businessman. No longer would he mark down prices; in fact, he swung violently in the opposite direction. Morgan was to become as adept at pumping water into properties as ever Dan'l Drew had been, even in his days as a drover.

He would start at the top, with a corporation whose capitalization would be measured, not in dozens of millions as the other amalgamations of the time were being valued, but in billion-dollar terms. The total amount of stock and bond certificates that Morgan had printed up to buy the components to create the United States Steel Corporation bore the face value of $1,402,-000,000.

More than half, or about $726,846,000, of the value engraved at the corners represented pure water, according to the United States Bureau of Corporations. In other words, the market value of the component companies making up this hydraulic wonder was estimated by the bureau at no more than $676 million. That meant that the component corporations would have to more than double earnings in the year beginning March 3, 1901, when U.S. Steel was formed, in order to stay even with the year before.

Morgan had to struggle with this great bag of water, which was like some soggy animal on a Mardi Gras float. He had plenty of help in getting the great hydrocephalic object to stand on its own waterlogged feet. There were thirty men in Andrew Carnegie's part of it alone whom the old Scotsman boasted of making millionaires overnight. They were all set to man the ropes and guy wires. And there were more corporations than Carnegie's involved, all of whose executives were quite ready to pitch in.

Of course, Morgan himself wasn't idle. Right outside his doorway, at the New York Stock Exchange across the street, the champion in this kind of corporate drum beating and flim-flammery, James R. Keene, was hard at work. Bearded and elegant, Keene was a daring manipulator on Wall Street, although he preferred the racetrack and sporting crowd at his hotel, first the Hoffman House near Madison Square, and later the Waldorf-Astoria. But it was for his talents as a bold rigger of market values, a creator of interest in stocks where none existed, that he was chosen by Morgan for the U.S. Steel operation.

He was badly needed. Despite his ability at "making a market"—in other words, flushing the public out into the open to take stock off the hands of Morgan and the others—the outrageously overcapitalized corporation was in deep trouble two years after it was put together. The four-dollar dividend on the common was suspended and the stock, which had been floated in the choppy waters whipped up by Keene at about 44, had dropped to 10. The preferred, 94 at the launching, had sunk to 50, but still paid its seven-dollar dividend.

The great hydraulic operation had been reversed; the value of the common and preferred together at the 1903 values came to $230 million, a drop from par of $638 million, which is fairly close to the estimate of fluid content made by the water diviners at the Federal Bureau of Corporations. To critics who found fault with Morgan's part in the water-letting, the financier said: "I was the company's midwife, not its wet nurse."

He might have been its embalmer, too. The prospect wouldn't have weighed too heavily with him. He did act in just that role in another scheme of his at the time, the International Mercantile Marine. Morgan imagined that this half-baked plot to form a trust of nearly all the shipping companies in the world would be foolproof for anyone in his commanding position in railroad transportation. He and the other bankers involved in the steel experiment offered prices so high, especially for such British lines as White Star and Leyland, that, one authority noted, the sellers were able to strike "an exceptionally good bargain, which it is probable the purchasers will soon find out."

They did, to such a degree that they let the former owners "buy back control of the whole unwieldy combination for one-third or one-fourth of the price paid originally by the Americans."

U.S. Steel might have gone the way of International Mercantile Marine, except for an industrial development that Morgan had no faith in. At this point, the automobile industry was practically nonexistent. Autos were playthings of the rich, like the *Corsair*. In fact, they were little more than the hated outward signs of a social cleavage dividing the haves from the have-nots, in part because the rich had the habit of running around the country in their expensively decorated horseless carriages, often over the bodies of the offspring of the poor.

But a change could be detected by those occupying the vantage points of industrial leadership. Since the Civil War, machinery—horse-drawn, it is true—had revolutionized agriculture.

In the early years of the nineteenth century, farming methods and tools, here and abroad, were little different from what they had been in Biblical times. In the first half of the century, the basic conceptions of the reaper, or harvester, which cut and bound grain, the thresher, the mower, and the binder had been worked out, and the Civil War intensified the process of putting them to work.

A great combination of the reaper and thresher was ready in the 1880s. It was drawn by twenty or thirty horses, surely a development whose lines were converging with the perfection of the internal combustion engine begun by Gottlieb Daimler in Germany at the end of that decade. However, tinkerers like Daimler were not the real founders of the automobile industry; that title can more properly be traced back before the Civil War to Simeon North and Eli Whitney, two riflemakers working a few miles from each other in Connecticut who independently established the principles of standardization and interchangeability of parts that were to be more important to automobiles as Americans produced them than any other development.

Whitney's cotton gin "made inevitable the Civil War" and a host of social and economic changes; his concept of interchangeability was to free manufacturers from dependence on skilled labor and was to lead to transformations more cataclysmic. Whitney's and North's processes were in operation in the early 1800s. Samuel Colt, another artificer of weapons, brought them to further perfection on the eve of the Civil War.

The processes languished while the demand grew for movable equipment that required the power of thirty horses. The natural and explosive fusion of these stages of industrial development and demand needed the touch of a genius, which was not to come from Pierpont Morgan or, for that matter, from any investment banker. It was to come from Henry Ford. In 1907, the year that Morgan's partner, insurance man George F. Perkins, turned down the opportunity to finance the organization of General Motors and laughed at William C. Durant's prediction of half a million cars a year, Ford, after more than a decade of pondering where to put the Whitney-North-Colt ideas to work, set up his automobile assembly line and turned out ten thousand cars, each a fulfillment of Eli Whitney's dream that they be "as much like each other as the successive impressions of a copperplate engraving."

Durant's goal was passed almost before Perkins had the chance to go back and tell the boss how he had put down that whipper-snapper. A decade later, the industry produced 1.5 million vehicles; in terms of value of product, it had become one of the three billion-dollar industries in the country. The other two were steel and food production.

The railroad industry, which the organizers of U.S. Steel had been counting on as the elixir to change their watered stock into gold, was about as big as it ever would be and was preparing to head downhill. Morgan's favorite transportation systems ultimately would be wrecked by an offshoot of the motorcar industry, the truck. But the silver lining on this cloud was the fact that the production of motor vehicles would transmute much of U.S. Steel's water into gold and the steel industry would go on growing because of it.

Morgan's stumbling vision of the future importance of the auto industry and its threat to his railroads has been called "an excusable oversight at the time." Whether oversights of such magnitude and economic importance by one who constitutes himself an all-knowing agent for the placement of wealth here and abroad can ever be truly excused is debatable. But questions of excuses, explanations, apologies, and the like aside, the stance Morgan took toward the automobile industry was symptomatic of the finance capitalism he helped produce and make so dominant.

Of course, he knew nothing of automobiles. He knew nothing of railroads, either, other than that they would get him to the Episcopal Triennial conventions on time and in comfort. And he knew nothing of barbed wire, although U.S. Steel owed its origin to that humble product, nor of bridge building, although that was a considerable part of the success of the Carnegie works.

It is worth noting that no excuses are needed for a more primitive type of capitalist, Henry Ford, who, as a fabricator and artificer, early saw that mass production made possible by the old riflemakers' methods held unlimited promise. He had, as a young man, first considered putting these processes to work in the making of watches. He would give the mass of workingmen either an inexpensive watch or an inexpensive car. It didn't make much difference to him. The end product wasn't the important thing. He had his eyes on industrial processes. Under the circumstances, it was lucky for Morgan and Big Steel that he was flexible enough to adapt his ideas to the automobile industry rather than watchmaking, which uses little of everything, especially steel.

The idea of a steel trust, an organization that would practically monopolize the industry and whose enormous capitalization could be effectively deposited in the hands of a few, did not originate with Morgan and, in fact, for a long time he refused to take any part in promoting it. His resistance was overcome largely because of his dislike of two men, Andrew Carnegie and John W. Gates, and his desire to get them out of American business.

There are indications that Carnegie became more obstreperous than usual in his freewheeling competitiveness in order to prod Morgan into buying him out; he may have planned the whole thing simply as a profitable way to retire. With Gates, the real prime mover, there was no planning. He was designed from the cradle to have attributes that Morgan would hate and would want to eliminate. Gates was an incorrigible gambler and early won the nickname "Bet-a-Million" because of the ease with which that expression would spring to his lips.

His business was located in Chicago, but from the mid-1890s, when he had amassed sufficient wealth, he spent most of his time at the Waldorf and, from 1897 on, when it was enlarged and hyphenated into the Waldorf-Astoria, at the new splendor on Fifth Avenue between Thirty-third and Thirty-fourth Streets. The new hotel, the site of the Bradley Martin ball and other of those upper-crust entertainments that were blooming into magnificence with the emergence of new millionaires, was the center of social activities for both the newer and older orders of society.

For the most part, the kind of money that checked into Charles C. Boldt's new structure wasn't in search of purely innocent entertainment. At 33 West Thirty-third, just down from one of the Waldorf-Astoria's side entrances, was a place known as "The House of the Bronze Doors," where the Fifth Avenue ambience gave way to the steamier atmosphere of the city's tenderloin on Sixth. A gambling resort much beloved of "Bet-a-million" Gates, it boasted a half-million-dollar interior decoration job, including the bronze doors, carried out by Stanford White. Not as fashionable or as exclusive as the better known palace of chance run by Richard Canfield further uptown at 5 East Forty-fourth Street, it had the advantage for high rollers like Gates of having no house limit. At Canfield's, in contrast, stakes could not be raised freely without getting the proprietor's special permission and he often refused.

But there were games even closer to home for Gates—in fact, right in the Astor family dining room, whose walls and furnishings had been preserved intact from the original Astor mansion and installed in the older part of the hotel. There the play would often start with a thousand-dollar limit, which could grow to double that at a time when the lower figure was more than twice the average annual wage for the fortunate, employed part of the working class. Losses and winnings for an evening often totaled $75,000 to $150,000.

Gates was one of a dozen tycoons who took part in a baccarat game at the hotel that ranks as the biggest ever held there, and possibly in any other gambling center. Baccarat is a complicated and fast game in which the banker plays what amounts to a hand of blackjack against two tables of players. When the game ended around five in the morning, and the chips were cashed in, they were found to total a million dollars.

But Gates didn't need the formality of a gaming room. Once, at the close of a day of poker-playing in his suite with a number of his Chicago associates, Gates and the group put aside the cards and flopped wearily into easy chairs. A rain came up. Gates, enthralled at the progression of drops down the window at his side, brightened. "Say, John," he called out to one of the tired players. "See them two raindrops? I'll bet that fellow on this side reaches the bottom before that one over there." Ten dollars was the first stake, but the ante jumped quickly to $100 for the duration of the storm.

Gambling wasn't the only Gates habit that Morgan frowned on. He was possessed of enough bad habits to make enemies anywhere; in this department he seemed almost to be a reincarnation of old Uncle Dan'l Drew or the flamboyant Fisk. He slurped and guzzled his way noisily through the heroic meals of the time, a large napkin wrapped around his neck. The napkin was a necessity because he usually used only one table implement, the knife.

One English hotel owner, faced with a visit from the then Prince of Wales, who had reserved the table next to the one habitually occupied by Gates, felt called upon to trick the American into taking another. H.R.H. shared one variety of fastidiousness with the rest of his subjects, who at the time popularized a line that went something like this: "If there's nothing else to do, let's drop into the Carlton and listen to the Americans eating soup." The trick of removing Gates far from the Prince cost the Carlton his patronage, a loss it seemed to survive. To complete the picture, Gates spat constantly, on or off expensive carpeting and inlaid parquetry and into or out of spittoons.

Gates had had his start in the beginnings of homesteading in the West, when the settlers were initiating a new kind of farming on the vast spreads that had formerly been frontier. They needed a new kind of fencing, something cheaper and more easily placed than the picketing or post-and-railing of eastern farms, and Gates had just what they needed. He was the chief salesman for Isaac L. Ellwood, the inventor of barbed wire. By the time Gates—and Ellwood—had found the Waldorf-Astoria, the latter had become his former boss's superior in one of the earlier steel combination flimflams that succeeded the barbed wire company. Ellwood was fond of puncturing the dignity of the portly Gates. "I went into steel . . . ," Gates would say, beginning one of his frequent reminiscences.

"John, how do you spell that?" Ellwood would interrupt.

The theft thus punningly alluded to apparently took place with the combination in 1892 of five small wire companies in Illinois into the Consolidated Steel & Wire Company. This deal brought Gates up to a level of financial potency that permitted him to take on a $20,000-a-year suite in the hotel.

Within a few years, Gates had parlayed this holding, along with seven steel mills, into one of the greatest trusts of the time, the American Steel and Wire Company of Illinois, by methods that he claimed were not even clear to him. At least they weren't clear when he was under oath.

In a suit in New York Supreme Court some years later, Gates went through an elaborate presentation on the witness stand about the formation of American Steel & Wire and its replacement, after the addition of seven more plants, by the American Steel & Wire Co. of New Jersey, a state whose complaisancy was winning for it the title of "Mother of Trusts." Gates was testifying grandly of capitalizations going from $24 million to $90 million when some cross-examiner who had been busy with pencil and foolscap at the opposing counsel table pointed out that $26 million was unaccounted for and asked where it went. Gates blandly replied that he did not know. The response fell far short of "It has gone where the woodbine twineth," Fisk's comeback of nearly three decades earlier. The rhetoric of insolence, like everything else, was in sharp decline.

If Gates preferred to forget how the water gathered in this instance, there is other testimony that sheds some light on the methods he employed. A Wall Street broker said that an officer of Chase National Bank told him around this time:

> I was up at the Waldorf last night and met John W. Gates with some of his crowd. While we were talking about the market, Gates said to someone who had just joined the party: "We're going to close our steel mills tomorrow morning."
>
> Somebody said, "What's the matter? Business falling off?"
>
> Gates answered, "No, we're short of the stock."
>
> . . . The next day announcement was made that the mills had closed down. The stock broke from in the 60s to the 40s and 30s.

Gates doubled his money on the way down, then reopened the mills, bought back the stock, and made more on the way up.

Thus Gates, whose table manners could be oppressive to innocent bystanders, developed business methods that could disrupt in widening circles, from the stock market outsiders to the wire spoolers and drawers in what was then one of the greatest of American corporations.

In 1898, the year the New Jersey combine was formed, Gates was in his early forties and ambitious to lock up the entire steel industry. McKinley, the so-called "advance agent of prosperity," was in the White House. Despite some feeling before his election that he would have the strength of character to be independent of his kingmaker, Hanna, the President's actions, if not his intentions, all combined to create for the business interests that Hanna had marshaled for the campaign the moldy kind of growth in which a Gates could flourish.

Early in the campaign of 1896, McKinley had impressed John Hay, who visited the Canton headquarters. Hay, law clerk, private secretary, and later biographer of Lincoln, and the very model of the diplomat in previous and subsequent service to his country, told about it in a letter to his friend Henry Adams. After a two-hour visit with the "Majah," as Hay transcribed McKinley's Civil War military rank, the caller wrote to Adams: "I was more struck than ever with his mask. It is a genuine Italian ecclesiastical face of the fifteenth century. And there are idiots who think Mark Hanna will run him!"

Hanna may not have lived up to the expectations of the idiots; he really didn't have to. It turned out that McKinley thought like Hanna, anyway. McKinleyism, as Adams said, was a "system of combinations, consolidations, trusts, realized at home, and realizable abroad." The expansive medium for commerce wasn't solely dependent, of course, on a reincarnated quattrocentro prelate offering his oily orisons and benedictions over the formations of capital and treaties of commercial penetration. There were tangible developments in the world, and in America in particular, that provided a nourishing climate for business.

Chief of them was the increase in the world's gold supply, through discoveries in the Transvaal and the Klondike. There had been a moderate rise in the world's store of gold during the half dozen years ending in 1896, a factor that, infinitely more than the futile efforts of Morgan and Belmont, aided Cleveland in building up the reserve and relieved McKinley of the need for any repetition of the bond sales. From 1892 to 1896, annual production doubled and then took off on a near-exponential climb, tripling the earlier figure by the close of the decade.

This inflationary move increased prices, particularly in countries like the United States whose output was predominantly agricultural. The effect, as noted, was to multiply the value of the American wheat crop during the failure of the India harvest and help defeat Bryan in 1896.

But the following year, drought in France, rains in Russia, and storms in the Danube Valley reduced the whole European output by nearly one-third, while favorable weather here smiled on a crop that had been increased anyway because of price rises. These may seem like unimportant country matters to be affecting such events as the amalgamating of steel companies, yet even now, when agriculture no longer dominates the economy, such movements still would be crucial, except that science has loosened the dependence of the food-producer on the whimsicalities of nature.

In any event, in 1897 America's good luck and Europe's bad brought to the former a tide of gold amounting to $120 million in the balance of trade. It was "the first natural movement of the kind in this direction since the autumn of 1891," said Noyes. By mid-1898, McKinley could count a total of $245 million in the government's reserve coffers. Thus insured against any return of the trouble that had haunted Cleveland and Harrison before him, he was able to make good two years later on the gold standard assurances that had brought him to the White House.

Both by natural forces and by the permissive stance of the administration, an overly placental environment was created for the capitalist. Sustained by its nourishing juices, combinations multiplied monstrously. In this uterine world, water, of course, played a great part. The financial community was big with trusts.

In the first three months of 1898 new industrial companies whose capitalization came to at least $1,586 million were formed. The remainder of the year brought the total to more than double that figure, or $3,593 million, of which $2,354 million was common stock, according to the New York *Financial Chronicle*'s year-end railway and industrial supplements. The common stock was all water, passed out to underwriters and trickled out by them to their distributors as a bonus for selling the fixed debt and preferred stock issues.

In the preceding decades the investing public had taken an interest only in railway stocks, but now it began to extend its attention to industrials. There was some reason for this, inasmuch as stock shares had demonstrated that they had some value, intangible in many cases, often only the equivalent of a glass of water. But many of them had begun to resume dividends that had been dropped in the panic. In this bracing business climate, William Jennings Bryan tried again in 1900 to win the presidency, but with almost all of his issues now academic, the country returned a plurality about a third greater than the monumental landslide of 1896 for McKinley.

Meanwhile, Gates had been busy trying to manufacture enough stock to satisfy the public demand. In his search for corporate containers to be filled with more water, he combined with two kindred spirits, William H. Moore, a former Utica, New York, jurist, and Daniel G. Reid. They made up an unholy trio whose very repulsiveness helped trigger the events that finally resulted in the formation of United States Steel.

Reid, a hanger-on of Moore's in Chicago, was a heavy drinker well known in that city for one notable habit. He regularly ap-

peared, every few months, at one of the Windy City's two principal pleasure palaces, spending a week each time regaling himself
and friends with wine, women, and song and then, marking his
departure in his own novel way, he would take an axe to the
piano in the parlor and any other part of the furnishings he could
reach. It was all part of his outing. The proprietor would have
the damage assayed and later would present his bill, which Reid
would promptly pay.

Reid was a supernumerary figure in the group headed by
Moore, as was Moore's brother, James Hobart Moore. Reid's
idiosyncrasies on the social scene were not matched by the other
members of the group, but in the financial sphere of Chicago, all
were equally capable wreckers.

They had organized the Diamond Match Company in 1896.
Their wild financial maneuverings in that trust-building venture
had forced the closing of the Chicago Stock Exchange for three
months and ended with their bankruptcy and that of many
others. But they recovered rapidly, set up the National Biscuit
Company, and then went on to form the American Tin Plate
trust, the American Steel Hoop trust, and the National Steel
companies. A congressional report later scored their operations.
"The Moore concerns were the most heavily overcapitalized and
suffered from a distinctly speculative backing," noted the report
in a day when overcapitalization was almost a national fad.

The distinction that the three were to achieve consisted in the
fact that their methods were abominable even to Andrew Carnegie, a man who could close his eyes, or repair to a bonny castle
in Scotland, when lesser abominations appeared. Carnegie had
shown his superiority to the rough business practices necessary to
running his company, so painful to an aspiring philosopher and
adviser to emperors, kings, and presidents, by hiding out abroad
during the murderous strike at his Homestead, Pennsylvania,
plant in 1892. The strike was really a small-scale war, complete
with atrocities on both sides, but Carnegie left everything to his
associate, Henry Clay Frick, who was thus not troubled in his
union-busting activities by the Scotsman's assertions of the rights
of man, especially the laboring man.

Frick thought the worker had no rights and spoke and acted
accordingly. His attack on unions at the Carnegie works took the
form of a policy of importing Slavic workers, a poor and
wretched addition to the melting pot who could be easily ex-

ploited. They were used to break strikes and weaken the union. The policy was profitable, but also nearly fatal. A Slav, the Latvian Alexander Berkman, an anarchist who was welcomed by Frick as an employment agent for eastern Europeans capable of fitting into that scheme, shot, knifed, and nearly killed him on July 22, 1892, during the strike.

It was Frick who brought the unholy trio of Gates, Moore, and Reid to Carnegie. Carnegie, who once was characterized by an Ohio congressman as "the arch-sneak of this age," engaged in a prodigious amount of double-dealing, much of it at the expense of his junior, Frick. He praised Frick privately for his handling of the Homestead strike while writing to Whitelaw Reid and others of how much better things would have been handled had he been on the scene. Understandably enough, Frick, who was generally a forthright man, found it necessary to develop a high degree of subterfuge in his dealings with his benefactor, Carnegie.

In falling in with the proposal of Gates and his associates, Frick's first step was to win over an old Carnegie associate, Henry Phipps, Jr. Through these dealings he concealed the identity of the Gates group from his chief, thereby setting in motion a train of events that led to his ouster as chairman of Carnegie Steel, estranged him completely from Carnegie, put a great strain on the latter's relations with his boyhood friend Phipps, generated a couple of expensive lawsuits, and set at each other's throats as bloodthirsty a crew of industrial pirates as ever had been seen.

The final act involved Carnegie's agreement at long last to retire and the creation of the United States Steel Corp. It should properly have been brought to life in the Caribbean, amid the swaying palms and sinister zephyrs of Tobago Island, where so many similar deals had been carried out by other buccaneers four hundred years earlier. For these men were freebooters, preying even on each other.

For example, one of the events leading up to the final break between Frick and Carnegie was a tricky maneuver by which Frick sought to enrich himself minutely in a small profiteering land sale at the expense of the company of which he was chairman. And Carnegie, when he uncovered the attempted fraud, endeavored to buy Frick's interest in Carnegie Steel and freeze him out completely on the basis of a truly Costerlike valuation in which the price was to be set on the "book" value of the stock of more than a decade earlier, before Frick had vastly increased it by union-busting and other piratical activities.

The break between them even led to the kind of near-murderous assault that characterized the breaks between previously amiable buccaneers in the Caribbean. The last meeting between the two took place at Frick's Pittsburgh office on January 8, 1900. The conversation brought Frick to a "towering rage" in which he shouted at Carnegie, "For years I have been convinced that there is not an honest bone in your body. Now I know that you are a goddamned thief. We will have a judge and jury of Allegheny County decide what you are to pay me."

Then the sixty-five-year-old Carnegie dashed out of the office into the hall, chased by Frick. Both men could be described as giants in the financial sense, but physically they were on the side of the pygmies. "The little white-haired devil" Andrew Carnegie was giving away fourteen years to his subordinate, but still managed to outdistance him to the stenographers and typists pool on his route to safety. The shock and possibly also the amusement set off there stopped Frick in his headlong rush to do bodily harm to his former boss and Carnegie made good his escape.

Whether Frick intended to murder or merely maim Carnegie has never been made clear. Such are the reticences permitted to roughnecks whose net worth is counted in the hundreds of millions. In any case, Frick's later action has all the characteristics of a badly conscience-stricken man seeking out a confessor. That afternoon, he called on a friend of his and Carnegie's, John Walker. "John, I lost my temper this morning," he said, in the opening of his *mea culpa*.

"Oh, well," Walker responded ,"I knew you had one."

Frick then told him of the morning's events, Frick and Carnegie both died in the same year, 1919, but neither ever spoke to the other in the interim.

Before this final break, Carnegie had become aware that Frick and Phipps, were going to help him retire by selling his interest to the Moore-Gates group. He also had some suspicions that they were going to enrich themselves by splitting $5 million worth of stock out of the reorganized company. Carnegie was to get $200 million, but when he discovered the swirl of plots and counterplots, he did some plotting of his own, insisting that the group post 1 percent of that sum as an option to run for a limited time. He later scaled down the amount to $1,180,000, of which $1 million was supplied by the Moore group, the rest by Frick and Phipps.

Before option time had run, there was a short-lived panic in the New York money market sufficient to cause Moore, Gates, and the rest to default. The forfeit, including the contributions of his partners, went to the canny Scots steelmaker.

At the Stanley Committee investigation of U.S. Steel in 1912, Carnegie was asked if he hadn't promised a refund to Frick and Phipps. Moore was the key to his decision to mousetrap the combination, he answered, and the self-help being indulged in by Frick and Phipps confirmed him in his intention to foreclose. "Chicago adventurers," he called the Moore brothers, and he told the committee that "I never knew Judge Moore was a party to the proposal. If I had known it, I would not have given them an option upon any account." Further, he said, "If Mr. Frick and Mr. Phipps entered into a contract with the Moore Brothers by which they assumed to make $5 million apiece [sic], and never told me about it, why, I do not think I am obligated to pay them anything now."

The same point was made more directly to visitors to his castle at Skibo in Scotland, which he had refurbished at a cost of $1 million in the year of the Moore-Frick-Phipps proposal. "The whole thing is just a nice little present from Mr. Frick," he told them.

After the collapse of the proposal Carnegie grew very busy. Morgan apologists diligently claim that the great steel amalgamation was originated by Morgan, with a little prodding from Gates' protégé, Elbert H. Gary, a onetime Illinois county judge, and from Carnegie's new heir-apparent, Charles M. Schwab.

However, Carnegie's actions up to the time he unloaded the Carnegie Steel operation—then the biggest steel producer in the country—on Morgan bear all the earmarks of the kind of "salting" indulged in by a country store owner who is interested in making a quick sale to a reluctant prospect. One of the chief saline indicators was the corporate report of the doubling of profits by Carnegie Steel from the $21 million of 1899, a fabulous enough figure, to the incredible amount of $40 million in 1900. Other devices in the campaign to stampede Pierpont Morgan included a return by Carnegie to his former ruthlessness in setting up industries and transportation companies in competition with well-watered organizations in which Morgan was interested.

Carnegie well knew the hydraulic nature of these properties.

In a letter to an associate he once paid tribute to the ability of one of the Morgan ventures to make profits despite its inability to make steel products: "I think Federal [Steel Company] the greatest concern the world ever saw for manufacturing stock certificates—we are not in it—but they will fail sadly in Steel," he noted.

Besides aqueous stock certificates, the major product of Federal Steel was Elbert H. Gary, a watery creature himself in his slippery crawling after power. He had been a prominent businessman and lawyer in his birthplace, Wheaton, Illinois, organizing a bank there and serving as mayor following a four-year term as county judge. Yet in 1891, at the age of forty-five, he attached himself to Gates, nine years his junior, when the flamboyant Chicagoan was organizing Consolidated Steel & Wire.

He was rewarded for his faithful servitude by being made chairman of Federal Steel on its organization in 1898, but, like most parasites, he had had to put up with much from the arrogant Gates in the meantime. Gates used often to allow his underling to play cards with him at the Astor dining room, but during one of the two-thousand-dollar-a-chip sessions he loudly barred the judge. To a waiter Gary had sent in to announce his arrival, Gates said: "Tell Judge Gary the game is going to be so high, it will be over his head." Gary slipped quietly away to try his luck another time.

For all his servility, Gary seemed strangely able to charm others into adopting an equally obsequious attitude toward him. For example, the woman with the muck rake, Ida Tarbell, who had turned out such a devastating indictment of the Rockefellers and Standard Oil, was completely undone by him and obliged him with a fawning biography.

At about this time, Morgan was developing an appetite for boneless bootlickers of the Gary sort and was captivated by the judge, despite his relationship with the hated Gates. Thus Gary was in a position to be instrumental in infecting Morgan with the idea of a steel combination. He himself got the idea from Gates, who had outlined the monumental scheme during a meeting at the Waldorf Men's Café.

Gary was aided by a powerful ally from the Carnegie camp, Charles M. Schwab, also of the courtier class, but of a bluffer and somehow more appealing type than the former judge. Schwab gave a speech at the University Club in Morgan's presence on

December 12, 1900. It has been called "magnificent," "splendid," and the like by people who, at the same time, don't bother quoting any parts of it. It seems to have been a twenty-minute dissertation on the obvious, for its theme was that the control of America's steelmaking capacity concentrated in the hands of a few would be a wonderful thing for those few indeed.

Schwab, only thirty-eight at the time, and a man who had begun in his teens as a dollar-a-day stake driver with Carnegie and was now the chosen successor to the perfidious Frick, was a compelling personality, a considerable improvement as a human being over both his superior and the man he supplanted. But it is not likely that his chalk talk played any great part in changing Morgan from his former indifference to the steel combination. Morgan's shift largely was the product of a desire for "the elimination of disturbing personalities" and the desire to pick his own nondisturbing "right men to run the great corporation."

Carnegie had become very disturbing indeed, and Gates was not one of the right sort. Gary was though. It is amusing that Gary, in his years of hanging around Gates, had tried to be as much of a high-living gambler as Gates and probably owed his success with Morgan to the fact that Gates frequently refused to permit him to take his place at the Astor dining room or the House with the Bronze Doors.

As Carnegie, to Morgan's increasing annoyance, continued to develop his disturbing personality, he did not neglect to reevaluate his holdings in accordance with the then-popular science of hydrodynamics. Like Rockefeller, Carnegie had always refinanced internally, through the surpluses of earnings, and for the same reason. Both had wanted as little as possible to do with banks, except those they could control, and nothing whatever to do with the money market on Wall Street dominated by Pierpont Morgan.

It had been a good system, except that the insulation from the stock market had meant that there was now no current evaluation of his holdings. He set about to rectify that. He had set a price of $157,950,000 for the group represented by Frick and Phipps. Sometime later he had inflated that to $250 million when John D. Rockefeller displayed some interest in buying him out, whereupon the oil magnate dropped out of the running.

Carnegie then proceeded to step up the personality disturbances to the point where there was a flurry of panic in Wall

Street. Besides a direct challenge to Morgan's National Tube, which consisted of letting contracts for $12 million for a competing plant on Lake Erie, he also increased pressure on John W. Gates' American Steel & Wire Company by announcing that a gigantic rod-mill would be built in Pittsburgh.

For good measure, he lashed out with a threat to Rockefeller, ordering the construction of a large fleet of ore-carrying steamships to operate on the Great Lakes in opposition to the Rockefeller interests there. And he frightened the life out of the Pennsylvania Railroad by fanning out a corps of surveyors to lay out a railroad route from Pittsburgh to the Atlantic. To further agitate the Pennsylvania, he announced plans for an ore-carrying railroad from Lake Erie to Pittsburgh. When Charlie Schwab breezed into town to give his little talk at the University Club, all of Wall Street was united in trying to get Morgan to buy out the troublemakers.

This was the Carnegie of thirty years earlier all over again, a man who had known every dirty street-fighting trick of the corporate world. Some part of it was surely bluff. But where the old Carnegie would have had to look for financial backing and thus have left himself vulnerable to pressure from the banking world, this new version had all his defenses in order as he mounted his attack. He was making more than a quarter of all the Bessemer-process steel being produced in the country and half of its structural steel and armor plate. He had no debts, was on the way to profits of $40 million in 1900, which, even allowing for a little salt, was more than adequate to make good on all his threats.

He had also, under the benevolent laws of New Jersey, "the Mother of Trusts," put together a new company in March 1900, with a capitalization more in tune with the times. The Carnegie Company, combining the old Carnegie Steel and the Frick Coke companies, was capitalized at $320 million, half in stock and half in 5 percent first mortgage bonds. Carnegie's interest was set at $174,526,000. He carried out his own watering operation to bring it more into line with the high-flown concepts of Gates, the Moores, and Gary.

With a little prodding from Gates, Morgan was ready to meet with Schwab and the way was opened to do business with Carnegie. A month after the University Club talk, Pierpont Morgan agreed to Carnegie's demand for the equivalent of $447 million for a complex that the steelmaker had valued at about half that figure just a few months earlier and at about 70 percent of that figure in the window-dressing reorganization less than a year before.

The sum consisted of $303,450,000 in 5 percent bonds and stock with a market value of about $144 million. Carnegie, as his price for withdrawing from the business arena, took most of the bonds—about $226 million worth—together with a mortgage on the entire steel corporation, a detail that nearly put him back in possession of it when the great waterlogged monstrosity began to leak a few years later.

He left the rest of his associates to grapple with the common stock and the remainder of the bonds. One of them, Henry Phipps, a lifelong friend who was never at ease with Carnegie's competitive methods, was on his sickbed when word came that his share would come to about $43 million and he would be out of the business at last. Choked with emotion, he murmured: "Ain't Andy wonderful!"

Carnegie's insistence on bonds was said to have indicated his conviction that the stock in the new $1.403 billion combine, which also took in Gary's Federal Steel and Gates' American Steel & Wire, consisted of "not merely water but air." However, like most people who have driven a hard bargain, there came a time when he began to feel uneasy, to suspect that, given the mechanism of hydraulic finance, with its gauges, piping, and valves all under steady manipulation, he could have demanded even more.

A year or two later, Morgan and Carnegie met aboard ship. Carnegie said, "I made one mistake, Pierpont, when I sold out to you."

Morgan, who was said invariably to wince when the elfin Scot addressed him by the name he reserved only to associates who were close and nearly equal, asked, "What was that?"

"I should have asked you for a hundred million more than I did."

Then came the nightmare response hard-driving bargainers dread.

"Well," said Morgan, "you would have got it if you had."

The formation of Big Steel called forth the usual amount of burbling that the movement of capital in excess of about one hundred dollars always seems to evoke. Typical was the comment of John Brisben Walker, editor of the *Cosmopolitan* magazine, then a publication on the fringes of the muckraking group that circulated widely at ten cents a copy. In the April 1 issue, he wrote:

> The world, on the 3d day of March, 1901, ceased to be ruled by . . . so-called statesmen. True, there were marionettes still figuring in Congress and as kings. But they were in place simply to carry out the orders of the world's real rulers—those who control the concentrated portion of the money supply.

On the whole, Walker thought it was for the best.

Some Americans, aware of the relationships between big business and the legislatures during the preceding thirty-five years, might have thought Walker was slow in grasping post-Civil War realities, so that his conclusions were roughly equivalent to a 1901 headline announcing the victory at Appomattox. It often seemed that special training would be necessary to bring most lawmakers up to marionette status.

In contrast to Walker's acquiescent spirit, overseas publications saw Armageddon and Doomsday. The London *Chronicle* declared: "It is little less than a menace to the commerce of the civilized world. It sets the seal to the triumph of the millionaire." The Berlin *Kreuz Zeitung* saw the extension of "morganization" overseas, with eventual consolidation of the continental iron and steel industries under American control. It would be "the last humiliation of Europe by the young giant of the West," the paper declared.

Despite all the planning and the profligate meeting of the most inflated values in order to ensure the completeness of the steel trust, there was one important element that had been left out— the vital Lake Superior iron ore and shipping companies owned by John D. Rockefeller. This point was raised by the spanking new chairman of U.S. Steel, Judge Gary. He was answered with a growl by Morgan that they "had all they could attend to." Gary kept on though, finally convincing Morgan that the Rockefeller interests would provide the sort of menace to U.S. Steel that must be avoided. But Morgan insisted he wouldn't think of going to Rockefeller.

"Why?" Gary asked.

"I don't like him," said Morgan.

"Mr. Morgan," said the judge, "when a business proposition of so great importance to the Steel Corporation is involved, would you let a personal prejudice interfere with its success?"

Morgan grudgingly agreed to see Rockefeller and buy the ore lands and shipping lines from him, but it was an arduous task. Rockefeller, two years younger than Morgan, was in retirement and in the process of beginning that vast public relations expenditure to change his image as the most hated man of American business. It is a process continuing to this day, long after his death.

Like Carnegie, he appreciated the corner Morgan was in and was ready to squeeze him somewhat. First, he refused to journey to 23 Wall Street and insisted that the older man make the journey to the Pocantico Hills preserve inhabited by himself and his family. But he also set down an advance condition that business would not be discussed.

The sixty-four-year-old Morgan consented to the mild humiliation by traveling to the upstate lair of Rockefeller, who continually interrupted him whenever he tried to bring up the subject of mines and ships. Rockefeller told him to get in touch with his son, John D., Jr., on such matters.

The younger man, twenty-seven at the time, duly and respectfully reported at Morgan's office, whereupon the somewhat put-upon financier got down to business, in his brusque fashion.

"I understand that your father wants to sell his Minnesota ore properties and has authorized you to act for him. How much do you want for them?"

Young John D. was as maddeningly elusive as his father.

"It is true I am authorized to speak for my father in such matters," he replied, "but I have not been informed that he wishes to sell these properties. In fact I am sure he does not." The young man hastened home to report to his proud parent and ask if he had done the right thing.

"Time alone," the older man answered, "can tell whether you acted wisely or not. But I may say to you, my son, that had I been in your place I should have done precisely what you did."

After the humility of standing hat in hand at Pocantico Hills, to be told by a younger man who had already retired that he must confine himself to nonbusiness matters, being then told to await the call of a mere stripling, and then having the whole thing

Pierpont Morgan and Friends

come to naught, Morgan was understandably vexed. He turned then to Carnegie's former chief aide, Henry Clay Frick, who had successfully defied Carnegie's attempt to force him to surrender his stock holdings for about $5 million. As a result of the translation of Carnegie Steel into a part of U.S. steel, he held stock and bonds in the combination worth about $60 million at this point.

Morgan got along well with Frick, who didn't try any unwanted familiarities comparable to Carnegie's flippant use of "Pierpont." Frick, in fact, was highly dignified, even repellent—so much so that even the bumptious Gates, who essayed a few "Pierponts" in public and referred to the great man in private as "Livernose," was extremely respectful before Frick, the only man Gates ever addressed as "Mister."

Physically compact and with a white Van Dyke-trimmed moustache and beard, Frick closely resembled his diminutive former boss. One writer fantasied him "seated on a Renaissance throne under a baldacchino and holding in his little hand a copy of the *Saturday Evening Post.*" The compelling picture is probably a libel. There's no evidence that Frick ever subscribed to the *Post,* a magazine of some vigor at the time. His tastes ran more to things like *Self Control: Its Kinship and Majesty,* according to one biographer, but he did build a $5.4 million Renaissance palace at One East Seventieth Street, where squatting beneath silk and gold canopies must have been the most readily performable act.

Morgan ordered Gary to prepare a valuation of the Lake Superior properties and sent Frick to Rockefeller with it as an "outside figure" he was prepared to pay. The wily oil magnate promptly turned Frick around, from Morgan's agent to his own, a feat that apparently no one has found particularly reprehensible. When Frick had explained the proposition, including the outside figure given by Gary, Rockefeller interrupted their walk around the Pocantico Hills vastness.

"I do frankly object . . . to a prospective purchaser arbitrarily fixing an 'outside figure' and I cannot deal on such a basis. That seems too much like an ultimatum," he said. "Now I want to ask you a question. Nobody is more familiar with those properties than you are. Do you or do you not agree with me that the price these gentlemen propose to pay is less by several millions than their true value?"

Frick agreed that Rockefeller was right—if payment was to be made in stock of the watery giant and considering what other stockholders had gotten in that flexible medium.

"I thought that would be your answer," said Rockefeller. "Now, Mr. Frick, I will tell you what I will do. I want only a just and fair price. You know what this is, certainly better than those gentlemen do, and quite likely than I do. I know your judgment is good and I believe you to be a square man. I am willing, Mr. Frick, to put my interests in these properties in your hands."

Frick was willing too, in spite of the fact that the interests Rockefeller was turning over to him would be in direct conflict with those of Morgan. In any case, he jacked up Gary's price by $5 million and was told by the judge: "That is a prohibitive proposition."

This time Morgan acted as Gary's persuader. "Judge Gary, in a business proposition as great as this would you let a matter of $5 million stand in the way of success?"

"But I told you, Mr. Morgan, that mine was the outside."

"Well, put it this way: would you let these properties go?"

"No."

"Well, write out an acceptance."

Thus the Rockefeller menace was neutralized. The full price, including the $5 million added by the double agent Frick, has always been something of a mystery, even to Rockefeller.

"It was either forty millions or sixty millions—I have forgotten which, but I think it was forty," the oil tycoon later told Thomas Hanly, a reporter for the *Herald,* whose mouth gaped open at the airiness of his estimate. Its value to the steel company was well understood by Rockefeller, who was asked by an interviewer years afterward what would have happened if the sale had not been made.

"Then, in my opinion," he replied slowly, "the United States Steel Corporation could not have survived the stress of its formative period."

And stress was what it had plenty of. One of the ballyhooers of the enterprise wrote breathlessly of the capitalization and the implications it held. "Consequently, when Morgan coolly announced that his new company would pay interest or dividends upon nearly fourteen hundred millions, the whole international world of finance was speechless with surprise."

Frick was a part of that world. Whether he or any other part of it was speechless matters little. But his actions show definitely that he was not so much in a state of surprise as in one of total disbelief.

For as the great carnival figure was being readied, he knew exactly what the presence of one of the men on the guy wires, James R. Keene, portended. Keene, then in his late fifties, was hired on for $1 million in cash and a percentage of the syndicate profits, which amounted to $40 million or 160 percent of the $25 million put up by the members.

Keene, whose proper sphere was the turf, either among his string of racehorses or at the betting window, was a legendary figure on Wall Street. A notable picture of him in action is given by Richard D. Wyckoff, a considerable operator himself and once associated with him. He wore a pointed gray beard, "a horsy expression, and the sharpest pair of eyes I have ever seen," said Wyckoff.

> His air was that of a Southern gentleman, and his handshake was limp. The front of his head was somewhat bald and the gray of his hair like the gray of his beard. His voice was pitched high. . . .
>
> I used to stand facing him, my left elbow on his ticker while talking to him. He would hold the tape in his left hand and his eye-glasses in his right as he listened to me, then on went the glasses astride his nose as he bent close to the tape in a scrutiny of the length that had passed meanwhile. I might be talking at the moment his eye began to pick up the tape again, but until he finished he was a person in a trance. . . .
>
> His deliberation process would include trips up and down the office, during which his hands would be closed and his forearms slightly upraised as though he were swinging himself along by their weight. He seemed to walk invariably the same number of steps, each exactly measured. He appeared to absorb a certain length of tape, and to devote to its analysis a specified interval measured by paces. Sometimes he returned to the ribbon for another examination, followed by more pacing. Often he would step to the telephone. . . . Then back to the tape, more examination, more pacing, and a completion of the mental digestion. All this may have required two or three minutes, but then

he could always answer my question as if nothing had happened between and it had been just propounded.

Keene was hired to "make a market" for U.S. Steel. In other words, he was to create so much technical interest in the stock that the more timid parts of the Street would enter the trading. It was also hoped he would stimulate totally new business out in the sticks. He did that part of his work so well that he almost ended his usefulness for future manipulating.

Up to this time Wall Street had been confined to the wealthy few, which meant New Yorkers and residents of other big cities. But on January 7, 1901, the Big Board experienced its first two-million-share day, a great milestone. And then, less than four months later, following the issuance of the stock in the great steel undertaking, the exchange celebrated its first three-million-share day! A quarter of that activity was in U.S. Steel common and preferred. Keene's buying and selling, largely sham transactions involving shares that weren't actually moving anywhere but were merely being traded back and forth in "wash sales" by pool brokers, plus the other hoopla launched in connection with the amalgamation, was bringing in people out in the hinterlands who had never thought of buying a share of stock before. In itself, opening up this new market for shares was a good thing, but Keene's exertions were increasing activity to the point where, he confessed later, he was no longer able to dominate trading.

The outburst of speculation during this period "was something rarely paralleled in the history of speculative manias," observed the New York *Post*'s Alexander Dana Noyes, who likened it to aberrant outbreaks like the South Sea Bubble of 1720 and the railway craze of 1844. The public "caught the speculative fever; even in thrifty Western towns and New England country villages, the gossip of an evening was apt to concern itself with 'Steel.' . . . The newspapers were full of stories of hotel waiters, clerks in business offices, even doorkeepers and dressmakers, who had won considerable fortunes in their speculations." Activity became so tumultuous that in May, two months after the launching, the exchange was forced to the unprecedented step of closing down for an extra holiday.

The waiters, clerks, and dressmakers who were profiting did so by getting in and out, like small fry around sharks, while the process of distribution was going on. Those who were nimble and rested content when they were able to cash in for a profit were able to hang on to their modest gains; it was otherwise with those who were tempted back for bigger profits.

Frick, a man-eater among man-eaters, played his own game in the distribution of all the stocks and bonds generated by Morgan. At the changeover to United States Steel, he came away with $15 million worth of the 5 percent bonds so prized by Andrew Carnegie, $23,767,940 in preferred paying 7 percent, and $21,832,440 in common stock. Not bad at all for one who, three and four decades earlier, had been looked on by neighbors in western Pennsylvania as a slightly bewildered youth because of his obsessive pawning of everything owned by himself, his parents, and any other unwary relative in order to buy lands that were useless for farming because of coke outcroppings.

He may have been bewildered, but no more so than many other amiable boobies of the day who were putting their money into this, that, or the other worthless piece of land, stock, or hare-brained invention. But then, through no fault of Frick's, who had neither the chemical nor metallurgical training to have foreseen it, this coke that made the land so cheap turned out to be just the stuff that was needed to produce the steel of the time. When Carnegie discovered that Frick owned just about all the supply in that part of the state, he took him in as an associate. In the time that had lapsed since receiving his first reward for befuddlement, he had learned a lot as he watched his own holdings expand and shrink in the catapulting and plunging economy.

For nearly a year, to the beginning of 1902, the syndicate was still able to maintain the inflated value of steel fairly effectively. Frick, whose value in Morgan's estimation had been immeasurably increased in the Rockefeller dealing, was made a director of U.S. Steel and remained so to the end of his life. But that didn't mean that all his wealth was tied up in the company. He knew the values were unrealistic and he had misgivings about the management. Convinced that a decline in earnings was inevitable, he began to liquidate his holdings.

Selling on rebounds and keeping volume low, he was able to distribute, to some not-so-fortunate waiters and clerks and possibly even some of the man-eaters, too, his entire block of 218,324 shares of the common and all but 10,000 of his original 237,679 preferred. Like Carnegie, he felt safe only with the bonds.

He apparently got clear before the bottom was reached in

January 1904, when the common hit 8¾, the preferred about 50, and dividends were not being earned on either class of stock. Frick probably took some losses, strictly on paper, but he did his own analyzing and, in a metaphor borrowed from his pastime of collecting old masters for his Seventieth Street palazzo, concluded: "Railroads are the Rembrandts of investment." With the bulky wad of cash he had realized after the great shark barbecue, he was able to buy an average of $6 million par value of stock in each of seven roads and soon became the largest individual railway stockholder in the world.

The first sickening flop of Big Steel found him with almost unimpaired fortunes. Less informed insiders, as well as the employees of Morgan's greatest triumph, were not in such a fortunate position. Twenty-one thousand of them, more than 12 percent of the total force of 168,000, were dismissed from their jobs as drastic internal efforts were made to keep the monster on an even keel. The remainder had their annual wages chopped from $716 to $677, a cut of over 5 percent.

That wasn't all. Thousands of them had been inveigled into a "profit-sharing" plan, part of the syndicate's mechanism for unloading the preferred stock offered at 82¼ that had since come down to 50. "The 'profit-sharing' plan seemed to have resolved into a 'loss-sharing' plan devised by Wall Street promoters to unload their worthless shares upon their own working men," observed George Brinton McClellan Harvey, Frick's biographer and a man as typical of American literary big business as Frick and Morgan were of financial big business.

Writing in 1928, he had grown much more caustic about a Morgan venture than he would have dared to allow himself to be during the financier's life, when it had been his habit to touch the great Pierpont regularly for a subsidy to keep his magazine, *Harper's Monthly*, going. But by whatever tortuous path he came ultimately to the truth, he at least did come to it. And he did take note, if only briefly and long after the fact, of a consequence that should be, but seldom is, taken into account in any toting up of the supposedly brilliant achievement of launching the country's first billion-dollar business.

Frick's complete sellout of his United States Steel holdings constitutes a fitting epitaph for the formation of the billion-dollar trust, far more appropriate than the awed burblings of publicists of the time and since. But there is something more dangerous to this Morgan fad of overvaluation than the effect Harvey noted that it had on the holdings of the wealthy, the near-wealthy, and even the unfortunate employees who must get the sack when the great confection careens alarmingly in the ordinary ups and downs of business.

Such a great bag of wind and water as U.S. Steel was in 1901 is a powerful force for disequilibrium. Getting it into motion in the sunshine of the regular business parade was a frightening task for Morgan and the other promoters, a job of prodding and bolstering, of patching the leaky skin, of tugging and hauling on the guy ropes. But the awesome job of taking it through panic and depression can only be likened to skipping across Niagara Falls on a tight-wire, bearing the awful Mardi Gras concoction on one's back. The steel combination was helped eventually in righting itself by the long-term inflationary trend and, particularly, as noted, by a development that Morgan not only did not foresee, but actively discouraged—the emergence of the auto industry.

Thus its exact social cost in great panics, such as the one that occurred in 1907 and the more severe depression of 1932, is masked and difficult to measure with any accuracy. But it is obvious that an overvalued U.S. Steel, barely able to produce earnings and dividends on its inflated capitalization in good times, would be a potent disorganizer of the whole economy in bad ones. It would act as an out-of-whack gyroscopic stabilizer which, instead of countering the forces that cause a ship to pitch, roll, and yaw, would accentuate such conditions. It could wreck the ship; at the very least, it would make everyone a lot more seasick than usual. That seems to have been what happened.

THE

MORGAN DECADE

FOLLOWING the assembly of the parts that formed the world's first billion-dollar corporation, Pierpont Morgan needed a rest. On April 4 he left aboard the White Star liner *Teutonic* for Europe. He had been preceded only three weeks earlier by Andrew Carnegie, who was well-heeled for his fling. At the close of the negotiations for the Carnegie properties, Morgan had grandly consented to meet the little man whom he wanted out of business at any price in order to tell him: "Mr. Carnegie, I want to congratulate you on being the richest man in the world!"

There had been a slight hitch, though. Carnegie, like most of the other great souls in the upper levels of business, never forgot a slight, no matter how minor. He remembered that way back, sixteen years earlier, Morgan had held a conference aboard one of the *Corsairs* that dealt with the South Pennsylvania Railroad, in which he was vitally interested. Yet he had been excluded from the meeting.

So, when he got the invitation from Morgan he reminded the man who was raising the money to buy him out so handsomely that the distance from the Carnegie home at 5 West Fifty-first Street to Morgan's office at 23 Wall Street was the same as that from 23 Wall to 5 West Fifty-first. Morgan got the point and went to Carnegie's.

Both men gravitated to a favorite watering spot, Aix-les-Bains, in the mountain-and-lake country near the Italian border, 350 miles southeast of Paris. Carnegie had headed directly for the resort, though, and apparently was gone before Morgan arrived. The financier had made a leisurely tour, stopping first in London to pick up an odd acquisition or two—one of them was the magnificent Gainsborough painting of the Duchess of Devonshire—then on to Paris and to Aix.

At this point, the absolute pinnacle of his career, he had just celebrated his sixty-fourth birthday and was in full magnificence physically. There is a tendency to picture him after the manner of the caricaturists—portly and aging, the popular image of a Croesus of the financial world. This tendency is fortified by the fact that no portraits of him except in a seated position date from this time. Any views of him walking were taken later, in his seventies, when he began to get rumpled looking, and most are from 1912, when news photographers had their only clear shots of him shuffling only a few months before his death to take the witness stand in the Money Trust investigation in Washington.

In the year of the steel merger, at the age of sixty-four and carrying only 210 pounds on his large, six-foot frame, he would have cut quite a figure. His nose brought him into contact with healers and semi-quacks and was much more of a problem than it had been in his younger days, but then even that went with the large-featured handsomeness of his wide mouth, walrus moustache, and the arresting, shaggy-browed eyes of deep blue.

The object of his vacation journey, Aix, had been a source of regeneration as far back as the days of the Romans and before. The baths, or aquae, had been named successively for Domitian, the first Roman emperor to style himself "Lord and god," who reigned in the first century, and for Gratian, a weak and indolent fourth-century ruler of only the western part of the empire. This emperor of a puny domain comprising all of Spain, France, and Britain, who preferred hunting to governing, was slain less than fifty miles to the west, at Lyon.

Also at Aix was one of those visible reminders of antiquity that Morgan was fond of observing. It was an arch, thirty feet high, twenty-two feet wide, standing in the center of the town, before the Etablissement Thermal. It had been built by a prominent member of the Pompey family, a Morgan of the Roman Empire, in the third or fourth century.

Morgan's partisans liked to emphasize the health-giving attributes of Aix, although Morgan, it is conceded, never exercised and only used such quantities of the sulphurous waters as he was obliged to. Unmentioned by the family chronicler are the far livelier attractions of Aix. It was not the gathering place of rachitic invalids in wheelchairs awaiting their turn at a healing dip in the warm, vile-smelling waters. The lame, the halt, and the afflicted did not journey to Aix unless they were in the upper reaches of the economic hierarchy.

For most of the pleasures provided by the resort, a stout and lusty constitution was desirable. Aix was the capital of the more privileged part of the international set of the time, when even modest journeyings required vast reserves of leisure and capital. During the season, its gambling rooms, as well as its seclusion from the better-known newsgathering centers like Paris or New York, drew those who wanted to play at roulette, baccarat, and chemin-de-fer but didn't want it known they had such yearnings. And the footloose men of wealth in semi-hiding around the gaming tables were an irresistible lure for just about every *poule* who hoped to be *de luxe* anywhere in the pretty young world. According to Albert Lewis Crockett, the café society Boswell who managed to extend his *Herald* beat to this opulent spa:

> There [were found] . . . men, interviewed about serious things—matters of finance, legislation and politics—seeking, rather than avoiding, the snares of notorious adventuresses, and openly parading their willingness to sign blank checks for their experience. . . . Almost every woman walked trailing clouds of scandal. . . . Truly the place provided a great spectacle for the merely moral who had come in good faith to take the baths.

Wives and daughters of visiting American capitalists, he added, "sat about in chairs, staring open-mouthed at the 'goings on,' swished aside their skirts as decorative protagonists of vice swept by in the latest modes, and kept one protective or minatory eye upon husbands or fathers, who sat as monuments of virtue . . . secretly resolved that their next trip to Aix would be made 'without the women folks.' "

It was even said that some of the beautifully turned out women who flocked to the casinos and hotels of Aix had been "decked out by expensive Paris dressmakers and milliners, either in speculation that such investment would be repaid out of the women's earnings, or else that rich advertisement would be reaped from the display of model frocks and hats, the names of whose makers their wearers would gladly reveal upon the slightest manifestation of interest."

Morgan was apparently unencumbered with his "women folks" on this trip to Aix. Gossip had it that he was enjoying the company of one of the foremost beauties of the time, although the name has not been preserved. His son-in-law Satterlee, who doesn't carry discretion beyond all bounds, records that he "customarily took a congenial party with him."

In any event, his sabbatical, whether holy in the strictest sense or not, was to be cut short. For dark doings were under way back home. Perhaps they were taking place even as he stood in the southern sunlight, a superb and commanding figure, the all-highest of finance, arms linked with a befitting beauty, musing on all that remained of Lucius Pompeius Campanus before the fifteen-centuries-old arch celebrating his eminence.

For even as he revelled in his living predominance, back in the dark canyons of Wall Street a spidery figure was working to bring him down from his pinnacle. The shadowy operator was Edward Henry Harriman. The son of a minister who had been forced to supplement the meager benefice of Hempstead, Long Island, with a part-time job, Harriman, then fifty-three, had fought and scrabbled his way to his own sort of pinnacle. Operating mainly as a market speculator, he had risen to the point where he was able to reorganize the most ambitious of the country's railroads, the Union Pacific, and to win control of it only three years earlier. In 1901 he was to add the Southern Pacific, and his ambition for further railroad control was bounded, in fact, only by the Atlantic and Pacific oceans.

Like the other bane of Morgan's life, Carnegie, he was undersized. Morgan often referred to him contemptuously as "the little fellow." He was otherwise unfavored as well. In contrast with the generous proportions of Morgan's stature, his eyes, jaw, and larger-than-life nose, Harriman's small features gave him a mean and shifty look. He enhanced this effect with a pair of perfectly circular rimless glasses that gave him the expression of an animal caught in some sneaking misdeed. And he crowned all these negatives with a drooping mop of a moustache that obscured his mouth and always appeared to be soaking wet, as though whatever animal he was trying to represent spent most of its time under water, perhaps around old pilings.

But he was no one's fool and, if anything, his goals were grander even than Morgan's. He may have started merely as a market manipulator, but he became truly absorbed in railroads and in their operations. His aim was to make them fulfill their own technical promise, and to enrich himself, of course, whereas it was characteristic of Morgan's more specialized and narrow conception of investment banking that the technical considerations came far down the roster of imperatives. Morgan's chief aim was to rid the parts of the business world in which he was interested of the dislocations and uncertainties of competition.

But there was a more immediate reason for Morgan to dislike Harriman. The railroad man was one of the few mortals who counted to have ever bested him, and he did it with trickery that Morgan affected to despise but was equally ready to use himself.

Morgan had clashed with Harriman back in 1887, at a time when Morgan was wielding the power of his father's house tentatively and when the minister's son, then thirty-nine, was just beginning his climb to railroad dominance. When Morgan dipped his toe into the transportation waters outside his home state, he ran into a denizen of that medium wired for high voltage shock. Harriman, he learned, was a vicious Moray eel equipped with batteries.

As a director of the Illinois Central Railroad, Harriman was authorized by the stockholders to try to get control of a leased portion of that line, a road known as the Dubuque & Sioux City Railroad. The lease was expiring and, rather than renew at a higher rate, the Illinois Central powers decided to buy it for cash or stock. But Morgan headed a group that owned a majority of the road's stock and was holding out for a high price. To that end, Morgan secured proxies from his associates and others under their influence until he controlled more than twice the amount of stock that would be voted by the Harriman group.

Morgan thus looked forward to a crushing victory as the time came for the annual meeting to be held at Dubuque. But Harriman held the trump; at the meeting his lawyers noted that Iowa law did not permit voting by proxy, a legal detail that had escaped the notice of Morgan's attorneys.

Harriman installed a board favorable to the Illinois Central at the meeting while Morgan, in a move that recalled some of the Jay Gould-Jim Fisk shenanigans he had so deplored, held a rump session and elected his own slate. The matter went to court, where Harriman was upheld and the Morgan group had to settle on Harriman's terms.

"This incident made Pierpont very angry," Morgan's son-in-law blandly reports. It also led to a lifelong coolness between Morgan and Harriman that was to be broken only on the latter's death-bed, when the financier accepted an invitation to the railroad man's kingdom in Arden, New York.

Morgan attributed his animosity toward Harriman to the latter's use of niggling legal technicalities to win control of the Dubuque & Sioux City. Such courthouse tricks stirred his hatred —when other people were guilty of them. But he had no hesitation in adopting them for his own purposes. For instance, during the absorption of the West Shore competition into Vanderbilt's New York Central in 1885, a stockholder of the former line tried to block the transaction by obtaining a court injunction against sale of the West Shore to the Central. Morgan got around the injunction and the fatal delay court action would have meant by the legal dodge of having the sale made to himself; and he tried to repeat the same deceptive device to foil a legal process in the South Pennsylvania case, as we have seen. Morgan could conveniently relax his stern sense of fair play when it was to his benefit to do so.

The second clash between Morgan and Harriman came four-teen years after the first, when both had grown to share an unequaled dominance in the country's transportation industry. Harriman, together with the investment banking firm of Kuhn, Loeb & Co., controlled most of the West through the Union Pacific and Southern Pacific railroads; Morgan, who had become closely associated with James J. Hill in securing the Great Northern and Northern Pacific, was as dominant in the East and just under the Canadian border in the West.

Harriman had links in the eastern trunk lines, too; Kuhn, Loeb had largely displaced J. P. Morgan & Co. as the Pennsylvania's banker, but Morgan retained hold of the Central, the Erie, and the railroads of New England and the South. When these two rival potentates collided, the days of Jay Gould were reborn. Despite Morgan's sanctimonious claims to have purged Gould-style iniquities from American business and his often expressed contempt for those who had indulged in them, he was ready to commit the same sins himself when his own interests were involved.

It was another variation on the theme of Comstockery for everyone else; Maxine Elliott and the pleasures of Aix for Morgan. And just as Comstock hurt and humiliated those more innocent than his paymasters, so the rage of Morgan against Hill spread and threatened the entire country, wolves and sheep alike, with financial panic. It was partially responsible for a dislocation that would be called "slight" by Morgan's defenders even though it amounted to a total drop in production of nearly 5 percent, the termination of employment of a few tens of thousands of industrial workers, and the ruination of a few thousand speculators. All this interruption of productive activity was in the interest of the free play of capital and capitalists, a freedom supposedly justified, it should be noted, by the economic activity it created.

The key to the Morgan-Harriman clash was the relative isolation of the Hill railroads. Harriman had tried to join forces with Hill a few years earlier but was rebuffed. The only reason that he failed to retaliate was the peculiar weakness of the Great Northern and Northern Pacific. The Hill-Morgan lines lacked a link to the all-important Chicago terminal, with its outlets through the eastern trunks to the Atlantic ports and through the Illinois Central to the great Mississippi cities and the port at New Orleans. The missing linkage made for weak competition for Harriman, whose Illinois Central provided the Chicago connections to points east and south for his Union Pacific and Southern Pacific via the Dubuque and Sioux City line that he had wrested from Morgan back in 1887.

But when the burly, one-eyed Hill, who was as ruthless, as expansionary, and as good a railroader as Harriman, moved to buy the link that connected his lines to Chicago—the Chicago, Burlington & Quincy Railroad—Harriman realized he would be faced with a competitor who would then hold a very sharp knife at his throat. He first tried his bluff method of demanding representation in the Burlington management, but Hill would not even consider the proposition.

"Very well," Harriman said. "It is a hostile act and you must take the consequences." He then reacted with his customary audacity and wiliness, not against the Burlington, but against the great Northern Pacific line which was the repository for Hill's controlling shares!

He was aided in this scheme by a number of factors, including his own ability to move stealthily among the pilings of the financial waters, but above all by several considerations over which he had no control. They were thrown his way by that chance or fortune that favors the daring, and he knew how to take full advantage of them.

The first was the absence of Morgan, far off in the south of France, taking his ease and pleasure far from the sooty canyons of Wall Street in a resort that had served Caesars and first citizens of the Roman Empire. The second factor was avarice, the cardinal sin that all mankind is prone to, but particularly that portion that already possesses great wealth and cannot bear to pass up the chance of increasing it.

Such were the Morgan associates, who held from $35 million to $40 million worth of Northern Pacific stock as of April 1, 1901. This constituted a little over 25 percent of the $155 million worth outstanding and was sufficient to vest control in Morgan's hands in the lopsided world of publicly held corporations. Sufficiently wide distribution and dilution of stock can ensure control with even less, as Hill himself boldly and baldly admitted when he said, in connection with his other major holding, the Great Northern:

> I may say that I think I controlled the policy of the Great Northern Railway Company and its predecessor as fully as the policy of any railway ever was controlled in this country, and I never owned more than 10 or 12 percent. I never owned a majority of the stock, but I always had a following of good, loyal stockholders, and the men who were most active, covering about 33 or 35 millions out of 125 millions, practically formed the company. . . .

Hill did not carry his reflection out fully to the most important part of the equation by which a onetime backwoods general store clerk could grasp power beyond all his deserts. He left out of consideration the key element, the supine stockholder of the remaining 90 or 92 millions who was being victimized. The recollections of bank robbers are similarly lacking; their memoirs present the exciting doings of only two classes of protagonists, cops and robbers. Never is the reader of these memoirs reminded of the dull truism that he is the ultimate sap who is forced to support both factions.

In any case, such minority control is precarious, and the domination of Hill and Pierpont Morgan in Northern Pacific began to slip as Harriman enlisted the services of mankind's great acquisitive vice. The Morgan group had bought the Northern Pacific shares at prices that averaged about sixteen dollars during the preceding two or three years; it closed on April 1, presumably as Harriman began his foray, at ninety-six. The quantity and variety of hormones and other body fluids set loose in the avaricious by a sixfold increase in the price of a stock are frightening; and the Morgan partners and associates must have been awash in seas of endocrine fluids. The temptation was irresistible. By the first of May, they had sold from 25 to 35 percent of their holdings, leaving only $26 million in the portfolio.

The principal agent playing into the hands of Harriman was Robert Bacon, whom Morgan had left in charge when he departed for the playground of upper-crust Europe on April 4. Bacon illustrated perfectly the irritating inability of those in charge of the power structure, like Morgan, to choose subordinates. He was a Morgan partner for all the wrong reasons.

He was handsome, a *sine qua non* for leading men but otherwise a quality of little use. He had been outstanding on the football field, which meant that his triumphs had come quickly and relatively cheaply in the golden autumnal glow of Saturday afternoons and did not necessarily fit him for the week after week grittiness, far from the howls and cheers of the stadium, that was needed to hold great enterprises together. He was from the same New England stock as Pierpont Morgan, from among the Higginsons, the Lees, and the Washburnes, and, not least, he had gone to Harvard. Both conditions go far toward establishing a man's pedigree for serving as, say, a prospective dinner companion or even the more wearing companionship of a two-day hunting trip. But when it comes right down to it, they are little more than an assurance that their possessor will conform to accepted sanitary practices; they are not guarantees that he may not be a very great bore, or even a danger, such as one addicted to smoking in bed.

Morgan hadn't learned these elementals of character judgment, though, and took Bacon in as a partner and replacement for the truly able Coster. His weakness was to cost Pierpont Morgan a great deal of money and Bacon his partnership, plus other emoluments thought fit for a geneologically correct Harvard graduate, such as the directorship in the newly formed U.S. Steel.

For Bacon, whether intentionally or not, sold Morgan out. The truth of the matter is not the kind of thing the Morgan class likes to share with the public, the ultimate victims of the whole affair and the ones who in the last analysis have to pay the bill. For this reason, sources connected to any of the principals tend to slide by Bacon's role, implying that, at worst, he had been guilty only of a lapse of attentiveness as Harriman began his end run around the Burlington by buying Northern Pacific stock.

But it seems likely there was something more to it than a tired footballer simply letting the opposition gain a first down while he husbanded his strength for more vigorous defense. The indications are that he played a more active part, possibly even passing the ball into the hands of the archenemy, Harriman.

The Morgan method in a holding like Northern Pacific was not to distribute the stock into the hands of his associates for them to sell or hold as the spirit of avarice moved them. On the contrary, such holdings would be under the control of Morgan's firm, either by an informal "gentleman's agreement" or by the formal trust or holding company device.

That handsome Bob Bacon, who was Morgan's surrogate at this time, could be simply inattentive over the period of more than a month during which the Morgan group put from 90,000 to 140,000 shares into the hands of Harriman could be believed only by someone with the same background as Bacon. The likelihood is that he had to approve the transfer of every one of those shares. Some of the stock even came from the Northern Pacific treasury, a transfer that would almost certainly have had to have had the signature of the man in charge of J. P. Morgan & Co.

In any case, Bacon did nothing while the control of the railroad was passing to Harriman. The infinitely abler James J. Hill was the first to note what was happening while he was far off from Wall Street, inspecting his lines in Seattle. In the meager reports of local papers and from his own informants, Hill learned of the activity in the stock of the railroad that he had wrested from Henry Villard with the aid of Morgan. The price in those first few days of May had gone up to 115.

Hill ordered a clear track for himself on his Great Northern and sped on a special train to St. Paul, from where he proceeded on to New York, arriving on Friday, May 3. He further displayed his shrewdness by not bothering to call on the ornamental and temporary head of J. P. Morgan & Co. Instead, he followed where his suspicion led and ended up in the offices of Jacob H.

Schiff, head of Kuhn, Loeb & Co., Harriman's investment banker.

Schiff, who had once been a director of Hill's Great Northern and who made it a practice to be amiable, not to say obsequious, to all factions in a dispute, admitted he was doing much of the buying and it was for the Union Pacific.

"But," said Hill, "you can't get control. The Great Northern, Morgan, and my friends were recently holding $35 million or $40 million of the Northern Pacific stock, and so far as I know none of it has been sold." Schiff did not enlighten him, but told him that the action was in retaliation for Hill's refusal to permit Harriman representation on the Burlington board.

Hill then went on to 23 Wall Street, where a look at the stock transfer records presumably disabused him of any doubts as to the enemy's success. He and Bacon conferred the next day, Saturday, May 4, and wired Morgan at Aix when the market closed at noon.

Morgan gave this account of his reaction later:

> Somebody must have sold. I knew where certain stocks were and I figured it up. I feel bound in all honor, when I reorganize a property and am morally responsible for its management, to protect it, and I generally do protect it; so I made up my mind that it would be desirable to buy 150,000 shares of stock. . . .

Morgan's buy order, duly forwarded to his agents in New York, followed by a day a similar decision by Harriman and the two titans of finance were off on the mighty struggle to corner Northern Pacific stock. The battle would culminate in the incredible rise of the stock to 1,000 in the following week and the sale of 78,000 more shares of it than actually existed by "shorts" who were operating on promises to deliver at lower prices.

Schiff went immediately to Harriman that Friday after Hill had visited him and reported the conversation. He told Harriman that he now possessed "about 370,000 shares of the common stock and about 420,000 of the preferred." Much was made in financial accounts of the time of the fact that Harriman, while owning a clear majority of the preferred, lacked about 30,000 or 40,000 shares of a majority of the common and therefore had no clear control. However, this is just part of the mythology of corporate finance.

Harriman, it can be seen, had more than the Morgan group had owned on April 1 and that group had clearly controlled the Northern Pacific. Indeed, the fractionalization of ownership and the distribution of the fractions widely had developed precisely in response to the desire for control of people like Harriman and Morgan who did not otherwise possess the financial means to accomplish it.

An example of the system in full flower is provided by the purchase of the Burlington, the act that set off the whole Northern Securities corner. Earlier in 1901, Harriman had tried to buy shares from the estimated 15,000 small holders whose holdings averaged 68 shares worth eighty dollars each. He found himself blocked in attempts to locate them and buy directly from this pool of 1,020,000 shares whose total value came to over $80 million. Harriman backed off, but the stock had more than doubled in the meantime, to 180, when Hill and Morgan drove for control of the road.

In the wonderful naïveté of financial writing, Hill's biographer, James Gilpin Pyle, says: "Messrs. Hill and Morgan preferred to deal directly and openly with the authorized officers of the road, not indirectly and covertly upon the market (as Harriman had)." The deal that they made with the controllers of the road, rather than with the vast number of owners whose shares were listed on the market, was the payment of close to a quarter billion dollars for 1,075,772 shares, or two hundred dollars a share, twenty dollars more than the small holders were willing to take.

How Harriman's method of buying in the free market at prices set by that market can be metragrabolized into an "indirect and covert" operation while the under-the-counter deal at a premium not being offered to the true owners can be described as the "direct and open" Hill-Morgan deal is a secret known only to authorized biographers. At any rate, their action in paying an inflated valuation of 180 plus a premium of 11 percent for less than a clear majority of stock is a revealing example of how control is one thing while the possession of money enough to own is totally different—and totally unnecessary. To Hill and Morgan and their world, it was just one of the tricks of the trade.

But there are exceptions to this. While the true owners are somnolent and content, easily tricked by late proxy statements, annual meetings in inaccessible places, and other advanced devices worked up by management, control can rest in a single large percentage of stock and great influence can be brought to bear by those with only fractions. But Harriman, on that Saturday morning after Schiff's visit, was uneasy.

His state of mind was only partly due to financial causes. He was in that mood of many generals about to start a battle, who would feel infinitely more sure of themselves if they had 11.3 men for every one the enemy had. In addition he was ill, with the debilitating agonies of a condition that would later be diagnosed as appendicitis, an ailment of considerably greater terror then than now. He was convinced that he had control, yet he gave way to his anxieties as he recounted later:

> I made up my mind that we would have a majority of the common shares, and on that morning [May 4], I called up Heinsheimer [a junior partner at Kuhn, Loeb] and gave him an order to buy 40,000 shares of Northern Pacific common for my account. He said: "All right"; and as dealings for that day in Northern Pacific common shares continued to be very heavy, I felt that, come what might, I had control of Northern Pacific, common stock and all.

But he hadn't. Through one of those chance occurrences that can upset even the plots of titans, the order was never executed. On Monday, May 6, Harriman called Heinsheimer to ask why he had gotten no confirmation. "He told me that before giving out the order he had to reach Schiff, who was at the synagogue. Schiff instructed him not to execute the order and said that he [Schiff] would be responsible," Harriman recalled.

The pious Schiff had more faith in their plan than Harriman had. Actually he was right, but Harriman entered the fray with Morgan on that Monday morning anyway, with the two of them bidding the stock up and up. Morgan had once more called on James R. Keene to help him. On Monday, Northern Pacific rose to 127½, on Tuesday to 143¼, on Wednesday to 180. By this time the two warring factions were out of it, the Morgan group having achieved its objective and Harriman withdrawing.

This outcome resulted because charging into the middle of the battle came the Wall Street breed known as the shorts, responding to some deep conditioned reflex. Every previous roaring bull market in one stock of this sort had been due to manipulation by individuals or pools in search of great profits. It was thus possible for the short seller to intervene, borrow stock that belonged to someone else, and then replace it when the pool had withdrawn and the stock had fallen. The short interest in Northern Pacific, as noted, totaled 78,000 shares ultimately, and it was likely that some of the 143,000 shares that were all that Keene and others were able to buy for the Morgan group were thus encumbered. In other words, they were not deliverable because they did not exist.

This Northern Pacific bull market was different from the previous rises the shorts had enjoyed. It was carried on by two factions that wanted the actual stock and the control that went with it and cared nothing for profit or loss. There would be no withdrawing by either side. Thus the shorts were squeezed by demands for delivery of their shares and the stock soared astronomically as they sought to replace their borrowed shares.

On Thursday, Northern Pacific stock for immediate delivery for cash opened at 190 and within the first few hours went to a high of $1,000. The panic, with its short covering, had produced an anomaly in Northern Pacific shares. Alone of all stocks on the New York Stock Exchange list, it was being quoted as two classes of stock: one for normal transactions for payment or delivery a few days later, the other for immediate transfer for cash on the barrelhead.

The two contenders were at an impasse. Either had enough for control if it weren't for his rival. At this point the two arrogant powers, hitherto absorbed totally in their respective private concerns, had the opportunity to look at and reflect on what their struggle for the control of a small link in the country's transportation system had unleashed.

One of the immediate effects they were able to deal with and relieve. This was the disastrous dive of every other stock on the list. While Northern Pacific was enjoying its rampant bull market, other stocks were in the hands of the bears. Declines of 50 percent and more took place in some of the soundest shares. Traders were selling everything in order to get in on the supposed windfall of the Morgan-Harriman clash. Whatever money was available was being loaned for that purpose.

Although their partisans would argue for years as to who had won, Morgan and Harriman and their close cronies realized they had touched off a blaze that could send up in flames everything that made up their respective empires. A series of meetings was held by representatives of the two factions, where the parties arranged a settlement of the bloody war.

In the outcome, Harriman was clearly the victor. He was recognized as part of the "community of interest" that Morgan maintained in the country's railroads. This term was defined later by Morgan during the litigation that followed. Asked what the theory behind it was, Morgan replied: "that a certain number of men owning property should do what they like with it. . . ."

In the new arrangement, Morgan, still vacationing in Europe, had to make the considerable concession of taking into partnership a man he hated. Harriman, in his turn, won the assurance that the Great Northern, the Northern Pacific, and the Burlington would not act unilaterally to undercut him, and that the Burlington would not penalize his lines for transshipments to Chicago. It was all he could ask, and except for a brief return of the old railroad warfare days in the penetration of Oregon by Hill and Harriman, all was well with the western railroads.

With the truce under way, Morgan's associates were able to give closer attention to the immediate problems that afflicted the markets on that May 9. For that purpose, both factions agreed to lend stock to the shorts at 150, a move that immediately brought the price of Northern Pacific down. The Morgan group also organized a syndicate of banks to provide $20 million to the money-starved market, which helped rekindle trading in other issues.

These moves brought a measure of stability to the financial markets, but there was a longer term consequence, one that might be said to be still moving toward its resolution. For out of this clash of two self-willed men came the public realization that Morgan and Harriman were like two backwoods brawlers in some mining town saloon whose flailing efforts to gouge each other's eyes out or to plant some disabling kick might easily bring down the whole ramshackle structure of the building that served as their arena or even the entire jerrybuilt town.

For the private battle had spread beyond Wall Street. Morgan was able to provide instant relief of a sort, but he was unable to halt the frightened withdrawal of capital by London, Paris, and other European centers. A "foreign credit balance" of $200 million had been reposed in domestic securities a year earlier; in mid-1901, just after the Northern Pacific battle, it was estimated that

that had all been recalled and a foreign debt of equal size had been run up by financial institutions in the United States. That debt was being recalled during the autumn of the year, at harvest time when the need for capital to finance what was a poor harvest anyway became most acute. As Noyes remarked:

> The reaction from the excesses of 1901 continued during the two ensuing years; for although speculation again grew rampant in 1902, with resumption of promoters' activities and stock-jobbing exploits, the signs of public abstention and over-strained credit were visible throughout the year.

That was all evident enough to the public in the consequent distress and hardship that followed a fight between selfish rivals. But another event was to occur that would immeasurably help to focus the attention of everyone on the outsize effects that could follow a thoughtless action on the part of men of the Morgan class.

Sometime during the summer a man named Leon Czolgosz, engaging a tailor friend in small talk on a subject they both apparently found congenial, said he had decided he would kill a priest.

"Why kill a priest?" the tailor asked. "There are so many priests; they are like flies—a hundred will come to his funeral."

The thought struck home with Czolgosz. He changed his mind and went to Buffalo, New York, to the city's newly opened Pan American Exposition, where he fatally shot President McKinley. The result of Czolgosz' loss of animus toward priests was to put Theodore Roosevelt into the White House. One of Morgan's class, Mark Hanna, ruefully described the outcome: "I told William McKinley it was a mistake to nominate that wild man at Philadelphia. I asked him if he realized what would happen if he should die. Now look, that damned cowboy is President of the United States!"

In opposing Roosevelt's nomination at the Philadelphia convention the previous year, the Ohio industrialist, now a United States senator, had used even stronger language: "Everybody's gone crazy! What's the matter with all of you? . . . Don't any of you realize there's only one life between that madman and the Presidency?"

Roosevelt, as one who brought a concept of power to the presidency, became a larger than life figure to both supporters and opponents. He was a piddling ameliorist, a contemptible "reformer," to those who thought the system he gave his attention to was full of contradictions and ought to be swept away. To those at the opposite end of the philosophical scale, financiers and industrialists like Morgan who would brook no interference, he was a wild-eyed radical, a "damned cowboy," a madman who should be checked.

One thing all were clear on, though. He measured the temper of his time with uncanny accuracy, seized on those issues that the majority of the public agreed or could be taught to agree were worth battling about, and clearly established for all time the fact that the office of the presidency, the executive function of the government, was the superior of shopkeepers, pickle-makers, sundries manufacturers, and bond salesmen like Morgan. His lesson has not always been clear to his successors, but the text has been there for people like Woodrow Wilson and Franklin Delano Roosevelt to read when they wanted to. The judgment of Henry Adams smacks of eulogy, but there is little in it to be quarreled with: "Roosevelt . . . showed the singular primitive quality that belongs to ultimate matter—the quality that mediaeval theology assigned to God—he was pure act." To turn around an expression Roosevelt himself popularized, every day was seen in terms of Armageddon and there was no question to him that his shield and buckler were being bloodied in the service of the Lord.

He was full of inconsistencies, of course. He was great; he settled world conflicts. But he was petty; he got into arguments with nature writers so that one day a poor writer of outdoor trash for boys awoke to find the President of one of the world's major powers pelting him with eight-inch shells of literary criticism. But even in his pettiness there was a certain style that stands out in a day when a successor of his can demean himself by commenting on a sordid, sorry, and most insignificant murder trial and allow himself a slip of the tongue that prejudged the guilt of a defendant. Roosevelt was a conservationist, yet he shot elephants. It's true that there were more elephants then, but that is a poor justification. He could invite a great black man, Booker T. Washington, to lunch, and name a black to the post of collector of the port of Charleston, of all places; yet he could explain both actions away in an unbecoming manner.

And he could wage war against "the malefactors of great

wealth"—a term he coined virtually right under the terrible shaggy brows of J. Pierpont Morgan—and yet see nothing wrong in being put in a position of trying to squeeze a campaign contribution from the same malefactor. His character was complicated, filled with crosscurrents, inconsistencies, contradictions, so that judgment of him will always be hedged with reservation. Yet there must be general agreement that he met and discharged the great duties of his office with verve, gusto, vitality—with, in the last analysis, life; qualities that had not been evident in the country's Chief Executive for years.

Theodore Roosevelt began with reassurances of the continuity of his administration with that of his predecessor. Lulled by this, Morgan and Harriman continued with their work of parceling out the territories of the West among each other, binding the Northern Pacific, the Great Northern, and the Burlington into a new super-package, a trust along the old lines that was called the Northern Securities Company. Capitalized at a watery $400 million, and with Harriman's participation secured as in the preceding arrangement, it came into being in New Jersey on November 13, one day after Bob Bacon was for all practical purposes cut loose from all significant connection with Morgan.

He still retained various directorships, on the Northern Securities board, for instance, where he was seated along with Daniel W. Lamont, Cleveland's factotum and an acquaintance from the gold contract days seven years earlier; and he was to figure in the negotiations to end the coal strike in 1902. Other than that, though, he was to move on to a new phase of his career, the harmless posturing in the full-dress uniform of a State Department appointee and the more resplendent plumage of aide-de-camp to various Allied generals in the First World War.

Northern Securities was a trust pure and simple, the divvying up of territory among a small group that had set up the edifice for one simple reason—because it neutralized all powers of the actual owners of its components and substituted tight control by those who had contributed little or nothing in the way of capital. It was a violation of the Sherman Act of 1890, but the legal forces working for Morgan and Harriman knew that the act had never been enforced against corporations.

The man now in the White House, though not always reassuring to big business, seemed to present no threat. Only three days before the formation of the trust he had addressed Congress in words that both menaced and then drew back. The financiers figured it was all for effect and probably agreed with the assessment by Finley Peter Dunne's Mr. Dooley:

> "Th' trusts," says he [Roosevelt], "are heejous monsthers built up by th' inlightened intherprise iv th' men that have done so much to advance progress in our beloved counthry," he says. "On wan hand I wud stamp thim undher fut; on th' other hand not so fast. . . ."

There was another reason for Morgan to be reassured. A few years after the half-hearted preparation and passage of the Sherman Act, President Cleveland tried to give it meaning by ordering dissolution proceedings against the American Sugar Refining Company for its monopoly of sugar manufacture. In 1895 the Supreme Court handed down a farcical decision that effectively nullified what little force the act had: a monopoly of manufacture, the judges solemnly declared, was not a monopoly of commerce and therefore not illegal.

The collection of judicial luminaries that had rendered that decision included an old friend of Morgan's, Justice Rufus W. Peckham, who had been so helpful back in the fight over the Albany & Susquehanna with Jay Gould and his judge, Barnard, and George Shiras of Pennsylvania, who had given him short-lived satisfaction on one occasion. Shiras had distinguished himself in the celebrated flipflop by which the Court a half-dozen years earlier had outlawed the Cleveland administration's income tax law. He had been the one who had flipped, having favored the law in April, when the Court divided equally on the question, and wholly shifted his philosophical outlook a month later following rehearing, casting the pivotal vote in the five to four decision against the tax. This same crew still occupied places in the highest court in the land, so there was little reason for fear in the Morgan-Harriman camp.

But they had misread Roosevelt. His message to Congress had not been intended as an "on-the-other-hand" straddling of issues. Moreover, they had misread his character, a blend of mature doggedness and determination together with the kind of childlike slyness that made him choose a startlingly direct method: he would go back to the same Court and make them come up with the decision he wanted.

The earlier decision "had, with seeming definiteness, settled that the National Government had not the power" to control big business, he noted in his autobiography. He added, with a touch of the triumph of a child besting his elders: "This decision I caused to be annulled by the court that had rendered it; and the present power of the National Government to deal effectively with the trusts is due solely to the success of the Administration in securing this reversal of its former decision by the Supreme Court."

He was to be foiled of complete triumph over the entire bench by the death of two of the judges before the final decision. To replace one of them, Roosevelt named Oliver Wendell Holmes, who turned out to be one of four dissenters in the minority against the government. For a brief time, Roosevelt was brought to the point of considering half seriously whether he ought not dismantle the whole court because of this perfidy of Holmes's.

The hoop that Roosevelt chose for the Supreme Court to jump through in reversing its earlier stand was the Northern Securities Company. The government's action against the trust was begun under circumstances that must have delighted Roosevelt. His Attorney General was Philander C. Knox, one of the "old men" of the McKinley era who had been continued in office by the forty-three-year-old President.

Knox, moreover, was essentially a party hack and fund-raiser who had refused the same appointment in the first McKinley administration because he hadn't yet made enough money. He consented to enter the second in 1900 when that desideratum no longer existed. He had been a Carnegie Corp. lawyer and remained a close associate of men like Henry Clay Frick.

Roosevelt, though, had faith in his legal aide. One of the battery of Hill-Morgan lawyers, united in their opinion that the Supreme Court would never reverse the eight-to-one decision the same members had made only six years earlier, sneered at Knox. The President, he told a Roosevelt associate, had been led into an act of folly on the advice of "an unknown country lawyer from Pittsburgh." The remark was relayed to Roosevelt, who said, "They will know this country lawyer before this suit is ended."

Another of the adolescent notes in the initiation of the suit was Roosevelt's imposition of absolute secrecy, even from other members of the Cabinet, like Elihu Root, also a holdover from the

McKinley administration as Secretary of War, but a fellow Harvardian and close friend of Roosevelt's. But the President knew of his ties to Wall Street, and probably it was as much to prevent Root's tipping off Morgan as for any other reason that Knox was told to proceed in fog and gloom. The result was that Morgan, less than three months later, after the formation of the trust, was stunned to hear from a newspaper source on February 18, 1902, that Knox had announced that he was preparing to file the action.

Morgan's reaction was typically swift and direct—and futile, for he misjudged the character of the man he was dealing with. He went to Washington and complained to Roosevelt and Knox about the ungentlemanly oversight of the administration in failing to give him advance notice of its complaint against his newest trust. "That is just what we did not want to do," said Roosevelt, whereupon Morgan came back with a revealing response. "If we have done anything wrong," he said, "send your man [meaning the Attorney General] to my man [naming one of his lawyers] and they can fix it up."

Morgan did not realize that his world was undergoing a profound change at about this point. No longer were things "fixed up" by big businessmen over their cigars and brandy in forbidding New York clubs, with small concessions, or perhaps even a campaign contribution, to set straight the trifling concerns of politicians and the public. Through a mixture of considerations, a demogogic realization that his action would be hailed by rabble and soldier citizen alike, and a genuine desire to lead in smoothing this growing inflammation between big business and government, Roosevelt had taken a bold step that would forever open a vulnerable spot in Morgan's hitherto unchallenged realm.

The President answered his suggestion with: "It can't be done," and Knox, the Pittsburgh corporation lawyer, chimed in with "We don't want to fix it up, we want to stop it."

Morgan then betrayed further anxiety and got cold comfort. "Are you going to attack my other interests, the Steel Trust and the others?" he asked.

"Certainly not," said Roosevelt, adding a characteristic hedge, "unless we find out that in any case they have done something that we regard as wrong."

When Morgan left, the President summed it up. "That is a most illuminating illustration of the Wall Street point of view.

Mr. Morgan could not help regarding me as a big rival operator, who either intended to ruin all his interests or else could be induced to come to an agreement to ruin none."

The suit, begun in St. Paul on March 10, ended in complete victory for Roosevelt's point of view on March 14, 1904. By that time, two of the judges whom he intended to make leap backward through the hoop they had created in the 1895 sugar decision were dead. One of them was the justice who had been so able to see both sides of the income tax question within an incredibly short period. Shiras.

Shiras had gladdened Morgan's heart during one of the many ancillary actions, a question of whether the state of Minnesota had a right to intervene. Morgan was in Washington and dropped in to hear the judge announce that it hadn't the right, but that was about the only part of the whole long proceeding that had gone his way and its effect was wiped out by the final decision, five to four, upholding the lower court order to dissolve the trust.

It was a signal triumph for Theodore Roosevelt and a double defeat for Pierpont Morgan. Not only was his trust ordered to dismantle itself, but the decision even came at a time when it forced him to delay sailing on his annual visit to England for a week. As he told Stetson, "You will have a pretty job, unscrambling the eggs and putting them into their shells and getting them back to the original hens!" In the course of the unscrambling, though, the once-hated Harriman retained the position he had fought for and won in the Northern Pacific-Great Northern complex.

It was during this period that Morgan suffered another defeat, the foundering of the grandiose International Mercantile Marine combination, its ultimate dehydration, and sale of the components at bargain prices back to their original owners, largely British shipping interests. What was worse, he was the butt, or at least he shared the straight man role with a limited supporting cast, in another of Roosevelt's jokes by which the President ended the paralyzing anthracite coal strike of 1902. The strike, extending from May to October, began to worry politicians like Henry Cabot Lodge of Massachusetts, who gave way to "squeaky hysteria" over the possibility that its continuance would make the difficult job of electing Republicans in the November midterm elections for Congress almost impossible. Roosevelt was being importuned to take a part by Lodge and others, but he resisted because there were circumstances that made it likely that political interference could do more harm than good.

Appeals were also being made to Morgan, but he remained aloof, claiming that he had now power over the mine operators, although most of them were the managers of his railroad interests in Pennsylvania. One of the principals among them was George F. Baer, president of the Philadelphia & Reading, a line that Morgan had long been associated with. Baer outraged everyone during the course of the struggle and helped set the stage for considerable concessions to the miners by refusing any kind of outside arbitration. The reason, he said, was that God had put him in charge of the mines! He expressed his startling view in a letter in which he said:

> The rights and interests of the laboring man will be protected and cared for—not by the labor agitators, but by the Christian men to whom God in His infinite wisdom has given the control of the property interests of the country, and upon the successful Management of which so much depends.

The letter was widely circulated and drew clerical lightning down on the heads of Baer and other mine operators for espousing "the divine right of plutocrats."

Ultimately Roosevelt was drawn in—in the month before the election—and so was Morgan. The President was about to impose the solution that Cleveland had used in the Pullman strike a decade earlier, but with a difference. Troops would be used, but this time not merely to maintain order while the operators continued to profit. The difference now was that the government also would take over the operation of the mines, a considerable change in philosophy since Cleveland's time.

The plan had little justification in law, a point brought to Roosevelt's notice by Knox, but that was not the reason for its not being implemented. Knox recalled being asked to make a number of such futile researches, and on one occasion he tried to save his staff the trouble by asking Roosevelt, "Ah, Mr. President, why have such a beautiful action marred by any taint of legality?"

In any case, there was no test of the proposal. Instead, Roosevelt decided to impress the reluctant Morgan into service. This time he let Elihu Root, his Secretary of War, in on the plan because he wanted to use Root's connection with the financier. He had Root arrange a meeting with Morgan, which took place aboard the *Corsair* on October 11. There Root told Morgan that the operators must either submit to arbitration or Roosevelt would seize the mines, a suggestion that filled the financier with fears of socialism that he communicated to the mine operators. The result was that arbitration was agreed to, but the owners, with Morgan backing them, continued their arrogant stand and set stupid limitations on the makeup of the arbitration commission that gave the President an opportunity to exercise his sense of humor.

He knew that to make the commission acceptable to the miners it had to contain one union representative. He also named a clergyman, Bishop John L. Spalding of Illinois, one of many men of the cloth sympathetic to the plight of the workers. To get his union man on the panel he resorted to a bit of trickery so sly that, to his surprise and, no doubt, his chagrin, no one, not even the newspapers, noticed it.

The operators' highhanded agreement had conceded one place on the board to "a man of prominence eminent as a sociologist." In his autobiography Roosevelt took care of the oversight of press and public in not getting his joke. Following the last lengthy wrangle about the composition of the group, Roosevelt says, "it dawned on me that they [the operators] were not objecting to the thing, but to the name. I found that they did not mind my appointing any man, whether he was a labor man or not, so long as he was not appointed *as* a labor man, or *as* a representative of labor; they did not object to my exercising any latitude I chose in the appointments so long as they were made under the headings they had given."

Roosevelt had a sufficient appreciation of Lewis Carroll, Edward Lear, and other nonsense writers. In fact, he had even imitated them in some of the delightful illustrated letters he had written for his children. More important, though, was his understanding of when the fantasist's nursery world became appropriate to the reality before him:

I shall never forget the mixture of relief and amusement I felt when I thoroughly grasped the fact that

> while they would heroically submit to anarchy rather
> than have Tweedledum, yet if I would call it Tweedle-
> dee they would accept it with rapture; it gave me an il-
> luminating glimpse into one corner of the mighty
> brains of these "captains of industry." . . . All that
> was necessary for me to do was to commit a technical
> and nominal absurdity with a solemn face. This I
> gladly did. I appointed the labor man I had all along
> had in view, Mr. E. E. Clark, the head of the Brother-
> hood of Railway Conductors, calling him an "eminent
> sociologist"—a term which I doubt whether he had ever
> previously heard.

This "utter absurdity," he wrote a week after the conference,
was accepted by Morgan's representatives, George F. Perkins
and Robert Low Bacon, the latter of whom had been momentarily rehabilitated because of his friendship with the President.
Thus "Messrs. Morgan and Baer gave their consent by telephone
and the thing was done."

Roosevelt expressed disappointment, though, that his inclusion
of Clark as an "eminent sociologist" had "merely furnished material for puzzled comment on the part of the press." He had done
his best to tip the editors off in an elaborate, winking explanation
when he released his selection. When he came to Clark's appointment he added that he was being named "as a sociologist—the
President assuming that for the purposes of such a Commission,
the term sociologist means a man who has thought and studied
deeply on social questions and has practically applied his
knowledge."

Between the Northern Securities victory and the success he
had in imposing a union man on Pierpont Morgan and company,
Roosevelt lost whatever illusions he may have had about the
potency of businessmen. His biographer, Henry Pringle, sums up
his attitude following that night of October 15, 1902, in these
terms: "Political expediency might, in the future, dictate caution,
but the nation's business leaders were not, after all, dangerous
foes."

Roosevelt reached that conclusion at about the same time the
public arrived at a similar judgment. This came about through
the incredible arrogance shown by coal operators like Baer, but
the disillusionment was to be increased a few years later in the

greater arrogance and irresponsibility that would be shown in revelations by Pulitzer's *World* of widespread insurance scandals in New York.

The disclosures developed out of a quiet struggle that had been seething in the Equitable Life Assurance Society, one of the three companies that dominated the country's insurance industry and, like them, located hard by the financial rulers' turf in Wall Street. The insurers controlled a hoard of gold, with assets of more than $400 million, gathered in nickels and dimes from small policyholders. It was, in short, "other people's money."

This pile of nearly half a billion, an enormous sum then and still a considerable holding, was totally insulated from those who contributed it, except if they complied with their part of their contract—by dying. Even at that another half billion or so was set aside under the primitive insurance laws of the time that was ample to cover those easily and exactly predictable contingencies.

The key to this treasure house had been left by Equitable's founder, Henry Baldwin Hyde, upon his death in 1899, to his son James Hazen Hyde, then only twenty-three years of age. This was a galling condition to one Equitable director, James W. Alexander, who had festooned the company with his relatives, but still had to bow to Hyde, the holder of 501 shares out of the thousand that made up the capitalization of the company.

Hyde was a youth of flamboyant and extravagant tastes of a decidedly Gallic turn. He made spectacular copy for the press, especially on January 31, 1905, when he presided at a ball at Louis Sherry's restaurant, two floors of which had been transformed into a replica of Versailles in the time of Louis XV and adorned with a popular French actress, Mme. Gabrielle Rejane, and $28,500 worth of roses. The ball, which it later developed cost a total of $200,000, all of which came out of the stack of "other people's money," was just what Alexander needed in his fight to unseat young Hyde, especially when photographs taken during the festivity began to appear in the *World*.

But as galling as Hyde was to Alexander, the unseemly squabble between the two and their factions was completely intolerable to the real beneficiaries of the Equitable hoard, the Wall Street tycoons who, in exchange for a few favors, directorships, or shares of stock, were able to gain access to the money that was neither their's nor Equitable's. Alarmed, they assembled the board of directors and appointed an investigating committee headed by Henry Clay Frick, who had been a director since 1901 but had never attended a meeting until a week after the Versailles ball. The Frick group recommended on May 31 that both Hyde and Alexander be deposed, but it was too late. By this time, the public, through Pulitzer's *World*, had heard enough to be convinced of deep mismanagement and misuse of funds. The result was a legislative inquiry into the doings of all insurance companies.

In the confusion preceding the inquiry that began in the fall of 1905, Hyde sold his controlling interest in the billion-dollar insurance company for an extraordinary knockdown price of $2.5 million to Thomas Fortune Ryan, a gangling country boy turned financier-politician whom William C. Whitney had called "the most adroit, suave, and noiseless man" he had ever known.

The investigation was put into the hands of Charles Evans Hughes, a then unknown lawyer who was as purposeful, as remorseless, and as colorless as an adding machine. Appointed at the behest of Pulitzer, Hughes was, as a result of his success, to find his way to the governorship of New York, to get as close to the White House in 1916 as any defeated candidate has ever been, and ultimately to reach the chief judgeship of the land. He was able to bring out the kind of instant corruption that would delight the public, such as the admissions that Hyde's entertainments had been paid for by the grindingly poor policyholders that his firm battened on. But in the course of the fifty-seven public hearings from September 6 to December 30, he was also able to lay out what amounted to a primer on high finance and the way in which the Morgans, the Harrimans, and the rest were able to fling around vast sums that came actually from the scrapings of the poor.

Such complex financial finagling could only be carried across to the busy wage earners who were its victims by the kind of tedious day-after-day procedure that was open to the Hughes investigators. Joined with the Equitable in the public grilling were the other two dominant insurers, the Mutual Life Insurance Company of New York and New York Life. All of them were shown as "financial annexes to Wall Street interests," in the words of an Equitable director.

Policyholders' money, the inquiry revealed, was used to back favored candidates, to form slush funds to generate favorable newspaper and other publicity, to establish a "House of Mirth" in

Albany to tempt susceptible lawmakers, and to finance lobbying in Washington, including $20,000 a year to the then Senator Chauncey M. Depew. The directors and their friends in the financial community were able to dispose in their own interests of millions in supporting bank deposits at rates that shortchanged the policyholders. Favored financiers were able to sell shares in their dubious enterprises to the group.

In the case of the Morgan group, two outstanding examples were flushed out. Followers of the hearings were edified by the belated explanation of the part played by New York Life in the hydraulics of that aqueous wonder, United States Steel. George W. Perkins, a Morgan partner since 1901, while still retaining his offices with the insurance company, including the chairmanship of the finance committee, explained condescendingly to the Hughes investigators that New York Life had saved $400,000 by buying from Morgan securities with a par value of $39,200,000 for only $38,800,000. Included were United States Steel shares, forbidden holdings for the insurance company even in that time of primitive regulation and obtained only by the evasive tactic of having a subsidiary do the purchasing—the cheapjack type of ruse that was a Morgan hallmark. Those shares were a bargain only in the sense of a tired old vaudeville turn such as: "I saved you $200 today, dear." "How?" "I bought a $1,500 mink coat that was on sale for $1,300."

Perkins's condescension did not extend to instructing the investigators that United States Steel stock was priced at at least double its worth when his company bought it and that it had been selling in recent markets at a quarter of his knockdown bargain price. It is disquieting for those who like to think that men in power must have some acumen and that any wrongdoing by them must grow out of a conscious, malevolent choice to realize that it is just barely possible Perkins really believed he had struck a bargain. In other words, he may not have had the kind of financial astuteness required to operate a successful candy store, in which case the wrong he did could only be attributed to a defect of reason such as would absolve him of all responsibility. Bearing this out is the fact that he sat in a witness chair giving this explanation to Charles Evans Hughes and, through the thorough newspaper coverage, to many knowledgeable Wall Streeters who would well know of the gyrations over the preceding four years of the "bargain" he was talking about.

The second example by which Morgan's "wealth" was shown to consist of the pennies of the poor was the revelation of how he caused New York Life to take on the even shakier promotion of his International Mercantile Marine. Over a two-year span the insurance company bought $4 million worth of this ill-starred "Shipping Trust," concealing part of the transaction by another one of the ruses. Then IMM foundered and went back as such a bargain to its original holders that New York Life lost $80,000. And the loss would have been double that figure, were it not for the fact that the amount seemed excessive even to Perkins, with his slippery concept of the duty he owed to his policyholders. He took on half the loss personally.

Platoons of other financiers appeared before the investigating committee to admit speculations as great or worse than those of Pierpont Morgan's men. The admissions were open, even naïve, and the belief has grown up that therefore the businessmen of the time were somehow innocent in an age that wasn't setting the high standards for business ethics that have come to be demanded since. Such a view is difficult to credit. Ethics of this kind have been preoccupations of mankind since the days of St. Augustine, and even farther back, to Moses. Perkins, for instance, would surely have known that it would be impossible to have used the word honesty to describe his actions.

The only reason for the ingenuousness of the witnesses was that they were caught relatively by surprise. They had never been forced to explain these matters before, nor had their fathers or grandfathers. They were thieves playing fast and loose with other people's money and they knew it. When forced to explain under oath, they hadn't the time to make more than feeble efforts to dissemble. Later would come the shoals of apologists, the acolytes who would impart an odor of sanctity to what couldn't be erased, and who would explain what remained in terms of the "primitive conditions" of the business world.

The investigation produced some beneficial results. The vast "never-failing reservoirs of capital" were removed to a certain extent from easy availability to promoters. But essentially they still provided financial support for Wall Street, as was demonstrated by Morgan's continuing interest in them. Already a power in New York Life through Perkins, he had interests in Equitable and in 1910, after the furor of the investigation had died away, he forced Thomas Fortune Ryan and the Harriman estate to yield up the control of the insurer to him. The transaction was revealed in the following exchange between Morgan and the redoubtable Samuel Untermyer in the Money Trust investigation much later:

Q. Untermyer: Did Mr. Ryan offer this stock to you?

A. Morgan: I asked him to sell it to me.

Q. Untermyer: Did you tell him why you wanted it?

A. Morgan: No; I told him it was a good thing for me to have.

Q. Untermyer: Did he tell you that he wanted to sell it?

A. Morgan: No, but he sold it.

Q. Untermyer: What did he say when you told him you would like to have it, and thought you ought to have it?

A. Morgan: He hesitated about it, and finally sold it.

Untermyer later got around Pierpont Morgan's evasiveness by spelling out the real reason the financier paid $3 million to the Ryan-Harriman interests for stock that paid dividends of $3,710 a year, or about an eighth or a ninth of a percent. "No sufficient reason has been given for this transaction, nor does any suggest itself, unless it was the desire of these gentlemen [Morgan and his associates] to control the investment of the $504 million assets of this company, or the disposition of the bank and trust company stocks which it held and was compelled by law to sell within a stated time," Untermyer reported to Congress.

Two years after Pierpont Morgan was exposed along with the rest of the financiers with the scrimpings of scrubwomen, letter carriers, and other laborers in their hands, he had his greatest triumph. During the Panic of 1907, Morgan, in his seventy-first year, truly manipulated vast sums and groups of men in a commanding fashion. But even this must be looked at against its background. The year formed the nadir of the first decade of the twentieth century, a ten-year period that, of all others, deserves to be called "the Morgan decade." And it was not a prosperous decade, for all Morgan's passion for order and his desire to have everything in hands whose reliability he had verified in advance.

The best available index of production of the time shows manufacturing growing by about 55 percent from 1901 to 1910, but with extraordinary dips in between. During 1904 and again in 1908, the index stagnated, returning to the 1902 level, so that there were almost alternate annual ups and downs until the end of the period, when most of the gain was recorded. Not too much can be expected of the statistical data of the time, but there would seem to have been rampant inflation during the period.

To the inflationary forces depriving the great masses of any gains in income they may have made was added unemployment, peaking at 8½ percent the year after the panic and cresting at just under or a little over 5 percent in three of the other years. Whatever gains there were for everyone were largely illusory. The hectic rise in the last three years of the decade led to a slide that continued on into the depressed period of 1914, until that ultimate savior, a first-rate war being waged by others, began to help out.

The Morgan decade was a period, as noted before, of pyramiding inflation, to which he contributed with his U.S. Steel, International Mercantile Marine, and other adventures such as the Northern Pacific corner. But there was a larger background for the inflationary forces, spreading across the decade and across the entire world, so that the Panic of 1907 occupies only a small portion of the total spectacle.

Hence Morgan's commanding role is diminished in the larger perspective. In an international sense it was a decade of unbalance, largely because of the cross-currents of the inflationary pressures. To put the matter in its simplest form, industry responds to price rises by heavy borrowings for capital improvements so as to be able to produce more efficiently and cheaply and to do it today rather than at tomorrow's higher prices. At the same time, individuals respond by putting off buying—the wealthy by a conscious choice, the poor and those on small fixed incomes because prices have carried goods up beyond their reach. This dries up the source of funds available to industry at the very time when corporations are driven to the credit markets to a greater extent than in more stable periods.

The rise in prices that would intensify this precarious balance became somewhat alarming early in the Morgan decade. Worldwide, according to the London *Economist*'s index, the increase in the three-year period ending in 1907 was double that of the eight years from 1897 to 1904; in other words, the annual increment was more than quadrupling.

Pierpont Morgan was making his contribution in this field, too. Three years after the formation of the billion-dollar trust, the country got a glimpse of the kind of savings it would get through the efficiences of large-scale production. Steel prices went from $22.18 a ton to $27.45 in 1906, a rise of nearly 24 percent. To be sure, there were other causes of this price rise besides the need for pumping some sort of value into the enterprise, causes that operated on all manufacturers of all lands and on their climate-dependent agriculture and on the source of their money.

Chief of these was the epidemic of belligerency throughout the world from 1898, when America and Spain fought through the first half of the Morgan decade, when first the British and the Boers were at war, and then the Russians and Japanese. The total cost of these came close to the staggering sum for the day of over $3 billion, with the bulk of it ascribable to the Russo-Japanese War and pressing down hard on the credit markets of Paris, London, and New York in competition with the other demands in mid-decade.

The billion-dollar Boer War added another vector to upset the equilibrium. About 25 percent of the world's gold, or $75 million, came from the Transvaal in 1899, but during the 1900–1901 conflict that source yielded only ounces. The shutdown was a strain in itself, and then the rebound to nearly one and a half times the 1899 figure by 1906 added to the inflationary pressures and, even more important, to the speculative fever that was strong in Europe and in America despite the rich-man's panic that followed the Northern Securities corner. This speculation was epidemic on the two continents for the first time in over three decades. Since the 1870s, America and Europe had taken turns in exporting capital to each other, because depressed conditions alternated between them, but in this decade they were moving in tandem, a doubling of a destructive force.

The effect was evident in the activity on the New York Stock Exchange during the decade. Never was such speculative frenzy seen before or since. The turnover rate on the Big Board, a measure of the rate at which stocks are bought and sold relative to the total list and the best available indicator of speculative interest, was 172 percent in 1900. There were 102,386,252 transactions out of a total listing of 59,579,694 stocks. During a recent wildly speculative year, 1968, the rate got up to a post-World War II high of 24 percent, but ordinarily in recent years it has run around the 20 percent mark or lower. In 1901, with the help of the United States Steel wash sales by Morgan's manipulator, James Keene, the rate rose to an incredible record that still stands, 319 percent.

"In terms of the turnover rate," says one market student, "1901 would see days in which more than three million shares were traded, or 5 percent of the stocks listed. This would be equivalent to a 200-million-share day in 1968 [when trading never got above 21,351,000]." It was a dangerous situation that was being matched in Europe, in Japan, and in Chilean and Egyptian bourses.

Onto this ledge of loose rocks and quicksand stuck with birdlime to the side of a precipice moved the undersea creature, Edward H. Harriman, to erect still another jiggery-pokery structure. For the task he brought with him nearly $142 million, part of which—i.e., nearly $56 million—came from the profitable sale of the securities he had gotten when Morgan "unscrambled" the Northern Securities omelet by order of the Supreme Court. The other $86 million he pulled out of the hard-pressed securities market.

With this cash he proceeded to buy such shares as New York Central, Atchison, Topeka & Santa Fe, and Baltimore & Ohio— speculative favorites all. His market activity served to whoop up the trading in these issues between June 30, 1906, and February 28, 1907. While the soufflé was still trembling, in August of 1906, he blandly had Union Pacific raise its dividend from 6 to 10 percent, a move that had the effect of nearly doubling the value of the common, "and a speculation of excessive violence ensued on the Stock Exchange." Union Pacific rose thirty-five points over a two-week span; other stocks rose ten points or thereabouts.

Now everything was in place. The stars of the most rickety tumbling act of all time, Morgan, Harriman, and scores of lesser lights, stood atop each other, chairs balanced on chins and skulls, balancing rods at the ready. It was an incredible performance reaching far up into the proscenium, where the last man held not one but two complete baby grand pianos. Now everyone held his breath, hoping that the pair of virtuosi who were to mount from shoulder to shoulder to the top to render a concert duet of "My Country 'Tis of Thee" would make the ascent gracefully. But the two who made the climb were just the types who would be wearing deep-cleated track shoes for such a task. They lacerated everyone and brought the whole act down in a great crash. They were Charles W. Morse and F. Augustus Heinze, associates in a copper speculation and, even more important, in a new tricky style of chain bank known as a trust company and not to be confused with the trusts in which Morgan, the Rockefellers, and other financiers used to lock up control of steel, oil, sugar, and other industries.

The trust company was a device that, through a loophole in the New York State law, was able to operate with little or no reserve requirement. One such, the Lincoln Trust Company, with eight thousand depositors and $16 million in deposit liabilities, maintained, as a sort of courtesy to banking practice rather than the law, an $11 million reserve on the threshold of the panic. It thus was in a position in the event of stringency to return a depositor about seven cents for each dollar he had entrusted to the bank. The Trust Company of America, a larger institution, with twelve thousand depositors, $42 million in deposits, and $3.2 million in reserve, could muster seven and a half cents on the dollar. These trust company devices, it had been shown in the Hughes insurance investigation a year earlier, had been used to multiply assets for the big three insurers and to evade laws governing them.

Morse was an out-and-out crook who had been exposed a few years before in collusive arrangements between city officials and his ice trust. Richard Rovere hilariously noted in his biography of the shysters Howe and Hummel that Morse "died in 1933, but Congressional committees were still discovering evidences of his outrageous operations in 1936."

Posthumous crookery was matched by what was proved against him in his lifetime. He was given a fifteen-year sentence for banking frauds during this period, but won a pardon from President Taft after two years by taking generous draughts of soapsuds and other potions that induced in him symptoms of the last extremities of Bright's disease.

Even in his private life, Morse adopted the methods he was using in business. For instance, he wanted an annulment from his second wife, his boarding house landlady, and hired Howe and Hummel to do it by proving that she had not validly been divorced from an earlier mate.

Abe Hummel carried out the contract with some plain and some fancy perjury and by virtually kidnapping the earlier husband so that he could not be forced to disclose the plot. The transporting of the man, which Morse would have had to have been privy to since it involved expenditures of possibly a million dollars, was carried out pleasurably to the victim; he was supplied with wine, women, and song in New Orleans and other pleasure centers and he became "debauched until his teeth fell out."

Morse's sidekick, Heinze, had some training as a mining engineer. More of a dilettante in crookery, he was indicted in connection with the bank fraud but never brought to trial. Heinze died about seven years after the crash, after losing a judgment of $1,250,000 in connection with the bank hanky-panky. He died broke.

Morse and Heinze each made a unique contribution to the crash. Morse had pioneered the form of finance known as chain banking, a variation of the old check-kiting scheme that worked especially well with the trust companies, where control hinged on such modest reserves. Morse had the controlling interest in the Bank of North America. Using its assets, he bought control of the Mercantile National Bank and then pyramided that into control of the Knickerbocker Trust. Heinze was associated with him in these moves, but his chief contribution was a scheme to corner copper with a firm known as Union Copper.

He also brought to the combination a more unfortunate ingredient—the enmity of the Standard Oil group, which he had incurred some years before when the Rockefeller associates were constructing the powerful copper trust, Amalgamated Copper. In mid-October, when Heinze and Morse began to try to corner the stock of their Union Copper corporation, using the pyramidal bank and trust company assets, the Standard Oil crowd saw the opportunity to even the old score.

By this time, Morse and Heinze had gained allies, the most important of which were the Trust Company of America, headed by Oakleigh Thorne, and the Lincoln Trust, whose president was George C. Boldt of the Waldorf-Astoria. These two were banks with only seven or seven and a half cents on hand for each dollar that had been entrusted to them, but a third ally, the Knickerbocker, whose president, Charles T. Barney, was friendly with Morgan, was even more precarious.

The Morse-Heinze combination, spreading their finances thin, managed to bull the price of United Copper to about sixty early in October, when the well-financed Standard Oil group began taking revenge. On Tuesday, October 15, United Copper dropped to thirty-six and the next day to ten. The copper issue had previously been one of the few to show any strength during the period, and when it began to sag a general decline set in, affecting particularly Morse's interests, such as American Ice and Knickerbocker Ice.

Wall Street well knew that the Morse-Heinze combination was using bank funds, and as United Copper headed down to ten, knowledgeable people in the financial center began withdrawing their money from Mercantile National, a Morse affiliate with $11.5 million in deposits. The bank had to appeal for help to the member banks of the Clearing House. The following day, Thursday, a committee from the Clearing House agreed to extend aid, but in terms that intensified the uneasiness by publicly identifying the culprits.

Among the conditions was the requirement that Morse and Heinze get out, posthaste, effective the following day. The reason for the demand was the committee's confirmation that depositors' funds had been used in the copper speculation. The Clearing House action effectively spotlighted the troubles the group was having and set the stage for a general run.

It was at this point that Pierpont Morgan got a clear view of the crisis and decided to do what he could in the developing panic. He had gone on October 1 with a considerable party in two private railroad cars to attend the general Episcopal Convention that was being held in Richmond. During the closing week of the meeting, the week of the copper manipulating and the decline of prices, he began getting telegrams more frequently. The Bishop of Massachusetts, William Lawrence, recalled:

> If one came during a meal, he tore it open, read it; then putting the palms of both hands on the table, a habit of his, he looked straight ahead with fixed eyes and deep thought for a few minutes. One day a member of the party said, "Mr. Morgan, you seem to have some bad news." He shot his eyes across the table at the speaker and said nothing. No question of that sort was asked again.

The convention was to end Saturday afternoon, October 19, but Morgan told Bishop Lawrence he was going back to New

York a few hours earlier, at noon. The clergyman asked why and Morgan responded: "They are in trouble in New York: they do not know what to do, and I don't know what to do, but I am going back." The Bishop pointed out, though, that he'd be getting to New York in the middle of the night and that it would be more sensible to leave with everyone else on the early evening train.

Morgan agreed, the Bishop recorded in his diary, and the next view the clergyman had of him, as the train drew into Jersey City the following morning, was a startling arabesque: "We went into Mr. Morgan's car for some bread and coffee before arrival, and found him sitting at the table with a tumbler turned upside down in each hand, singing lustily some tune which no one could recognize."

Later that day, Morgan set up headquarters at his recently finished mortarless library alongside his own home on Thirty-sixth Street. It was to be the night command post for him, with his office at 23 Wall Street serving by day, as he took control during those weeks of panic. He would decide the fate of many financial institutions, dispose of great quantities of money, some of which he would order raised by others, some of which he would procure himself in the form of shipments of gold from England. A very large part, about $35 million, would come to him courtesy of the man in the White House who, only as recently as the preceding August, had lashed out at the "malefactors of great wealth."

But there had been great changes since Theodore Roosevelt had exhibited that summer ferocity. Among them were the failure of the city of New York to finance two bond issues in late summer, then, in September, the bankruptcy of two vast enterprises, the $52 million street railway system of New York and the $34 million Westinghouse electric complex. As the avalanche began to get underway, Roosevelt became a very frightened man.

With the Clearing House decision getting the fullest possible dissemination over the weekend, pressure began to mount against the three remaining Morse-Heinze affiliates at the Monday morning opening. It was strongest at the largest of them, the Knickerbocker Trust Company, hundreds of whose seventeen thousand depositors had begun lining up early in the morning. By mid-morning the worst had happened. The National Bank of Commerce, a business bank that had been honoring checks of the trust companies and whose interests were strongly allied with Morse's enemies, "the Standard Oil crowd," announced that it was withdrawing the privilege from the Knickerbocker. The trust company closed its doors at noon.

It was to be the beginning of a test for the country's credit system, largely set up by, or under the direction of, Pierpont Morgan. Much has been said of Morgan's dislike of trust companies like the Knickerbocker. They had mushroomed since the closing years of the preceding decade, in lockstep with his own ventures in steel, farm equipment, and further railroad manipulations. However, his distaste wasn't strong enough, for instance, to move him to object to the dabblings of insurance companies under his control, like Mutual of New York, in setting up such evasive devices. Nor did it keep him from owning stock in the Knickerbocker. The wholesale leveraging of other people's money made possible by these rickety structures had been welcomed by him, up until this perilous moment, when he decided to let some of them bear the brunt of the panic.

He began his work in earnest this day, Monday, October 21, after a preliminary look at the situation at his library that kept him up a good part of the night following his arrival from Richmond. The week ahead was to be one of assembling groups to study individual credit institutions that were in danger, of pleading with men in safe positions for funds, and, not least, of turning whatever he could to his own advantage.

Session followed session at his palatial library and at his office in the heart of the financial district. He said at one of them: "Why should I get into this? My affairs are all in order. I've done enough. I won't take all this on unless—" and he had ended with a gesture which those around him understood to mean, "unless I get what I want out of it."

He did get what he wanted out of it, in a small, selfish way. What he wanted was the ownership of one of United States Steel's major competitors, the Tennessee Coal & Iron Company, and he got it at about a thirtieth of its value. But in the wider sense, he was to demonstrate that neither he nor any other private individual or group was capable of managing the country's credit structure and his handling of the situation merely added to the demand for governmental control.

Although he had earlier been ready to use the trust companies when his insurance allies needed them, he was now ready to cut them loose and would have done so except for the intervention of one man, James Stillman. Stillman feared that such drastic surgery would bring on a total hemmorrhage of the banking industry and his influence prevailed on Pierpont Morgan and the Rockefeller interests, a group that Morgan had earlier fought as a rival.

As head of the National City Bank, Stillman was the money man for the Rockefeller's Standard Oil complex, his bank had been built up by that organization when internal financing no longer sufficed. He also had been closely associated with another onetime Morgan enemy, Edward H. Harriman, "the little fellow."

But Morgan was drawn, personally and as a matter of business, to the astute banker, a "little fellow" himself, in contrast to Morgan's height, and of a strange sardonic manner that often led him into twenty minute silences before replying to questions in private meetings.

He was to end oddly a decade or so after the panic, a voluntary exile from the country from which he had often flown when public investigations threatened. Separated from his wife, Stillman was to develop a peculiar interest in the very young, buying clothing, including underthings, for small relatives and friends and flitting about the countryside of France in a chauffeured car, stopping to gather children about him by distributing quantities of small candies wrapped in paper. In the countryside of Gilles de Raiz, the sinister forebear of the Pied Piper, "Papa Bonbon," as he was to be known, must have started up some uneasy recollections.

In the year of the panic Stillman was fifty-seven and at the height of his financial power. He managed to convince Morgan that some of the trusts should be shored up, but his influence, naturally, was not being exerted too strongly on behalf of the Morse-Heinze group, the upstart financiers who were being pounded by the Standard Oil faction. The Knickerbocker Trust was allowed to go under the following day, Tuesday, October 22, despite an attempt by Charles T. Barney to see and appeal to Morgan.

Morgan's aloofness led Barney to a nervous breakdown, which he terminated three weeks later by shooting himself. If anything, Morgan hastened the wrecking of the Knickerbocker by advising the directors of the trust company to hold a meeting Monday night at Louis Sherry's popular and well-attended restaurant. He

sent George W. Perkins along as an observer. It was a highly
unlikely spot. Sherry's regulars, all people of substance and many
of them Knickerbocker depositors, quickly learned of the gathering and moved in and out among the long-faced bankers. They
also learned that the National Bank of Commerce had that day
revoked its practice of honoring checks on the Knickerbocker and
that doom was in the air. There would have been a continuation
of Monday's run anyway, but this all-but-public meeting intensified the crisis.

On that Tuesday the line doubled and redoubled outside the
bank on Fifth Avenue, just across from the Waldorf in what was
then an elegant residential district of the city. Two directors of
the trust company made another try at appealing to Morgan, but
were rebuffed, as Barney had been. "I can't go on being everybody's goat," Pierpont Morgan said, "I've got to stop somewhere." The Knickerbocker went under at noon that day.

During the next few days, three more trust companies and a
half dozen banks failed. But a strange immunity shrouded one
Morse-Heinze institution, the Trust Company of America, which
was also being subjected to the full intensity of the banking
run.

An odd thing happened in connection with that institution on
Tuesday night. George W. Perkins, one of the Morgan partners
most active throughout the panic, gave an interview to a group of
reporters that almost seemed to be directed at increasing the
possibility of a run on the Trust Company of America. It occurred at the Hotel Manhattan, just after Perkins, with a group of
other bankers, had met in one of the rooms with Theodore
Roosevelt's Treasury Secretary, George B. Cortelyou, to impress
upon the man from Washington the need for immediate government intervention—and cash.

What Perkins said to the newspapermen has been the subject
of controversy since, controversy that easily could have been
dissipated when, as was inevitable, the whole matter moved into
the congressional arena and he denied under oath the statements
said to have been made by him. It would then have been
ridiculously simple to have called in the reporters to make their
statements under oath, but as always Congress had no heart for
proving perjury against one of the earth's shakers and nothing
was done about it.

At any rate both *The New York Times* and the *Sun* printed
accounts agreeing that the Trust Company of America had been

singled out as "the sore point." It was like marking the trust company with the Black Hand, even though Perkins was said to have added that money would be forthcoming to salvage it. The whole statement apparently was intended to mark off the trust company as the target for frightened depositors on Wednesday when the papers would be on the street. The head of the Associated Press, Melville E. Stone, recalled later that the Perkins statement had been considered so inflammatory that the wire service refused to carry it. At the inevitable hearing, Perkins denied everything except supplying the reporters with such information as he thought it was "proper to give, of a reassuring and helpful nature."

Thorne told the same congressional group that withdrawals from his bank had mounted from $1.5 million on Tuesday to over $13 million on Wednesday and that the "sore point" statement had been the cause. The whole episode seems to fit with what Morgan wanted to bring about, but it may have been that Perkins, like many overzealous underlings, had been led into an injudicious exposure of the Morgan hand.

In any event, like Bacon after the Northern Pacific fiasco, Perkins was flung out of the Morgan orbit before the end of the year, to be replaced by Henry Pratt Davison. "Perkins' ten-year contract with Mr. Morgan expired soon after this, and he went into private life," notes Morgan's Boswell, Satterlee, in the same detached way that, say, the West Point morning report of September 25, 1780, might have recorded, matter of factly, the departure of General Benedict Arnold right after getting both breakfast and the news that Major John André had been captured.

The nature of the Trust Company of America's immunity from the vengeance being wrought on other Heinze-Morse ventures became clear about eleven o'clock, Wednesday, October 23, when the reports of the Perkins interview began to circulate widely. The trust company saw a duplication of the crowd scenes at the Knickerbocker.

President Oakleigh Thorne shouldered through the lengthening line in front of his bank on Wall Street and headed for "the Corner" of Wall and Broad. He had none of the trouble of Barney and the Knickerbocker directors in being ushered into Pierpont Morgan's presence, where he made an urgent plea for help.

Morgan then reversed his previous indifference toward Heinze-

Morse banking difficulties. He told Thorne to get together everything he had in the way of collateral and bring it to a temporary command post in the nearby Mills Building. If the collateral was good, he promised that J. P. Morgan & Co., Baker's First National, and Stillman's National City would provide a loan to rescue the trust company.

Thorne did as he was told and a group of Morgan lieutenants went over the paper he supplied, finally pronouncing it adequate security. Morgan turned to Baker and Stillman, who had joined him at the Mills Building headquarters and said: "THEN THIS IS THE PLACE TO STOP THE TROUBLE!"

It was all very thrilling to Morgan's son-in-law Satterlee, who was with him almost constantly, but what Satterlee failed to observe was the inclusion in the stack of paper pronounced adequate of stock that represented the control of Big Steel's major competitor, the Tennessee Coal & Iron Company. That detail did not, of course, escape the ferocious eye of Pierpont Morgan. Now he had an answer to that gesture that seemed to mean "what's in it for me?"

What was in it was the possible ascendancy over a company that, unlike other competitors, controlled its own iron ore and coal deposits, and all within a radius of about thirty-five miles of the main plant at Birmingham, Alabama, a promising sector that had not been exploited the way the Mesabi Range deposits had been. Moreover, the ore was of a superior quality and the plant was the last word in efficient, low-cost, open-hearth production, the method of steel preparation that was to largely supplant the Bessemer system.

The controlling stock had been posted with the trust company for loans to the investment banking house of Moore & Schley during the panic. As the panic deepened, the firm's John Moore had been trying to sell it directly to Morgan at $90 a share compared with the current market price of $130, but the financier turned the offer down. He may have been deterred by the antitrust possibilities of the purchase, but he certainly saw, as Thorne delivered the securities to his Mills Building outpost, an opportunity for a better bargain.

He was ultimately able to buy it in at less than $74 a share in United States Steel bonds. The actual value has been estimated at more than $250 a share and the potential worth, when fully developed, at more than ten times that figure. This, then, truly was the place to stop the trouble, and it occurred on a day when Morgan was in acute physical distress.

He had been developing a cold since Sunday and on this particular morning he had been comatose when Satterlee tried to awaken him. Only the ministrations of a physician with gargles and sprays, followed by the elation produced by Thorne's appearance in his office, nerved Pierpont Morgan to a day of shuttling between the corner and the Mills Building among the panic-stricken traders in Wall Street and a night of tense sessions among equally panicky big money men amid the baronial splendors of Chigi family wall fabric and Ghirlandaios smiling from the walls at the Library.

Thanks to Tennessee Coal & Iron, the Trust Company of America now had its safe conduct signed and countersigned. The Lincoln Trust was shored up and other banks saved by means of millions that Morgan was able to bulldoze out of the more solvent parts of the trust company and banking community, from sums he was able to advance from his American and English branches, and from an unprecedented use of script or certificates that the banks agreed to accept in place of money.

The money substitute lasted for twenty-two weeks and, with the country banks also adopting the strategem, reached a total of $238 million. But at the start, something besides all these was needed: seed money from the federal government.

Cortelyou, communicating the sense of panic to his chief in Washington, was able to move some millions into New York business banks, but that failed to stem the flight of currency that brought the markets tumbling further on Thursday, October 24. The stringency had brought "call money," the money that could be borrowed at a sort of anteroom to the New York Stock Exchange from Morgan and other Wall Street moneylenders, to a cost of 100 percent.

What happened that day took a long time to unravel. Ransom H. Thomas, president of the New York Stock Exchange, testified at the Money Trust hearings in 1912 that he had gone to Morgan's office to ask his support in shutting the place down. He was kept waiting twenty minutes, he said, before he was admitted. Morgan then told him that the Big Board could not be closed and to go back with the announcement that help in the form of $25 million was on the way.

He didn't know where the assistance had come from, Thomas

said, but in a few minutes J. P. Morgan & Co. and the national banks were back at their posts at the call market stand, and the rate had dropped to 10 percent for loans for stock. It should be added that the whole market structure was so leveraged at this time that a dollar down payment could buy up to ten dollars' worth of stock, a margin requirement that helped produce the dizzy pace of speculation in the markets up to the 1930s.

In the 1912 hearings, the Money Trust investigators were able to get some slight further enlightenment about what had happened from Cortelyou. He told them that the deposit had consisted of government funds that he had deposited for "the relief of the community generally" and that he had not differentiated "the stock market from the community generally." He was unable to give any details of the conferences that he had had with Morgan, Perkins, and the rest and couldn't recall whether the call money matter had been raised. He was even foggy on which banks received the funds. His evasiveness rubbed the bristly Money Trust counsel, Samuel Untermyer, the wrong way.

Q. [by Untermyer] You considered it important to relieve the stock market, did you not?

A. [by Cortelyou] Yes, I felt it was important that the stock market should be relieved.

Q. Did you not know, Mr. Cortelyou, that this money was used to loan out that afternoon to brokers in order to relieve the stock market?

A. I have understood since that time that considerable of the money was so used.

Q. Was it not so used by Mr. Morgan?

A. I did not understand so.

Q. By whom was it used?

A. I have no idea.

It was not to be the only time in this crisis that Pierpont Morgan would use the man in the White House.

Pierpont Morgan, the amateur hymn-singer, now found himself before the whole organ keyboard, working the pedal bass before bringing on the crashing diapason that would reverberate over the weekend. During the Friday night conference at the library, it was suggested to Morgan that, with all the secular lines of communication in order—to the press, Washington, and so on—it would be a good idea to open up an ecclesiastical avenue. Satterlee says that this was his personal contribution, but it was probably a routine matter for the Morgan organization to leave no opiate untried in reaching the people at times like these.

A committee was formed and the word went out to archbishop, bishop, priest, minister, and rabbi.

On Sunday, parishioners at St. Patrick's Cathedral heard Archbishop Farley conduct a special mass for businessmen at which he intoned, "I have confidence in the banks." Few, if any, realized that the day's homily had its inspiration not in the customary pipeline, whatever it was, between His Eminence and the Divine Will, but in temporary plumbing that led from a wellspring of white, Anglo-Saxon Protestantism at Thirty-sixth Street near Madison.

And rabbis and ministers were equally pliable. Over in Brooklyn, the Reverend John F. Carson spoke reverentially of "that magnificent and praiseworthy leader, J. P. Morgan."

In passing, it might be noted that whatever sidereal forces the archbishop and the others had contact with were powerless in this instance. Throughout the following week the crisis deepened, banks outside of the city suffered runs, railroads laid off workers and retrenched on construction plans, and the City of New York began a staggered system of paydays to lighten the demands its employees would impose on the meager money supply.

Hardly had the rolling bass tones of the clergyman died away that Sunday than Morgan, stymied both materially and spiritually, began to give thought to "what's in it for me?" Late that night, he took full advantage of the frightening progress of the panic to that point by having his chief incense swinger of the moment, Judge Elbert Gary, arrange a most urgent conference with the President, who had just returned from a bear-hunting trip. Gary, together with Henry Clay Frick, was dispatched on a midnight special to Washington, where, still insisting on the gravity of the situation, they forced Roosevelt to interrupt his breakfast to hear them.

The resulting conference has been the occasion for argument from barroom to boardroom, from party clubhouse to the highest groves of academe. The outcome was to give Morgan relief from any fears he may have had of antitrust harassment as he closed the United States Steel trap on Tennessee Coal & Iron.

Despite the labyrinthine denials of Gary, it was clear that he and Frick exaggerated the importance of the Tennessee Coal & Iron situation in the course of the panic and tricked Roosevelt into believing that a more important institution than Moore & Schley was menaced whose fall could vastly widen the developing panic. Testifying before the Stanley Committee, Roosevelt said that he had felt "it was necessary for me to decide on the instant, before the Stock Exchange opened, for the situation in New York was such that any hour might be vital." He declared that he "felt it no public duty of mine to interpose any objections" to the absorption of the Birmingham company into Big Steel and that the merger was needed to "save one big trust company." No one told him which one it was and, he said, "I thought it just as well that I should not ask."

If he had, of course, he might have discovered that it was just a mere brokerage house, one that had been in trouble before and probably would be again, that he was being asked to salvage with all the power of his great office. And he would have further discovered that he was just submitting to the Morgan whip in a race that had no other goal than to increase the otherwise watery value of U.S. Steel.

But then, such discovery might also easily have been withheld from him by the Morgan connivers. Roosevelt had displayed ability in handling crises of various sorts, but, as his biographer Henry Pringle noted, the peculiarities of the financial panic that bedevilled him in this year of 1907 had badly frightened him.

Theodore Roosevelt, like so many Chief Executives before and since, was easily awed by economic dislocations. He might have been cool in the face of belligerence by the British, Russians, Japanese, or Germans, and he had always been able to face down political opposition whether it came from a Senator Foraker or from the most vicious wardheeling plug-ugly of the streets of New York. But the consequences of the blunderings and self-serving moves of a Pierpont Morgan would always unship him. To a former economics teacher who had tried to initiate him into the mysteries of supply and demand at Harvard, he wrote: ". . . when it comes to finance or compound differentials, I'm all up in the air."

11

"I'VE GOT TO
GO UP THE HILL"

FOLLOWING the Panic of 1907, Pierpont Morgan busied himself in trying to patch up the banking system he had helped create and that had proven so inadequate during the Morgan decade. His efforts in this direction were as much of a futility as his great spending sprees.

By now he was looting antiquities and national treasure on a grand scale. These forays all seemed faintly inebriate. He was like some tipsy dowager with unlimited credit moving down Fifth Avenue on a riotous shopping trip.

His stumbling failure to improve the banking system was beginning to draw national attention that would ultimately lead to a great congressional investigation at which Pierpont Morgan was to make what amounted to a deathbed appearance late in 1912. He spoke foolishly to the committee as his powers waned; and he had been acting foolishly in the application of his methods in business, notably in the management of the New York, New Haven & Hartford Railroad system. Only a week before his appearance, the New Haven had passed its dividend for the first time in forty years in the most effective form of comment on his management that the world of finance knows.

The senility of his utterances before the Money Trust investigation by Congress escaped the notice of everyone except the organizer of the monumental project, Samuel Untermyer. Editorial opinion throughout the world generally agreed that Morgan had comported himself superbly, but by the close of his life it was becoming hard to defend the disinterestedness of editorial opinion about him.

Around this time the Morgan firm was choosing the top executives for the old and troubled Harper & Brothers publishing house. Among those being considered was the great promoter of muckraking, S. S. McClure. His stable of writers were scourges to most of the capitalistic freebooters but his Morgan specialist was John Moody, a man who treated his subject with much delicacy.

In the newspaper field, Pierpont Morgan at this period was in effective control of the New York *Sun,* whose editor, Edward Page Mitchell, spoke so reverentially of him: "What a whale of a man!" Clarence W. Barron, of the Boston News Bureau, *Barron's* magazine, and the *Wall Street Journal,* was to turn waspish after Morgan's death, but while the old man was alive he was considered an ally.

We have seen how Pierpont Morgan was considered one of the Union Club's "sacred cows" in James Gordon Bennett the Younger's *Herald.* Frank Munsey, the great newspaper wrecker, chose for most of his victims papers that could embarrass Morgan, according to Ferdinand Lundberg, who presents some other leads that help explain the awe, in which the press held Morgan.

Given this delicacy on the part of the press, it is not difficult to understand how Pierpont Morgan's mishandling of the transportation system of New England escaped everyone's notice until after his death, when it was bared to the public in two Interstate Commerce Commission investigations. The ICC hearings, held in response to patient, plodding legal moves on behalf of stockholders by Louis D. Brandeis, revealed an incredible tale of financial stupidity.

It was a repetition of United States Steel's formation, but this time applied to a regional complex that was mature and, unlike the still-growing steel industry, unable to bail out a watery capitalization of its transportation system. New England was a place for caution, for conservative moves, not a place for speculative exploits. It was in equilibrium, but a genuinely competent financier was needed to keep it in that precarious state. Instead it got the watery wildcatting of J. Pierpont Morgan and his chosen agent, Charles S. Mellen, so that when the inevitable occurred—the movement of industry to more economical climes south and west—the transportation system was totally unprepared to deal with the crisis.

Twenty-two years after Morgan's death in 1913, the New York, New Haven & Hartford Railroad Company filed a petition in bankruptcy and it was noted that its financial straits were directly attributable to the Morgan reign of the early 1900s. There can be no doubt that the rates the operators had to set to pay for an inefficient and wasteful overcapitalization of the transportation system was one of the prime causes of the flight of industrial customers, although there were other elementals such as cheap sources of power and labor elsewhere.

The New Haven had grown almost cancerously from a capitalization of $93 million in 1903 to $417 million in the year of Morgan's death, according to the second and more searching ICC probe. This growth had the usual complement of water. According to Mellen, who was transferred in 1903 to the New Haven presidency by Morgan from James J. Hill's Northern Pacific, $10 million more than their value was paid for trolley lines in Connecticut. That was only one of many extravagant overpayments in the almost lunatic plan of controlling every form of transportation in the area.

An even more flagrant example of hydraulic financiering was the purchase of a loser, the New York, Westchester & Boston Railway. "The enormous sum" of $36,434,173.25 was paid, the commission report stated, for this line of about 18.3 miles of track that was being run at an annual loss of $1,250,000. Other examples of similar financial profligacies were amassed by the federal agency in its investigation of the tangled affairs of the New Haven. They had been laboriously concealed in a rat's maze of about three hundred corporations making up the transportation complex. The companies formed a "web of entangling alliances with each other, many of which were seemingly planned, created, and manipulated by lawyers expressly retained for the purpose of concealment of deception," the commission reported.

However, the Morgan management wasn't depending solely on legal quiddities. Many of the books and records had been burned in advance of the probe and many witnesses, in the classic pattern, put themselves beyond the reach of the commission by fleeing. But the probers pressed on and were able to present a convincing indictment of what they called "one of the most glaring instances of maladministration revealed in all of the history of American railroading."

Besides buying up shipping companies, railroads, and even unimportant branch trolley lines at prices that guaranteed that profitable operation would take decades to achieve, the New Haven system made "unwarrantable expenditures" in suborning newspaper reporters, editors, publishers, and even college professors to write favorable stories or deliver "lectures" on the advantages of a unified transportation system.

In five New England states, lobbyists and lawyers with no discernible connection with the railroad in any professional way were being subsidized, free passes were issued to legislators and their friends, and contributions were made to local branches of the major political parties. Among the more mysterious items was a contribution of $1.2 million to a New York police official for some unspecified help he had provided in fastening the unprofitable New York, Westchester & Boston on the system.

The investigation of the purchase of that particular railroad also provided information on how closely Morgan and Mellen worked. The link has become important, because after Morgan's death Mellen gave an unflattering picture of the great financier, first to the Interstate Commerce Commission examiners and later in a series of garrulities to Clarence W. Barron, publisher of Boston and Wall Street financial papers. Barron's information did not become public until after his death in 1928, when his notes were brought together in two volumes that were far more outspoken and specific than any of his editorial matter published in his lifetime had ever been.

So, some years later, when Morgan's son-in-law produced his "official" biography, Mellen was pictured as a renegade who had betrayed his benefactor, Pierpont Morgan, by keeping from him information about the running of the railroad during the last decade of his life and by reviling him after his death. This explanation was intended to clear Morgan and put the onus on Mellen.

But the commission showed that in the purchase of the 18.3-mile New York, Westchester & Boston, a special committee of the board had been set up, including Pierpont Morgan, and with the line's president, Mellen, as chairman. The committee contained only two other members and had been specially created to plan and execute this dubious purchase, so there is little likelihood that any part of the affair could have been concealed from Pierpont Morgan by Mellen.

Mellen was a sharp-tongued man and, like many coarse-grained titans of the period, was fond of pleasantries that gave off a gamy, barnyard smell. He said at one point: "The record of New Haven transactions with the elimination of Mr. Morgan would have been as tame and uneventful, as devoid of interest or incident, as would the record of a herd of cows deprived of the association of a bull." He also told the commission, "I had no more to do with the financial policy of the New Haven than I had with the editorial policy of the Boston *Post*." In the following exchange with the ICC's chief counsel, Joseph W. Folk, a former governor of Missouri retained for the investigation, Mellen detailed his relationship with Morgan:

Q. Mr. Mellen, were you Mr. Morgan's man as president of the New Haven?

A. I have been called by the newspapers his office boy.

Q. Would you say from your experience, whether you were his man or not?

A. I was very proud of his confidence. I desired to equip myself to meet his approval. I regarded the statement I was his man as a compliment.

Around this time, Mellen told his friend and publicist, Clarence W. Barron, that he was "proud" to wear the Morgan collar.

Mellen put the blame for buying the New York, Westchester & Boston at $2 million a mile—an extravagance that matched Morgan's overpayments for artworks, but with far less justification—directly on the supposedly astute financier. The purchase was pushed through the board of directors by Morgan despite reservations by Mellen, who added that one of the reasons for his disapproval was the inadequacy of the accounting he got of millions that were sent from "Special Account No. 2" at J. P. Morgan & Co. This account possibly was the one used to recompense the city police official for his unspecified but valued services.

Mellen told the investigators that he had complained of one report on account of its vagueness and Morgan answered him with "Didn't Stetson draw that report? . . . Well, doesn't Stetson know more about how it should be drawn than you do?"

Mellen, though, realized that, as head of the line, he was vulnerable: "I was a president," he testified, "and I knew, if trouble came, that lots of people would go to Carlsbad or some other place where they would be inaccessible, and I would have to stay and fight it out." He correctly foretold to newspapermen after his resignation that he would be cast as "the goat" and added with his characteristic barnyard humor, "I intend to go back to Stockbridge and raise goats. The demand for goats is growing."

The Interstate Commerce Commission hearings ended with loud words of opprobrium like "financial joy riding," "sham methods," "reckless and profligate transactions," "manipulation of securities back and forth" and laid a sort of blame on the dominance of Morgan and Mellen.

A little more to the point, the commission—greatly strengthened during Theodore Roosevelt's reign, which had ended five years earlier—directed the New Haven to give up control of the Boston & Maine, divest itself of its trolley line foolishness, and get rid of its steamship lines. Eleven of its directors were indicted for criminal conspiracy, but, of course, six were acquitted and the jury disagreed over five.

The names of the newspapermen and scholars subsidized by the transportation complex have never been publicized. One of the latter group of hirelings who offered his learned charms to the New Haven for a price was said to be a "Harvard professor." This vagueness might have been expected to irritate his colleagues sufficiently for them to demand that he come forward to clean their own academic skirts, which is usually what happens among the lower orders of mankind when besmirched—policemen, civil servants, and the like. But no such demand was made, which seems to indicate that there must have been spots aplenty on all the academic gowns.

The Interstate Commerce Commission investigation of the affairs of the New Haven portrayed a Pierpont Morgan who was reckless, small-minded in his plan for an area that happened to include his boyhood homes in Hartford and Boston, and totally oblivious to the larger effect of his design on the economics of the region or the country at large. But the portrayal was delayed until after his death and he had no opportunity to be questioned about the movements he had made. However, before he departed this life, he figured in a display in which a fairly clear picture of his power and the way he misused it was to be provided for those who would see it.

The mechanism for this public unveiling of Morgan was an investigation in 1912 and 1913 by a subcommittee of the House Banking and Currency Committee. The eleven-man group was charged with looking into "the concentration of money and credit" in the United States. It was headed by a fifty-two-year-old representative from New Orleans. Arsene Pujo, and was alternately known as the "Money Trust Investigation" and, because of the captivating sound of the chairman's onomatopoeic name, the "Pujo Investigation." But Pujo was a nonentity who, along with his generally indistinguishable colleagues, was rendered almost invisible by the abrasive initiator, organizer, promoter, and general ringmaster of the hearings, Samuel Untermyer.

Untermyer, fifty-five years old when he took charge of the investigation, was a striking opponent for his chief adversary, Pierpont Morgan. He was undersized, so that there was more than the suggestion of David and Goliath when the two got together in the hearing room. Untermyer, though, was as much a part of the financial system as was Morgan; he had been rumored to have received the monumental fee of three quarters of a million dollars in one case alone, the $100 million amalgamation of a group of copper companies only two years earlier.

Before that he had been profitably employed as personal counsel to the embattled Francophile, James Hazen Hyde, in the Hughes insurance investigation. He had also been active in the interest of various brewing combinations, a group not known for parsimony in rewarding their lawyers, and the same was true of another set of clients, the fabulously wealthy Meyer Guggenheim and his sons. With the Guggenheims, Untermyer's services even extended to the divorce court.

Although his clientele came to include the very rich, it hadn't always been that way. He was born in 1858, the year that Morgan had turned twenty-one. His father had emigrated to this country from Germany and had taken up tobacco planting in Lynchburg, Virginia. Like many Jews whose preferences or background had drawn them to the South, the older man was an ardent supporter of the Confederacy who invested heavily in its bonds. He was said to have died of shock on hearing of Lee's surrender—and his own consequent financial undoing.

The family tragedy and ruination had the result, though, of freeing Samuel from a destiny as a developer of tobacco strains and sent him, his mother, and two brothers north to New York. There he worked by day and put himself through the College of the City of New York and Columbia Law School by night. Admitted to the bar in his twenty-first year, he was one of the leading corporation lawyers in the country by the end of the 1890s.

In undertaking and inspiring the federal government's first great probe into the control of capital—an investigation that was bound to put Pierpont Morgan into the dock—Untermyer may have been motivated in part by recollections of his first brush with the financier.

Untermyer, too, was a sometime country squire, having bought in 1900 the Yonkers estate, Greystone, that had formerly belonged to that tarnished hero of 1867, Samuel J. Tilden. There, like Morgan, farther up the Hudson at Cragston, he raised collies, although his first love was gardening, particularly the cultivation of orchids.

Many years later he would tell newspaper reporters who were in the habit of visiting Greystone on Sunday afternoon that his life's ambition was to be commissioner of parks for his adopted city. He'd do it without pay and use his own money to help out with maintenance, he said. "It would be a pleasant job, working among flowers," he told them.

In February 1907 he had entered some of his collies in the Westminster Kennel Club show at Madison Square Garden, only to see the field swept by an offspring of one of Morgan's dogs, Cragston Blue Prince. Morgan stalked from the area, angered that his own dogs were being outclassed by their whelps, jostling Untermyer in the process. The incident rankled. The lawyer then cabled to England for a shipment of pedigreed collies, which he entered at a kennel show in Boston a few weeks later. He had the satisfaction of seeing them take the honors from the Morgan dogs.

It would be delightful to record that because of this incident the fiery little lawyer determined to bring the magnificent financier to heel, but his distaste for Pierpont Morgan and his high-handed financial methods went deeper than that. Untermyer was among many who had been frightened at the United States Steel adventure, the lunacies of spending that were then being exposed by the Brandeis suits against the New Haven, and the spectacular International Mercantile Marine fiasco, in which properties were bought from Englishmen at double their worth and then sold back to them at half of it, to the detriment of everyone except masters of capital like Morgan. He even had played a part in extracting some clients from one of those freebooting operations, the formation of United States Shipbuilding. Morgan apologists deny that the financier was active in the shipbuilding trust, but it was full of his friends and present or former associates, and in fact Untermyer criticized him by name in the course of a courtroom proceeding that followed.

The incident of the collies took place at the beginning of the panic year, a year that was to make many besides Untermyer undertake a reappraisal of Morgan and the power that he had amassed. The futilities of Morgan's attempts after the panic and the demonstrable powerlessness that he had shown during it were becoming evident to many. His trade, that of a merchant of money, was a gainful one, most were ready to admit, but the distribution and channeling of capital had developed into the source of that kind of absolute power that corrupts absolutely.

Morgan was supposed to be one of those who provide efficiency in the flow of money from individual and institutional savers to industry and services that were filling some need, extracting in the process a percentage that would leave him well paid. That had not been what had happened. Instead, he was sluicing capital into enterprises in which he was interested and the mass of people that ultimately could hobble or even destroy him was becoming disillusioned at the outsized profits he could take.

United States Steel had become his beneficiary because it satisfied his passion for order and harmony, not because it could produce steel more efficiently or cheaply. The shipping trust was created by his hydraulics out of his desire for absolute power and it had to be broken up—unscrambled, as he had said in the case of Northern Securities—at great loss to the true owners of the wealth whom he had disinherited. The New Haven transportation complex was the object of his questionable benevolence largely through the accident of serving his boyhood neighborhoods; the fact that his overcapitalization of the line almost criminally put an insupportable burden on New England's farms and factories did not figure in what he chose to call his plan. What is more, the automobile industry would not have developed if he had had his way. And so on through the list of the mistakes of the Morgan decade.

All these errors, miscalculations, misappropriations, stock waterings, and lost opportunities were, in the interconnected world of finance, interacting and cumulative, especially in periods of weakness like the Panic of 1907. More and more people were beginning to realize this. They were also beginning to

realize that Morgan and his fellow bankers were not only contributing to the dislocations—in fact, creating them—but also
that they were powerless to do anything to alleviate them when
they came.

The seeming heroics of providing a few million in 1895 were
tarnished almost immediately by the 1896 bond issue, floated
almost without any help from the supposed savior of the year
before. And increasingly, from the turn of the century, the federal government's unlimited resources had to be called on again
and again to relieve the financial strains of the Northern Pacific
corner, the mild upset that began after McKinley's assassination,
and, most recently, in Treasury Secretary Cortelyou's rescue
mission at the height of the 1907 trouble.

The disillusionment was more than a mere recoil from the
misuse of economic power. The general disgust with those who
constituted themselves the chosen of the Almighty in the control
of business and industry, and paid themselves accordingly, was a
considerable part of the ferment that developed on into the term
of Theodore Roosevelt's hand-picked successor, the highly conservative and unyielding William Howard Taft.

In the middle of Taft's only term occurred one of the typical
signs of the demand for social change. In the elections of 1910,
the power of the House of Representatives passed from the
Republicans to the Democrats for the first time in seventeen
years. This early warning signal was to be highly important in
shaping Samuel Untermyer's future, for the Democratic House
was to write out an extraordinary blank check for his investigation.

At the end of the first year in office for this Congress, on
December 27, 1911, Untermyer made an address to the Finance
Forum at the West Side YMCA in New York City. "Is There a
Money Trust?" was the title. In the talk, which takes up twenty-
eight pages in the printed pamphlet version, he laid out substantially all the points he was later to include in the investigation.
Sections of the talk run through the Pujo committee's final
report—of which, of course, he was the author—almost verbatim,
as for instance in his stylized oratorical device noting there is, yet
there is not, a money trust:

> If it is expected that any Congressional or other in-
> vestigation will expose the existence of a "Money

Trust" in the sense in which we use the word "Trust"
as applied to unlawful industrial combinations, that
expectation will not be realized. Of course, there is no
such thing. . . .

  If, however, we mean by this loose elastic term
"Trust" as applied to the concentration of the "Money
Power" that there is a close and well defined "community of interest" and understanding among the men
who dominate the financial destinies of our country
and who wield fabulous power over the fortunes of
others through their control of corporate funds belonging to other people, our investigators will find a situation confronting us far more serious than is popularly
supposed to exist.

In addition, he made eleven recommendations for regulating
the money power. Virtually the same words used in his speech
reappear in the report that followed months of investigation,
three volumes of testimony, and dozens of charts displaying the
power of the masters of capital.

  The following year, as Taft and Roosevelt were moving toward
the split over just such issues as the committee would explore
and thus assure the election to the Democratic candidate, Woodrow Wilson, Untermyer was called to Washington and offered
the job of chief counsel to the committee.

  As part of the blank check that he demanded, he was given the
unprecedented right to gag the congressmen and do all the questioning himself. Untermyer, who had prepared carefully for a
study of how capital had been allocated all the way back to the
Civil War, well knew that the whole effect of his presentation
could easily be spoiled by having some unschooled and inattentive or possibly even underhanded congressmen break in with
questions typical of such committees. Many a hearing before and
since has had its effectiveness vitiated by being led down some
rambling byway by an inept congressman from the sticks asking:
"Well, what is a stock market?" or some similar absurdity.

  Untermyer had the corrective. He alone was to be permitted to
ask questions of the collection of star witnesses that he would
assemble. The subcommittee members were to remain silent.

  One of the minority members complained that never before
had such a daring condition been imposed on the people's surro-

gates. The hearings, said Representative Henry McMorran of Michigan in a minority report that was sent to the House along with Untermyer's masterpiece at the end of the investigation, were of "an unusual character, entirely different from anything that I have ever witnessed during my experience in Congress. . . . I refer to the agreement under which no member of the committee has been permitted to interrogate witnesses upon subjects material to the investigation."

Untermyer was allowed to write his own check, but he had to make the collection himself and in one important particular he was balked. Although the country was rightly concerned over the bankruptcy of its business leaders and although their failures would help elect Woodrow Wilson even as the open hearings were being prepared later in the year, the money trust proved its potency in connection with one of Untermyer's requests, the right to subpoena bank records.

In asking for the power to compel the production of books and records, Untermyer had before him the example of the feeble investigation of stock speculation conducted two years earlier by a committee appointed by New York State Governor Charles Evans Hughes.

"That committee had . . . no power to subpoena witnesses or to send for books and papers," he noted in the introduction to his report. "It was compelled to rely largely on statements formulated by the governors of the [New York Stock] exchange in consultation with their counsel in answer to written questions."

That committee had been headed by Horace White, the economist-journalist who was getting on in years and was then engaged in writing such letters as we have noted to newspapers about who suggested what at meetings he had not attended. Its report was farcical, as it would have to be in view of the emasculation the committee had submitted to. Untermyer was to prove of such dimensions that an operation of that kind on him would need the facilities of a zoo infirmary, perhaps one attached to the elephant house. And he was not about to cooperate in it.

He got his subpoena powers for witnesses and a certain amount of power to compel the production of records, but he had had the grand design of circularizing no fewer than thirty thousand of the country's biggest banks with a detailed questionnaire. In this, he was thwarted. He got about twelve thousand responses, but he noted that most state banks and the principal national banks in the reserve cities of New York, Philadelphia, Boston, and St. Louis refused to answer. The money trust could show its power, too.

The big banks cited a law that they said denied jurisdiction over them to Congress, whereupon the egregious chief counsel tried to get Congress to change the law. Meanwhile, he attacked on another front.

In September, he went after Taft's controller of the currency to demand that he circularize the quiz. In the interim, the Pujo group had heard all the witnesses involved in two of the three major areas that interested Untermyer, the clearing house associations and the New York Stock Exchange, in the heated-up atmosphere of the impending presidential campaign. For his third topic, the concentration of control of money and credit, it was decided to avoid giving opponents of the committee any occasion to attack it on the grounds that it was trying to influence the November contest and hearings were adjourned until December.

The question of Untermyer's questionnaire had in the meantime been laid in the capacious lap of President Taft by the controller. Taft withheld his decision until the eve of the resumption of the hearings and, after Wilson's victory in November, as a very lame and defeated duck with no constituency to answer to, refused to take a hand in distributing the questionnaire. Taft claimed Untermyer could have whatever data the controller possessed, but the scrappy chief counsel charged in the Pujo commitee report that he didn't even get that.

> It is thus seen [Untermyer stated] that the refusal of aid by the comptroller, the failure of the [still Republican] Senate to pass the bill [that would spell out congressional jurisdiction over the banks], and the lack of any authoritative decision by the courts . . . have seriously embarrassed your committee in its efforts to present a complete disclosure of the extent, if any, to which the resources of the leading national banks in the cities of New York, Boston, and Chicago have been or are being exploited in the interest of banking houses and others with which they are affiliated through stock holdings, joint account, promotion, syndicate, and other financial relations and transactions.

For these reasons . . . [including the recess during the campaign, and the lack of time to examine a "large number of important witnesses"], your committee has been unable to complete its investigations and has deemed it best to present this intermediate report, accompanied by the urgent recommendation that the incoming Congress continue this inquiry into the important subjects set forth in the resolution.

Untermyer did not stress the point further, but nothing in his two-thousand-odd pages of hearings nor his beautifully organized report of about 250 pages does more to prove his contention that there was a "money trust," that it had real, palpable power that extended right on into the White House and was fully capable of diverting and blunting a congressional investigation at a time unique for its popular interest in bringing the masters of capital to some sort of accountability.

The questionnaire sought to bare the role of the banker, which at that time consisted of both business or commercial plus investment functions, in the economy. It sought information on the methods employed in financing transportation and industry, the influence the banker had as a result of this activity in the corporations whose stocks and bonds were merchandised, and the relationship of this function to the commercial or business one of lending money to these same entities.

Specifically, Untermyer asked for the size and number of deposits held for customers and the names of those customers; the number of their joint purchases and underwritings of corporate securities since the panic year of 1907 and the names of the associates; a list of the directorships held by the bankers' partners or officers; and a list of investments held in the names of the banking institutions themselves or of individual partners or officers in other financial institutions.

He didn't get all that, a failure he refers to repeatedly in his report. But he was by no means despoiled of his creative powers; he was able to interpolate much of the data from that supplied by cooperating institutions plus the admissions he was able to wring from his witnesses.

He was prophetic in calling his report an intermediate one, although it didn't seem so at the time. Congress did not follow up immediately, but the fires he lit still flare up from time to time in congressional sequels, in protracted antitrust cases, and in the formation of executive commissions that have grown out of the "Pujo Investigation."

Besides the insolence of the bankers in refusing to respond to the inquiries, there was the traditional flight of important witnesses that precedes any congressional investigation that promises to grow embarrassing. James Stillman once again felt the vague tuggings that assailed him on such occasions and embarked for France to dance and skip through his role as "Monsieur BonBon" among clusters of French children in the provinces.

Thus the committee was deprived of first-hand response from the man who, after Pierpont Morgan, could probably best have defined the tightening core of concentration of the money power. In every list, in every one of the laboriously hand-colored charts drawn up under Untermyer's direction, the final arbiter of who got how much for what and why was Pierpont Morgan, with chief henchman George F. Baker of First National Bank of New York basking in second place by virtue of Morgan's refulgence. Next in any hierarchical arrangement was James Stillman, the man who augmented his sphinxlike qualities by flight when necessary, and who wielded his power through the biggest bank in the country, the Rockefeller's National City Bank, with its quarter of a billion deposits.

But Morgan was on hand, along with enough of the others, to provide Untermyer with the material for a first-rate look into the incredible structure of power the financial leaders had built up for themselves out of other people's deposits, insurance policies, and stockholdings. It was a rickety structure, as shown in the panic that had taken place five years earlier, one that resembled more the vaudeville clownings of the era rather than an orderly assemblage of rational leaders.

Untermyer was too serious-minded to dwell at any length on the slapstick nature of the group before him. And of course he was correct in that. These buffoons weren't amusing; they could hurt—each other and the public—when they tripped over one another's outsize shoes and landed in the audience or hit one another with bladders that turned out to be loaded with shot. The subcommittee's chief counsel occupied himself with the bloodshed these entertainers caused and his hearings became a hinge opening the door so the public could take its first look at the doings of masters of capital like Morgan.

The part of the investigation dealing with the concentration of control of money and credit opened on December 9. A contemporary provides a description of the scrappy and pugnacious chief counsel at the time. A small figure crowned with a mane of silvery-white hair, Untermyer added to his dandified dress in a characteristic manner.

Each morning he would arrive at the hearing room, his buttonhole sporting an orchid grown by himself at his country place, Greystone. Accompanying him would be the orchid-cavalier, an aide with a damp paper bag containing a further selection of blooms to be brought forward at intervals as the predecessor wilted in the heat of forensics. Unfortunately, the horns and tinkling bells of Richard Strauss so appropriate to these floral effects were not permitted in the hearing rooms.

Untermyer had an eye for the "imponderables," as Henry Pringle has noted. Among them were his love of publicity, a passion that may have cost him the rewards that a more discreet co-religionist, Louis D. Brandeis, was to reap. After all, Brandeis stole much of his fire from Untermyer, even taking up the Adam Smith phrase Untermyer often used in his report; "other people's money," as a title for a series of articles, later a book, that relied heavily on the Pujo report. The work amounted to little more than a popularization of Untermyer's work in a magazine Brandeis was connected with as a lawyer.

Untermyer was such a newspaper fan during his investigations that he would wait up until three o'clock for the morning editions. Arrogant and overbearing, he used to order reporters around and didn't hesitate to call their editors about lapses in the copy that appeared in the papers. Once he went so far as to demand that no statement he made could be abridged. It was an onerous requirement, since, as one Park Row editor once remarked, "he couldn't turn around in less than two columns."

When one paper responded to his "all or nothing" requirement by opting for the space-saving alternative, he quickly altered his highhanded stand. Such conduct ordinarily would antagonize reporters and editors and would win him no concessions in the press, but he had more winning habits. In a day when the afternoon newspapers created circulation with a succession of editions built around hourly news developments, Untermyer would carefully program his investigatory climaxes in the hearing rooms to coincide with edition time. He seldom failed to produce some damaging statement in time for the first edition, another fresh and exciting admission in time for the early Wall Street run, and still another for the later afternoons. And if the reporters failed to rise like chorus boys for a quick step to the telephones with his timed exposé, he would often interrupt questioning a witness long enough to turn and glare at them until they responded.

He put one of his imponderables to work when Pierpont Morgan went on the stand before the Pujo group. Accompanied by members of his family, business associates, and no fewer than six lawyers, the aging financier arrived in Washington in response to a subpoena on Wednesday, December 18, 1912.

Surrounded by his retinue, he proceeded to the hearing room that day, passing on the way photographers and reporters and a queue stretching out of the House building and into the street. The line put his son-in-law, Herbert Satterlee, in mind of the crowds that ordinarily form for World Series contests.

As the commanding figure moved into the hearing room to take a seat, he was greeted courteously by his fellow collie-fancier, who signaled to the chairman that he was ready to begin. Falsely reassured by the friendly greeting, Pierpont Morgan rose from his chair, assuming that he was to be questioned immediately. "Somewhat foolish looking," he dropped back into the seat when Untermyer called out the name of some far more obscure witness. It was reported that he had become "almost apoplectic" by the time he was called late that December afternoon.

At last, Pierpont Morgan was face to face with an able opponent. But he was very old. He had put in a strenuous year, marauding the Valley of the Kings and European capitals in hasty anticipation of laws aimed at preventing him from doing just that. Only two months earlier, he had testified before the Senate committee raking over eight-year-old campaign contributions. In the next few months he would hasten back to the sites of ancient glory on his final visit to Egypt and Italy.

He and the orchidaceous Untermyer got into a widely publicized exchange almost at the start:

Untermyer: There is no way one man can get a monopoly of money?

Morgan: —or control of it. . . . No, sir; he can not. He may have all the money in Christendom, but he can not do it.

Untermyer: Let us go on. If you owned all the banks of New York, with all their resources, would you not come pretty near having a control of credit?

Morgan: No, sir; not at all. . . . What I mean to say is this— allow me: The question of control, in this country, at least, is personal; that is in money.

Untermyer: How about credit?

Morgan: In credit also.

Untermyer: Personal to whom—to the man who controls?

Morgan: No, no; he never has it; he can not buy it.

Untermyer: No; but he gets—

Morgan (interrupting): All the money in Christendom and all the banks in Christendom can not control it.

Untermyer: If you had the control of all that represents the assets in the banks of New York, you would have the control of money—of all that money?

Morgan: No, you would not. . . . But money cannot be controlled.

Untermyer: Is not the credit based upon the money?

Morgan: No, sir.

Untermyer: It has no relation?

Morgan: No, sir.

Untermyer: None whatever?

Morgan: No, sir; none whatever.

Untermyer: Is not commercial credit based primarily upon money or property?

Morgan: No, sir; the first thing is character.

Untermyer: Before money or property?

Morgan: Before money or anything else. Money can not buy it.

Untermyer: So that a man with character, without anything at all behind it can get all the credit he wants, and a man with the property can not get it?

Morgan: That is very often the case.

Untermyer: But that is the rule of business?

Morgan: That is the rule of business, sir.

Untermyer: Do you mean to say that when people lend, as when loans are made on stock exchange collateral, to the extent of hundreds of millions of dollars, they look to anything except the collateral?

Morgan: Yes, they do.

Many years later, in the 1930s, Morgan's son and heir, J. P. (Jack) Morgan was waiting to testify in Washington in connection with a very important piece of legislation, the Glass-Steagall Act, which, in fact, broke up the investment and commercial banking business he had inherited into two separate parts and severed all connection between them. At the same time, a troupe of midgets was playing the town and an enterprising news photographer brought one of them into the hearing anteroom, plopped him into Jack Morgan's lap, and snapped a wonderful photo of the financier and the freak. The resulting picture, reprinted around the world, is about all that most people can recall of the Glass-Steagall proceedings and a similar superficiality became the high point and principal surviving image of the Pujo hearings: Morgan's response that "character" came before collateral as the basis for commercial transactions. The assertion was bold and simple enough to be fitted into the myth of J. Pierpont Morgan. The arrogant response, which actually proved Untermyer's contention that the concentration of credit had brought control into the hands of a man who admittedly relied on highly subjective standards, appealed to the journalists covering the hearings and even more to their editors and publishers for its Old Testament qualities. Despite Pierpont Morgan's frequent invocation of Christendom, the words he spoke could have come from the clouds occupied by Yahweh. The communications networks, then greatly indebted to the money trust, found themselves accommodated by the revelation.

But not Untermyer. He had drawn such statements from Morgan by using a decidedly gentler manner than he did with the other witnesses. His exchange with the slippery Jacob Schiff, for instance, is a model of legal ferreting as he forced the banker to make admissions about the dangers of concentration that Schiff was by no means ready to grant.

But the fifty-five-year-old prosecutor handled the seventy-five-year-old Pierpont Morgan with great delicacy. When his report, equivalent to a summation before a jury, came out two months later, the reason became clear. Using the testimony of Baker, principally, and of other witnesses, he implied strongly that Pierpont Morgan was senile. "Peculiar" was the term he used several times to characterize Morgan's expressed views.

Commenting on the "character" response, he said, "None of the other witnesses who were interrogated on this subject were able to agree with Mr. Morgan as to the factors that enter into the current business of loaning money on collateral." The concept of character enunciated by Morgan was "an obvious economic fallacy," he said, and the financier's denial of "the slightest" economic power was "so peculiar as to invalidate all his conclusions based upon it." Again, his conceptions of the duties of bank officials "are peculiar to himself and represent neither the generally understood point nor do they correctly state the legal obligations resting on a [bank] director."

To destroy Morgan's contribution, Untermyer recalled the testimony of George F. Baker, in which his masterly cross-examination had squeezed a devastating response from the head of Pierpont Morgan's bank. Asked whether he thought the concentration of control of money and credit could be thought dangerous, Baker, after some vague meandering, finally answered: "I think it has gone about far enough." Pressed further, he said, "If it got into bad hands, it would be very bad."

Untermyer tightened his grip through a further exchange and then asked Baker: "Do you think that is a comfortable situation for a great country to be in?"

"Not entirely," said Baker.

In his report Untermyer noted: "On the proposition that there is not and can not be concentration of control of money or credit, it will be observed that Mr. Morgan is directly at variance with his associate, Mr. Baker, who deprecated further concentration in this regard, saying it has gone far enough, because in the hands of the wrong men 'it would be very bad'; that the safety of the situation lies in the personnel of the control."

None of this fitted into the hagiolatry that was building to a climax in these last months of Pierpont Morgan's life. In addition, then as now, time passes before the Government Printing Office gets out the organized, reasoned analysis such as Untermyer provided and the supporting documents of transcripts of actual testimony. The lights and cameras are gone, the flash powder burned. By February 28, 1913, when Congressman Pujo submitted the landmark study to his fellow representatives, all the excitement of having Morgan, Baker, Schiff, and the rest in the flesh submitting to the chief counsel's deft interrogation was gone.

By then, the ordained intermediaries of the press, magazines, and trade papers were off in search of new thrills for their publics. Untermyer's indictment went largely unheeded by them and Morgan had returned to the scenes of dynastic power for the second time in less than a year, this time to die.

He had left aboard the *Adriatic* on the morning of January 7 for a trip to the Mediterranean that was to end at Alexandria. It began with a false start: the *Adriatic* got down New York Harbor only as far as a shoal off Governor's Island, where the ship ran aground and had to wait for the twelve-hour run of the next high tide to free itself at 9:30 P.M.

In crossing the Atlantic, the ship passed close to the Azores. That started Morgan reminiscing of the winter six decades earlier that he had spent in those islands, an invalid, alone, who may have thought he had been sent out to die far from his family. He spoke of those times to his companions aboard the ship, of the orange groves and of his lonely walks and of Mount Pico, the distant beckoning peak he had wanted to climb.

The voyage continued and Pierpont Morgan's strength ebbed. On the trip up the Nile, he grew irritable at the snail's pace that the Thomas A. Cook steamer *Khargeh* maintained against the swift-flowing stream in a voyage that was expected to end far upriver at Khartoum in the Sudan.

His irritability was communicated to Cook's staff and the chef and waiter were replaced in an effort to mollify him. But he grew weaker. The trip had to be cut short just beyond Aswan and the party returned to Alexandria and then back to Shepheard's Hotel in Cairo while arrangements were made to get the ailing financier home. But he recovered sufficient strength to continue the journey to Naples and then Rome, where he put up at his accustomed apartments in the Grand Hotel.

That was as far as he was to get. Reporters set up a death watch as his strength ebbed. On Monday, March 31, at five minutes past midnight, Pierpont Morgan died. During his last period of consciousness, Satterlee recalled, he had said: "I've got to go up the hill."

He may have thought briefly at the last of Mount Pico, an elevation he hadn't climbed, but the lofty eulogies called forth by his death, running to front-page columns in New York and other world centers, the lengthy dirges floated from pulpits all over the world, left no impression of heights unscaled. Their burthen ran thus: he was the pinnacle himself, his career the inspiration for the entire nation. There was a suitable sliding over the inconvenient fact that he had begun with the slight edge of a $25 million fortune of his own, an advantage that did not accord with most acceptable myths.

But his true obituary had been penned by Samuel Untermyer, whose cunningly fashioned report would ring down the years far louder and more insistently than the mouthings of preachers and popular writers.

There were even those who saw in it an immediate cause of his death. A little over a month after Pierpont Morgan's funeral, a Boston banker and railroad executive who was often critical of Morgan, Frederick H. Prince, told Clarence W. Barron: "The Pujo Committee Investigation killed Morgan. Morgan was a very sensitive, shrinking man and his exterior bluff was simply a protective coating."

Untermyer, of course, denied having the power of life and death over the country's preeminent financier, and he was right. But Prince was talking figuratively. In that sense, Untermyer did "kill" Morgan's power in a process that has been going on in the decades since his actual death and which is not completed yet.

The lawyer laid out the details masterfully in the well-tempered set of Pujo hearings and in his report. In the seemingly inchoate structure of finance he was able to perceive form. And the form he saw was a pattern of widening concentric circles of interlocking directorates linked with further independent systems of concentric rings that gave the nuclear figure at the center, Pierpont Morgan, power that he himself was not fully aware of over men and events far removed from himself.

Pierpont Morgan's power could be as trivial as his dictation to the stock exchange that only the engraving company he owned could be used for stock certificates for companies listed there. It could be as complex and sinister as the display of 1902, when the perfidy or stupidity of one of his chosen trusted lieutenants together with his petty rivalry with E. H. Harriman threw men out of work and closed down factories and plants, along with ruining unfavored stock speculators as a less consequential side effect.

From harmony to unheavenly harmony Untermyer moved in making comprehensible the financial structure. His words perhaps lacked true inspiration; the going is heavy in his report. But there are well-tempered sonatas, Pindaric odes, ceiling paintings, verse dramas, and treatises in theoretical physics or biology that require great effort, attention, and patience on the part of the beholder—effort, attention, and patience that bring great rewards. A similar experience follows a close study of Untermyer's report.

He shows Morgan at the center, with the great concentric systems represented by George F. Baker's First National Bank and James Stillman's National City Bank revolving about him. Lesser orbits, still centered on Morgan, are occupied by Lee, Higginson & Co. of Boston; Kidder, Peabody & Co.; and Kuhn, Loeb & Co.

Through other satellite financial institutions, controlled "through stockholdings, voting trusts, interlocking directorates, and other relations," Pierpont Morgan had effective control of resources to the amount of $2.104 billion in pre–World War I values. This power structure, Untermyer noted, was further linked with all the major transportation, natural resource, industrial, and public utility corporations of the country, with total capitalization valued at $22.245 billion!

Literally no enterprise of consequence was initiated, expanded, or terminated in this period without the approval, or at least the sufferance, of frail and fallible mortals like Pierpont Morgan and his associates. The direction of industry—over- or undercapitalization of transportation systems, over- or underutilization of resources, the development or decay of power systems—was in their hands. A hiccup from one of them was enough to throw the United States into a panic. It was not, as Baker grudgingly admitted, a comfortable situation for a great country to be in.

Untermyer began to change it. There has been a great deal of argument, including much by him, over his responsibility for taking the banking system out of private hands and placing it under semi-public control, but surely his hearings helped create the kind of public mood of irritation and disgust that made the Federal Reserve system possible.

Of course, his demands for reform went too far too fast. One of these demands was the kind of reaction one would expect of a small-town crusader against betting parlors: he demanded that the telephones and other wire devices be yanked out of the New York Stock Exchange. But even that extreme exhortation was linked to the sensible suggestion that the threat of wire-cutting be used as a club to force the exchange to incorporate and disclose its activities more fully. That change is something that is only coming to pass now, nearly six decades after he propounded it.

Other of his legislative proposals continued to exert a strong influence, even after the Wilson Congress to which they were made ignored them. The Federal Reserve system, set up the year he wrote his report, served, as has been noted, to end the kind of death grip on the flow of capital enjoyed by private individuals like Pierpont Morgan, accountable to no one. It took longer to accomplish another of his objectives—the separation of commercial and investment banking. A great depression and a midget in the lap of Pierpont's son Jack was needed to bring that about, but ultimately the House of Morgan was divided into an investment banking firm, known as Morgan, Stanley, and the banking corporation of Morgan Guaranty Trust, with headquarters on the site of Morgan's old "Corner." The power that Pierpont Morgan and his successors had to lend money to or call in loans from corporations in which they had a financial stake has been greatly dissipated in the years since Untermyer noted it as one of the prime financial evils.

In this and other ways, Untermyer's obituary for Morgan is a living document, passing from generation to generation. The Glass-Steagall hearings of 1932–33 were a sequel to the Money Trust investigation. So were the hearings that brought about the Securities Exchange Act of 1934. And another depression, in 1937, brought about the creation of the Temporary National Economic Committee and more regulation of the sort Untermyer called for. A recent financial history describes the episode in a chapter called "Pujo Revisited: the TNEC."

More recently, Untermyer's proposals were evident in the 1952 antitrust suit against the Morgan, Stanley firm and others. That ended in a defeat for the trustbusters, but only after a trial so peculiar that it stands out even in America's disquieting judicial history. Among its more extraordinary features was a presiding judge who saw fit to enter his son on a legal career by allowing him to find an opening in one of the firms representing the defendants shortly before the case opened in court.

In any case, Untermyer's argument grows in influence; the extraordinary power created by Pierpont Morgan from the closing years of the last century to its apogee about the time of his death becomes more and more vestigial. One wonders if Morgan, hallucinating on that last hill he had to go up, had turned and seen gaining on him his last important adversary, whom he had encountered at the congressional hearings only three months earlier, the white-maned "little fellow," Samuel Untermyer.

BIBLIOGRAPHY

$\mathcal{T}$HE sources are given first. Where necessary, a key descriptive word is given in parenthesis. In the Notes on Sources, the author's last name together with this key is used to refer the reader to the full title.

Books

Adams, Charles Francis, Jr. *An Autobiography* (Autobiography), Cambridge: Houghton Mifflin Co., 1916.

————, and Adams, Henry. *Chapters of Erie* (Chapters). Ithaca: Cornell University Press, 1956.

Adams, Henry. *The Education of Henry Adams: An Autobiography* (Education). Boston: Houghton Mifflin Co., 1961.

Allen, Frederick Lewis. *The Great Pierpont Morgan* (Morgan). New York: Harper & Bros., 1949.

Andrews, Wayne. *The Vanderbilt Legend: The Story of the Vanderbilt Family, 1794–1940*. New York: Harcourt, Brace & Co., 1941.

Azey, A. C. M. *Signal 250: The Sea Fight off Santiago* (Signal). New York: David McKay Co., Inc., 1964.

Barnes, James A. *John G. Carlisle Financial Statesman* (Carlisle). New York: Dodd, Mead & Co., 1931.

Barrett, Walter. *The Old Merchants of New York City: Second Series* (Merchants). Carleton, N.Y., 1863.

Barron, Clarence W. *More They Told Barron* (More). New York: Harper & Bros., 1931.

Beard, Charles A., and Mary R. Beard. *The Rise of American Civilization*. New York: The Macmillan Co., 1930.

Beebe, Lucius. *The Big Spenders* (Spenders). Garden City, N.Y.: Doubleday & Co., 1966.

Belmont, Eleanor Robson. *The Fabric of Memory*. New York: Farrar, Straus & Cudahy, 1957.

Bishop, Joseph Bucklin. *Theodore Roosevelt and His Time* (Roosevelt). 2 vols. New York: Charles Scribner's Sons, 1920.

Bouguereau, William. *Cataloge Illustré des Oeuvres*. Paris, 1885.

Bowers, Claude G. *The Tragic Era* (Tragic). Cambridge: Literary Guild of America Inc., 1929.

Bibliography

Brandeis, Louis D. *Other People's Money.* New York: Harper & Row, 1967.

Breen, Matthew P. *Thirty Years of New York Politics Up-to-Date* (Thirty Years). New York, 1899.

Bridge, James H. *Inside History of the Carnegie Steel Company* (Carnegie). New York: Aldine Book Co., 1903.

Broun, Heywood, and Margaret Leech. *Anthony Comstock.* New York: Literary Guild of America, 1927.

Burgess, George H., and Miles C. Kennedy. *Centennial History of the Pennsylvania Railroad Company. 1846–1946,* Pennsylvania Railroad Co., Philadelphia, 1949.

Burr, Anna Robeson. *The Portrait of a Banker* (Portrait). New York: Duffield & Co., 1927.

Campbell, Edward G. *The Reorganization of the American Railroad System, 1893–1900.* Columbia University Press, New York, 1938.

Carnegie, Andrew. *The Autobiography of Andrew Carnegie.* Boston: Houghton Mifflin Co., 1920.

Carnegie, Andrew. *Miscellaneous Writings of Andrew Carnegie.* Volume I. Garden City, N.Y.: Doubleday & Co., 1933.

Carosso, Vincent P. *Investment Banking in America* (Investment). Cambridge: Harvard University Press, 1970.

Casson, Herbert N. *The Romance of Steel* (Steel). New York: A. S. Barnes & Co., 1907.

Clews, Henry. *Fifty Years in Wall Street* (Fifty). New York: Irving Publishing Co., 1908.

Corey, Lewis. *The House of Morgan* (Morgan). New York: G. Howard Watt, 1930.

Crockett, Albert Stevens. *Peacocks on Parade.* New York: Sears Publishing Co., 1931.

Daggett, Stuart. *Railroad Reorganization* (Railroad). Cambridge: Houghton Mifflin & Co., 1908.

Dunn, Arthur Wallace. *From Harrison to Harding* (Harrison). New York: G. P. Putnam's Sons, 1922.

Dunshee, Kenneth Holcomb. *As You Pass By.* New York: Hastings House, 1952.

Duveen, James Henry. *The Rise of the House of Duveen* (Rise). New York: Alfred A. Knopf, 1957.

Faulkner, Harold Underwood. *The Decline of Laissez Faire, 1897–1917.* New York: Rinehart & Co., 1951.

Flynn, John T. *God's Gold* (Gold). New York: Harcourt Brace & Co., 1932.

Forbes-Robertston, Diana. *Maxine.* London: The Quality Book Club, 1964.

Friedman, Milton, and Anna Jacobson Schwartz. *A Monetary History of the United States: 1867–1960* (Monetary). Princeton: Princeton University Press, 1963.

Haney, Lewis Henry. *Congressional History of Railways in the United States, 1850–1887.* Madison, Wis., University of Wisconsin, 1910.

Bibliography

Harvey, George. *Henry Clay Frick the Man* (Frick). New York: Charles Scribner's Sons, 1928.

Hendrick, Burton J. *The Age of Big Business* (Age). Yale University Press, 1919.

———. *The Life of Andrew Carnegie* (Carnegie). 2 vols. New York: Doubleday, Doran & Co., 1932.

———. *The Life and Letters of Walter H. Page* (Page). Garden City, N.Y.: Doubleday, Page & Co., 1926.

Hicks, John D. *The Populist Revolt.* Minneapolis: University of Minnesota Press, 1931.

Hidy, Ralph W., and Muriel E. Hidy. *Pioneering in Big Business 1882–1911: History of the Standard Oil Company* (New Jersey). New York: Harper & Brothers, 1955.

Holbrook, Stewart H. *The Age of the Moguls* (Moguls). Garden City, N.Y.: Doubleday & Co., 1953.

Hone, Philip. *The Diary of Philip Hone 1828–1851,* ed. Bayard Tuckerman. 2 vols. New York: Dodd, Mead & Co., 1889.

Hovey, Carl. *The Life Story of J. Pierpont Morgan* (Morgan). New York: Sturgis & Walton Co., 1911.

Josephson, Matthew. *The Robber Barons* (Barons). New York: Harcourt Brace & World, Inc., 1962.

Kennan, George. *Edward H. Harriman* (Harriman). 2 vols. Cambridge: Houghton Mifflin Co., 1922

Kirkland, Edward C. *Industry Comes of Age: Business, Labor and Public Policy, 1860–1897.* New York: Holt, Rinehart & Winston, Inc., 1961.

Kohlsaat, Herman Henry. *From McKinley to Harding* (McKinley). New York: Charles Scribner's Sons, 1923.

Lawrence, William. *Memories of a Happy Life* (Life). Boston: Houghton Mifflin Co., 1926.

Leech, Margaret. *In the Days of McKinley* (McKinley). New York: Harper & Bros., 1959.

Lehr, Elizabeth Drexel. *"King Lehr" and the Gilded Age* ("King"). Philadelphia: J. B. Lippincott Co., 1935.

Lundberg, Ferdinand. *America's 60 Families* (Sixty). New York: The Citadel Press, 1946.

Lynch, Denis Tilden. *"Boss" Tweed* (Tweed). New York: Boni & Liveright, Inc., 1927.

McCarthy, James Remington (with John Rutherford). *Peacock Alley.* New York: Harper & Bros., 1931.

McElroy, Robert. *Grover Cleveland: The Man and the Statesman* (Cleveland). 2 vols. New York: Harper & Bros., 1923.

Moody, John. *The Masters of Capital* (Masters). New Haven: Yale University Press, 1919.

Moody, John. *The Railroad Builders* (Railroad). New Haven: Yale University Press, 1919.

Bibliography

Morison, Samuel Eliot, and Henry Steele Commager. *The Growth of the American Republic* (Growth). 2 vols. New York: Oxford University Press, 1942.

Morris, Lloyd. *Incredible New York.* New York: Random House, 1951.

Mott, Edward Harold. *Between the Ocean and the Lakes: The Story of Erie.* New York: John S. Collins, 1901.

Myers, Gustavus. *History of the Great American Fortunes* (Fortunes). New York: The Modern Library, 1964.

Nevins, Allan. *Grover Cleveland: A Study in Courage.* New York: Dodd, Mead & Co., 1932.

Noyes, Alexander Dana. *Forty Years of American Finance* (Forty). New York: G. P. Putnam's Sons, 1909.

———. *The Market Place: Reminiscences of a Financial Editor.* Boston: Houghton Mifflin Co., 1938.

Oberholtzer, Ellis P. *Jay Cooke: Financier of the Civil War* (Cooke). 2 vols. Philadelphia: George W. Jacobs & Co., 1907.

Orth, Samuel P. *The Armies of Labor.* New Haven: Yale University Press, 1919.

Parrington, Vernon Louis. *Main Currents in American Thought.* New York: Harcourt Brace & Co., 1930.

Pringle, Henry F. *Big Frogs* (Frogs). New York: The Vanguard Press, 1928.

———. *Theodore Roosevelt: A Biography* (Roosevelt). New York: Blue Ribbon Books, 1931.

Pyle, James Gilpin. *The Life of James J. Hill.* Garden City, N.Y.: Doubleday, Page & Co., 1917.

Rienow, Robert, and Leona Train Rienow. *Of Snuff, Sin and the Senate.* Chicago: Follett Publishing Co., 1965.

Ripley, William Z. *Railroads: Rates and Regulations.* Longmans, Green & Co., New York, 1912.

Roosevelt, Theodore, *An Autobiography* (Autobiography). New York: Charles Scribner's Sons, 1920.

Rovere, Richard H. *The Weeper and the Blackmailer* (Original title: *Howe and Hummel*) (Weeper). New York: New American Library, 1950.

Satterlee, Herbert L. *J. Pierpont Morgan: An Intimate Portrait.* New York: The Macmillan Co., 1939.

Scheer, George F., and Hugh F. Rankin. *Rebels and Redcoats.* New York: New American Library, 1957.

Scott, James Brown. *Robert Bacon: Life and Letters* (Bacon). London: William Heinemann Ltd., 1924.

Seitz, Don C. *The James Gordon Bennetts: Father and Son* (Bennetts). Indianapolis: Bobbs-Merrill Co., 1928.

Smith, Henry Nash, ed. *Popular Culture and Industrialism: 1865–1890.* Garden City, N.Y.: Doubleday & Co., Inc., 1967.

Smith, Matthew Hale. *Twenty Years Among the Bulls and Bears of Wall Street*. Hartford: J. B. Burr & Co., 1870.

Sobel, Robert. *The Curbstone Brokers*. New York: The Macmillan Co., 1970.

———. *Panic on Wall Street*. New York: The Macmillan Co., 1968.

Staples, Henry Lee, and Alpheus Thomas Mason. *The Fall of a Railroad Empire* (Fall). Syracuse: Syracuse University Press, 1947.

Stoddard, Henry L. *As I Knew Them*. New York: Harper & Bros., 1927.

Straus, Oscar S. *Under Four Administrations*. Boston: Houghton Mifflin Co., 1922.

Sullivan, Mark. *Our Times* (Times). 6 vols. New York: Charles Scribner's Sons, 1927.

Swanberg, W. A. *Sickles the Incredible* (Sickles). New York: Ace Books, 1956.

Sykes, Christopher. *Four Studies in Loyalty* (Four). London: Collins & Co., 1946.

Tarbell, Ida M. *The Life of Elbert H. Gary*. New York: D. Appleton & Co., 1925.

Taylor, John M. *Garfield of Ohio: The Available Man* (Garfield). New York: W. W. Norton & Co., Inc., 1970.

Thayer, William Roscoe. *The Life and Letters of John Hay* (Hay). 2 vols. Boston: Houghton Mifflin Co., 1915.

Thomas, Lately. *Delmonico's: A Century of Splendor*. Boston: Houghton Mifflin Co., 1967.

Thompson, Holland. *The Age of Invention*. New Haven: Yale University Press, 1921.

Untermyer, Samuel. *Is There a Money Trust?* New York, 1911.

Vachon, Marius. *William Bouguereau*. Paris: A. Lahure, 1900.

Van Wyck, Frederick. *Recollections of an Old New Yorker* (Recollections). New York: Liveright, Inc., 1932.

Wall, Joseph Frazier. *Andrew Carnegie* (Carnegie). New York: Oxford University Press, 1970.

Wasson, R. Gordon. *The Hall Carbine Affair*. New York: Pandick Press, 1948.

Wechsberg, Joseph. *The Merchant Bankers*. New York: Pocket Books, 1968.

Welcome, John. *Cheating at Cards: The Cases in Court*, London: Faber & Faber, 1963.

Werner, M. R. *Tammany Hall* (Tammany). Garden City, N.Y.: Doubleday, Doran & Co., Inc., 1928.

White, Andrew D. *Autobiography*. 2 vols. New York: The Century Co., 1905.

Wilson, William Bender. *History of the Pennsylvania Railroad Company*. 2 vols. Philadelphia: Henry T. Coates Co., 1899.

Winkler, John K. *The First Billion—The Stillmans and the National City Bank*. New York: The Vanguard Press, 1934.

Winkler, John K. *Morgan the Magnificent*. New York: The Vanguard Press, 1930.

Bibliography

Wister, Owen. *Roosevelt: The Story of a Friendship, 1880–1919.* New York: The Macmillan Co., 1930.

Wyckoff, Richard D. *Wall Street Ventures and Adventures through Forty Years* (Ventures). New York: Harper & Bros., 1930.

Documentary Sources at the Library of Congress

Cleveland, Grover, *Presidential Papers.*

Curtis, William E., *Correspondence of,* Volumes 5 and 9.

Lamont, Daniel Scott, *Manuscripts.*

Hamlin, Charles S., *Scrapbook,* Volumes 31 and 78.

Olney, Richard, *Manuscripts.*

State, Federal, and Other Reports, etc.

1886 *Pennsylvania Railroad Co. and others v. the Commonwealth* (Three cases) (Supreme Court of Pennsylvania. October 4, 1886) Reported in the *Atlantic Reporter,* pp. 368–374 of 7 AT 368.

1886 Same title, court, and date as above. Reported in the *Atlantic Reporter,* pp. 374–377 of 7 AT 374.

1896 U.S. Senate Committee on Finance, *Investigation of the Sale of Bonds,* 54th Congress, Second Session.

1906 *Report of the Joint Committee of the Senate and Assembly of the State of New York Appointed to Investigate and Examine into the Business and Affairs of Life Insurance Companies Doing Business in the State of New York.* (Better known as the "Hughes Committee" after its special counsel, Charles Evans Hughes, or the "Armstrong Committee" after the senior legislator, William W. Armstrong of Rochester.)

1909 U.S. Senate Judiciary Committee, *Hearings Before the Subcommittee of the Committee of the Judiciary Relating to the Absorption of Tennessee Coal & Iron & Railroad Co.*

1910 *New York Committee on Speculation in Securities and Commodities, Report* . . . June 7, 1909 (Albany, 1910). (This was the utterly fangless investigation of the New York Stock Exchange by Horace White and others. It is reprinted in full as part of the "Money Trust Investigation." See entry for 1913.)

1911–1913 U.S. Bureau of Corporations, *Report of the Commissioner of Corporations on the Steel Industry.* 3 vols.

1912 U.S. Senate, *Committee on Privileges and Elections Hearing on Campaign Contributions* (known as the "Clapp Committee Hearings").

1912 U.S. House, *Committee on Investigation of the U.S. Steel Corporation Under House Res. 148,* 62nd Congress, First and Second Sessions (known as the "Stanley Committee Hearings").

1913 U.S. House, *Hearings and Report of the Committee Appointed Pursuant to House Regulations 429 and 504 to Investigate the Concentration of Control of Money and Credit,* 62nd Congress, Third Session (known variously as the "Money Trust Investigation" or the "Pujo Investigation").

1914 Interstate Commerce Commission, *Report of the Investigation of Finan-*

cial Transactions of the New York, New Haven & Hartford Railroad Co.

General References

Dictionary of American Biography; Encyclopaedia Britannica, 11th Edition, 1910; *National Cyclopedia of American Biography; New York Stock Exchange Fact Book,* 1971; *Historical Statistics of the United States: Colonial Times to 1957.* 1960, etc.

Magazines

The Bankers' Magazine, Commercial and Financial Chronicle, Congressional Record, Forum, Literary Digest, McClure's Nation, Public Opinion.

Newspapers

New York *Evening Post, Herald, Times, Tribune,* and (morning) *World.*

NOTES

ON SOURCES

Chapter I   The Gold Crisis

This and the following two chapters are based largely on the transcript of the Senate subcommittee hearings investigating the bond sales of the Cleveland administration; on the papers of Grover Cleveland; of his Attorney General, Richard Olney; his Secretary of War, Daniel Scott Lamont, and of the assistant secretary of the Treasury, William Edmund Curtis. The *Forum* estimate is from the November 1889 issue, pages 265–66. The evaluation of the monetary standard of the 1890s is based on Friedman and Schwartz, Monetary, p. 111.

For the background of the 1893 panic, I have relied on the account in Noyes, Forty, and Sobel, Panic, as well as more general histories of the time. The reconstruction of the events from January 24 to February 8, 1895, is based on the testimony of August Belmont, J. Pierpont Morgan, Francis Lynde Stetson, John G. Carlisle, and William E. Curtis at the bond sale hearings. Some details of Belmont's career are from Eleanor Robson Belmont's The Fabric of Memory.

Cleveland's remark on Carlisle's drinking is from Nevins, Cleveland, p. 446. Noyes, Forty, is the commentator who notes that the United States came into the money market hat in hand. The editorial survey from the Springfield *Republican* is cited in *Public Opinion* for February 7, 1895. The Conrad N. Jordan letters are to be found in the Curtis papers in the Library of Congress.

My reconstruction of the international climate of anti-Semitism is based on an article on the subject in the *Encyclopaedia Britannica* by Lucien Wold of the Jewish Historical Society of England, carried first in the 11th edition (1910). The cables exchanged between Morgan's offices in New York and in London are from Allen, Morgan. Frederick Lewis Allen was the only one of Morgan's biographers—or investigators of any kind, including those from Congress, for that matter—to be allowed the run of the firm's cable books. He saw them in 1948. I am informed by letter dated July 23, 1971, from Pierpont Morgan's great-grandson, Charles F. Morgan, that "almost all the papers which Mr. Allen used in making up this biography no longer survive." However, he wrote: "The Allen account is perfectly accurate" as far as he and his father, Henry Sturgis Morgan, are able to determine.

Chapter II   Morgan Is Brought In

The Rothschild loan to Queen Victoria is in Wechsberg, Bankers, p. 46. The Hambros reference is on p. 40 of the same work. The "angels of God" quote is from Burr, Portrait, p. 114, while the Walter Camp description is found in Scott, Bacon, p. 29. Stetson's relationship with Jacob Sharp is detailed in Myers, Fortunes, p. 579.

Cleveland's article is from the *Saturday Evening Post,* May 7, 1904. The Horace White incident is given in Barnes, Carlisle, pp. 380–81. Barnes, in his otherwise excellent book, strangely accepts the White claim for Curtis, though he agrees (p. 379) that Curtis wasn't even at the all-important conference of Tuesday, February 5, 1895. Pierpont Morgan's reaction to Cleveland's demand for a guarantee is given on p. 292 of Satterlee.

Various guidebooks, plus a retracement by me of the financiers' walk, went into the Lafayette Square reconstruction, together with reference to Swanberg, Sickles. In addition to the manuscript sources already cited, the analysis of the aftermath of the contract relies on the chapter, "The Bond Syndicate Operation," beginning on p. 234 of Noyes, Forty, together with material, as indicated, from his preface to the 1909 edition. (In the 1930s, a mellower, septuagenarian Noyes, in an autobiographical volume, Market Place, allows himself a much higher opinion of Morgan. I didn't find his later views convincing.)

Chapter III   A Respectful Inquiry

The account of Morgan's meeting with Herrick and Hanna is from Satterlee, pp. 316–17. Belmont the Younger's sartorial elegance is noted in Beebe, Spenders, p. 368; the reason for Belmont the Elder's duel is given in Van Wyck, Recollections, p. 371. Beebe is the source for the incident of the $60,000 ducks, on p. viii, and the Commodore as wine steward, on p. 371.

Chapter IV   Youth and Early Missteps

Here I am indebted to Satterlee. His biography is, of course, a respectful family chronicle, as it must be, coming from Pierpont Morgan's son-in-law only a quarter century after its subject's death. Even allowing for this, the account can be infuriatingly sloppy in details. But there are two compelling reasons for any student of Pierpont Morgan's life to hold it in considerable esteem.

The first is the intimate relationship Satterlee had with his father-in-law for a great part of the latter's public career, particularly in the Panic of 1907 and in his last illness. The biography contains many references, in direct quotations and indirect allusions, that have the fullest claim to being the authentic reactions of a man who unburdened himself to few in his lifetime. This consideration alone makes Satterlee invaluable—subject, though, to the reservation that it is difficult indeed to separate the genuine from the spurious.

Second, despite the family claims that all Pierpont Morgan's letters and papers went up the flue at Roehampton in 1911, Satterlee seems to have had no trouble in finding a fair number of both. We are forced to rely on him and be thankful for those he has seen fit to pass on.

Further, the evidence is strong that Satterlee had a daily journal, at the least, and possibly even scrapbooks or diaries to work from. The very slavishness of his organization, tied rigorously to a day-by-day system in the entire 583-page work, attests to this. Once again, we are forced to make do with what the family has permitted to come to light.

The Joseph Morgan diary entry and all the letters and diaries of Pierpont Morgan quoted are to be found in Satterlee's strict chronologic scheme under the appropriate dates. The Philip Hone diary entries are similarly arranged. Duveen's comment on Pierpont Morgan's deformity is in Duveen, Rise, p. 279.

I have used Lewis Corey, Morgan, as a corrective for Satterlee in this chapter and *The Medford Historical Register,* Volume VI, No. 4, October 1903, as a check on both. The comment on slavery is found in Myers, Fortunes, p. 243. The 1852 illness is found on p. 37 of Satterlee; the recollections of James Goodwin and James Burbank on p. 10.

As noted, the Hall's carbines details come from Satterlee. For the Gold Room account, I am indebted to Sobel, Panic; Sobel, Curb; Corey, Morgan and contemporary descriptions by the Reverend Matthew Hale Smith and others. The Lincoln anathema is in Sobel, Curb, p. 33. The description of Pierpont Morgan's first marriage is based on Satterlee; the incident of the Baker portrait is from Hovey, Morgan.

Chapter V   The Great Barbecue

The Union Club references are from Seitz, Bennetts, p. 218. New York's "round-the-clock trading" is described in Sobel, Curb, pp. 39–40. Garfield's comment on the staining of the presidential parlor is from Josephson, Barons, p. 148; that and Taylor, Garfield, p. 130, provide more background. The Noyes judgment on the era is from Noyes, Forty, pp. 17–18.

My major source on the Erie and its wreckers is a wonderful but neglected coffee-table book twelve inches high, ten wide, and two and a half thick called *Between the Ocean and the Lakes— The Story of Erie,* by Edward Harold Mott. It has all the outward signs of being an inspired, subsidized official business history. In fact, the copy I acquired contains the cover stamping: "Compliments of Arthur H. Page & Co. Bankers and Brokers, 44 Broad Street, New York." That's not ordinarily a sign under which the spirit of research conquers. Yet the book is a splendid reconstruction of the career of perhaps the most hapless railroad of all times. The volume reproduces all sorts of documentation, from actual superintendents' reports, on up through local as well as the more usual metropolitan newspaper accounts, to generous swatches from the numberless state investigatory findings. It all forms a stunning history of the tortured line from its beginnings in 1848 to about 1900. It even contains such minutiae as price, number of shares outstanding, etc., of Erie bonds and stock annually from 1848 on. Its biases are few and easily discernible.

The "watered stock" details are from Holbrook, Moguls, p. 21, while the cornering of Drew by Vanderbilt is in Moody, Railroad, p. 32. Henry Adams's reaction to Fisk is in Adams and Adams, Chapters, pp. 106 and 108; his brother's to all of the Erie gang, in the same, pp. 95–96. Gould's tearful tale was told to a Senate committee on education and labor in 1883. It is recounted in Smith, Popular Culture, pp. 132–33.

The account of Drew's printing press relies on Mott, pp. 148–49, and Adams and Adams, Chapters, p. 19. The description of Augustus Schell is from Werner, Tammany, p. 279, that of the committee headed by Astor from Lynch, Tweed, p. 347. Barnard is described by Werner on p. 126. His electric contributions to jurisprudence is from Adams and Adams, Chapters, p. 163.

The Erie accident that was fatal to seventy-five is in Mott, p. 443; the general superintendent's report on p. 156. For details of Sickles's career, I have used Swanberg, Sickles, with added information from Mott and Adams and Adams. Charles Francis Adams Jr.'s oft-quoted judgment on businessmen of the day is from his Autobiography, p. 190; his comments on Hooker, Sickles, and Butterfield, on p. 161. The summary of the Erie's bonded indebtedness is from Daggett, Railroad, p. 36. The description of the panic of September 24, 1869, is based on Adams and Adams, Chapters, p. 129, and contemporary sources. The "woodbine twineth" quotation is in Mott, p. 489.

For the Vanderbilt memorial celebration, I have referred to Dunshee, p. 207, and Smith, Popular Culture, pp. 92–95, together with Corey, Morgan, p. 103, and Andrews, Vanderbilt, p. 157. Bryant's firing of Nordhoff is in Lynch, Tweed, p. 355–56. "The great barbecue" is from Parrington, Main Currents, Volume III, pp. 23–24. The incident of the Albany & Susquehanna president's son is from Breen, Thirty Years, pp. 143–46.

Chapter VI   After the Feast

The Civil War's value to Jay Cooke and Grant is noted in Parrington, Main Currents, Volume III, p. 31. The extended trip by Pierpont Morgan is recounted by Satterlee, beginning on p. 149. Cooke's reminder to Salmon P. Chase is in Oberholtzer, Cooke, Volume I, pp. 143–44, the Union Pacific incident in Volume II, p. 409. Morgan's remark on sending "your man to my man" is in Bishop, Roosevelt, Volume I, p. 184. Morgan's feelings for the Arlington is from Satterlee, p. 157. Material on the House Ways and Means Committee hearings is from *The New York Times,* January 9, 1873, and Hovey, Morgan, pp. 75–76. Sobel, Panic, p. 173, was helpful for the account of the 1873 Panic.

Statistics on the growth of railroad mileage are from the indispensable *Historical Statistics*, pages 427–28. Corey's misreading of Clews is on p. 117 of Corey, Morgan, while the Carnegie anecdote comes from Carnegie, Autobiography, pp. 164–65.

The satirical Gibson drawing is reproduced opposite p. 225, Broun and Leach, Comstock. Simon Cameron's cynical definition of an honest politician is in Rienow and Rienow, Of Sin, p. 235. The Phelps, Dodge incident is from Myers, Fortunes, p. 431, while Morgan's reputation as a gallant is from Van Wyck, Recollections, pp. 286–87. The anecdote involving Anne Morgan is from Lehr, "King Lehr," pp. 17–18.

Pierpont Morgan's litany of favorite cities is from Satterlee, p. 545. Bowers, Era, calls the 1876 election plot "the most daring conspiracy." Andrew White's perverse eulogy of Garfield is in his Autobiography, Volume I, p. 190. The letter from Charles Francis Adams Sr. to Samuel Jones Tilden is in Bowers, Era, p. 537.

Chapter VII   Enter Coster

John Moody's description of Coster is in Moody, Masters, p. 33; Lord Kitchener's scolding of Morgan in Satterlee, p. 571. The material on Coster and his forebears is from Barrett, Merchants, pp. 190 ff., obituary notices at the time of his death, and from an interview with his son. Commodore Vanderbilt's protracted passing was described in his obituary in the New York *Herald*, January 5, 1877. His attitude toward the law is from Hendrick, Age, p. 22. Chauncey Depew's apologia for Billy Vanderbilt is from Josephson, Barons, p. 187, while the Gladstone comment to Depew is at p. 184 of the same work. The letter from General Scott is quoted in Satterlee, p. 167.

The 8 percent guarantee that ended abruptly is noted in Winkler, Morgan, p. 85. The background of industrial unrest during the 1870s and 1880s is based on Orth, Armies, pp. 66–67 and general histories of the period.

The information on the real risk-takers in railroad construction, the public at large, is from Ripley, Railroad, pp. 37–39, and the descriptive material from Moody, Railroad. The latter work, pp. 167–68, supplied the thirty-cent evaluation for the Dutch bondholders in Hill's early transaction, while the *Encyclopaedia Britannica* article on Hill in the 11th edition estimates that the Dutch investors got only a third of that amount. The sample of Carnegie's fawning personality is provided by Wall, Carnegie, pp. 310–11; the fawning by Tilden is from the New York *Tribune*, November 9, 1877. Pierpont Morgan's widening itinerary is given by Satterlee from the years 1878 through 1882. Morgan's letter to his wife is at p. 204. The comment on railroad building in 1880 and 1881 is from Hovey, Morgan, p. 97. Clews's remark on the Nickel Plate is in his Fifty Years, p. 362. General Horace Porter's part in the 1869 gold corner is told in Adams and Adams, Chapters, p. 122.

The rest of this chapter consists of information and misinformation from Satterlee; Hovey, Morgan; Wall, Carnegie; and others, with the misinformation corrected by a more rigorous look than any of them had apparently ever made of contemporary accounts, particularly those of the New York *Tribune* and the New York *Herald* from August through October 1885. Added correctives were the histories of the Pennsylvania Railroad by Burgess and Kennedy and by Wilson. The first was especially helpful and deserves special mention.

Nominally by George H. Burgess and Miles C. Kennedy, this volume is a sort of computerized history, based on a mangement study of the railroad's career by the engineering firm of Coverdale & Colpitts prepared for the centennial of the carrier in 1949. It was the only source that was able to lead me, after several frustrations in the law library of the commonwealth of Pennsylvania, to the actual 1892 decisions settling the Pennsylvania-South Pennsylvania case. With the information provided, I was able to get copies of the decisions.

The book speaks well for the engineering study methods that produced it. They are surely superior to the usual procedure followed in historical research, i.e., the dispatching by an aging professor of hordes of his young students, ostensibly in search of original data, but more often in pursuit of the handiest secondary sources that boast full bibliographies. The mainspring of the latter process usually consists of a foundation grant—or two or three—for the educator, good grades for the boys and girls.

Chapter VIII   Frightened Capitalism

The Satterlee version of Morgan on the legal profession is on pp. 226–27; the second reference is in Tarbell, Gary, p. 134. The 1888–89 conferences are reconstructed from Hovey, pp. 139–43.

Junius Morgan's attitude toward his son is related in Satterlee, p. 232; Moody, Masters, p. 20, likens the older man to the figure in an old play. Satterlee on Coster is at p. 234 and pp. 245–46. The $50,000 a mile cost of railroads is given in Haney, Congressional, p. 254. Railroad mileage, as noted, is from *Historical Statistics*. The Jeremiah Whipple Jenks reference is from an article he contributed on trusts to the *Britannica*, 11th edition. Rockefeller's desire to be independent of the "Street" is in Hidy and Hidy, Pioneering, p. 607. The Untermyer analysis is from Money Trust Report, p. 40. The outlawing of the early Standard Oil trust is from Hendrick, Age, p. 52, and the Thomas Fortune Ryan "tin box" quotation from the same, p. 139.

Archibald A. McLeod's expansionary plans are detailed by Myers, Fortunes, p. 363; Noyes, Forty, p. 218, and the "peanut-stand" remark is given in Hovey, Morgan, p. 136. Coster's method, as outlined by Thomas Fortune Ryan to R. Gordon Wasson, is to be found in Carosso, Investment, p. 40. The Interstate Commerce Commissioner's complaint of monopoly pricing is quoted in Faulkner, Decline, p. 199.

The incident of Morgan's naming the hymns is from Satterlee, p. 170; his love of *Trovatore* is at p. 164; his methods with art dealers, at pp. 432–34. Stillman's story of Morgan on temptation is given in Burr, p. 317. The death of Junius P. Morgan is from Satterlee, pp. 252–53. The yacht-building instructions are from Satterlee, pp. 254–55. The price Pierpont Morgan got from the Navy is cited by Azoy, Signal, p. 52.

The amusements of Albert Edward, Prince of Wales, and later Edward VII, are catalogued in Sykes, Four; others are added in Welcome, Cheating, pp. 63 and 105. The account of the Maxine Elliott-Pierpont Morgan shipboard interview is in Forbes, Maxine, p. 180. Testimony to Miss Elliott's business acumen is found on pp. 4 and 177 of that work and her comment on Morgan's yacht on p. 180. The account of her seduction of the King is at pp. 200–201. Morgan's encounter with the Kaiser is told by Satterlee at pp. 383–84; his abrupt response to Edward VII is from the same source, p. 434.

I have taken the "Mr. Dooley" passage on Morgan's way with spiritual and temporal royalty from Sullivan, Times, Volume II, p. 355. Satterlee describes the Chamber of Commerce dinner at p. 306, and relates the Myron Herrick-Mark Hanna meeting at pp. 315–17. Hanna's initial contempt for Wall Street is given in

Stoddard, As I Knew Them, p. 239. Hanna's shifting of the McKinley pledge to embrace the gold standard is from Leech, McKinley, p. 79. Noyes, Forty, pp. 264-65, provides the economic background of the 1896 election. Pierpont Morgan and the railroad coach are described in Satterlee, p. 103; Morgan and the climb up the side of the *Oceanic* on p. 337.

Chapter IX The Parade Starts: U.S. Steel

The evaluation by the U.S. Bureau of Corporation is cited in Myers, Fortunes, p. 602. Wyckoff, Ventures, pp. 106 ff. is the source for the 1903 aftermath of the U.S. Steel flotation and of Morgan's "midwife" remark. The *London Annual Shipping Review* for 1901 commented on the "exceptionally good bargain" British sellers struck with Morgan's International Mercantile Marine. Noyes, Forty, p. 303, notes their second bargain.

The account of industrial development is drawn largely from Thompson, Age, pp. 180–82, and Hendrick, Age. Perkins's turndown of the General Motors financing is in Carosso, Investment, p. 133, where it is described as an "excusable oversight." The subsequent growth of the automobile industry is given in Hendrick, Age, pp. 171 and 183.

For the description of the Waldorf-Astoria, I am indebted to Crockett, Peacocks, an excellent social history of the time by a man who prowled the hotel and nightlife beat for the New York *Herald*. Gates's betting on raindrops is from Crockett, Peacocks, p. 126; the trick played on him at the Carlton in London, on pp. 207 ff., and the Ellwood-Gates banter on p. 84.

Gates's response to the question of where the $26 million went is cited from the court hearing by Noyes, Forty, p. 288, while the shorting of his steel stock is recounted in Wyckoff, Ventures, pp. 77–78. The John Hay description of McKinley is in a letter from Hay to Henry Adams, dated October 20, 1896, cited in Thayer, Hay, Volume II, p. 153, while the Adams definition of McKinleyism is from Adams, Education, p. 423. Gold production figures are U.S. Mint estimates for 1892 and later as cited by Noyes, Forty, p. 259.

Daniel G. Reid's bordello-wrecking is described in Crockett, Peacocks, pp. 114–15. The "arch-sneak" epithet is quoted from Bridge, Carnegie, p. 47. The quotation from Henry Clay Frick beginning "For years, I have been convinced . . ." is cited by

Wall, Carnegie, p. 753, while the struggle between him and Carnegie is in Harvey, Frick, pp. 230–31. The "nice little present" is from Hendrick, Carnegie, Volume II, p. 88. Carnegie's remark on Federal Steel's ability to produce stock certificates is quoted in Wall, Carnegie, p. 767.

The incident in which Gates barred Gary from the card game is from Crockett, Peacocks, p. 126. The March 1901 capitalization of Carnegie Steel is from Wall, Carnegie, p. 763, and the "Ain't Andy wonderful!" remark is from the same source, p. 791. The meeting at which Morgan told Carnegie he could have gotten a hundred million more for his steel interests is described in Hendrick, Carnegie, Volume II, p. 142.

The turndown of Pierpont Morgan's offer for the Lake Superior properties owned by Standard Oil is based on Flynn, Gold, p. 351; the success of Frick is described in Harvey, Frick, pp. 265–66. The post mortem, in which Pierpont Morgan convinces Judge Gary, is from Tarbell, Gary, p. 266. Crockett, Peacocks, p. 114, tells of Rockefeller's total lack of recall of the price paid.

Casson, Steel, pp. 220–21, is the source for the speechlessness of the world of finance at Morgan's U.S. Steel announcement. The description of Keene, together with the details of his profits, are from Wyckoff, Ventures, pp. 81–82, while his method of working is given on pp. 147–48 of the same source. Frick's profits are described in Harvey, Frick, pp. 268 and 271–72; his remark on railroads as "the Rembrandts of investment" is at p. 276.

Chapter X   The Morgan Decade

The habitues of Aix-les-Bains are described by Crockett, Peacocks, pp. 217 and 223–24. Harriman's remark on "a hostile act" is from Kennan, Harriman, Volume I, p. 296; the Morgan group's holdings in Northern Pacific is from Moody, Masters, p. 102, and Hill's analysis of what was needed for control is from Pyle, Hill, Volume II, pp. 142–43. Hill's dash to New York and meeting with Jacob H. Schiff is from Kennan, Harriman, Volume I, pp. 303–4.

Hanna's "damned cowboy" remark is from Kohlsaat, McKinley, p. 99, his stricture on "that madman" from Dunn, Harrison, Volume I, pp. 334–35. TR as "pure act" is from Adams, Education, p. 417; Finlay Peter Dunne's Mr. Dooley on TR and the trusts is from Sullivan, Times, Volume II, p. 411. Roosevelt on his determination to have the Supreme Court reverse itself is from his Autobiography, p. 426; his "they will know this country lawyer" from Bishop, Roosevelt, Volume II, p. 183, and the "send your man to my man" incident is from the same source, as noted earlier.

The George F. Baer letter on the divine right of money is reproduced in Sullivan, Times, Volume II, pp. 425–27; the Philander C. Knox comment on "any taint of legality" is from the same volume, at p. 438. TR's explanation of his joke is from his Autobiography, pp. 468–69. The interchange between Samuel Untermyer and Pierpont Morgan on the sale of the Thomas Fortune Ryan stock to Morgan is at pp. 1069–70 of the Money Trust Hearings and at p. 137 of the Money Trust Report. The production, employment, and inflation figures for the "Morgan Decade" are from *Historical Statistics*. The steel price rises are noted by Noyes, Forty, p. 316. The comparison between 1901 and 1968 trading is from Sobel, Panic, pp. 279–80.

Charles W. Morse's posthumous thievery is noted in Revere, Weeper, p. 119; his marital misadventure from the same, pp. 108 ff. The recollections of the Bishop of Massachusetts are from Lawrence, Memories, pp. 251–52. Morgan's "Why should I get into this?" is from Burr, Portrait, p. 235; his "I've got to stop somewhere" from the same, p. 225. The squeeze on the Trust Company of America is from testimony of Oakleigh Thorne and George F. Perkins and the letter of Melville E. Stone in House Investigation, U.S. Steel, Volume III. "Then this is the place to stop the trouble!" is from Satterlee, p. 469; the valuation of Tennessee Coal & Iron is based on Sobel, Panic, p. 318; the Samuel Untermyer-George Cortelyou exchange from Money Trust Hearings, pp. 442–43. TR on the mysteries of economics is from Pringle, Roosevelt, p. 432.

Chapter XI   "I've Got to Go up the Hill"

Morgan's relations with the publishing world is from Hendrick, Page, Volume I, p. 64; Mitchell, Memoirs, (cited in Sullivan, Times, Volume II, p. 346), and Lundberg, Sixty, pp. 252 ff. Mellen's testimony at the Interstate Commerce Committee hearing is cited in Staples and Mason, Fall, pp. 182–83; his remark to Barron in Barron, More, p. 153. In sketching Samuel Untermyer's personality and career, I am indebted to the chapter on him in Pringle, Frogs. The description of Pierpont Morgan's first appearance at the Money Trust hearings is from this source, p. 150. The long exchange between Untermyer and Morgan beginning "There is no way . . ." is condensed from the longer extract presented by Untermyer in Money Trust Report, pp. 136–37; Untermyer's analysis of Morgan's responses is at pp. 137–38; the George F. Baker testimony in full is in Money Trust Hearings, pp. 1567–68. The Frederick H. Prince claim that the investigation "killed" Morgan is in Barron, More, p. 157. Morgan's control of resources is outlined in the Money Trust Report, pp. 86 and 89. Carosso, Investment, titles his chapter on the Temporary National Economic Committee: "Pujo Revisited: The TNEC."

Index

Index